For Reference

Not to be taken

from this library

CHRONICLE OF THE ROMAN EMPERORS

CHRIS SCARRE

CHRONICLE OF THE ROMAN EMPERORS

THE REIGN-BY-REIGN RECORD OF THE RULERS OF IMPERIAL ROME

WITH **328** ILLUSTRATIONS
111 IN COLOUR

THAMES AND HUDSON

To Judith

Author's Note
I should like to thank all those who have helped in the preparation of this book, notably Professor Roger Wilson, Dr Roger Bland for his help in checking the coin drawings and above all Professor Anthony Birley for his detailed and invaluable comments. Needless to say, any faults which remain are the author's alone.

(*Half-title*) Onyx cameo of the Roman eagle, with symbols of victory, late first century BC. Kunsthistorisches Museum, Vienna.
(*Frontispiece*) Augustus, the first emperor of Rome, shown in the uniform of a Roman general. Vatican Museum.

Any copy of this book issued by the publisher as a paperback is sold subject to the condition that it shall not by way of trade or otherwise be lent, resold, hired out or otherwise circulated without the publisher's prior consent in any form of binding or cover other than that in which it is published and without a similar condition including these words being imposed on a subsequent purchaser.

© 1995 Thames and Hudson Ltd, London
Text © 1995 Chris Scarre

All Rights Reserved. No part of this publication may be reproduced or transmitted in any form or by any means, electronic or mechanical, including photocopy, recording or any other information storage and retrieval system, without prior permission in writing from the publisher.

British Library Cataloguing-in-Publication Data
A catalogue record for this book is available from the British Library

ISBN 0-500-05077-5

Printed and bound in Slovenia by Mladinska Knjiga

CONTENTS

Augustus

Caligula

Septimius Severus

Diocletian

92839

PREFACE: IMPERIAL LIVES

Bust of Trajan (AD 98–117) in old age. One of the greatest and most renowned of Roman emperors, Trajan pushed the frontiers of the empire to their widest extent. Archaeological Museum, Ankara.

Which Roman emperor threatened to make his horse a consul? Which took part in no fewer than 735 gladiatorial combats? Was Hadrian really a homosexual? The personalities of the men who governed the Roman empire have never ceased to fascinate later generations. From Augustus to Constantine, the empire was ruled by some 54 'canonical' emperors, not to mention a host of rivals and rebels who claimed the imperial title, and their successors of the divided empire.

Contemporary writers relished the opportunity to dig up scurrilous and extravagant tales about their imperial subjects: how Caligula drank pearls dissolved in vinegar, or how Nero seduced his own mother. Christian writers provide gruesome accounts of the deaths of emperors who persecuted them, as evidence of divine vengeance: of Galerius, for instance, eaten away by a hideous disease, or of Valerian, flayed alive by the Persians. *Chronicle of the Roman Emperors* presents these and other colourful accounts as part of the surviving evidence, but takes a critical approach. For we are now able better than ever before to distinguish between fact and fiction, between the scandal-mongering of writers such as Suetonius and the real substance of the imperial achievement. Indeed we must not forget that, whatever their individual failings, these men and their officials sustained an empire stretching from Britain to the Sahara and from the Atlantic to the Euphrates for over 400 years.

When we talk of emperors we are using the very word invented by the Romans. 'Imperator' was the cry raised by the legions to salute a victorious general. It was the cry which greeted each emperor on his accession. These men were not merely military leaders, however, but also politicians, builders and husbands. *Chronicle of the Roman Emperors* assesses each of these aspects, detailing dynastic squabbles, family intrigues, and the troubled question of relations with the senate, the people who, despite the rise of emperors, still felt that it was they who should govern the state.

Some of the most famous monuments of ancient Rome are linked with imperial names: the Baths of Caracalla, the Arch of Constantine, Trajan's Column and Hadrian's Villa, to name but a few. Building projects in the provinces likewise bear the stamp of individual emperors: the great baths at Carthage, Hadrian's Wall in Britain, and Constantine's new capital at Constantinople (modern Istanbul). Buildings are one material legacy; more evocative still are the portraits that allow us to recognize emperors as individuals. Imperial sculptors rarely employed a realism which showed their distinguished subjects warts and all; but the best portraits are clearly

(*Above*) Tiberius (AD 14–37), the efficient but somewhat grim and gloomy successor of Augustus, who eventually withdrew to the island of Capri, giving rise to much speculation about sexual depravity in his villa there.

(*Right*) Commodus (AD 180–192) has gone down in history as a monster and a megalomaniac, who delighted in playing the gladiator in front of the assembled Roman populace.

taken from life, and provide an important additional insight which helps us to see these long-dead rulers as real people.

Also considered is the role of emperors as authors, and the cultural life over which they presided. The *Meditations* of Marcus Aurelius are well known, but several other emperors have left us fragments of their literary output. We have a poem by Hadrian; some lines from the song Nero sang while Rome burned, as well as letters from Trajan. In these writings the emperors speak with their own voice.

Another compelling theme that emerges is the varied and complex role of women in the imperial household: as mothers, sisters, wives and mistresses. Many were major figures in their own right. Livia, wife of Augustus, is credited with poisoning a whole series of potential successors to the imperial throne in order to make the way clear for her own son Tiberius. Agrippina attempted to rule Rome through her son Nero. Early in the third century two Syrian princesses effectively managed affairs of state while the emperor Elagabalus indulged in religious and sexual excesses.

Here then is a history of Rome as seen through the lives, relationships and achievements of its rulers. In countless ways, from roads and cities to laws, languages and literature, the empire they created fundamentally shaped the character of Europe, and ultimately the Renaissance and modern worlds.

INTRODUCTION: THE BACKGROUND TO EMPIRE

Rome was an empire long before it had an emperor. An emperor is the individual who wields supreme power; an empire, however, is a series of territories welded into a single unit by political and military might. It consists of a core territory plus conquered provinces or dependencies. In this sense, the Roman empire originated in the third century BC. In the sixth century, Rome had been a mere city-state. By the end of the third century, it controlled the whole of Italy and had taken possession of Sicily, its first overseas province. This acquisition set a trend, and during the last two centuries BC a succession of new provinces were added, until by the time of Augustus the Roman empire stretched from the Atlantic in the west to the Syrian desert in the east, and from the Nile cataracts to the North Sea. This was without question a great empire; but the office of Roman emperor did not appear until the 20s BC, arose out of a particular political crisis, and was essentially the creation of Augustus.

According to tradition, confirmed by archaeology, Rome was already over 700 years old when Augustus came to power. For the first two centuries or so the city was ruled by kings. In 510 BC the last of the kings, Tarquinius Superbus, was expelled, and Rome became a republic. After a series of constitutional adjustments power came to rest jointly in the hands of the senate, a council of leading citizens chosen by birth and rank, and in the assembly of the people, composed of all free male citizens. The senate provided the senior magistrates of the republic, including the two consuls who were elected each year. The assembly of the people had their own representatives, the tribunes, who theoretically had the power to veto any legislation. It was on to this traditional constitution that the position of emperor was grafted.

The uneasy balance between the power of the people and the power of the senate led to serious problems during the last century of the Roman republic. The leading figures in the struggle were all senators, but some took the part of the propertied classes while others sought to increase their power by championing the cause of the common people. At the same time, the responsibilities of governing a growing overseas empire placed a major strain on the traditional administrative arrangements. The success of Rome's armies gave unprecedented power to a series of leading generals: first Marius, then Sulla, then Pompey and Julius Caesar. Centralized rule, with government in the hands of one man, was perhaps the inevitable outcome, the only way of restoring peace and stability to an empire riven by civil feuds between over-mighty generals. But centralized rule did not arise without its own prolonged birth-pangs.

By 50 BC the political question had resolved itself largely into rivalry between Pompey 'the Great', now the defender of senatorial authority at Rome, and Julius Caesar, who had just completed the conquest of Gaul and had a powerful army at his back. In 49 BC Caesar crossed the Rubicon and invaded Italy, pursuing Pompey and his supporters to the Balkans where they were defeated at the Battle of Pharsalus in June the following year. Caesar became dictator, absolute ruler of Rome, but failed to establish his power on an acceptable footing and was assassinat-

The murder of Julius Caesar in 44 BC provided lessons from which Octavian (the future emperor Augustus) could learn when framing his own constitutional settlement.

Antony and Cleopatra. By favouring Cleopatra and her ambitions Mark Antony alienated conservative Roman opinion and squandered his support in the west.

Augustus as the god Jupiter, detail of the 'Gemma Augustea' (Kunsthistorisches Museum, Vienna). Beside him sits the goddess Roma and between their heads floats a sun-disc bearing the figure Capricorn, his natal sign. The symbolism proclaims Augustus supreme ruler of the inhabited world.

ed five years later (15 March 44 BC: the famous Ides of March). His death was followed by a second civil war in which his assassins led by Brutus and Cassius were defeated by Mark Antony and Octavian, Caesar's adoptive son. In the settlement which followed Mark Antony took the east and Octavian the west, but Octavian had already set his sights on supreme power, Mark Antony played his hand badly, and Octavian emerged victorious at the Battle of Actium (31 BC).

Four years later Octavian reached an arrangement with the senate at Rome which gave him supreme power under the guise of republican forms. Now named Augustus, he became the first Roman emperor. Caesar's murder served him as a cautionary tale, but over the 45 years of his rule Augustus succeeded in establishing the institution of emperor in the form it was broadly to retain for several centuries. Thus the emperor was supreme military commander, with sole control over most of the army. He was protected by a special military unit, the praetorian guard, whose commanders (usually two at any one time) came to wield considerable power themselves. The emperor also appointed most of the provincial governors, presided at public games and ceremonies, and proposed laws and edicts.

As his role developed during the first century AD, the emperor built up a household of officials and civil servants, many of whom were freedmen (former slaves). Emperors also came to place growing reliance on the *equites* or knights, the social class immediately below the senators which included the landed gentry as well as many wealthy and successful businessmen. Imperial patronage and public generosity also allowed the emperor to reinforce his constitutional position by broad-based popular support, and it is essential when reading the histories of Tacitus, Suetonius or Cassius Dio to remember that these were senators, the guardians of the old republican order and the one class of men who lost out significantly in the new imperial scheme.

Historians such as these paint lurid pictures of debauchery and intrigue, and seem often to find great difficulty in saying anything at all complimentary about their subjects. Yet the evidence shows that the empire was kept on a steady keel, despite the eccentricities of individual emperors. We may perhaps doubt much of what we are told by the hostile sources. In many cases, indeed, they were writing long after the events which they described: Cassius Dio on Augustus is as distant in time as a modern biographer on Napoleon. A hostile tradition does not necessarily mean an irresponsible ruler. On the other hand, there are few events more serious than death, and the manner of their deaths may serve as a commentary on the men themselves and on the perils of imperial office. Of the first 12 emperors (Augustus to Nerva), only 4 died peacefully in their beds: 4 were assassinated, 2 committed suicide, and 2 more were most likely murdered, one by poison, one by suffocation. And those that died peacefully were not spared conspiracy. In this hothouse world of wealth and intrigue the emperors of Rome held supreme power, but only at supreme risk.

THE ROMAN EMPIRE IN THE TIME OF AUGUSTUS

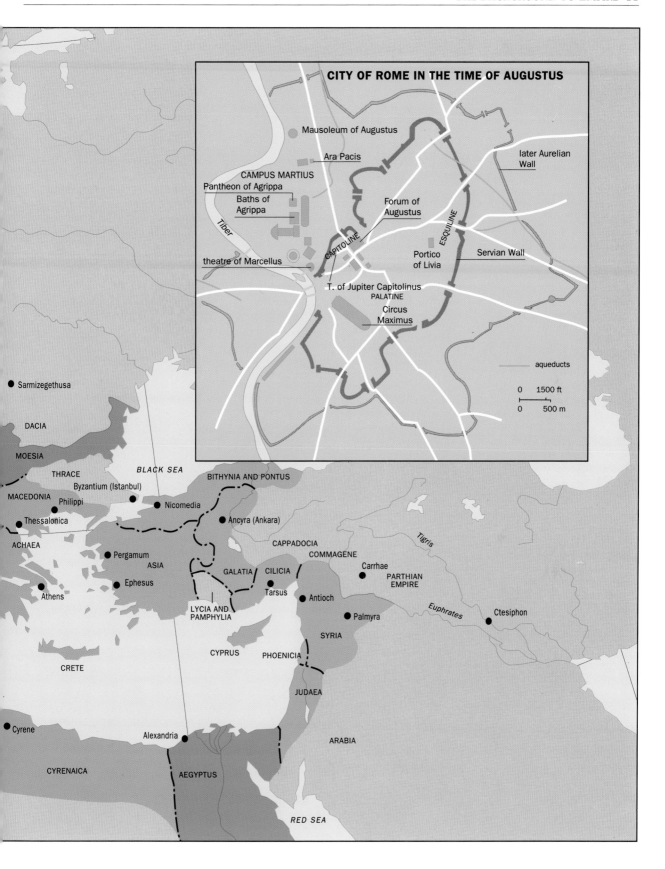

CITY OF ROME IN THE TIME OF AUGUSTUS

Mausoleum of Augustus

Ara Pacis

later Aurelian
Wall

CAMPUS MARTIUS

Pantheon of Agrippa

Baths of
Agrippa

Forum of
Augustus

CAPITOLINE

ESQUILINE

theatre of Marcellus

Portico
of Livia

Servian Wall

T. of Jupiter Capitolinus

PALATINE

Circus
Maximus

Tiber

aqueducts

0   1500 ft

0   500 m

Sarmizegethusa

DACIA

MOESIA

THRACE

BLACK SEA

BITHYNIA AND PONTUS

Byzantium (Istanbul)

MACEDONIA

Philippi

Nicomedia

Thessalonica

Ancyra (Ankara)

ACHAEA

CAPPADOCIA

COMMAGENE

Tigris

Pergamum

ASIA

GALATIA

CILICIA

Carrhae

PARTHIAN
EMPIRE

Ephesus

Tarsus

Antioch

Athens

Euphrates

Ctesiphon

LYCIA AND
PAMPHYLIA

Palmyra

SYRIA

CYPRUS

PHOENICIA

CRETE

JUDAEA

Cyrene

Alexandria

ARABIA

CYRENAICA

AEGYPTUS

RED SEA

THE PRINCIPAL TEXTUAL SOURCES

The key Roman historians who provide accounts of Roman emperors and their reigns from Augustus to Constantine are the following:

AURELIUS VICTOR

Sextus Aurelius Victor was a fourth-century African who was appointed governor of Pannonia by Julian in 361 and became prefect of Rome under Theodosius in 389. He completed a series of short imperial biographies, the *Liber de Caesaribus* (from Augustus to Constantius II) in the early 360s. Useful as a source for the third and early fourth centuries.

CASSIUS DIO

Lucius Cassius Dio, sometimes known as Dio Cassius, was a Bithynian and son of a Roman senator who had been governor of Cilicia and Dalmatia. He was born around 160, entered the senate around 180, and was consul in 205 and 229. He wrote a massive history of Rome from the origins to the reign of Alexander Severus, but only certain sections survive. Cassius Dio is a staunch supporter of the dignity and tradition of the senate and severely critical of imperial encroachments.

EUSEBIUS

Bishop of Caesarea in modern Israel, Eusebius was a Christian historian and admirer of the emperor Constantine. His *Ecclesiastical History* is the earliest extant history of the Christian church, carrying the story down to the fall of Licinius in 324. A harsh critic of anti-Christian emperors, he wrote a eulogistic *Life of Constantine* after the latter's death in 337, and died himself two years later.

EUTROPIUS

Eutropius was the author of the *Breviarium ab urbe condita*, a brief history of Rome from its origins to the death of Jovian in 364. Born around 320, Eutropius served as a high official under a whole series of emperors from Constantius II to Theodosius.

HERODIAN

Born probably in Asia Minor around 175, Herodian wrote a history of his own times from the death of Marcus Aurelius to the accession of Gordian III. It is particularly valuable for its apparent eyewitness accounts of events in Rome during this period, though these may be based on other writers and Herodian's own imagination. Herodian as a minor (perhaps local) official not a senator, writes without the pro-senatorial bias of his contemporary Cassius Dio.

HISTORIA AUGUSTA

A series of imperial biographies purporting to have been written by six different authors and dedicated to Diocletian and Constantine. It is now thought to be the work of a single writer in the late fourth century. The biographies span the period from Hadrian to Numerian but are very variable in quality and contain invented names and many passages of pure fiction.

LACTANTIUS

Born in Africa around 250, Lactantius was summoned to Nicomedia by Diocletian to teach rhetoric in his new eastern capital, but soon converted to Christianity and was forced to flee to the western provinces during the Great Persecution of 303. There in 314 he wrote *De Mortibus Persecutorum* 'The Deaths of the Persecutors', an account of the years 303–313 which showed how the emperors who had persecuted Christians had all met an unpleasant end.

SUETONIUS

Gaius Suetonius Tranquillus, a friend of the younger Pliny, began life as a lawyer then turned his hand to writing. He entered the imperial secretariat under Trajan but was dismissed by Hadrian in 122 for being too familiar with the empress Sabina. Suetonius's main work, the *De Vita Caesarum*, 'Lives of the Caesars', is a series of 12 biographies from Julius Caesar to Domitian. Suetonius's position would have given him privileged access to official archives and though he is keen on rumour and gossip his testimony is considered generally accurate.

TACITUS

The most famous of Roman imperial historians, Cornelius Tacitus was born in northern Italy or southern Gaul around AD 56 and rose to become consul in 97. His major works were the *Annals*, 'from the death of the Deified Augustus', covering the period 14–68; and the *Histories*, which continued the story up to the assassination of Domitian in 96. Only the first books of the *Histories* survive, however, and the *Annals* too have significant gaps. Tacitus is the quintessential senatorial historian, regretting the death of the republic and the power of the emperors. Though vivid and detailed, his writings can hardly be considered an impartial account. He died probably during Hadrian's reign.

ZOSIMUS

Zosimus was a Greek courtier and treasury official who wrote a *Nea Historia* 'New History' around the year 500. It begins in the third century and since the author was a militant pagan it provides a useful counterpoise to the writings of early Christian historians.

Alongside the works of these individual historians there is the vast mass of inscriptional and epigraphic material, some of it available in English translation (see bibliography).

A GUIDE TO IMPERIAL TITLES

Greek and Roman historians are just one of the sources which give information about Roman emperors. Another major category of evidence is the imperial titles. These appear on coins and inscriptions, and give valuable information about the chronology of a reign. They can help to date military campaigns and other historical events by giving the regnal year of a particular event or honorific title. Imperial titles are given for each of the emperors in the pages which follow, but it may be useful here to introduce the principal elements and their significance.

A typical imperial title – in this instance of the emperor Trajan – takes the form:

Imperator Caesar Divi Nervae Filius Nerva Traianus Optimus Augustus Germanicus Dacicus Parthicus, Pontifex Maximus, Tribuniciae potestatis XXI, Imperator XIII, Consul VI, Pater Patriae

The order of individual elements varies slightly from emperor to emperor, and even between different inscriptions of the same emperor.

Imperator, with which most imperial titles begin, was traditionally the honorific title granted to a Roman commander by his soldiers after a victory. Augustus was the first to use it as a permanent part of his name, to emphasize his unique and unrivalled military authority.

Caesar originated as the family name of Julius Caesar, and was assumed by Augustus on his adoption. It was then passed by adoption to Tiberius and Caligula, and was assumed by subsequent emperors either on their accession or on their adoption or nomination as heir-apparent. From a family name implying descent from Julius Caesar it hence became a mark of status. Diocletian built on existing practice when he created a tetrarchy of two senior emperors (Augusti) and two junior emperors (Caesars).

The formula *Divi Nervae Filius* (son of the deified Nerva) was used by several emperors to indicate their descent (sometimes through adoption – or merely by pious assertion) from a previous emperor, usually an immediate or close predecessor, whose memory was held in particular respect. It was often a political statement: thus Septimius Severus assumed the title 'son of the deified Marcus' in 195 to proclaim and strengthen his legitimacy, though he had never been (nor is ever likely to have been) adopted by Marcus Aurelius, who died 15 years before.

The personal name in this case is *Nerva Traianus*, i.e. the emperor Trajan; *Optimus* (best) is an additional honorific, specific to this emperor who was held in high regard by the senate.

The title *Augustus* usually follows directly after the personal name. It was a title conferred on Augustus by the senate in 27 BC as part of the constitutional settlement following his victory at Actium. This, rather than *Imperator*, was the Roman equivalent of the English term 'emperor': the Augustus was the emperor of Rome.

Following *Augustus* are the 'Victory titles', which relate to specific military successes won by that emperor or his commanders. The custom began under Domitian, who adopted the title *Germanicus* after his German war of 83. It was taken to great lengths by later emperors such as Diocletian, who had no fewer that 17 victory titles in his official list, or Galerius, with almost 30.

The title *Pontifex Maximus* or chief priest was adopted by Augustus on the death of Lepidus in 13 BC, and assumed (with the office) by all later emperors on their accession. Its use continued even under the first Christian emperors but was abandoned by Gratian in 383.

Tribuniciae potestatis refers to the tribunician power which each emperor was given on his accession and which was renewed every year, either on the anniversary of the first conferral or, from the time of Trajan, on 10 December. Tribunician power gave the emperor immunity from prosecution and the right to introduce legislation and to veto laws, elections or the actions of other magistrates. Since it was renewed every year, the number following the tribunician power on a coin or inscription dates it precisely to a particular 12-month period. In the example given above, the emperor Trajan had had his tribunician power renewed for the 21st time on 10 December 116, eight months before his death.

Imperator makes a second appearance in imperial titles towards the end, where it is accompanied by a numeral. This refers to subsequent acclamations by the army, following particular victories during the reign. They are often difficult to date precisely. Trajan was acclaimed *Imperator* a total of 13 times (once on accession, six times during the Dacian Wars and six more during the Parthian War).

Consul was the title of the two leading magistrates of the Roman republic, elected annually. Under the emperors the consuls retained some prestige and some official duties but had little real power, and the office was often given by emperors to reward their supporters. The frequency with which the emperors themselves chose to hold the consulship varied considerably from reign to reign. Most held it in the year after their accession, but some showed little interest in it thereafter, while Domitian, on the other hand, was consul for 10 of his 15 years as emperor. Trajan was consul first in 91, before his accession, and five times during his reign.

Pater Patriae was a purely honorific title granted by the senate originally to the leading statesman Cicero in 63 BC, and later to Julius Caesar. It was held by Augustus and most later emperors and from the reign of Pertinax onwards was assumed routinely on accession. Before then, it was a title granted only after some years of rule, and short-reign emperors such as Galba, Otho and Vitellius never received it at all.

Augustus

Tiberius

Caligula

Claudius

THE JULIO-CLAUDIAN DYNASTY	THE CIVIL WAR OF 69	THE FLAVIAN DYNASTY
Augustus 31 BC–AD 14	Galba 68–69	Vespasian 69–79
Tiberius 14–37	Otho 69	Titus 79–81
Caligula 37–41	Vitellius 69	Domitian 81–96
Claudius 41–54		
Nero 54–68		

Augustus

Tiberius

THE JULIO-CLAUDIAN DYNASTY

| 40 | 30 | 20 | 10 | BC | 0 | AD | 10 | 20 |

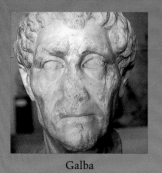
Galba

Otho

Vespasian

Titus

THE FIRST EMPERORS
The Julio-Claudian Dynasty 31 BC–AD 68
The Flavian Dynasty AD 69–96

THE FIRST FIVE EMPERORS OF ROME are among the most famous names known to us from antiquity. Who has not heard of Nero, who played and sang while Rome burned? Or Caligula, who said he would make his favourite racehorse a consul? The imperial court was indeed a place of extravagance and intrigue, but this should not obscure the real achievement of the period: the establishment of imperial government, controlled by a single individual whose power passed at death to the nearest male relative.

Despite the hereditary principle, it is a curious fact that none of the Julio-Claudians was succeeded by his own son. Augustus passed on the imperial purple to his stepson Tiberius; Tiberius to his brother's grandson Gaius (Caligula), who in turn was followed by his uncle Claudius. Yet the prestige of the family was such that for a hundred years it was accepted that the emperor should be one of the descendants of Augustus. Only at Nero's death was that tradition broken, and the consequence then was bitter civil war.

The civil war of AD 69 revealed dangerous divisions within the empire. First the praetorian guard murdered one emperor, Galba, in order to proclaim another, Otho. Then the armies of Upper and Lower Germany marched south to impose their candidate, Vitellius, on the Roman people. Stability returned only with the victory of the armies of the Danube and of the east, and the founding of a new imperial dynasty – that of the Flavians.

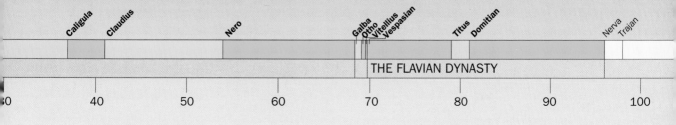

THE FLAVIAN DYNASTY

Caligula Claudius Nero Galba Otho Vitellius Vespasian Titus Domitian Nerva Trajan

40 50 60 70 80 90 100

Augustus

Imperator Caesar Divi Filius
Augustus
27 BC–AD 14

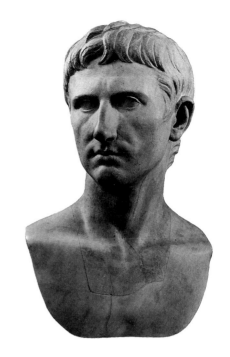

According to Suetonius Augustus 'had clear, bright eyes, in which he liked to have it thought there was a kind of divine power. . . . His teeth were wide apart, small, and ill-kept; his hair was slightly curling and inclining to golden; his eyebrows met.' Marble head of the young Augustus, now in the British Museum.

May it be my privilege to establish the State in a firm and secure position, and reap from that act the fruit that I desire; but only if I may be called the author of the best possible government, and bear with me the hope when I die that the foundations which I have laid for the State will remain unshaken.

Augustus, in Suetonius *Life of the Deified Augustus* XXVIII

He was unusually handsome and exceedingly graceful at all periods of his life, though he cared nothing for personal adornment. He was so far from being particular about the dressing of his hair, that he would have several barbers working in a hurry at the same time, and as for his beard he now had it clipped and now shaved, while at the very same time he would either be reading or writing something.

Suetonius *Life of the Deified Augustus* LXXIX

The emperor Augustus stands Janus-like between the Roman republic and the Roman empire. He was both a culmination of the old order, last of the over-mighty generals, and the beginning of something entirely new. That he succeeded in creating a new type of government was partly because he stayed in power for almost half a century and died in his bed. He was also a shrewd politician who realized the importance of masking his power under traditional republican forms. Augustus can hardly be hailed the saviour of the republic, as he claimed; nor can the rule of one man be expected to have pleased the senate. Yet Augustus restored order to a Rome wracked by decades of civil war, and his advent was a blessing to most ordinary Romans. Whether he was hero or villain is a more difficult question to answer.

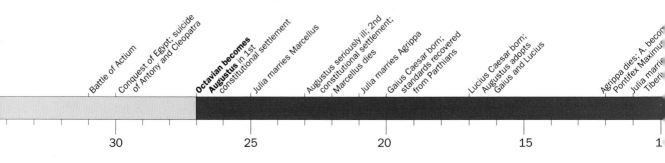

Battle of Actium

Conquest of Egypt; suicide of Antony and Cleopatra

Octavian becomes Augustus in 1st constitutional settlement

Julia marries Marcellus

Augustus seriously ill; 2nd constitutional settlement; Marcellus dies

Julia marries Agrippa

Gaius Caesar born; standards recovered from Parthians

Lucius Caesar born; Augustus adopts Gaius and Lucius

Agrippa dies; A. becomes Pontifex Maximus; Julia marries Tiberius

30   25   20   15   1

AUGUSTUS

The titles adopted by Augustus remained the basis of the imperial titles of all subsequent Roman emperors.
Born at Rome 23 September 63 BC
    Gaius Octavius (Octavian)
On adoption by Julius Caesar (8 May 44 BC)
    Gaius Julius Caesar. 'Caesar' became a title rather than a family name for later emperors.
On deification of Julius Caesar in January 42 BC
    Gaius Julius Caesar Divi filius Imperator
From 40 BC Octavian dropped the name Julius and his own forename Gaius, and switched the title 'Imperator' from the end to the beginning
    Imperator Caesar Divi filius.
    'Imperator Caesar' became standard nomenclature for all subsequent Roman emperors up to the fourth century AD
New title 'Augustus' conferred by the senate on accession 16 January 27 BC
    Imperator Caesar Divi filius Augustus, this became a standard part of the imperial title, usually following the personal name
On 6 March 12 BC, after death of Lepidus
    'Pontifex Maximus' (chief priest)
	Conferred by the senate on 5 February 2 BC
	    Honorary title 'Pater Patriae' (Father of his Country)
	Consul first in 43 BC, then II (33 BC), III (31 BC), IV (30 BC), V (29 BC), VI (28 BC), VII (27 BC), VIII (26 BC), IX (25 BC), X (24 BC), XI (23 BC), XII (5 BC), XIII (2 BC)
	
	Acclaimed 'Imperator' (the title given by the troops to a victorious general) 21 times first in 43 BC
	
	Tribunician power first in 23 BC (under second constitutional settlement); renewed annually on 26 June
	
	Full titles at death
	    Imperator Caesar Divi filius Augustus, Pontifex Maximus, Consul XIII, Imperator XXI, Tribuniciae potestatis XXXVII, Pater Patriae
	
	Wives
	    (1) Claudia 43 BC
	    (2) Scribonia 40 BC
	    (3) Livia Drusilla 38 BC
	Children
	    Julia (by Scribonia)
	
	Died of illness at Nola in Campania 19 August AD 14; buried in the Mausoleum of Augustus

The rise to power

The future emperor Augustus was born plain Gaius Octavius (Octavian) at Rome on 23 September 63 BC. His father (another Gaius Octavius) was the first in the family to become a senator, but died when Octavian was only four. It was his mother who had the more distinguished connection. She was the daughter of Julia, sister to Julius Caesar, and it was through this connection that Octavian made his first steps to prominence.

Octavian served under Julius Caesar in the Spanish expedition of 46 BC, and was designated to take a senior military command in Caesar's projected Parthian expedition of 44 BC, although only 18 years old. Octavian was in Illyricum (modern Albania) preparing for this expedition when news reached him that Caesar had been assassinated. He at once returned to Rome, learning on the way that Caesar had adopted him in his will. The news sharpened his resolve to avenge Caesar's murder, but when he arrived at Rome he found power in the hands of Mark Antony and Aemilius Lepidus, who were urging compromise and amnesty. Octavian refused to accept this, and succeeded in undermining Antony's position by winning over many of Caesar's supporters, including some of the legions.

Many of the senators, too, were opposed to Antony, and during the summer of 44 BC their leader, Cicero, delivered a series of fulminating speeches against him (known as the Philippics). Cicero saw the young Octavian as a useful ally, and when in November 44 Antony retired from Rome to take command in northern Italy, Octavian was dispatched with Cicero's blessing to make war on Antony. Antony was forced to retreat westwards to Gaul, but if Cicero had planned to control Octavian he signally failed to do so. In August 43 Octavian marched on Rome with his army, and compelled the senate to accept him as consul. Three months later he met Antony and Lepidus at Bologna and the three reached an agreement, the Triumvirate, which entirely excluded the senatorial party from power. Cicero died in the proscriptions which followed, and late the next year the Triumvirs defeated Brutus and Cassius, Caesar's assassins, at Philippi in northern Greece.

The victors of Philippi reached a new agreement in October 40 BC by which the Roman empire was to be divided between them, Antony taking the east, Octavian the west, and Lepidus (no longer an equal partner) the province of Africa. To seal the pact, Antony married Octavian's sister. Octavian's own standing had been heightened by the deification of Julius Caesar two years earlier; no longer addressed as Octavian but as

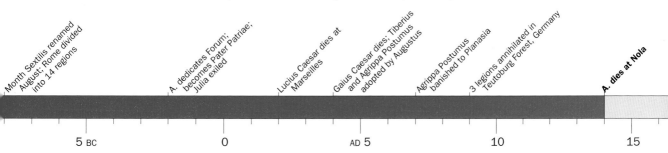

Month Sextilis renamed August; Rome divided into 14 regions

A. dedicates Forum; becomes Pater Patriae; Julia exiled

Lucius Caesar dies at Marseilles

Gaius Caesar dies; Tiberius and Agrippa Postumus adopted by Augustus

Agrippa Postumus banished to Planasia

3 legions annihilated in Teutoburg Forest, Germany

A. dies at Nola

5 BC   0   AD 5   10   15

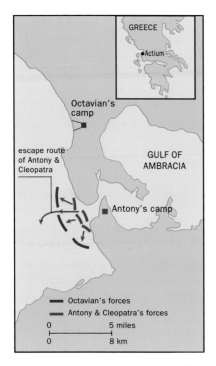

Then came the day of the great conflict, in which Caesar and Antony led out their fleets and fought, one for the safety, the other for the ruin, of the world.

Velleius Paterculus *Roman History* II 85-86

The Battle of Actium on 2 September 31 BC brought an end to the long period of civil war and gave Octavian undisputed mastery of the Roman empire. Actium itself is a promontory on the western coast of Greece, at the mouth of the broad Gulf of Ambracia. Antony established his camp on the south side of the entrance, while Octavian took up position on the northern promontory, some five miles back from the mouth of the Gulf. Their land forces were fairly evenly balanced, but at sea Octavian had the advantage of a larger battle-hardened fleet led by the outstanding Marcus Agrippa. By the end of the summer Agrippa's blockade had seriously weakened Antony's position, and he determined to attempt a break-out by sea. Cleopatra's squadron broke through the line of enemy ships, and Antony followed her with a few more vessels, but the bulk of his fleet surrendered. When Antony's land army capitulated a few days later, Octavian's victory was complete.

'Caesar', he could now also style himself 'Divi filius' or 'son of a god'.

He spent the following years consolidating his hold over the western provinces and delivering Italy from the piracy of Sextus Pompeius, a son of Pompey the Great, who was using Sicily as a base for his fleet. Octavian's faithful friend and able commander Marcus Agrippa brought the campaign to a successful conclusion with a naval victory off Mylae in 36 BC. Lepidus had crossed from Africa to take part, but caused his own downfall by trying to seize command of the victorious legions from Octavian. He was neutralized as a political force, though he remained Pontifex Maximus until his death in 13 BC.

The breach with Antony

This left Antony and Octavian the two rulers of the Roman world. While Octavian was building up his reputation in the west, Antony lived openly with Cleopatra, queen of Egypt, more in the style of a Hellenistic monarch than a Roman commander. Oriental monarchs were not popular at Rome, and Octavian was able to turn the situation to his own advantage. Furthermore, though Antony carried out a useful reorganization of the eastern provinces (which were retained by Octavian), his prestige had been seriously weakened by a failed campaign against the Parthians. In July 32 BC Octavian illegally gained possession of Antony's will and read it out in public; it promised large legacies to his children by Cleopatra, and asked for his body to be returned to Cleopatra for burial should he die in Italy. This was hardly the will of a true Roman, and the senate declared war.

The fateful battle took place at Actium on the west coast of Greece on 2 September 31 BC. Antony's fleet tried to break through Octavian's encirclement but only a few ships escaped, the remainder, and the large land army, surrendered to Octavian. Antony and Cleopatra fled to Egypt, but Octavian resumed the offensive the following year. When he captured Alexandria, Antony committed suicide, followed by Cleopatra a few days later. The treasure of Egypt's rulers, the Ptolemies, fell to Octavian, and Egypt itself became a new province of Rome.

The new constitution

The victory at Actium left Octavian undisputed master of the Roman world, but did not solve the question of his constitutional position. He had no intention of relinquishing power, yet the murder of Julius Caesar warned him to come to some arrangement with the senate. He could not in any case govern entirely on his own; he needed men experienced in administration and public affairs.

Thus in January 27 BC Octavian went through the pantomime of giving up power to the senate, and receiving most of it back again. The whole proceedings were carefully stage-managed by his agents and associates. Octavian retained Egypt, Cyprus and the important military provinces of Spain, Gaul and Syria, for 10 years in the first instance. He continued to be elected consul, as he was every year from 31 to 23 BC. He

Cameo of the emperor Augustus, attributed to the Greek engraver Dioscurides who also carved Augustus's signet ring. From the St Denis treasure, now in the Bibliothèque Nationale, Paris.

also received the name 'Augustus', a slightly archaic word meaning sacred or revered. It was translated in the Greek half of the empire as 'Sebastos' and became the title used by all later emperors. Augustus himself preferred the term 'Princeps' or 'first citizen', though he also retained the title 'Imperator' to underline his position as supreme military commander.

Augustus claimed that in this so-called 'First Settlement' of 27 BC he had restored the republic. The powers he now held were exceptional, mainly in that they were all held by one person, but none of them was entirely without republican precedent. His great achievement, however, lay in persuading the senators to accept his position as head of state, and to find adequate scope for their ambitions without directly threatening his own political aims.

In the summer of 27 BC Augustus left Rome for Gaul and Spain, and did not return until 24 BC. The following year, 23 BC, he fell so seriously ill that he thought he was dying. When he recovered he decided to alter his constitutional position. He resigned the consulship, only holding it twice in later years. In its place, the senate awarded him tribunician power for life. This gave him the right to convene the senate, to propose legislation in the popular assembly, and to veto any enactments. At the

THE HOUSE OF AUGUSTUS

He lived at first near the Forum Romanum, above the Stairs of the Ringmakers, in a house which had belonged to the orator Calvus; afterwards, on the Palatine, but in the no less modest dwelling of Hortensius, which was remarkable neither for size nor elegance, having but short colonnades with columns of Alban stone, and rooms without any marble decorations or handsome pavements. For more than forty years too he used the same bedroom in winter and summer.

Suetonius *Life of the Deified Augustus* LXXII

The residence of Augustus on the Palatine was large for this crowded part of Rome, but not palatial. The remains which have been unearthed form two sides of a colonnaded courtyard, and included dining and reception rooms and a pair of libraries. Augustus probably acquired the house during the proscriptions of 42–41 BC, when its previous owner Hortensius was executed. He planned to extend it considerably, and bought up adjacent properties for the purpose, but changed his mind and used most of the land instead for a splendid Temple of Apollo. Other parts he retained for the use of himself and his family. This included the so-called 'House of Livia', a suite of four rooms decorated with elaborate wall-paintings.

Wall paintings from the so-called 'House of Livia', c.30–25 BC.

THE IMPERIAL IMAGE

Statues and sculptures played an important part in creating the new public image of Augustus as first citizen, emperor and priest. As priest *(below)*, he is represented with modest or reflective gaze, his toga drawn over his head. The portrayal lays stress on Augustus's piety rather than his power, and was the type he preferred in later years. As emperor, the most striking image is the marble statue from Livia's villa at Prima Porta, just north of Rome *(above)*. Here we see Augustus as a military leader, with right arm outstretched in gesture of command. He wears a ceremonial breastplate, decorated in low relief with a scene showing the return of captured Roman standards by the Parthians. The figure is over 6.5 ft (2 m) tall, rather more than life-size, and there are traces of painting and gilding, but the facial expression, conveyed, is one of gravity rather than vainglory.

same time, his command over the provinces was renewed for a further period, with the modification that it was now formally 'maius' (superior), and overrode that of any other provincial governor.

This so-called 'Second Settlement' got off to a rather troubled start, for the following year there was plague and famine at Rome and the people offered Augustus first a dictatorship and then an annual and perpetual consulship. At last in 19 BC he agreed to accept not the consulship but consular power. His authority thus became equal to that of the consuls in Rome and Italy, and much greater than theirs in the provinces. In addition, he controlled the army. It was a position of unassailable power, backed up by the immense moral authority he had acquired.

The success of Augustus's policy is shown by the fact that there was only one serious conspiracy against him. He handled the senate with firmness but respect, setting a model for later emperors. Senators and others were recruited to his cause, to form the nucleus of an imperial civil service. The culmination came when in 2 BC they gave Augustus a new honour, that of 'Pater Patriae' (Father of his Country), in recognition of his benevolent despotism.

The Augustan age

Augustus was keen to present the victory at Actium as the end of the civil war and the beginning of a new era. A key part of the programme was the rebuilding of Rome itself. This included the restoration of existing structures which had been neglected during the civil war; Augustus claimed to have restored 82 temples in one year alone. There were also grandiose new buildings: the Theatre of Marcellus, the Temple of Apollo on the Palatine, the Horologium or sun-dial (which used an Egyptian obelisk as its pointer), the great circular Mausoleum, and the massive Forum of Augustus with its Temple of Mars Ultor 'the Avenger'. Augustus's own efforts were aided by those of Agrippa, who embarked on several major building projects in the Campus Martius region of the city. Among these was the Pantheon, later rebuilt by Hadrian. Agrippa was also responsible for repairing the city's water system and building two new aqueducts, the Aqua Julia and the Aqua Virgo. Augustus himself took responsibility for the all-important corn supply and reorganized Rome into 14 administrative regions.

One building is lacking from Augustus's reign: an imperial palace. He continued to live in a modest but spacious house on the Palatine, avoiding the overt trappings of monarchy. He was equally careful in the question of the imperial cult. Subjects in the eastern provinces had long been accustomed to worshipping their rulers during their lifetimes. Augustus forbade worship of himself alone, but outside the capital he was happy enough to encourage the cult of Rome and Augustus, where his own name was linked to the fortunes of the state. The cult soon spread to the western provinces, including Italy itself. Officially, however, Augustus firmly refused all suggestion of divine honours while he lived, though he continued to style himself 'Divi filius', son of the deified Julius Caesar.

THE DARK HAND OF LIVIA

Cameo of Livia, now in the Royal Coin Collection at the Hague.

In domestic virtue she was of the old school, though her affability went further than was approved by women of the elder world. An imperious mother, she was an accommodating wife, and an excellent match for the subtleties of her husband and the insincerity of her son.

Tacitus *Annals* V.1

Livia Drusilla, the redoubtable lady whom Augustus married in January 38 BC, proved an able and powerful consort. She won a reputation for generosity, and encouraged Augustus to show clemency towards his opponents. She was also tolerant of his numerous infidelities. On the darker side, she was suspected of murder and intrigue, procuring the deaths of Marcellus, Gaius and Lucius so that her own son Tiberius would succeed Augustus. The most remarkable accusation against Livia concerns the death of Augustus himself. In his final months he made a secret visit to Planasia where his last-surviving grandson, Agrippa Postumus, was in exile. Livia may have feared that Agrippa was about to be reinstated as a rival to Tiberius. To pre-empt any such occurrence, 'she . . . smeared with poison some figs that were still on trees from which Augustus was wont to gather the fruit with his own hands; then she ate those that had not been smeared, offering the poisoned ones to him.' Livia survived Augustus by 15 years, dying in AD 29 at the grand old age of 86.

Augustus the man

According to Suetonius, Augustus was short in stature, 'but this was concealed by the fine proportions and symmetry of his figure'. Suetonius goes on, 'It is said that his body was covered with spots and that he had birthmarks scattered over his breast and belly . . . also numerous callous places resembling ringworm, caused by a constant itching of his body and a vigorous use of the strigil. . . . He complained of his bladder, too, and was relieved of the pain only after passing stones in his urine.' He was tolerant of criticism, and won genuine popular support by hosting games, by new buildings, and by measures for the general good. He saw that his personal standing and security would be strengthened by governing in the public interest as well as his own. Though he possessed supreme power, he was in a sense a constitutional monarch.

Augustus had a particular fondness for playing dice, but often provided his guests with the money to place bets. He also had a good sense of humour and a liking for homely turns of phrase, such as 'quicker than you can cook asparagus'. In the literary field Augustus's accomplishments were relatively modest. We know that he wrote an autobiography in 13 volumes, taking his life story up to the time of the Cantabrian War (26–25 BC), but nothing of it has survived. He also composed epigrams in the bath and began a tragedy called 'Ajax'. When asked later what had become of it he replied that 'his Ajax had fallen on his sponge' (the sponge used to erase writing in ink) as the mythical Ajax had fallen on his sword. On the other hand Augustus did not have a fluent command of Greek, and if he needed to speak in the language he would write what he wished to say in Latin first and have it translated. He was an educated man, but no scholar-emperor.

The central figure in Augustus's private life was Livia Drusilla, whom he married in his mid-twenties and remained married to until his death. She was in fact his third wife, after Claudia, stepdaughter of Mark Antony (43–41 BC), and Scribonia, a relative of Sextus Pompeius (40–39 BC). Livia was already married when Augustus met her, but her husband obligingly divorced her at Augustus's request. Suetonius tells us that Augustus 'loved and esteemed her to the end without a rival', but also had the reputation of an inveterate womanizer. Livia turned a blind eye to his string of mistresses, but it cannot always have been easy. For instance, some said that when Augustus left Rome for Gaul in 16 BC his real aim was to live openly with his mistress Terentia. This was ironic in a man who was keen to legislate on public morals, and banished his daughter and granddaughter to small islands for adultery.

Conquests and frontiers

Augustus was no great military leader, and had the good sense to recognize the fact. In his early years he relied heavily on Marcus Agrippa, his faithful friend, who had commanded the fleet at Actium. After Actium, Augustus took a personal lead in only one further campaign, the Cantabrian War of 26–25 BC in Spain; but even there it was one of his

MONUMENTS OF A DYNASTY

He built many public works, in particular the following: his forum with the Temple of Mars the Avenger, the Temple of Apollo on the Palatine, and the shrine of Jupiter the Thunderer on the Capitol.

Suetonius *Life of the Deified Augustus* XXIX

Augustus is famous for his boast that he found Rome brick and left it marble. Some of his buildings were directly connected with his dynastic ambitions. The Mausoleum, for example, was a dynastic monument on a massive scale, almost 295 ft (90 m) across and 131 ft (40 m) wide, capped by a bronze statue of Augustus himself. The stated aim of the Forum which Augustus dedicated in 2 BC, was to provide better facilities for the administration of the provinces, but it was also a powerful family statement. At its focus was the massive Temple of Mars Ultor, 'the Avenger', a reference to Augustus's avengement of Caesar's murder. One of the outstanding features of the Forum of Augustus was the wealth of statuary. In the colonnades on one side were statues depicting members of the Julian family; on the other, statues of all the greatest men of Rome, from Romulus founder of the city to late republican leaders such as Marius, Pompey and Sulla. Augustus and his family thus took their proper place among a whole gallery of worthies who had made Rome great.

The Mausoleum of Augustus in the Campus Martius at Rome. (Left) Reconstruction showing the tree-planted slopes above the lower drum, and the bronze statue of the emperor on the summit. The structure was largely of concrete faced in opus reticulatum (small triangular blocks of tufa), but the outer surfaces were finished in gleaming white marble. Only the denuded core remains today (below right). The ashes of Augustus, Tiberius, Livia, Claudius and many other members of the Julio-Claudian family were deposited in the burial chamber at the centre of the Mausoleum. The first person to be buried here was Marcellus, Augustus's nephew, in 23 BC; the last was the emperor Nerva, in AD 98.

The Forum of Augustus and the Temple of Mars Ultor. (Left) In the foreground, the steps of the temple and the column bases of the frontal colonnade. Behind rises the massive screen wall of tufa blocks, over 98 ft (30 m) high, which shielded the buildings from the crowded tenement blocks of the Subura beyond and acted as a fire break. In its original form (below) the Forum served as a portrait gallery of famous Romans from Aeneas to Augustus.

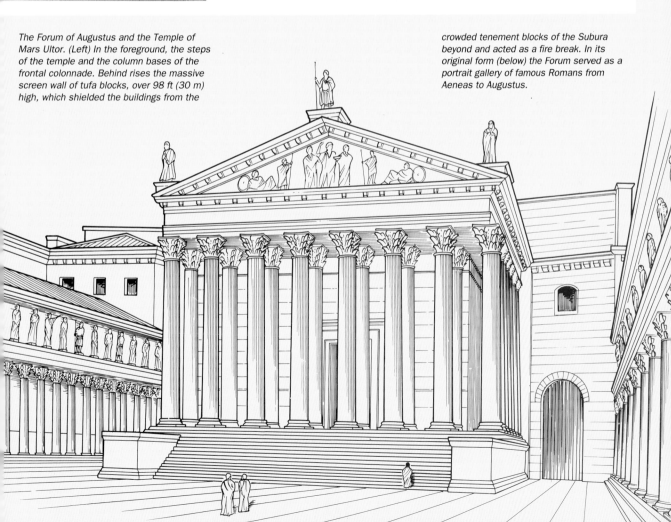

generals who brought the war to a successful conclusion.

The reign was marked nevertheless by some notable Roman successes. First and most important was the conquest of Egypt in 30 BC. That province soon became the principal source of the crucial free grain supply for the population of Rome. Augustus achieved a diplomatic victory in 20 BC, when he recovered the legionary standards captured by the Parthians at the disastrous battle of Carrhae in 53 BC. It was frontiers, however, which were the main military preoccupation of the reign. In the east, the Syrian desert and River Euphrates formed a natural boundary. To the north, Julius Caesar had already conquered Gaul in the 50s and established a new frontier along the Rhine. Augustus made the Danube his Balkan frontier after some hard-fought campaigns conquering the Alpine tribes and pacifying the northern Balkans. He then had to decide how best to carry this line to the North Sea. Following the Danube and Rhine to their sources created an awkward re-entrant in the Alps; a much shorter frontier would result if Roman rule could be carried forward to the Elbe. This Augustus determined to achieve, and in 12 BC he gave his stepson Drusus command of the Rhine legions with orders to advance to the Elbe. When Drusus died in 9 BC the task was transferred to his other stepson Tiberius. The work was steadily carried forward by others when Tiberius went into self-imposed exile on Rhodes, but Tiberius resumed command in AD 4. He was planning to conquer Bohemia and Moravia in AD 6 when he was called away to deal with a serious Balkan revolt. Then in AD 9 came the disaster of the Teutoburg Forest.

Quintilius Varus, commander of the Rhine legions, had spent the summer of AD 9 on the banks of the Weser. Germany was by now considered pacified and Varus took no special precautions when moving back to winter quarters on the Rhine. In September that year he was ambushed by the Germans in the Teutoburg Forest (near Osnabrück) and his three legions annihilated. Tiberius moved swiftly to the Rhine frontier to prevent any German invasion of Gaul, but Augustus himself was deeply shocked. It was said that for several months afterwards he went in mourning, cutting neither his beard nor his hair, and from time to time hitting his head against a door, crying 'Quintilius Varus, give me back my legions!'

Plans for an Elbe frontier were abandoned, and so cautious did Augustus become that when he died five years later, he left Tiberius a document in his own hand advising him to keep the empire within its present frontiers.

The military establishment

It seems curious that the loss of three legions could so seriously upset Augustus, but there was no reserve army, and reinforcement of one frontier meant transfer of legions from another. Augustus's overall policy was to keep the military establishment at the minimum necessary to ensure peace within the empire and guard the frontiers. Soon after

THE INTENDED HEIR

Portrait bust of Gaius Caesar from the Museum of Art and History, Geneva.

Augustus was extremely fond of his grandsons Gaius and Lucius, and adopted them as his own children in 17 BC. He intended them to succeed him, but was thwarted by their early deaths. The following letter to Gaius, written while the latter was in Syria in AD 1, shows the warmth of Augustus's feelings for the young prince:

The ninth day before the Kalends of October [23 September]. Greetings, my dear Gaius, my dearest little donkey, whom, so help me! I constantly miss whenever you are away from me. But especially on such days as today my eyes are eager for my Gaius, and wherever you have been today, I hope you have celebrated my sixty-fourth birthday in health and happiness. For, as you see, I have passed the climacteric common to all old men, the sixty-third year. And I pray the gods that whatever time is left to me I may pass with you safe and well, with our country in a flourishing condition, while you are playing the man and preparing to succeed to my position.

Aulus Gellius *Attic Nights* XV.7

Actium, he reduced the number of legions to 28, most of which were stationed on the imperial frontiers. After the Varus disaster eight of the remaining 25 legions were based along the Rhine, seven along the Danube, and four in Syria.

Their control was crucial to Augustus's power. The soldiers swore loyalty to him as imperator, not to the senate or the state. He was the first to give them fixed terms of service and pay. To further consolidate his position Augustus established the praetorian guard, nine élite cohorts, each of 500 (or perhaps 1000) men, based in Rome and its vicinity, whose sole function was to protect the emperor.

The succession

Augustus's reign was more successful than he could ever have foreseen; indeed he lived long enough to make his family seem the natural rulers in the eyes of the Roman people. The problem became how to ensure that the imperial mantle did in reality pass to one of his kin. The plans he made were not helped by a whole series of untimely deaths.

Augustus tried first to keep the succession in his own (Julian) bloodline. He did not consider Livia's sons of her previous marriage, Tiberius and Drusus, on an equal footing, since they belonged to the Claudian blood-line. This was fine in principle, but foundered since he himself lacked a male heir. Save for a baby born prematurely, his marriage to Livia produced no children of either sex, but Augustus did have a daughter, Julia, by his previous marriage to Scribonia. His dynastic plans therefore focused on Julia's husbands and children.

In 25 BC Augustus married Julia to Marcellus, the son of his sister Octavia. Marcellus was only in his late teens at the time, too young to share real power. When Augustus thought he was dying in 23 BC, he passed his signet ring not to Marcellus but to his trusted friend and lieutenant Agrippa. There was all the makings of a power-struggle between the two, but late in the same year Marcellus himself fell ill and died.

This left Agrippa the obvious candidate for the succession, and in 21 BC Augustus had him divorce his existing wife and marry the widowed Julia. Agrippa was 25 years her senior, had already been married several times, and was a striking change from the youthful Marcellus, but the marriage succeeded in producing three sons and two daughters. The eldest was Gaius, born in 20 BC; when a younger brother Lucius followed three years later Augustus adopted the two of them as his own. His long-terms plans for the succession were henceforth pinned on his two young grandsons, though while they were still mere children Agrippa retained the position of heir-apparent.

Agrippa died in 12 BC, leaving Julia widowed once again. Augustus realized that if he himself should die, her young sons would be left without a guardian. Now for the first time his thoughts were directed towards Livia's adult sons Tiberius and Drusus. Augustus obliged Tiberius, the elder of the two, to divorce his present wife Vipsania (daughter of Agrippa by the latter's first marriage) and marry Julia, and

THE JULIO-CLAUDIAN FAMILY

Augustus was adopted by Julius Caesar in his will, and thus became a member of the Julian family, which claimed its origins from the legendary hero Aeneas. The Claudian connection came with Augustus's marriage to Livia Drusilla in 38 BC. Her own father had been a Claudius, and her first husband (before Augustus) was Tiberius Claudius Nero. Augustus tried to keep the succession in the Julian line through his only daughter Julia, but his chosen heirs died before reaching maturity leaving Tiberius as the eventual successor. He was Livia's son from her first marriage, and hence a Claudian (though Augustus made him a Julian by adoption). Tiberius's successors, too, were Claudians, descendants of his brother Drusus, down to the death of Nero in AD 68.

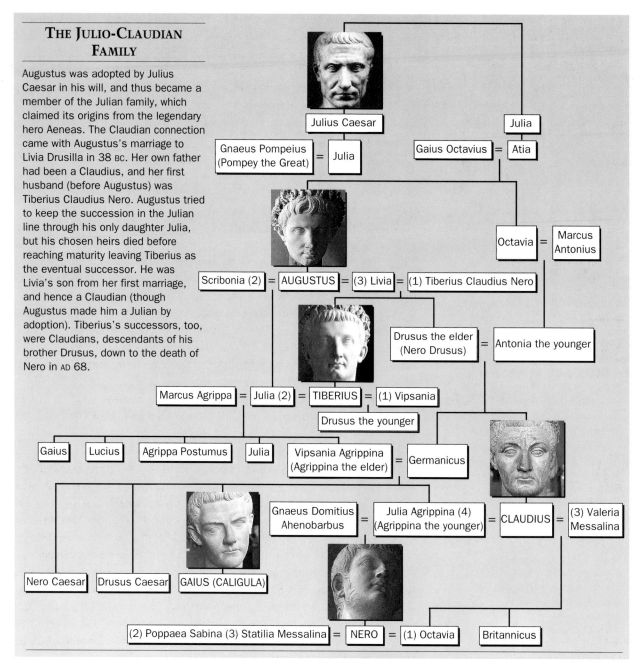

become protector for the young princes. Tiberius was deeply attached to Vipsania and strongly resented the move, but the marriage went ahead on 12 February 11 BC.

Gaius and Lucius were popular, but spoiled and precocious. In 6 BC Augustus sought to check their ambitions by giving Tiberius tribunician power for five years, but Tiberius refused to be drawn into a feud with his stepsons. Already at odds with his wife Julia, he retired from public life to self-imposed exile on the island of Rhodes.

Gaius's star continued to rise. He became consul in AD 1, and was sent

THE AUTHORIZED VERSION

Below is a copy of the acts of the Deified Augustus by which he placed the whole world under the sovereignty of the Roman people, and of the amounts which he expended upon the state and the Roman people, as engraved upon two bronze columns which have been set up in Rome.

So runs the heading of the 'Res Gestae', an official account of Augustus's achievements as he himself wished them to be remembered. Thus we read 'In my sixth and seventh consulships [28–27 BC], when I had extinguished the flames of civil war, after receiving by universal consent the absolute control of affairs, I transferred the republic from my own control to the will of the senate and of the Roman people.' The idea that he was a constitutional ruler rather than a conquering general was one which Augustus tried hard to promote. The bronze original of the Res Gestae was set up after his death on pillars in front of the Mausoleum. What survives today is a copy inscribed on the inside walls of the Temple of Rome and Augustus at Ancyra (modern Ankara) in Turkey.

with special powers to Syria to reassert Roman authority in Armenia. Then in AD 3 he was wounded in a siege, became ill and depressed, and set out back to Italy. He died at Limyra in south-west Turkey on 21 February AD 4. His brother Lucius had been carried off by a sudden illness at Marseilles two years before. Augustus's plans for the succession were once more in disarray.

The final choice

The deaths of Gaius and Lucius left Augustus only one viable successor: Tiberius, son of Livia. At last, on 26 June AD 4, he adopted the 44-year-old Tiberius, along with his last-surviving grandson the 15-year-old Agrippa Postumus (younger brother of Gaius and Lucius). At the same time Tiberius adopted Augustus's great-nephew Germanicus. Agrippa Postumus proved a violent and unpleasant character, and was sent into permanent exile on the islands of Planasia three years later. This left Germanicus the final hope for the Julian blood-line, though he was too young to succeed Augustus directly.

Tiberius continued to prove himself an able general, but Augustus never really liked him as a person. It was only the deaths of Marcellus, Gaius and Lucius, and the exile of Agrippa Postumus, which gave Tiberius his chance. There were not lacking those who saw in this turn of events the hand of Livia, Tiberius's mother. Rumour had it she had killed off the other heirs, one by one, until only her son was left. Good luck and disease are a less colourful but more likely explanation.

A peaceful end

During his final years Augustus began to withdraw from public life, excusing himself from banquets and regular senate meetings on grounds of old age. He left Rome for the last time in the summer of AD 14, intending to travel with Tiberius to Capri and then on to Beneventum (inland from Naples) whence Tiberius would continue alone to Pannonia. While they were sailing south towards Capri, Augustus fell ill with diarrhoea. He spent four days resting and feasting on Capri, but when they crossed back to the mainland Augustus could go no further. He died at Nola on 19 August AD 14, 44 years after Actium, and only a month short of his 76th birthday.

The body was carried to Rome, given a splendid funeral on the Campus Martius, and the ashes placed in the great Mausoleum nearby. The Res Gestae, an account of Augustus's achievements, was inscribed on a pair of bronze pillars set up at the Mausoleum entrance. His true legacy, however, was the institution of Roman emperor. Tact and discretion had created a basis for imperial government far stronger than could have been forged by naked power alone. At the end, on his death-bed, Augustus joked about the play-acting which had been involved. He called for a mirror, had his hair combed and his jaw set straight, then asked his friends to applaud as he departed the comedy of life; he had played his role well.

Tiberius
Tiberius Caesar Augustus
14–37

Suetonius records that Tiberius 'was of fair complexion and wore his hair rather long at the back so much as even to cover the nape of the neck'. Tacitus on the other hand, tells us that the emperor had a head 'without a trace of hair, and an ulcerous face generally variegated with plasters.' Naturally, neither baldness nor ulcers find any place in official portraits, such as this bust from the Louvre, Paris.

Cameo showing the emperor Tiberius with his mother Livia, wife of Augustus; now in the Boston Museum of Fine Arts.

He was large and strong of frame, and of a stature above the average. . . He strode along with his neck stiff and bent forward, usually with a stern countenance and for the most part in silence, never or very rarely conversing with his companions. . . . All of these mannerisms of his, which were disagreeable and signs of arrogance, were remarked by Augustus, who often tried to excuse them to the senate and people by declaring that they were natural failings, and not intentional.

Suetonius *Life of Tiberius* LXVIII

The emperor Tiberius is an enigmatic figure. Tacitus and Suetonius portray him as a mean-spirited tyrant, a man ever-ready to spill blood, living a life of odious seclusion on Capri while Rome was riven by treason trials and innocent deaths. That is not the whole truth. For in Tiberius, rather than deep-seated villainy, we may perceive a profound sense of inadequacy. Here was a ruler who shunned public life even before his accession, and had spent his active years not as a politician in Rome but as a field commander in Germany and the Balkans. We should not forget either that he was 54 when he became emperor, 67 when he retired to Capri, and 77 when he died.

Tiberius's progress from infant to emperor was far from smooth. He

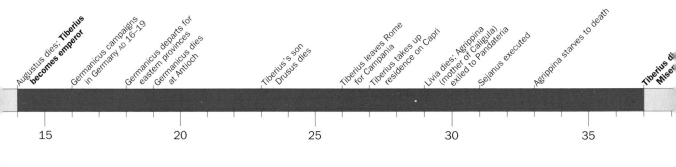

Augustus dies; **Tiberius becomes emperor**

Germanicus campaigns in Germany AD 16–19

Germanicus departs for eastern provinces
Germanicus dies at Antioch

Tiberius's son Drusus dies

Tiberius leaves Rome for Campania
Tiberius takes up residence on Capri

Livia dies; Agrippina (mother of Caligula) exiled to Pandateria
Sejanus executed

Agrippina starves to death

Tiberius di Miser

15   20   25   30   35

TIBERIUS

Born at Rome 16 November 42 BC
Tiberius Claudius Nero
On adoption by Augustus (AD 4)
Tiberius Iulius Caesar
On accession 19 August AD 14
Tiberius Caesar Augustus
Added March AD 15
'Pontifex Maximus'

Frequently styled 'son of the deified Augustus' (Divi Augusti filius)

Tribunician power first on 26 June 6 BC, for a period of five years to 25 June 1 BC; then continuously from 26 June AD 4, renewed annually

Imperator first in 9 BC, then II (8 BC), III (AD 6), IV (AD 8), V (AD 9), VI (AD 11), VII (AD 13), VIII (AD 16)
Consul I (13 BC), II (7 BC), III (with Germanicus, AD 18), IV (with Drusus, AD 21), V (with Sejanus, AD 31)

Full titles at death
Tiberius Caesar Divi Augusti filius Augustus, Pontifex Maximus, Tribuniciae potestatis XXXIIX, Imperator VIII, Consul V

Wives
(1) Vipsania Agrippina 16 BC
(2) Julia 11 BC (divorced 2 BC)
Children
Nero Claudius Drusus (by Vipsania)
A son by Julia died soon after birth

Died (smothered?) at Misenum 16 March AD 37; ashes placed in the Mausoleum of Augustus

was born in a house on the Palatine (then a fashionable residential district) on 16 November 42 BC. His father was Tiberius Claudius Nero, a member of the distinguished Claudian house, his mother the redoubtable Livia Drusilla. The older Tiberius fought against Octavian in the Civil War and in 40 BC was forced to flee to Greece. He returned to Italy the following year, and then divorced his wife Livia so that Octavian could marry her. Within a dozen years Octavian had become Augustus, and Tiberius found himself stepson of the first Roman emperor.

The troubled succession

As Augustus's stepson Tiberius was powerfully placed, but he did not automatically become heir to the empire. In 25 BC he had his first posting as an officer in Cantabria. Five years later he campaigned against the Parthians and won back the legionary standards lost by Crassus at Carrhae 33 years before. In 16 BC he was appointed governor of Gaul, and in 15 BC with his brother Drusus he conquered new territory in the Alps.

The reward was Tiberius's first consulship, in 13 BC. The joy did not last, however, since the following year he was forced to divorce his beloved wife Vipsania Agrippina in order to marry Augustus's widowed daughter, Julia. This match made him guardian of the young Caesars Gaius and Lucius, the heirs-apparent, and the scheme was strengthened by the fact that Julia had already taken a liking to Tiberius. The attraction was not mutual, and the marriage proved a disaster. Tiberius himself spent most of his time away from Rome on campaign. By 6 BC he decided he had had enough. Suetonius records that he felt 'disgust at his wife, whom he dared neither accuse nor put away, though he could no longer endure her'. He asked permission from Augustus and Livia to withdraw from public life and go into voluntary retirement.

The eventual heir

Tiberius retired to the island of Rhodes, where he lived quietly for almost eight years. In 2 BC Julia was banished to Pandateria for adultery and her marriage to Tiberius dissolved, but Gaius Caesar, the heir apparent, would not permit him to return to the capital. For a while Tiberius went in fear for his life. Then in August AD 2 he was allowed back to Rome on the firm understanding that he took no part in public affairs.

Within days of his arrival news came of Lucius's death in Marseilles, followed early the next year by that of Gaius. This left Augustus without an heir, and opened the way for Livia to plead her son's cause. Quite what Augustus felt about Tiberius is unclear. One tradition has Augustus exclaim on his deathbed 'Alas for the Roman people, to be ground by jaws that crunch so slowly!' He certainly thought Tiberius austere and stiff, and when adopting Tiberius on 27 June AD 4, he added the words 'This I do for reasons of state'. Tiberius was an adequate successor, perhaps, but not one he embraced with any enthusiasm.

Soon after his adoption Tiberius was back with the legions on the

Silver cup, one of a pair from a small villa at Boscoreale, near Pompeii, showing Tiberius riding a chariot in a triumphal procession. He grasps an eagle sceptre in one hand and a laurel branch in the other, while the attendant behind him holds the triumphal crown over his head.

Rhine, campaigning deep into Germany. Then in AD 6 he went to suppress a serious Balkan revolt. Hardly was that over than news arrived of Varus's disaster in Germany, and Tiberius was back on the Rhine shoring up the defences. He returned to Rome to celebrate a triumph in October AD 12, and remained in Italy during Augustus's final months. Of his military prowess there was no doubt, but he still had almost no experience of running the empire. Nor was much effort made to give him any. Tiberius was on his way back to the Balkans when an urgent message called him to Augustus's deathbed.

The new emperor

When Augustus died on 19 August AD 14, Tiberius was the clear successor, yet there was no precedent for the peaceful transfer of power from one man to another. Previous leaders, such as Sulla, Julius Caesar, or Augustus himself, had seized power by force, not by inheritance. There was, in addition, a dynastic problem which demanded urgent action. Agrippa Postumus, younger brother of Gaius and Lucius, had also been adopted by Augustus in AD 4, and though later imprisoned on the island of Planasia he still constituted a dangerous rival.

Agrippa was soon disposed of, but the constitutional question was less straightforward. Tiberius had been granted supreme power alongside Augustus in AD 12, and was heir to Augustus's enormous personal fortune. It was for the senate to decide which of Augustus's honours should be offered to Tiberius. Tiberius showed some reluctance to assume power, but his reticence merely irritated the senate. Tiberius wished to preserve Augustus's fiction that the emperor was merely First Citizen; he was in a sense a supporter of the old republican tradition; but there was never any doubt where real power lay.

Next Tiberius had to deal with the legions. These had sworn their loyalty to Augustus rather than the state, and saw the change of ruler as an opportunity to extract a pay rise. Tiberius sent his son Drusus to pacify the Pannonian legions, but the mutiny of the Rhine army proved dangerous, and was only with difficulty suppressed by Tiberius's adoptive son Germanicus.

The first decade

Drusus and Germanicus played an important role during Tiberius's early years as emperor, Germanicus drawing considerable prestige from his ancestry: not only was he adoptive son of Tiberius, but he was also great-nephew of Augustus, had inherited Julian blood from his mother Antonia, and was married to Augustus's grand-daughter Agrippina the elder. Livia, on the other hand, was a less welcome partner in power, and Tiberius took steps to limit her influence. She had been made Augusta in Augustus's will; but Tiberius refused to allow her the title 'Mother of her Country' or the honour of a lictor.

IMPERIAL INTENTIONS

Senators, I am a human being performing human tasks, and it is my ambition to fulfil the role of princeps [emperor]. I want you to understand this, and I want future generations to believe it; you and they will do more than adequate service to my reputation if I am held to be worthy of my forebears, careful for your interests, steadfast in danger, and not afraid to be unpopular if I am serving the national good. As far as I am concerned, if you hold these opinions of me, they will stand as my temples and my finest statues, and they will last.

Tiberius, quoted in Tacitus *Annals*
IV.38

Germanicus remained with the Rhine army from AD 14 to 16, leading the legions deep into Germany in successive campaigns. He managed to recover two of the three legionary standards lost at the Teutoburg forest, and buried the remains of the Roman dead. There was no longer any idea of permanently advancing the Roman frontier east of the Rhine, however, and Tiberius cut short expensive and unnecessary operations by recalling Germanicus to Rome. He celebrated a triumph there on 26 May 17, and the following year became Tiberius's colleague as consul.

This marked out Germanicus as the chosen successor. By the time he became consul, however, he was already on his way to the east, with special powers to settle various problems in the provinces. There he fell into conflict with Gnaeus Piso, the new governor of Syria, and overstepped his authority by visiting Egypt without imperial permission. When Germanicus fell ill and died at Antioch on 10 October AD 19 it was thought that Piso had poisoned him. Piso was tried for murder and forced to commit suicide, but there was suspicion he had been acting on Tiberius's orders.

Tiberius's own son Drusus now became heir-apparent. He too had been sent abroad with special powers as governor of Pannonia in AD 17, and returned to celebrate a triumph on 28 May AD 20. The following year

THE VIRTUOUS PRINCE

It is the general opinion that Germanicus possessed all the highest qualities of body and mind, to a degree never equalled by anyone; a handsome person, unequalled valour, surpassing ability in the oratory of Greece and Rome, unexampled kindliness, and a remarkable desire and capacity for winning men's regard and inspiring their affection.

Suetonius *Life of Caligula* III

Germanicus is painted by Suetonius in such glowing colours that he seems hardly human. The reality was rather less perfect. He was the son of Tiberius's brother Drusus, and was adopted by the latter when Drusus died in 9 BC. Germanicus's first major role was suppressing the mutiny of the Rhine legions after Augustus's death. Tacitus would have us believe that the soldiers offered to make him emperor instead of Tiberius; but what they really wanted was better pay and conditions. Tacitus also alleges that Germanicus was recalled in AD 16 because Tiberius had become jealous of his success. This too is propaganda, designed to show how much better an emperor he would have made than Tiberius. Germanicus was only a moderately competent general and his second campaign into Germany very nearly ended in disaster. When he died in AD 19, however, he became a popular hero, the focus for all those discontented with Tiberius's rule.

Detail of the 'Grand Camée' showing Tiberius enthroned and Germanicus in full armour.

SEJANUS AND THE GUARDS

The power of the prefectship, which had hitherto been moderate, he increased by massing the cohorts, dispersed through the capital, in one camp, in order that commands should reach them simultaneously, and that their numbers, their strength, and the sight of one another, might in themselves breed confidence and in others awe.

Tacitus *Annals* IV.2

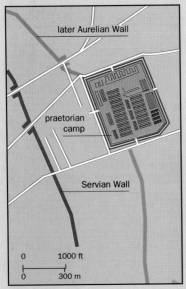

Thus Tacitus credits Sejanus with the decision to concentrate the praetorian guard in a single camp on the eastern edge of the city. This was of standard playing card shape (slightly distorted on the south-east side), with walls of brick-faced concrete enclosing a regular arrangement of barrack blocks. It covered an area of 40 acres, a little less than a normal legionary camp, and housed the nine élite cohorts of the praetorian guard and the three 'urban' cohorts of the city police. Remains of the camp walls can still be seen where they were built into the later city wall by Aurelian.

he in turn shared the consulship with Tiberius. Yet he, too, met an untimely end, dying at Rome on 14 September 23 while still in his late 30s. Eight years later it was revealed that he had been poisoned by his wife, Livilla, acting in concert with her lover Lucius Aelius Sejanus, commander of the praetorian guard.

The infamous Sejanus

The murder of Drusus was but one of the many crimes imputed to Sejanus, who openly entered the dynastic struggle two years after Drusus's death when he asked Tiberius for permission to marry Livilla. Tiberius warned him that he was looking above his station, since he was only a knight, not a senator. But though Sejanus did not succeed in his marriage plans, his power increased considerably when Tiberius left Rome for Campania in AD 26. The following year the emperor settled on the island of Capri, and never visited the capital again. This meant that he was not on hand to oversee business in the senate, and access to the emperor on Capri was entirely under Sejanus's control. He thus gained a stranglehold over official appointments, and an unrivalled position which set him way above consuls and senators.

Relations between Tiberius and his mother Livia remained at a low ebb. Their disagreements were among the reasons he left Rome for Capri. When she died in AD 29 at the grand old age of 86 he refused to attend the funeral, forbade her deification, and disregarded the provisions of her will.

That same year saw the arrest of Agrippina, widow of Germanicus, and her eldest son Nero. They were accused by Sejanus of plotting to succeed Tiberius (which might well have been true), and exiled to the Pontian islands. Agrippina, banished to Pandateria, was so badly beaten that one of her eyes was destroyed. She starved herself to death on 18 October 33. Nero, sent to a different island, was forced to commit suicide. Two years earlier Agrippina's second son, Drusus, was also arrested. Convicted of treason he was starved to death in a palace cellar; in his extremity he even tried to eat the stuffing of his mattress. The great event of that year, AD 31, however, was the fall of Sejanus. Tiberius had raised him to senator and made him his colleague as consul at the beginning of the year. Within a few months he had begun to doubt the wisdom of this act. It may be that Sejanus really was planning to seize power for himself. He certainly had many enemies who were ready to sow suspicion in Tiberius's mind. The crucial argument was a letter from Antonia, Tiberius's sister-in-law, warning him of his danger. Tiberius decided that Sejanus must go, but since Sejanus controlled the praetorian guard he had to act with great caution.

Tiberius's solution was to enlist the aid of Naevius Sertorius Macro, who was promised Sejanus's command. At the senate meeting on 18 October Macro replaced the guard of praetorians by soldiers of the night watch, then handed over Tiberius's letter ordering the arrest of Sejanus. The move took Sejanus completely by surprise, and he was quickly

*What public buildings did he construct
in his own name or that of his family!
With what pious munificence,
exceeding human belief, does he now
rear the temple to his father! For a
feeling of kinship leads him to protect
every famous monument.*

Velleius Paterculus II.130

The enthusiastic words of Velleius
Paterculus are sadly contradicted by the
monuments themselves, which show
Tiberius was responsible for very few
buildings during his long reign. He built
a temple just outside the Forum to the
Deified Augustus, but either never
finished or did not bother to consecrate
it; no remains have been found.
Conversely the Domus Tiberiana, the
palace platform on the Palatine which
bears his name, was probably the work
of Claudius. This lack of spending on
buildings and games gave Tiberius a
reputation for miserliness. Before
coming to power, however, Tiberius had
used the spoils from his victories to
rebuild the Temple of Castor in the
Forum (*right*). The massive podium and
three surviving columns, over 46 ft (14
m) tall, have been a familiar landmark
since the 15th century and are a
testament to Tiberius if not his reign.

hauled away to his death. His son and daughter were killed a few days
later, and his wife Apicata driven to suicide, but not before she had written a statement accusing Livilla of complicity in the death of Drusus. In
the weeks which followed, friends and supporters of Sejanus were hunted down and killed with a ferocity which shocked contemporaries.

A private man

Like that of so many emperors, the character of Tiberius's rule changed
as the years went by. At first, he followed the model set by Augustus,
regularly attending senate meetings, appearing at games and shows, and
distributing gifts and largesse on occasion. He lacked Augustus's tact,
however, and had little aptitude for social gatherings, gaining a reputation for stiffness and arrogance. Public dislike of Tiberius spread to the
populace, who were displeased at his unwillingness to hold lavish games
in later years, and his refusal to allow others to do so.

Tiberius's growing distaste for public life culminated in the move to
Capri. He surrounded himself with astrologers, and continued the literary interests which had always been among his favourite pursuits. In the
early part of his reign, he was noted for speeches 'obscured by excessive
mannerisms and pedantry.' He also tried to restrict the use of Greek
loan-words in Latin, and on one occasion consulted experts about the
propriety of using a foreign word in an official edict. Yet he was profi-

After traversing Campania . . . he went to Capri, particularly attracted to that island because it was accessible by only one small beach, being everywhere else girt with sheer cliffs of great height and by deep water.

Suetonius *Life of Tiberius* XLII

The rocky island of Capri had been acquired by Augustus as an imperial seaside retreat not far from the fashionable Bay of Naples. Tiberius spent most of his last decade here, choosing the craggy eastern summit for his inaccessible Villa Jovis. This was a masterpiece of architectural ingenuity on a confined and uneven site. Reception rooms, baths, and luxurious private apartments were clustered around a square central courtyard raised high above enormous vaulted cisterns. The private apartments led to a loggia providing panoramic views over the bay, while a little way downslope to the north was a long terraced walk with a pleasant seaview dining room. On this rocky summit it is easy to imagine condemned men being thrown into the sea, as Suetonius describes, where any who survived the fall were beaten to death with boathooks and oars. (*Below*) Reconstruction of the Villa Jovis on Capri.

cient in Greek as well as Latin, even to the point of composing verses in the style of his favourite Greek poets.

Tiberius's greatest interest was mythology, and his favourite pastime was quizzing grammarians with obscure or unanswerable questions. These included 'Who was Hecuba's mother?' and 'What was the song the Sirens sang?' He must have been a difficult dining companion.

Senate and empire

Tiberius's basic approach to government was one of laissez-faire, keeping control of affairs without intervening more than was necessary. This earned him the accusation of hypocrisy, in that he seemed to allow the senate freedom of action but continued to hold all the real power himself.

Tiberius often claimed he was following the policies laid down by Augustus. He nonetheless left provincial governors in office far longer than his predecessor had done, the record being the 25 years of Poppaeus Sabinus, governor of Moesia. On the other hand, Tiberius was capable of firm action where governors overstepped their authority. When the prefect of Egypt delivered more taxes than he was asked, Tiberius rebuked him with the words 'I want my sheep shorn not shaved.' He also provided generous disaster relief when Rome was hit by serious fires in AD 27 and 36. Yet in his later years Tiberius had to raise taxes, especially the hated sales tax of 1 per cent, introduced by Augustus, reduced by half in AD 17, but restored again to its former level in AD 31.

It was in relations with the senate that Tiberius's reign was most troubled. He was in political terms a traditionalist, a scion of the old sen-

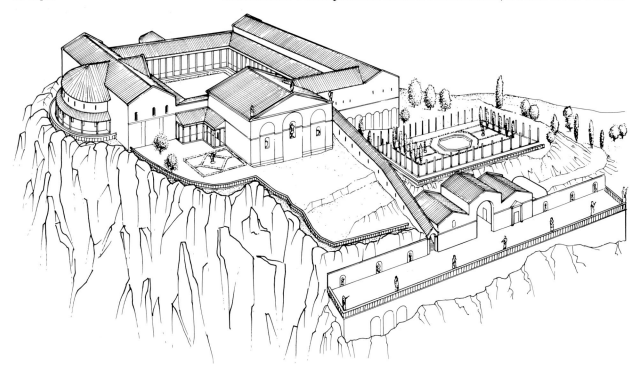

Tiberius in old age, a portrait-bust from the Capitoline Museum. He was widely credited with sexual perversions in his retirement on Capri; according to Suetonius, the abuse extended even to infants: 'unweaned babies he would put to his organ as though to the breast, being both by nature and age rather fond of this form of gratification.' His very seclusion fed the rumours which made him out to be a vulgar old libertine.

atorial aristocracy, and wanted to rule with their co-operation. Despite good intentions, however, he was by turns frustrated when they refused to act on their own initiative and annoyed with them when they did. Tiberius and the senate grew steadily further apart.

Tiberius's growing fears and suspicions led to an upsurge in treason trials which gave an air of terror to his later years. Even flippant accusations were sufficient to achieve convictions. One distinguished ex-consul was condemned for carrying a coin of Tiberius into the toilet: 'With my coin in your bosom you turned aside into foul and noisome places and relieved your bowels.' It was an easy way for unscrupulous senators to settle scores with their opponents.

Old age and death

While treason trials raged at Rome, Tiberius spent much of his final years at his island-refuge of Capri. Legends grew up of his homosexual practices, how he surrounded himself with troops of young boys known as 'spintriae' and indulged in promiscuous pederasty. The bedrooms were said to be decorated with erotic paintings and statues, 'in case a performer should need an illustration of what was required'. Most of this is later invention – Tiberius was in any event in his 70s by this time – but it illustrates the growing odium and disrespect in which the old man was held.

The question of the succession was still to be resolved. The two remaining candidates were Gaius (Caligula), the only son of Germanicus, and Tiberius Gemellus, son of Tiberius's son Drusus. Caligula was in his 20s, Gemellus 10 years younger. Furthermore Tiberius suspected Gemellus of being the offspring of Livilla's adultery with Sejanus, and not his own grandson. Hence it was Caligula who became heir-apparent as Tiberius entered his declining years.

Early in 37, Tiberius fell ill while travelling around Campania. In typical fashion he tried to ignore the illness and soldier on as usual, but he was eventually laid low in his seaside villa at Misenum. There he died on 16 March, aged 77. Tacitus tells a colourful tale of how Tiberius was thought to be dead, and how Caligula drew the ring from his finger and was greeted as emperor by the crowd. Then news came that Tiberius had recovered and was calling for food. Caligula was terrified, but Macro, commander of the praetorians, hurried in and smothered the old man with a cushion.

News of the death provoked tears of joy rather than grief. There were calls for the body to be thrown into the Tiber like that of a common criminal, but Caligula arranged for it to be carried under armed escort to Rome and cremated by the soldiers. On 4 April the ashes were placed in the Mausoleum of Augustus, but this was followed by neither deification nor official condemnation: an ambivalent end to an ambivalent reign. Tiberius had kept the empire on a steady keel for 23 years but was remembered only as one who had been despised, even in his youth, as 'bloodsoaked mud'.

Caligula
Gaius Caesar Augustus Germanicus
37–41

Caligula's self-love sat uneasily with his personal ugliness and his thinning hair. Surviving portraits carefully hide any sign of either defect. (*Right*) Portrait bust from Thrace, now in the Louvre, Paris.

CALIGULA

Born at Antium (Anzio) 31 August AD 12
  Gaius Julius Caesar Germanicus
On accession 18 March AD 37
  Gaius Caesar Augustus Germanicus
Added in 37
  'Pontifex Maximus'
  'Pater Patriae'

Consul I (1 July-31 August 37); II (39); III (40); IV (41)

Tribunician power first on accession; renewed annually on 18 March

Imperator once, on accession

Full titles at death
  Gaius Caesar Germanicus

Augustus, Pontifex Maximus, Consul IV, Imperator, Tribuniciae potestatis IV, Pater Patriae

Wives
(1) Junia Claudia AD 33
(2) Livia Orestilla AD 37
(3) Lollia Paulina AD 38
(4) Milonia Caesonia AD 39
Children
  Julia Drusilla (by Milonia)

Assassinated on the Palatine at Rome 24 January AD 41; buried in a temporary grave in the Lamian Gardens; later transferred to the Mausoleum of Augustus

He was very tall and extremely pale, with an unshapely body, but very thin neck and legs. His eyes and temples were hollow, his forehead broad and grim, his hair thin and entirely gone on the top of his head, though his body was hairy. Because of this to look upon him from a higher place as he passed by, or for any reason whatever to mention a goat, was treated as a capital offence.

Suetonius *Life of Caligula* L

The emperor Gaius, commonly known as Caligula, has not fared well in the pages of history; nor in truth does he deserve to. A capricious young man, cruel, insecure and highly strung, the best that can be said about him is that he was devoted to his family and showed a ready wit. Whether he was mad or merely bad, however, depends on how much we trust the sources. Should we believe the startling stories told by Suetonius and Cassius Dio, or do they simply reflect the hostility of the Roman senate? It is clear that some of Caligula's actions were cruel jokes, and others empty boasts or mere play acting. But ultimately we cannot escape the impression that the third emperor of Rome was a dangerous and unpleasant individual, verging on the megalomaniac.

Gaius Caesar Germanicus was born on 31 August AD 12 at Antium

Germanicus (father of Caligula) dies at Antioch

Tiberius takes up residence on Capri

Agrippina (mother of Caligula) exiled to Pandateria

Nero (brother of Caligula) commits suicide

Drusus (brother of Caligula) dies in prison; Agrippina starves to death

Tiberius dies; **Caligula becomes emperor** Drusilla dies

C. travels to Germany

British invasion abandoned

Caligula murdered at Rome

20   25   30   35   40

Bronze coin showing Caligula's elder brothers Nero and Drusus.

LITTLE BOOTS

There was also her little son, born in the camp and bred the playmate of the legions; whom soldier-like they had dubbed 'Bootkins' – Caligula – because, as an appeal to the fancy of the rank and file, he generally wore the footgear of that name.

Tacitus *Annals* I.1

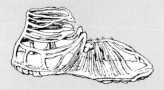

It is a curious thing to find an emperor of Rome named after a boot. The caliga was a hob-nailed boot worn by soldiers up to the rank of officer. The young Gaius was given the nickname 'caligula' ('little boot') during a mutiny of the Rhine legions in AD 14, when he was only two years old. According to one account he was taken hostage by the mutineers for a short time, while he and his mother were being sent out of the camp to safety. This story later became overlaid by sentimentality and it was claimed that the soldiers had abandoned their mutiny when they beheld the affecting sight of the young child dressed up in a miniature version of full military gear. It is not surprising that Gaius disliked the nickname and when he became emperor he punished anyone who used it. But then he did not like the name Gaius either!

(modern Anzio), some 25 miles south of Rome. His father was Germanicus, nephew of the emperor Tiberius. Before his suspicious death in AD 19 Germanicus won a considerable reputation for himself and became a kind of hero. This reputation was to help Caligula in his own rise to power. At birth, however, he was a long way from the succession. He had five elder brothers (though only two were still alive at his birth), and three younger sisters, for whom he developed a strong (perhaps improper) affection.

Caligula's childhood was overshadowed by the fate of his mother Agrippina and his brothers Nero and Drusus. They were accused of plotting against Tiberius, and their deaths between AD 31 and 33 must have been highly disturbing to Caligula. He took care to hide his emotions, however, and his reward was Tiberius's friendship and a chance of the succession. At the age of 18 he went to live with Tiberius on Capri. The emperor finally named Caligula his heir, boasting that, 'he was rearing a viper for the Roman people'. Macro, commander of the praetorian guard, made sure that Caligula succeeded without opposition when the old emperor died on 16 March 37.

A promising start

Caligula's accession was greeted with rejoicing by the people of Rome, including even the senate. On 18 March 37 they invested Caligula with sole power. Here at last was an end to the suspicion and miserliness which had characterized Tiberius's later years, a youthful emperor to revive all the hopes embodied by his father Germanicus.

One of Caligula's first actions was to take ship for the Pontian islands off the coast of Italy, and bring the ashes of his mother and brother back for proper burial in the Mausoleum of Augustus. Claudius, his uncle, was made consul, while Antonia, his grandmother, was granted the same honours and privileges as Livia had enjoyed. There the family harmony seems to have broken down. Caligula and Antonia simply did not get on, and when she died on 1 May 37 rumour had it that she had been forced to commit suicide.

That was a small cloud on an otherwise bright horizon. The early months of the new reign were a time of hope and relief. Caligula abolished treason trials, paid generous bequests to the people of Rome and a specially large bonus to the praetorian guard who had helped him to power. There was little warning of what was to follow.

The honeymoon ends

Six months after becoming emperor Caligula fell seriously ill. One possibility is a nervous breakdown, but a physical ailment is just as likely. He was said to have suffered from epilepsy in his youth, and was badly afflicted by insomnia in later life. Suetonius tells us he slept no more than three hours a night, and was troubled by terrifying nightmares. Instead of sleeping he would wander through the palace colonnades, calling out for dawn and daylight.

Bronze coin showing Caligula's sisters Agrippina, Drusilla and Julia Livilla. Drusilla was his favourite, and her death in 38 caused him great distress. The other two sisters were exiled the following year for their part in a conspiracy, along with Drusilla's husband Lepidus.

His recovery, in October or November 37, marked the end of the honeymoon period. Some argue that the illness caused serious mental deterioration. More likely it brought to Caligula's attention the fact that he was not indispensable and that others were waiting to step into his shoes. The most obvious of these was Gemellus, whom Tiberius had named joint heir (though the will was set aside) and Caligula had marked out for the succession. Caligula now suspected that Gemellus had been plotting against him, and had him killed. Another casualty was Macro, tricked into giving up his command of the praetorians and then forced to take his own life.

Wives and sisters

The following year was marked by a serious personal loss: the death of his sister Drusilla. It is a curious irony that Caligula was criticized for showing no emotion on the execution of his mother and brothers but was later accused of incest with his sisters. Suetonius tells the story that while still in his teens he was caught in bed with Drusilla. The story is probably an invention, but Drusilla was Caligula's favourite sister, and when she died on 10 June 38 he ordered her deification. A period of public mourning was announced, and Caligula left Rome to seek solace in a journey through Campania to Sicily.

Alongside Caligula's sisters there were his four wives. He married the first, Junia Claudia, in 33, but she died soon after in childbirth. The second was Livia Orestilla, who was already engaged to Gaius Calpurnius Piso when (late in 37) Caligula stepped in, during the very wedding celebrations, and took her for himself. Within two months, however, he had cast her aside, and the following year married Lollia Paulina. She too was soon divorced. Caligula was luckier in his fourth and final wife, Milonia Caesonia. She was several years his senior, but had the added surety of a trial period as mistress. The marriage took place in the late summer of 39, and a daughter, named Julia Drusilla in memory of Caligula's sister, was born a month later. Whatever his faults, Caligula was devoted to Caesonia and his daughter.

Shows and spectacles

One of the most famous stories told about Caligula, concerns his favourite racehorse Incitatus. This animal lived in great luxury, with a marble stall, an ivory manger, purple blankets and a collar of precious stones. Guests were invited to dinner in his name, and he too was invited to dine by the emperor, who offered him golden barley to eat. Caligula was even heard to say he would make him consul.

The most lavish of all his spectacles was the bridge of boats built at Baiae during the summer of 39. Merchant ships were requisitioned, and new ships built on the spot, to form a continuous double line across the Bay of Naples from Bauli to Puteoli, a distance of over 2 miles. A road was then built on top, including lodges and resting places, to serve as the stage for a two-day spectacular. On the first day, Caligula donned the

So much for Caligula as emperor; we must now tell of his career as a monster.

Suetonius *Life of Caligula* XXII

Caligula was a passionate devotee of chariot racing, and enjoyed shows and spectacles of any kind. He would participate as well, appearing in the arena as a Thracian gladiator. The circus provided ample outlets for both his cruelty and wit. On one occasion there was a shortage of cattle to feed the wild beasts, so Caligula ordered criminals to be fed to them instead. When they were lined up for him to choose, he said 'from baldhead to baldhead', there being a bald-headed man at each end of the line. On another occasion, when the spectators at the games supported an opposing faction, he burst out, 'I wish the Roman people had but a single neck.' In this first-century terracotta plaque (*right*), now in the British Museum, a Roman chariot race is depicted. The charioteer is approaching the turning posts at one end of the course, while a horseman rides in front to set the pace.

breastplate of Alexander (supposedly looted from the tomb at Alexandria) and rode as fast as he could from Bauli to Puteoli. The second day, he drove back the other way in a chariot. The whole event was an enormously costly extravaganza, on a par with his practice of drinking pearls dissolved in vinegar and building gem encrusted pleasure boats for coasting along Campania.

The slide towards tyranny

The lavish expenditures of Caligula's early years soon exhausted the enormous legacy of around 3000 million sesterces left him by Tiberius. To make up the deficit, he fell to the age-old expedient of confiscation and extortion. He also raised new taxes, including one on prostitutes, and is said even to have opened a brothel in a wing of the imperial palace to raise money. Another dodge was to auction gladiators at enormous prices to wealthy senators. Caligula also began to rake in legacies, not always by reasonable means.

Relations with the senate rapidly deteriorated. Early in 39 Caligula delivered a searing address, accusing the senators of complicity in the executions of Tiberius's reign, including those of his mother and brothers. September saw the first serious trouble, when Caligula dismissed both the consuls from office. No reason is given, but treachery is the likeliest explanation. This was only a prelude, however, to a much more dangerous conspiracy in which both of Caligula's surviving sisters, Agrippina and Livilla, were involved. A third party was Marcus Aemilius Lepidus, formerly husband to Drusilla. Lepidus was executed, while the sisters were imprisoned on the tiny Pontian islands off the Italian coast.

The German expedition

In September 39, shortly after the affair of the consuls, Caligula left Rome for the north. His aim was no less than the conquest of Britain, and with that in view he had set about the recruitment of two new legions. That the scheme did not succeed is not entirely Caligula's fault, though he showed no great ability as soldier.

The first problem was the poor discipline of the Rhine army and the incompetence of Cornelius Lentulus Gaetulicus, the regional commander. Gaetulicus was charged with conspiracy and executed on 18 October 39. Caligula himself arrived at the Rhine early the following year after spending the winter at Lyons. The future emperor Galba was installed as commander in Upper Germany in place of Gaetulicus, and there were operations against the Germans, but no major victory. Caligula marched to the Channel coast and ordered his troops to gather seashells, but the expected invasion of Britain never materialized. Perhaps the risk was simply too great. The one lasting testimony to his ambitions was the lighthouse built at Boulogne.

It was a bitter and disappointed emperor who arrived back in Rome in May 40. When senators met him on the way he slapped his sword-hilt and exclaimed 'I will come, and this will be with me'. He warned that he was coming back to those who wanted him, the common people and the knights, 'for to the senate he would never more be fellow-citizen or prince.' It did not bode well for the future.

The living god

During the final months of his reign Caligula began to assume the trappings of divinity. In the eastern provinces, the cult of the emperor as a living god was not new, but at Rome it was an unpopular innovation. Caligula built a temple to himself on the Palatine, and forced leading citizens to pay enormous sums for the honour of becoming his priests. 'At

LUXURY AFLOAT

He also built Liburnian galleys with ten banks of oars, with sterns set with precious gems, particoloured sails, huge spacious baths, colonnades, and banquet-halls, and even a great variety of vines and fruit trees, that on board of them he might recline at table from an early hour, and coast along the shores of Campania amid songs and choruses.

Suetonius *Life of Caligula* XXXVII

No Liburnian galleys have survived, but dramatic evidence of Caligula's pleasure fleet was revealed by the draining of Lake Nemi in the late 1920s. Remains of two vessels were found, both dating from the reign of Caligula and equipped to the very height of luxury. The decks were paved with mosaics, lead pipes carried running water, and there were even heated baths. Columns of African marble bear out Suetonius's reference to colonnades. Other fittings were in bronze, or in painted and gilded wood and terracotta. These floating palaces are remarkable testimony to the extravagant lifestyle of Caligula's court.

Roman pleasure barge from Lake Nemi.

IMPERSONATING THE GODS

In his clothing, his shoes, and the rest of his attire he did not follow the usage of his country and his fellow-citizens; not always even that of his sex; or in fact that of an ordinary mortal. He often appeared in public in embroidered cloaks covered with precious stones, with a long-sleeved tunic and bracelets; sometimes in silk and in a woman's robe; now in slippers or buskins, again in boots, such as the emperor's body-guard wear, and at times in the low shoes which are used by females. But oftentimes he exhibited himself with a golden beard, holding in his hand a thunderbolt, a trident, or a caduceus, emblems of the gods, and even in the garb of Venus. He frequently wore the dress of a triumphing general, even before his campaign, and sometimes the breastplate of Alexander the Great, which he had taken from his sarcophagus.

Suetonius *Life of Caligula* LII

Caligula shocked conservative Roman taste by his delight in impersonation and in dressing up to suit the part. It comes as little surprise to find that these parts included gods and goddesses, and that transvestism presented no obstacle. Fancy dress was for special occasions, but even for ordinary events Caligula enjoyed wearing gaudy clothing, including silks which Tiberius had forbidden for use by men. Caligula's exotic dress put people in mind of oriental despots, and his jewels and silks were criticized as effeminate.

night he used constantly to invite the full and radiant moon to his embraces and his bed, while in the daytime he would talk confidentially with Jupiter Capitolinus, now whispering and then in turn putting his ear to the mouth of the god, now in louder and even angry language; for he was heard to make the threat: "Lift me up, or I'll lift thee."'

Whether Caligula himself believed any of this nonsense is open to question. Once, when he claimed to be conversing with the Moon, he asked one of his courtiers whether he could see the goddess. The courtier kept his eyes resolutely fixed on the ground and replied in a whisper 'Only you gods, lord, may behold one another.' It sounds like an elaborate joke. Less frivolous was the command that the temple at Jerusalem be turned into an imperial shrine; but Caligula was dead before that could happen.

Assassination

By the final months of 40 Caligula had lost support almost everywhere by his capriciousness and cruelty. Late in the year another conspiracy was uncovered and several more senators were executed. The plot which eventually killed Caligula was more wide-ranging. The principals were Cassius Chaerea and Cornelius Sabinus, officers of the praetorian guard, but behind them were their commander Arrecinus Clemens, the powerful Callistus, a palace official and several members of the senate.

The assassination was planned for 24 January 41, when Caligula was attending the last day of the Palatine Games in a temporary auditorium in front of the imperial palace. It was his custom on these occasions to retire for a bath and lunch before returning for the afternoon. The idea was to set upon him as he left the theatre through one of the narrow passageways. On this day, however, he delayed his exit since he was suffering a stomach upset brought on by over-indulgence the night before. Senators privy to the plot at last persuaded him to leave, and as he made his way through a narrow passageway he was assassinated. According to one account his neck was slashed by Chaerea from behind, while Sabinus stabbed him in the chest. He fell to the ground, writhing in pain, and was finished off by some thirty blows from the other conspirators, some of whom 'even thrust their swords through his privates.'

The work was completed by the killing of his wife Caesonia and daughter Drusilla later the same day. Caligula's body, meanwhile, was carried secretly by Herod Agrippa to the Lamian Gardens on the Esquiline Hill where he had it partially cremated and the remains buried under a thin covering of turf. When Caligula's sisters Agrippina and Livilla were recalled from exile they gave what was left a full cremation and deposited the ashes in the Mausoleum of Augustus. They had little cause to love their brother after what he had done to them. His name was erased from the official acts, and his statues pulled down and destroyed. The memory of Caligula was not so easily forgotten, however, and slowly transformed itself into the archetype of the mad ruler, equalled only by Nero in the popular imagination.

Claudius
Tiberius Claudius Caesar
Augustus Germanicus
41–54

Suetonius describes Claudius as being 'tall but not slender, with an attractive face, becoming white hair, and a full neck. But when he walked, his weak knees gave way under him and he had many disagreeable traits . . . he would foam at the mouth and trickle at the nose; he stammered besides and his head was very shaky at all times.' Surviving portraits, such as this one from the Louvre, give Claudius a dignified appearance; it was only when he moved that his disability became apparent.

Cameo showing Claudius as the god Jupiter. The association of gods with emperors did not end with Caligula's death. A contemporary writer, indeed, refers to Claudius as 'our god Caesar'.

In great terror at the news of the murder, he stole away to a balcony hard by and hid among the curtains which hung before the door. As he cowered there, a common soldier, who was prowling about at random, saw his feet, and intending to ask him who he was, pulled him out and recognized him; and when Claudius fell at his feet in terror, he hailed him as emperor.

Suetonius *Life of Claudius* X

The murder of Caligula plunged Rome into chaos. A general massacre was narrowly averted as the Germans of the imperial bodyguard hunted down the assassins and killed many innocent people by the way. The senate, meanwhile, attempted to take power into its own hands and restore the republic. They counted on the support of the urban cohorts. Their ambitions were quickly thwarted by the praetorian guard, who had no interest in the restoration of the republic (who then would be their master?). One of their number came by chance across Caligula's uncle Claudius, hiding behind a curtain in the imperial palace. They hauled him forth and carried him off to the praetorian camp, where he was proclaimed emperor the same day (24 January).

The senate had little option but to acquiesce in his elevation. They

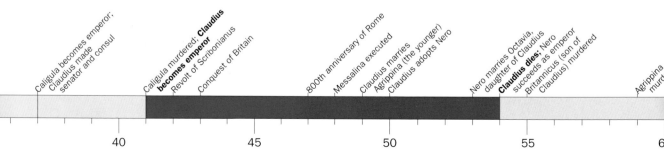

CLAUDIUS	
Born at Lugdunum (Lyons) 1 August 10 BC Tiberius Claudius Drusus *On adoption of his elder brother Germanicus by Tiberius (AD 4)* Tiberius Claudius Nero Germanicus *On accession 24 January AD 41* Tiberius Claudius Caesar Augustus Germanicus, Pontifex Maximus *Added January 42* 'Pater Patriae' Consul I (37), II (42), III (43), IV (47), V (51) Tribunician power first on accession, renewed annually on 25 January Imperator first on accession, then II-III (41), IV-VIII (43-45), IX-XIV (45-47), XV-XVIII (47-50), XIX-XXVII (50-52)	*Full titles at death* Tiberius Claudius Caesar Augustus Germanicus, Pontifex Maximus, Tribuniciae potestatis XIV, Consul V, Imperator XXVII, Pater Patriae *Wives* (1) Plautia Urgulanilla (2) Aelia Paetina (by AD 28) (3) Valeria Messalina AD 38 (4) Julia Agrippina AD 49 *Children* Claudius Drusus (by Urgulanilla) (died in childhood) Claudia (by Urgulanilla) (not recognized by Claudius) Antonia (by Messalina) Britannicus (by Messalina) *Died (poisoned?) at Rome 13 October AD 54; buried in the Mausoleum of Augustus*

did send an embassy, urging him to submit to their authority, but he was easily persuaded by his advisers to hold on to what he had won. A huge bribe of 15,000 sesterces per man helped to reinforce the loyalty of the praetorians, and the defection of the urban cohorts closed the matter. Within 24 hours of Caligula's death, Claudius was firmly in power.

The wilderness years

Claudius had been born at Lyons on 1 August 10 BC, and was 50 years old when he became emperor. He had distinguished parents: his father was Drusus, son of Augustus's wife Livia, his mother Antonia, daughter of Mark Antony. Despite his high birth, however, Claudius was kept out of the public eye because his disability was considered an embarrassment. His movements were jerky, he had a speech impediment, and he had a tendency to dribble, symptoms which have been diagnosed as cerebral palsy. His mental faculties were not impaired, but his family seem not to have understood this; not at least until his nephew Caligula drew him out of obscurity and made him a senator and consul in 37.

Claudius received little love from his mother, who described him as 'a monster of a man'. He took refuge in other pursuits, drinking, gambling and womanizing (he may have been an alcoholic). He also became immersed in historical research, and was the author of books on Etruscan and Carthaginian history, and an autobiography 'lacking in good taste', though none of these have survived. Claudius was no shrinking violet, however, and when opportunity presented he showed himself as avid for power as the rest of his family, though fearful of the dangers.

The shadow of fear

One of Claudius's first actions as emperor was to deal with Caligula's assassins. His revenge was carefully limited to those who had actually struck the blow: Cassius Chaerea, the ringleader, and Julius Lupus, who had killed Caesonia and the child. They were executed. Sabinus, on the other hand, was allowed to go free, but promptly committed suicide out of loyalty to his co-conspirators.

The violent death of Caligula was not a warning to be ignored, and throughout his reign Claudius took elaborate precautions to avoid the same fate. He tried to win popularity by abolishing treason trials, burning criminal records and destroying Caligula's extensive stock of poisons. He also returned many of Caligula's confiscations, and repealed his legislation concerning legacies to the emperor. At the same time, all those entering his presence were carefully searched for weapons. Even this did not give complete security, however, and several attempts were made on his life. On one occasion Gnaeus Nonius, a Roman knight, was discovered with a dagger at the emperor's public audience. On another occasion Claudius was attacked with a hunting knife outside the Temple of Mars.

Claudius's fearfulness drove him to act quickly and cruelly whenever he felt his life was threatened. No fewer than 35 senators and over 300

THE FOUR WIVES

. . . a remark let fall by Claudius in his cups, that it was his destiny first to suffer and finally to punish the infamy of his wives.

Tacitus *Annals* XII.64

Cameo of Messalina with her children Britannicus (right) and Octavia (left).

Nobody could call Claudius a fortunate husband. He was first betrothed at about the age of 15 to Aemilia Lepida. She was the daughter of Augustus's granddaughter, the younger Julia, but the match was broken off when her parents fell into disfavour. Next came betrothal to Livia Medullina, who had the ill-luck to die on the day of the wedding. The first woman he actually married was Plautia Urgulanilla, but she had to be divorced in around AD 24 for adultery and suspicion of murder. The children of the marriage were no luckier: the son, Claudius Drusus, was choked by a pear he had thrown into the air and caught in his mouth; the daughter Claudia was disowned by Claudius while still a child. Soon after Plautia Urgulanilla came Aelia Paetina, who bore him another daughter, Antonia. But Claudius divorced her, too, in 38 in order to marry a more prestigious bride, the young Valeria Messalina, then only 18 years old compared to Claudius's 50. She bore Claudius two children, Britannicus who was killed by Nero and Octavia who married Nero, before Messalina's faithlessness caught up with her and she was executed in October 48. Within a year of her death Claudius married his fourth and last wife, his niece Agrippina, who poisoned him five years later.

knights were executed in this way. Some of these were victims of his wives and freedmen, who found it easy to manipulate his fear. An early example was the case of Appius Silanus, recalled from Spain to marry Domitia Lepida, mother of the empress Messalina. He was executed shortly afterwards, accused by Claudius of having tried to murder him. Rumour had it differently, that he had refused to share Messalina's bed and that she had engineered his death in revenge.

The climate of fear reached crisis level in AD 42 when a full-blown rebellion was raised by Lucius Arruntius Camillus Scribonianus, governor of Dalmatia. It collapsed within five days, but carried with it a number of leading senators at Rome who were shown to be implicated in the plot.

The scheming Messalina

The fears and failings of Claudius were bad enough in themselves, but were made much worse by the machinations of his wife. Messalina was Claudius's third wife yet was the first to bear him a son. This was Tiberius Claudius Germanicus (later renamed Britannicus), born in February 41, just a month after Claudius's accession. Messalina clearly felt her position as mother of the emperor's heir made her secure against any accusations. With this assurance she set about killing off rivals and enemies, including a number of distinguished senators, by laying false charges against them. Among her early victims was Julia Livilla, sister of Caligula, who had been recalled from exile in 41 only to be sent back again and killed later that year.

Messalina soon became notorious not only for her killings but also for her adulteries. Her lovers ranged from leading senators to lowly actors, and Claudius appears either not to have known or to have turned a blind eye to her infidelities. At last, however, she went too far. In October 48, while Claudius was sacrificing at Ostia, Messalina married Gaius Silius, one of her lovers. The reason for this incredible act of folly is a mystery. It may have been cover for a coup d'état on Messalina's part, but certainly did nothing to make her position more secure. When Claudius was told the news he feared he had been overthrown, and many men hesitated before taking sides. It was the resolute action of Narcissus, the Chief Secretary, which saved the day. Claudius was hurried to the protection of the praetorian camp, where Silius was hauled before him and executed. Messalina too was executed, without being given a chance to appear before Claudius in case he let her off.

Freedmen and government

The story of Messalina illustrates one of the key criticisms made of Claudius, that he allowed himself to be dominated by his wives and freedmen. The most powerful officials were indeed imperial freedmen, former slaves who had risen to high office during this and previous reigns: Narcissus, the Chief Secretary; Pallas, the Financial Secretary; and Callistus, Secretary of Petitions. How far they controlled the emper-

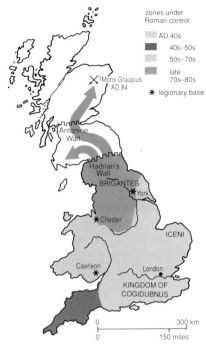

The Roman conquest of Britain, initiated by Claudius in AD 43, took several decades to complete, and even then the northern part of the island remained beyond Roman control.

Claudius as a mythological hero overcoming the fallen Britannia. Relief from the Sebasteion (a special shrine to the Julio-Claudians) at Aphrodisias in Asia Minor.

or it is difficult to say; but it was convenient to blame them, or the dead Messalina, for unpopular actions which in fact originated from Claudius himself.

The tendency throughout Claudius's reign was to increasing centralization. He avoided the overt conflict with the senate in which Caligula had engaged, and acted courteously and properly towards it, but was careful to reduce rather than increase its powers. He took a close personal interest in justice and finance, and spent part of almost every day in the law-courts hearing cases. This did not earn him the respect it might, however, since his judgments were criticized for capriciousness and unpredictability.

Claudius was also a great patron of the games. In fact, he gained a reputation for cruelty and blood-lust, taking particular pleasure in watching the faces of combatants as they died. He coupled this with the unfortunate habit of making feeble jokes in public. Even his holding of the Secular Games in 47 to mark the 800th anniversary of the founding of Rome did not escape criticism. Augustus had held them last in 17 BC, claiming that the 'century' should be reckoned as 110 years. The people laughed when Claudius's herald announced that his were games that nobody had ever seen before or would ever see again.

Britain and the provinces

It is ironic that a man so little suited in mind or body to military affairs should be credited with one of the few acts of Roman expansion during

CLAUDIUS THE BUILDER

Tiberius Claudius, son of Drusus, Caesar Augustus Germanicus, Chief Priest, holding Tribunician Power for the twelfth time, Consul for the fifth time, acclaimed Imperator twenty-seven times, Father of his Country, took charge of the waters of the Claudia, leading them into the city from the springs called Caeruleus and Curtius at a distance of forty-five thousand feet at his own expense, and likewise the waters of the Anio Novus from a distance of sixty-two thousand feet.

Inscription above the Porta Maggiore

Claudius's major building works involved engineering more than architecture. He completed two aqueducts, the Aqua Claudia 43 miles long and the Anio Novus 54 miles long, which Caligula had begun. At the approach to the city these aqueducts ran one above the other, crossing the junction of the Via Labicana and Via Praenestina on a monumental double arch. The inscription above records the length of the aqueducts and their completion in the twelfth year of Claudius's reign (AD 52).

Claudius's most important efforts, however, were directed towards the grain supply on which the free citizenry of Rome had come to depend. There had been trouble on his accession, when it was said that only eight days' grain was left in the city, and again in 51, when the imperial guard had to rescue him from a hungry crowd in the Forum. To alleviate shortages, Claudius undertook two huge civil engineering projects. The first of these was the draining of the Fucine Lake to create more farmland, a project which employed 30,000 men for eleven years, but ended in disaster. The second, was the building of a new deep-water harbour, known as Portus, at the mouth of the Tiber near Ostia.

He constructed the harbour at Ostia by building curving breakwaters on the right and left, while before the entrance he placed a mole in deep water. To give this mole a firmer foundation, he first sank the ship in which the great obelisk had been brought from Egypt, and then securing it by piles, built upon it a very lofty tower after the model of the Pharos of Alexandria, to be lighted at night and guide the course of ships.

Suetonius *Life of Claudius* XX

Hitherto, vessels bringing the all-essential grain to Rome had had to dock at Puteoli and transfer their cargoes to smaller vessels for the last leg of the journey along the coast and up the Tiber. The new harbour was situated some way north of the Tiber mouth so as to avoid the problems of silting which were affecting the river itself. In the event, it did begin to silt up soon after its construction, and also proved too exposed to be a safe and sheltered anchorage: 200 vessels were wrecked there in a storm in AD 62.

(Left) Merchant ship sailing into the Claudian harbour near Ostia. Note the stepped lighthouse behind. The she-wolf of Rome is depicted on the sails of the vessel, and Neptune with his trident stands ready to greet the crew. Relief slab c. AD 200 found near Trajan's Harbour. (Below) Second-century mosaic from the main commercial square (so-called Piazzale delle Corporazioni) at Ostia showing warship, merchant ship and lighthouse. (Bottom) Fanciful 16th-century reconstruction of the imperial harbours at Ostia. The hexagonal harbour (left) is the work of Trajan; the semicircular harbour (right) is that of Claudius.

(Left) The Porta Praenestina (now Porta Maggiore) at Rome, built by Claudius to carry the Aqua Claudius and Anio Novus over two of the arterial roads of Rome, the Via Labicana and Via Praenestina. The structure was later incorporated into the Aurelian Wall, visible to either side.

the first century AD: the conquest of Britain. This was something which Caligula had contemplated in 40, but was eventually left until Claudius's campaign three years later. Command of the invasion force was put into the hands of Aulus Plautius, though Claudius himself travelled north to Gaul and spent 16 days in the island once a safe bridgehead had been established. This was his moment of greatest glory. After his brief stay in Britain he returned to Rome, where he celebrated a magnificent triumph the following year.

The successful invasion of Britain gave a great boost to Claudius's regime in its early years. The other wars of the reign – in Mauretania and the Crimea, in Armenia and on the Rhine – were relatively minor affairs by comparison, and did not attract the emperor's presence in person. Claudius was no great traveller, indeed, and apart from the British expedition spent the whole of his reign in the neighbourhood of Rome. Nonetheless, by the time of his death he had annexed no fewer than five new territories for the empire: Britain, Thrace, Lycia, Mauretania and Noricum. Within the frontiers, too, there were changes of policy towards the provincials, notably Claudius's great generosity with grants of Roman citizenship. Particular favour was shown to Gaul, and to Claudius's birthplace Lyons. Claudius went further, and against some opposition made one group of Gallic leaders senators at Rome. Claudius's own speech on the subject is preserved in an inscription from Lyons, and in condensed form by Tacitus, who saw it as the beginning of a momentous change in the relationship of Italy to the provinces.

Agrippina and the succession

After the sorry affair of Messalina the 58-year-old Claudius swore he would never marry again. He was soon persuaded otherwise by the arguments of Pallas, his influential freedman, and the blandishments of Agrippina, Caligula's younger sister. Claudius married Agrippina in 49, with special dispensation from the senate since the pair were in fact uncle and niece.

Agrippina soon showed herself a powerful and scheming young woman, taking over where Messalina had left off. Her main objective was to ensure that it was Lucius Domitius Ahenobarbus, her own son by a previous marriage, rather than Britannicus (son of Claudius and Messalina) who inherited the empire on Claudius's death.

In 50 Agrippina and Pallas (who were rumoured to be lovers) persuaded Claudius to adopt Lucius Domitius officially; the boy took the family name Nero, the name he was to make famous (or infamous) in the years to come. Three years older than Britannicus, he was soon promoted far beyond Claudius's own son. In 51 Nero was given the title Princeps Iuventutis ('Leader of Youth'), marking him out as heir apparent. Agrippina, meanwhile, removed the praetorian commanders Lusius Geta and Rufrius Crispinus, replacing them with the more amenable Afranius Burrus. Nero's pre-eminence was sealed by his marriage in 53 to Claudius's daughter Octavia.

It only remained for Claudius to die for Agrippina's scheme to be complete. He had already been ill, perhaps gravely so, in late 52 or early 53. Now in 54 he was heard in his cups to say 'that it was his destiny first to suffer and finally to punish the infamy of his wives.' Agrippina decided she could not risk waiting any longer and enlisted the services of Locusta, an expert poisoner kept on the palace payroll. Halotus, the imperial taster, sprinkled the poison on an exceptionally fine mushroom, which Claudius (ever the gourmand) took no persuading to eat. At first he felt no ill-effects, then was seized by diarrhoea. Fearing the attempt would fail, Agrippina had Xenophon, the doctor, drop a second dose of poison down Claudius's throat on a feather which he was using to help him vomit.

Claudius died on the night of 12/13 October 54, leaving his stepson Nero to succeed him. Why he left his own son Britannicus in such a weak and dangerous position remains something of a mystery; perhaps he found it difficult to accept him as heir after the painful affair of Messalina. It should in any case be remembered that Nero was not yet exhibiting the megalomaniac traits which subsequently brought him into such disrepute. He made sure that Claudius was deified as one of the first acts of the new reign. At a banquet some years later, however, he came close to confessing his role in Claudius's death. 'He declared mushrooms to be the food of the gods, since Claudius by means of the mushroom had become a god.'

Statue of Claudius as the god Jupiter, now in the Vatican Museum.

CLAUDIUS THE GOD?

One of the most curious documents relating to Claudius is the *Apocolocyntosis*, a scurrilous pamphlet purporting to describe his fate after death. The title itself, 'the gourdification of the deified Claudius', is a pun, meaning that though declared a god, all Claudius was really fit to become was a gourd, a dry and empty vegetable. The pamphlet is attributed to Seneca, a famous stoic philosopher who was exiled to Corsica by Claudius and thus held no great love for him. Seneca was recalled to Rome after Claudius's demise and probably wrote the pamphlet for the amusement of Nero and his court. It contains savage indictments of Claudius's many executions and pokes fun at his physical disabilities and speech impediment.

In the following passage the deified Augustus expresses outrage to his fellow gods at the very idea that Claudius might seek admission among them:

The specimen you see, lurking under my name for so many years, paid me such thanks as to kill two Julias, my great-granddaughters, one by the sword, the other by starvation, and one great-great-grandson, L. Silanus. . . . And he got angry with his wife and hung her up . . . Gaius had killed his father-in-law, Claudius killed a son-in-law as well. Gaius forbade Crassus' son to be called 'the Great'. Claudius gave him back his name but took away his head. In one family he killed Crassus, Magnus and Scribonia. . . Is this the man you now wish to make a god? Look at his body, born when the gods were in a rage. In short, let him utter three words in quick succession and he can take me as his slave. Who will worship this man as a god? Who will believe in him? . . . My proposal is that he be severely punished and not given exemption from due process of law, and that he be deported as soon as possible and leave Heaven within thirty days and Olympus within three.

Seneca *Apocolocyntosis* 10-11

Nero

Nero Claudius Caesar
Augustus Germanicus
54–68

Suetonius describes Nero as 'having his hair arranged in tiers of curls', a feature very evident in this marble head from the British Museum. The hairstyle was a direct borrowing from Hellenistic royal portraits. The individuality of the face, too, marked a break in tradition; Nero is the first emperor we can easily recognize from his portraits.

For Nero, in fact, spent the rest of his life so disgracefully, that it is disgusting and shameful to record the existence of anyone of this kind, let alone that he was ruler of the world.

Aurelius Victor *Book of the Caesars* 5

He was about the average height, his body marked with spots and malodorous, his hair light blond. . . . His health was good, for though indulging in every kind of riotous excess, he was ill but three times in all during the fourteen years of his reign.

Suetonius *Life of Nero* LI

Nero is one Roman emperor of whom everyone has heard. Books and films portray him as a monster, a self-indulgent monarch who burned Rome to provide space for his country mansion, who tortured and killed his opponents, and who led a pampered life of great extravagance. The truth behind this image is more complex. The real Nero was indeed a cruel man. He murdered two wives, a step-brother and a mother, and condemned others to exile or suicide. But he was also a patron of the arts, and the first five years of his reign were looked back to as a golden age of moderate and responsible government.

He was born on 15 December AD 37 at the small Italian seaside town of Antium. His father was Lucius Domitius Ahenobarbus, from one of the leading families of the old republic. It was his mother, however, who provided his main claim to fame; for Agrippina was the daughter of Germanicus and sister of Caligula.

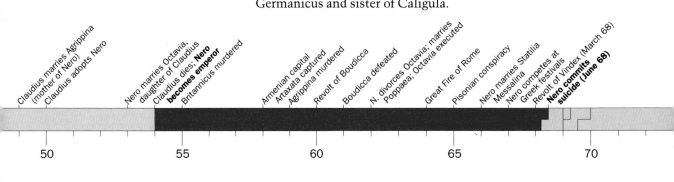

Claudius marries Agrippina (mother of Nero)
Claudius adopts Nero
Nero marries Octavia, daughter of Claudius; **Nero becomes emperor**
Claudius dies;
Britannicus murdered
Armenian capital Artaxata captured
Agrippina murdered
Revolt of Boudicca
Boudicca defeated
N. divorces Octavia; marries Poppaea; Octavia executed
Great Fire of Rome
Pisonian conspiracy
Nero marries Statilia Messalina
Nero competes at Greek festivals
Revolt of Vindex (March 68)
Nero commits suicide (June 68)

50   55   60   65   70

NERO'S MURDER OF HIS MOTHER

Nero's mother Agrippina exercised enormous influence over her son, and sought to rule the empire through him. At first he treated her with great deference, choosing 'best of mothers' as the watchword on the first day of his reign. There was even a rumour that Agrippina seduced Nero to strengthen her hold over him. Early in 55, however, her guards were dismissed and she was expelled from the imperial palace. Finally, four years later, Nero decided that she too had to be removed. Abandoning the idea of poison, since Agrippina was alert to the danger and took careful precautions, he hit upon the scheme of an 'accident' at sea.

During the festival of Minerva in March 59 Nero invited Agrippina to dine with him at Baiae. For the return journey he put her aboard an especially fine vessel, as if to do her honour. The ship had gone only a little way, however, when the mechanical death-trap came into play: a lead-weighted canopy collapsed on top of her, and she was only saved by the height of the couch sides. The ship was then intentionally capsized, but Agrippina was a strong swimmer. She managed to make it to the shore and reached one of her own villas, but soldiers were sent to finish her off. We are told that a soothsayer had once prophesied that Nero would live to be emperor and kill his mother. Agrippina retorted, 'Let him kill me, only let him rule!'

Cameo portrait of Agrippina the younger.

Nero's father died when he was only three years old and his mother was exiled by Caligula to the tiny Pontian islands off the Italian coast. The family fortunes revived in 41 with the accession of Claudius, who recalled Agrippina to Rome. He eventually married her in 49, and adopted Nero the following year. Claudius named Nero heir-apparent in 51, and wedded him to his own daughter Octavia in 53. Thus when Claudius died on 13 October 54, the 16-year-old Nero was accepted as emperor with little opposition.

The early years

The new reign began well. Nero offered an enormous donative to the praetorian guard and delivered a speech to the senate promising a return to the principles of Augustus. The senate would be given a greater role in the government and more freedom to express their views. These winning words were written by Seneca, a distinguished stoic philosopher who had been exiled to Corsica by Claudius but recalled to serve as Nero's tutor. Seneca was aided in his efforts to guide and restrain the young emperor by Afranius Burrus, commander of the praetorian guard.

Yet there was the problem of Britannicus. As Claudius's natural son he was a powerful rival; many people could not understand how Nero had gained supreme power and pushed Britannicus into the background. It comes as no great surprise, then, to learn that Britannicus was poisoned at dinner on 11 February 55, less than four months after his father's death. When Britannicus suddenly collapsed at table, Nero claimed he was suffering an epileptic seizure. He had the body carried outside and quietly buried the next day.

Passions and pastimes

The murder of his mother Agrippina (see box above) in 59 was the single

NERO

Born at Antium 15 December AD 37 Lucius Domitius Ahenobarbus *On adoption by Claudius* Nero Claudius Caesar Drusus Germanicus *On accession 13 October AD 54* Nero Claudius Caesar Augustus Germanicus *Added 55* 'Pontifex Maximus' and 'Pater Patriae' *From late summer 66 (after investment of Tiridates)* Imperator Nero Claudius Caesar Augustus Germanicus Tribunician power first on 4 December 54; renewed annually on 13 October Consul I (55), II (57), III (58), IV (60), V (68)	Imperator first on accession, then II (56), III-IV (57), V-VI (58), VII (59), VIII-IX (61), X (64), XI (66), XII-XIII (67) *Full titles at death* Imperator Nero Claudius Caesar Augustus Germanicus, Pontifex Maximus, Tribuniciae potestatis XIV, Imperator XIII, Consul V, Pater Patriae *Wives* (1) Octavia AD 53 (2) Poppaea Sabina AD 62 (3) Statilia Messalina AD 66 *Children* Claudia (by Poppaea Sabina) *Committed suicide at Rome 9 June AD 68; buried in the family tomb of the Domitii on the Pincian Hill*

NERO'S GOLDEN HOUSE

Nero turned to account the ruins of his fatherland by building a palace, the marvels of which were to consist not so much in gems and gold, materials long familiar and vulgarized by luxury, as in fields and lakes and the air of solitude given by wooded ground alternating with clear tracts and open landscapes.

Tacitus *Annals* XV.42

The Golden House (Domus Aurea) which Tacitus describes here was built by Nero on land cleared after the Great Fire of 64. It was essentially a country park in the heart of the city, covering some 125 hectares of the most expensive real estate in Rome. Contemporaries regarded the waste of space as a crime. Suetonius gives further details: 'The vestibule was large enough to contain a colossal statue of the emperor 120 ft (37 m) high; and it was so extensive that it had a triple colonnade a mile long. . . . There were dining-rooms with fretted ceilings of ivory, whose panels could turn and shower down flowers and were fitted with pipes for sprinkling the guests with perfumes. The main banquet hall was circular and constantly revolved day and night, like the heavens.' The banqueting hall is probably the domed octagonal room incorporated in the substructures of the Baths of Trajan, and does indeed show traces of a device which would have made the ceiling revolve by water-power. Though the Domus Aurea was never completed, Nero is said to have remarked 'that he was at last beginning to be housed like a human being.'

(Right) Plan of the Golden House and its park. The main entrance led from the Sacra Via at the eastern end of the Forum. Here in the entrance court of the palace stood the colossal bronze statue of Nero which later gave its name to the Colosseum (the Flavian amphitheatre built on the site of Nero's lake). Nero demolished the unfinished Temple of the Deified Claudius and had its massive platform reworked to provide ornamental cascades and fountains.

(Far right) The principal remains of the Golden House lie buried beneath the Baths of Titus on the Oppian Hill (the southernmost lobe of the Esquiline), opposite the later Colosseum. It was designed with a long frontage overlooking the ornamental lake. The octagonal dining room lay at the centre point of a symmetrical façade, which originally extended much further to the east.

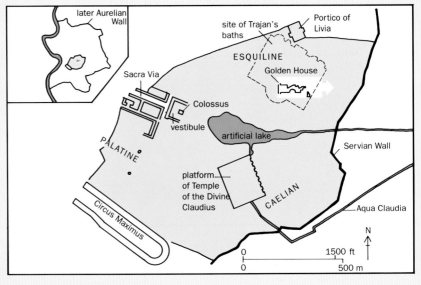

Wall paintings in Nero's Golden House. (Above) Painted and stuccoed ceiling of the transverse passage; (left) imaginary landscapes and architectural trompe-l'oeils in room 114.

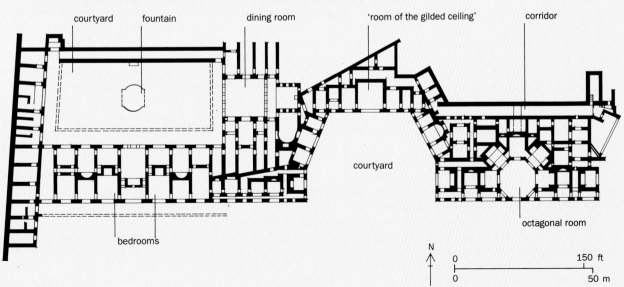

courtyard   fountain   dining room   'room of the gilded ceiling'   corridor

courtyard

bedrooms

octagonal room

N

0   150 ft

0   50 m

SENECA'S ADVICE TO A PRINCE

Lucius Annaeus Seneca (*above*, Staatliche Museen, Berlin) was one of the leading philosophers of the age. Born at Corduba in Spain around 1 BC, he came to Rome in his youth and became popular in court circles until he was exiled by Claudius for alleged adultery with Caligula's sister, Livilla. He was recalled in 49 and appointed tutor to the young Nero, remaining one of his principal advisers until he was accused of complicity in the Pisonian conspiracy in 65 and forced to commit suicide. Seneca composed a number of plays and moral essays, including 'On Mercy' addressed directly to Nero:

I have undertaken, Nero Caesar, to write on the subject of mercy, in order to serve in a way the purpose of a mirror, and thus reveal you to yourself as one destined to attain to the greatest of all pleasures. For, though the true profit of virtuous deeds lies in the doing, and there is no fitting reward for the virtues apart from the virtues themselves, still it is a pleasure to subject a good conscience to a round of inspection, then to cast one's eye upon this vast throng – discordant, factious, and unruly, ready to run riot alike for the destruction of itself and others if it should break its yoke – and finally to commune with oneself thus: 'Have I of all mortals found favour with Heaven and been chosen to serve on earth as vicar of the gods?'

Seneca *On Mercy* I.1

most notorious act of Nero's reign, but it was not alone. Rumour had it that he used to roam the streets after dark, visiting taverns with his friends, mugging people in the street, attacking women, and thieving from shops and stalls. He was also accused of abusing married women and freeborn boys. The most famous sexual excesses, however, were his 'marriages' to his homosexual lovers Pythagoras and Sporus, the latter a boy whom he had castrated. It was said that Nero acted as husband to Sporus and wife to Pythagoras.

Little better in many people's eyes was Nero's passion for music, for singing his own compositions while accompanying himself on the lyre. He hired the greatest living master of the lyre, Terpnus, as his teacher, and gave private performances for his friends. His own public début he put off until 64, choosing not Rome but Naples as the venue. It was an inauspicious event, since the theatre was hit by earthquake and collapsed shortly after the recital. How good a performer Nero was is difficult to say. Suetonius describes his voice as weak and husky; Dio calls it slight and indistinct; but he may indeed have been a skilled and effective musician. In Rome the following year Nero performed in full tragic garb before the populace, singing a song of Niobe and other roles both male and female, going on late into the afternoon, while the praetorian guard stood by to carry his lyre. It was not the image of power the people had come to expect.

Octavia and Poppaea

In the year 58 Nero developed a passion for Poppaea Sabina, a lady of great beauty. She was married to Marcus Otho, one of his closest companions, who used frequently to boast of his wife's accomplishments. Soon Otho was appointed governor of Lusitania and Poppaea was sharing the emperor's bed. The problem was that he was still married to Octavia, Claudius's daughter, and the link with Octavia (though she was barren) was politically important. Only in 62 did Nero feel secure enough to divorce Octavia and marry Poppaea.

Octavia was first sent to Campania, then imprisoned on the island of Pandateria on a trumped-up charge of adultery. She was killed later in the year, and in a refinement of callousness her head was brought back to Rome for Poppaea to gloat over.

Poppaea herself did not survive long. She bore Nero an infant daughter Claudia on 21 January 63, but the child survived only four months. Then in the summer of 65, while pregnant a second time, Nero kicked her to death in a temper tantrum. He married Statilia Messalina the following year, but then took up with the boy Sporus because he resembled Poppaea in appearance.

The gathering cloud

A gradual change came over Nero's reign as the years progressed. The beginning was marked by prudence and moderation, under the guidance of Seneca and Burrus. On being asked to sign his first death warrant Nero

IMPERIAL EPIC

He affected also a zeal for poetry and gathered a group of associates with some faculty for versification but not such as to have yet attracted remark. These, after dining, sat with him, devising a connection for the lines they had brought from home or invented on the spot, and eking out the phrases suggested, for better or worse, by their master; the method being obvious even from the general cast of the poems, which run without energy or inspiration and lack unity of style.

Tacitus *Annals* XIV.16

Nero fancied himself as a poet, but opinion was divided on his literary ability. Tacitus is scathing, but Suetonius had inspected the manuscripts themselves and was adamant that Nero had composed his own poetry. Very little survives for us to judge for ourselves, the longest fragment being three lines from 'Nero's First Book':

*Quique pererratam subductus Persida Tigris
deserit et longo terrarum tractus hiatu
reddit quaesitas iam non quaerentibus undas.*

'. . . and the Tigris too, which traverses Persia but then forsakes it, vanishes, and runs in a long subterranean cleft,
eventually returning its sorely-missed flow only to peoples who set no store by it.'

These lines may belong to Nero's famous epic on the Fall of Troy, which he was much blamed for singing during the Great Fire of Rome. This gave rise to the legend that Nero fiddled while Rome burned. If he did anything, it would have been to accompany himself on the lyre.

remarked (with more art than sincerity?), 'How I wish I had never learned to write!' After the death of Burrus in 62, however, Seneca slipped into the background. The dominant figures henceforth were Poppaea and Ofonius Tigellinus, Burrus's successor as praetorian commander. Tigellinus came to be regarded as the evil genius behind many of Nero's later actions. Treason trials were resumed, and as money began to run short, taxes were raised, the coinage was debased, and wealthy men had their estates confiscated as a source of easy revenue.

The Great Fire which ravaged Rome in 64 further damaged Nero's standing. It broke out in the neighbourhood of the Circus Maximus on 19 July, and spread rapidly to leave only 4 of the city's 14 regions untouched. Much of the city centre, including part of the imperial residence on the Palatine, was completely destroyed.

Nero was at Antium when the fire began, but hurried back as soon as the scale of the disaster became clear. He organized relief measures, opened public buildings as temporary shelters and provided cheap grain. Once the flames were out he gave funds for restoration work and issued strict regulations to reduce the risk of any future recurrence. Despite all this, people became convinced that Nero had started the fire himself in order to clear land for his new Golden House. Nor was this helped by the story that at the height of the fire, 'viewing the conflagration from the tower of Maecenas and exulting, as he said, in "the beauty of the flames", he sang the whole of the "Sack of Ilium" [one of his own compositions] in his regular stage costume.' Few people were fooled when he blamed the fire on the Christians.

Conspiracies betrayed

The Great Fire placed an enormous financial burden on Nero at a time when revenues were already stretched. The resumption of treason trials led to exiles, executions and suicides which spread fear and resentment in court and senatorial circles. The conspiracy of Gaius Calpurnius Piso was a direct result. A sizeable group of senators and others planned to assassinate Nero during the Circensian Games of 12–19 April 65. The scheme was betrayed when a servant of Flavius Scaevinus, the man chosen to strike the blow, became suspicious of his master's preparations. In the witch-hunt that followed, 19 people died and 13 were exiled. A particularly worrying feature was the complicity of several officers of the praetorian guard, on whom the emperor's personal safety depended.

The following year a second conspiracy was unmasked while Nero was on his way to Greece. Again, leading senators were implicated, including the distinguished general Gnaeus Domitius Corbulo. It was the final straw in Nero's relationship with the senate; henceforth, he said, he hated them all.

The Grand Tour of Greece

The visit to Greece was the clearest expression of Nero's love and admiration for Greek culture, and was the only foreign excursion of the entire

Bronze statuette of Nero in military dress, decorated with inlays of copper, silver and niello. One of Nero's crucial weaknesses was his failure to win military glory.

reign. One of his aims was to compete in the major Greek festivals at Olympia, Nemea, Isthmia, and Delphi. The Olympic and Nemean Games were even brought forward from their usual year for Nero's convenience. He naturally carried off the prizes, though he also bribed the judges and the best performers to be doubly sure. The audience were forbidden to leave their seats while he was performing, and since this could last several hours it gave rise to difficulties. The future emperor Vespasian fell asleep during one of Nero's performances and was dismissed from his entourage. Women were said to have given birth in the theatre, and some feigned death in order to be carried outside.

Nero regarded his Greek tour as a great success, although the spectacle of the emperor performing on stage in fancy dress did nothing for the imperial reputation. Victories on the stage were all very well, but they were no substitute for victories on the battlefield. The reign was not without its military successes: the suppression of Boudicca's rebellion in Britain in 61 and Corbulo's victories over the Parthians in Armenia. These, however, were won by his generals, and did little to dispel Nero's playboy image.

Despair and death

When Nero returned to Rome late in 67 relations with the senate were at an all time low. Support in the provinces was also weakening under the onslaught of increasingly repressive taxation. Then in March 68 came the revolt of Julius Vindex, governor of Gallia Lugdunensis. It was a curious uprising, since Vindex had no legionary forces at his command, nor did he claim the title of emperor for himself. But he did gain the adherence of Servius Sulpicius Galba, governor of Hispania Tarraconensis, who drew on the widespread dissatisfaction with Nero's rule.

The armies of the Rhine defeated Vindex at Besançon in May 68 but showed no enthusiasm for Nero. They tried instead to proclaim their own commander, Verginius Rufus, emperor. Rufus refused, but the bandwagon began clearly to run in Galba's favour. While Galba waited in Spain, his agents went to work in the capital, chipping away at Nero's

The rebellion of Julius Vindex at Lugdunum in March 68 was easily suppressed by the Rhine legions at Vesontio two months later, but by that time Galba had been proclaimed emperor in Spain. The map shows the events of March 68 to January 69. ①Vindex rebels against Nero and attacks Lugdunum (March 68) ②Vindex defeated at Vesontio (May 68) ③Galba proclaimed emperor at Carthago Nova (April 68) ④Galba learns of death of Nero at Clunia (June 68) ⑤Galba leaves Tarraco for Rome (late summer 68) ⑥Rhine legions declare for Vitellius at Colonia Agrippina (2 January 69) ⑦Otho overthrows Galba at Rome (15 January 69)

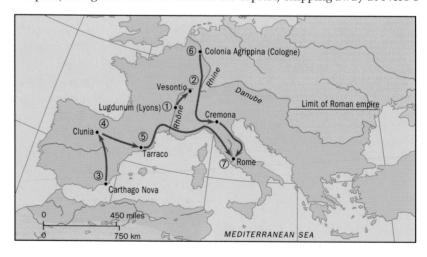

THE FIRST PERSECUTION

Nero substituted as culprits, and punished with the utmost refinements of cruelty, a class of men, loathed for their vices, whom the crowd styled Christians. . . . Vast numbers were convicted, not so much on the count of arson as for hatred of the human race. And derision accompanied their end: they were covered with wild beasts' skins and torn to death by dogs; or they were fastened on crosses, and when daylight failed were burned to serve as lamps by night.

Tacitus *Annals* XV.44

When Nero was accused of having ordered the Great Fire of Rome he blamed the Christians instead. The result was a flood of summary trials, some victims ending their days as human torches to illuminate Nero's circus games. St Paul had been executed at Rome earlier in 64, and this may have brought the Christians to mind when a scapegoat was being sought. Tradition holds that Peter the apostle was one of those crucified in this first great persecution, though whether he really died at Rome is open to doubt.

St Peter arrested, from the sarcophagus of Junius Bassus at Rome. Fourth century AD.

remaining support. Finally, on 8 June, with Nero openly planning to flee, the praetorian commander Nymphidius Sabinus abandoned him as a lost cause and switched his allegiance to Galba.

Nero's hope was to take ship at Ostia and seek refuge in the eastern provinces. The guards refused to help him, however, and he had to return to the palace. He woke around midnight to find himself abandoned even by the palace attendants. Going out into the street, he came across Phaon, one of his freedmen, who led him in disguise to his villa a few miles north-west of the city. This was a curious escape route, and it looks very much as though Phaon betrayed Nero in order to save his own life. Nero was hiding in one of the back rooms of the villa when the soldiers came to arrest him. Self-pitying to the last, he exclaimed 'What an artist the world is losing!' before stabbing himself in the neck. His private secretary Epaphroditus finished off the job.

Thus died the infamous Nero, only 30 years old, on 9 June AD 68. His body was taken for burial to the tomb of the Domitii (his father's family) on the Pincian Hill. It escaped the indignities visited on later emperors who fell from power, and was honoured with a porphyry sarcophagus and marble altar set within a stone balustrade. Hated by the senate, Nero remained popular with the common people, and for years afterwards the tomb was regularly decorated with spring and summer flowers.

Why did Nero fail, after such a promising start? Largely because he alienated the senatorial élite. Nero's growing insecurity led him to liquidate rivals, whether real or imagined, and the lavish expenditures of his later years encouraged him to confiscate property. These measures weighed heavily only on the rich, however, and it was the traditional aristocracy, too, who disapproved most strongly of his public displays and love of things Greek. In the crisis of June 68, Nero failed to realize that he still commanded wide popular support. Had he stood firm in 68, all might have been well. An emperor who ran before he was pushed had only himself to blame.

Galba

Servius Galba Imperator
Caesar Augustus
68–69

Otho

Imperator Marcus Otho
Caesar Augustus
69

Vitellius

Aulus Vitellius Germanicus
Imperator Augustus
69

The emperor Galba: portrait-bust from the Capitoline Museum, Rome.

GALBA

Although Nero's death had at first been welcomed with outbursts of joy, it roused varying emotions, not only in the city among the senators and people and the city soldiery, but also among all the legions and the generals; for the secret of empire was now disclosed, that an emperor could be made elsewhere than at Rome.

Tacitus *Histories* I.4

Servius Sulpicius Galba, governor of Hispania Tarraconensis, was already 70 years old when he succeeded Nero as emperor of Rome. It was no peaceful transfer of power. Julius Vindex, governor of Gallia Lugdunensis, had rebelled against Nero in March 68, and cast about for a

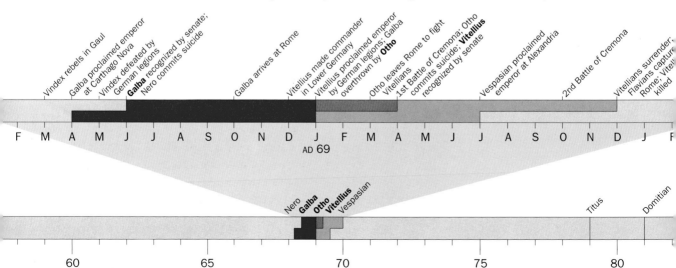

Vindex rebels in Gaul

Galba proclaimed emperor at Carthago Nova

Vindex defeated by German legions

Galba recognized by senate; Nero commits suicide

Galba arrives at Rome

Vitellius made commander in Lower Germany

Vitellius proclaimed emperor by German legions; Galba overthrown by **Otho**

Otho leaves Rome to fight Vitellians

1st Battle of Cremona: Otho commits suicide; **Vitellius** recognized by senate

Vespasian proclaimed emperor at Alexandria

2nd Battle of Cremona

Vitellians surrender; Flavians capture Rome; Vitellius killed

F M A M J J A S O N D J F M A M J J A S O N D J F

AD 69

Nero **Galba** **Otho** **Vitellius** Vespasian

Titus

Domitian

60 65 70 75 80

GALBA

Born 24 December 3 BC near Tarracina *Accession 8 June 68* Servius Galba Imperator Caesar Augustus	*Children* two sons (names unknown) *Killed in the Forum at Rome 15 January 69; buried near the Via Aurelia*
Wife Aemilia Lepida	

OTHO

Born 28 April AD 32 at Ferentium *Accession 15 January 69* Imperator Marcus Otho Caesar Augustus	*Children* none known *Suicide at Brixellum, south of Cremona, 16 April AD 69; burial nearby*
Wife Poppaea Sabina	

VITELLIUS

Born 7 (or 24) September AD 12 (or AD 15); place uncertain *Accession 2 January AD 69* Aulus Vitellius Germanicus Imperator Augustus. Vitellius tried to alter the imperial title in order to make a break from the Julio-Claudian past. He may have intended to make Germanicus a hereditary title, conferring it on his son in 69. This title was in recognition of the part played by the German legions in bringing	Vitellius to power. Vitellius did eventually assume the title Caesar, when he needed all the support that the imperial tradition could give. *Wives* (1) Petronia (2) Galeria Fundana *Children* a son Petronianus (by Petronia) a son Vitellius (by Galeria Fundana) a daughter Vitellia (by Galeria Fundana) *Murdered in the Forum, 20 December 69; body thrown into Tiber*

suitable candidate to head his revolt. Galba was a man of considerable ambition, even at his advanced age, and he avidly accepted Vindex's invitation, having himself proclaimed emperor at Carthago Nova on 3 April. He gained the immediate support of the governors of Lusitania and Baetica, followed soon afterwards by those of Egypt, Africa and Mauretania. It looks, indeed, as if he had already made the necessary alliances and that his revolt was no mere accident of circumstances.

Galba had only a single legion at his disposal, and in purely military terms his bid for power was foolhardy in the extreme. Nero, however, was no favourite with the troops. When the Rhine legions crushed Vindex's rebellion at Vesontio (Besançon) in May 68, they tried to make their commander Verginius Rufus emperor. Rufus declined the position, nor would he throw in his lot with Galba. It was not military secession but the perfidy of Nymphidius Sabinus, commander of the praetorian guard, which eventually drove Nero to despair and suicide.

The new administration

Galba was still in Spain when he was declared emperor by the senate on 8 June 68. He arrived in Rome in October, accompanied by a reputation for severity and avarice. He had shown himself a stern disciplinarian on several occasions, but his avarice came largely from the urgent need to recover the reckless expenditure of Nero's last years. He ordered that of all gifts of money or property made by Nero (amounting to 2,200 million sesterces) 90 per cent should be returned, and he refused to pay the customary bounties to the army, telling them it was his habit to levy troops, not buy them.

A still greater problem was the corruption among the officials he appointed. The numerous people who had supported Galba's rise to power now demanded places in the new administration. Many of them were greedy and unscrupulous individuals whose behaviour seriously undermined Galba's standing with the senate and the army. One of the worst was the ex-slave Icelus, rumoured to be Galba's homosexual lover and to have stolen in 7 months more than all Nero's freedmen had taken in over 13 years.

A violent ending

The beginning of the end came in January 69, when the armies of Upper and Lower Germany threw down Galba's images and declared Aulus Vitellius their new emperor. This defection made Galba painfully aware of the need for an heir; the two sons born to him by his wife Lepida were both dead before his accession. He decided therefore to adopt Lucius Calpurnius Piso Frugi Licinianus, a young man of distinguished family, then around 30 years old. The adoption took place on 10 January, and Piso was taken to the camp of the praetorian guard, where he was presented to the soldiers as Galba's heir. Once again, however, Galba lost what support he might have gained by refusing to pay the soldiers the bounty expected on these occasions. Furthermore Piso, though apparent-

Vespasian
Imperator Caesar
Vespasianus Augustus
69–79

Titus
Imperator Titus Caesar
Vespasianus Augustus
79–81

Vespasian was a man of action who
preferred a more forceful and
characterful portrait than the rather
expressionless faces of the Julio-
Claudians. The knotted brows and
firmly set lips of the marble head shown
here aptly convey the impression of a
tense and determined ruler.

VESPASIAN	
Born 17 November AD 9 at Falacrinae Titus Flavius Vespasianus *On accession 1 July 69* Imperator Titus Flavius Vespasianus Caesar *From August 69* Imperator Caesar Vespasianus Augustus *Added 70* 'Pontifex Maximus' and 'Pater Patriae'	Tribunicia potestas, first on accession, then renewed annually on 1 July *Full titles at death* Imperator Caesar Vespasianus Augustus, Pontifex Maximus, Tribuniciae potestatis X, Imperator XX, Pater Patriae, Consul IX
Consul I (51), II (70), III (71), IV (72), V (74), VI (75), VII (76), VIII (77), IX (79)	*Wife* Flavia Domitilla *Children* two sons Titus and Domitian a daughter Flavia Domitilla
Imperator first on accession, then II-V (70), VI-VIII (71), IX-X (72), XI (73), XII-XIV (74), XV-XVIII (76), XIX (77), XX (78)	*Died Aquae Cutiliae 23 June 79; buried first in Mausoleum of Augustus, later transferred to T. of the Flavian Family*

VESPASIAN

He, unlike all his predecessors, was the only emperor who was changed for the better by his office.

Tacitus *Histories* I.50

Vespasian was a new kind of Roman emperor: middle-class rather than patrician, and a man with wide experience in the provinces and the army, rather than a mere urban courtier. He gave the empire a period of stable and efficient government after the disturbances of the year 69. His tolerance and humour won him friends, and his conscientious attention to the welfare of Rome and the provinces set the empire on a new and firmer footing. The pity is we lack many details about the chronology and events of the reign. On the other hand, the testimony of Tacitus and Suetonius does afford us an image of the man himself, an able and determined individual who ended his days maintaining that the emperor should die on his feet.

A varied career
Unlike most of his predecessors, Vespasian's earlier career had given

Titus serves as military tribune

Vespasian made governor of Africa by Nero

T. divorces Marcia Furnilla after Pisonian Conspiracy

Vespasian becomes governor of Judaea

Nero dies

V. proclaimed emperor

Titus becomes Caesar

Jerusalem falls to Titus; V. arrives at Rome

V. begins Forum of Peace at Rome

Fall of Masada; end of Jewish War

Forum of Peace dedicated; Colosseum begun

Agricola begins conquest of Scotland

V. dies; Titus becomes emperor; Vesuvius erupts

Colosseum inaugurated

Titus dies; Domitian becomes empe

60   65   70   75   80

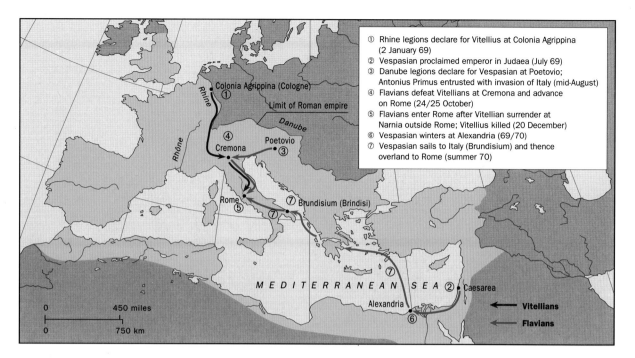

① Rhine legions declare for Vitellius at Colonia Agrippina (2 January 69)
② Vespasian proclaimed emperor in Judaea (July 69)
③ Danube legions declare for Vespasian at Poetovio; Antonius Primus entrusted with invasion of Italy (mid-August)
④ Flavians defeat Vitellians at Cremona and advance on Rome (24/25 October)
⑤ Flavians enter Rome after Vitellian surrender at Narnia outside Rome; Vitellius killed (20 December)
⑥ Vespasian winters at Alexandria (69/70)
⑦ Vespasian sails to Italy (Brundisium) and thence overland to Rome (summer 70)

Vespasian had been sent to the east by Nero to suppress the Jewish rebellion. In 67 he recovered Galilee and the coastal cities of Judaea, and the following year captured Jericho and Emmaus, leaving Jerusalem increasingly isolated. Then in July 69 Vespasian was proclaimed emperor by the eastern legions, and a few months later departed for Alexandria, leaving the completion of the Jewish War to his son Titus. The intention may have been to force Vitellius to surrender by blocking the Egyptian grain supply on which Rome depended, but the Danube legions which declared for Vespasian knew nothing of this plan. They invaded Italy, defeated the Vitellians at the second Battle of Cremona, and captured Rome in December 69. Vespasian did not himself arrive in the capital until October 70.

him first-hand experience of just about every corner of the Roman empire. He was born on 17 November AD 9 at Falacrinae near Reate, in the Sabine hill-country north-east of Rome, though he was brought up by his father's mother on her estates at Cosa on the west coast of Italy. He and his brother were the first generation of their family to enter the senate. Under Tiberius he served as military tribune in Thrace and quaestor of Crete and Cyrene. He was praetor under Caligula and displayed some disturbing sycophantic tendencies. His military career received a boost when he commanded the Second Legion 'Augusta' in the conquest of Britain in 43–47. He was rewarded with the consulship in 51, then the governorship of Africa some 12 years later.

Under Nero, Vespasian became an official 'companion' of the emperor and travelled with him to Greece. There he incurred imperial displeasure for falling asleep during one of the emperor's musical performances. Nero soon had need of him to deal with the Jewish revolt, however, and in 67 Vespasian was appointed governor of Judaea, with an expeditionary force of three legions. He was bringing the war steadily to a successful conclusion when news broke of Nero's suicide and the events of the fateful year 69 were set in train.

In 39 Vespasian married Flavia Domitilla, daughter of one Flavius Liberalis. It was not an especially good match for a man with ambition. Flavia Domitilla was not even a full Roman citizen, and had been mistress of a Roman knight, Statilius Capella, at Sabratha in Tripolitania. Nonetheless she bore Vespasian three children: a daughter, also called Flavia Domitilla, who was dead by the time Vespasian became emperor; and two sons, Titus and Domitian, who succeeded Vespasian in turn.

The elder Flavia Domitilla was not Vespasian's first love, for when

The map shows: 0 — 200 m scale, N (north arrow), Roman circumvallation, BEN YAIR VALLEY, MASADA, siege ramp, MASADA VALLEY, Roman camps, aqueduct.

she died he resumed relations with Caenis, who had been his mistress before. Caenis had been secretary to Antonia (daughter of Mark Antony and mother of Claudius), and is described as 'exceedingly faithful and gifted with a most excellent memory'. She had considerable influence over Vespasian, who treated her, while emperor, almost as if she were his lawful wife. He does not seem to have been as faithful to her as she was to him, however. We learn that on one occasion Vespasian gave a gift of 400,000 sesterces to a woman who was mad with passion to sleep with him!

The Jewish War came to an end in spring 74 when the Roman commander Flavius Silva besieged the fortress of Masada, the last rebel outpost. The Romans erected an encircling wall with attached forts, but eventually captured the rocky citadel only by building a great siege ramp against its western face. The defenders committed suicide rather than fall into their hands.

The Flavian victory

Vespasian was still engaged in suppressing the Jewish revolt at the time he was proclaimed emperor. The war dragged on for a further 12 months and more, though Vespasian left its conduct in the hands of Titus, his elder son and trusted lieutenant, while he himself travelled to Alexandria. His aim in moving to Egypt was perhaps to stop the grain supplies on which the city of Rome depended, and so force Vitellius to come to terms. At the same time, Mucianus, governor of Syria, led his

The Seven-Branched Candlestick from the Temple at Jerusalem born in triumphal procession at Rome. Relief from the Arch of Titus in the Forum.

main army westwards for a direct military confrontation. Before Mucianus had even crossed the Bosphorus the Danube army had declared for Vespasian, and it was they, rather than Mucianus, who invaded Italy and toppled Vitellius. Mucianus nonetheless played a key role in Vespasian's administration, lining his own pockets and claiming that Vespasian owed his position to him.

Another prominent and perhaps over-mighty subject was Vespasian's younger son Domitian. He had been in Rome during the last days of Vitellius, and had gone into hiding. When the Flavians took control, he and Mucianus governed jointly in Vespasian's name, appointing prefects, governors and consuls. So great were Domitian's pretensions that on one occasion Vespasian wrote to him 'I thank you, my son, for permitting me to hold office and that you have not yet dethroned me.' It was Mucianus who exercised real power, however, and it was he who ordered the execution of Vitellius's son and his notorious freedman Asiaticus. It was Mucianus, too, who sent forces north to suppress the revolt of the native chieftain Julius Civilis and restore order along the Rhine frontier.

Meanwhile Vespasian stayed on in Alexandria, waiting for Jerusalem to fall. It did not do so until 26 September 70, by which time Vespasian had lost patience and left Egypt for Rome. The capture of Jerusalem brought the Jewish War effectively to a close (though the stronghold of Masada held out until 74), and Vespasian and Titus celebrated a joint triumph for their victory in June the following year. Later years saw fighting in Britain, against the Brigantes, Silures and Ordovices, and in the east, where the kingdom of Commagene was annexed in 72. On the whole, however, Vespasian's reign was a time of peace.

Vespasian at Rome

Vespasian entered Rome early in October 70. He soon found he preferred to live not in the imperial palace on the Palatine but in the Horti Sallustiani, the pleasure gardens founded by the historian Sallust the previous century. This was a garden estate, with palaces and pavilions, near the northern edge of the city – in concept not very different from the notorious Golden House built by Nero. Vespasian did not travel far from Rome during the rest of his reign, though he spent every summer at Reate. Suetonius gives us a sketch of the emperor's daily routine. He rose before dawn every day, and spent the first part of the day meeting friends and officials, and reading official reports. Then he would have a drive and a sleep, after Caenis's death usually with one of his concubines. After his siesta he would go to the baths, and then have dinner.

Vespasian had already given his sons Titus and Domitian the rank of Caesar, and had marked out Titus, the elder, as his chosen successor. He chose Titus as his colleague for seven out of his eight consulships while emperor, and fully intended to found a ruling dynasty equal to the Julio-Claudians. In the senate he declared openly that either his sons would succeed him or no-one would. One means of promoting the new dynasty

A PORTRAIT IN RELIEF

He was well-built, with strong, sturdy limbs, and the expression of one who was straining. A propos of which a witty fellow, when Vespasian asked him to make a joke on him also, replied rather cleverly: 'I will, when you have finished relieving yourself.' He enjoyed excellent health, though he did nothing to keep it up except to rub his throat and other parts of his body a certain number of times in the ball court, and to fast one day in every month.

Suetonius *Life of Vespasian* XX

was an ambitious building policy at Rome. Most famous of all was the Flavian Amphitheatre (Colosseum), built on the site of the ornamental lake of Nero's Golden House. He also completed the massive Temple of the Deified Claudius on the Caelian Hill. This marked him as the legitimate heir of the Julio-Claudians, but distanced him from Nero, the last of that line, who had had parts of the half-built temple demolished.

Running the empire

These buildings represented a considerable financial outlay, but even before he became emperor Vespasian had gained a reputation for avarice. Suetonius tells us that 'The only thing for which he can fairly be censured was his love of money.' His governorship of Africa had been hated because of his financial extortion, and during his stay at Alexandria in 69–70 he had generated considerable animosity by his imposition of new tax burdens on the Alexandrians. At that time he was in the throes of a civil war, and the need for money was desperate. As Mucianus said, 'Money is the sinews of war.'

When the war was over, Vespasian found the imperial treasury considerably depleted, and declared that forty thousand million sesterces were needed to set the state upright. To restock the coffers he resorted to new taxes and increased old ones, and was not averse to selling public offices. The new tax for which Vespasian was best remembered was one on public urinals. When Titus objected that such a source of income was beneath the imperial dignity, the emperor picked up some gold coins and said 'See, my son, if they have any smell.' On the other hand, it was claimed that Vespasian never executed anyone merely in order to confiscate his wealth.

Vespasian was indeed noted for his justice and leniency. He helped Vitellius's daughter to make a good marriage and even provided the dowry. He also reformed the membership of the senate and set up a special commission to speed through the many lawsuits which had arisen during the civil war. He was not quick to take offence at criticism, though when Helvidius Priscus refused to desist from personal attacks he had him banished and then executed. Vespasian was also refreshingly unassuming and had a disarming honesty and good-humour. When he began to tire during a long triumphal procession, he joked, 'It serves me right for wanting a triumph in my old age.' In a lawsuit, where a senator was complaining about the disrespect of a Roman knight, Vespasian replied, 'Unseemly language should not be used towards senators, but to return their insults in kind is proper and lawful.'

Vespasian was in fact renowned for his witticisms, though Suetonius warns that these were 'of a low and buffoonish kind'. This extended to quoting from the Greek classics. When talking of a tall man with 'monstrous parts', Vespasian recited a line of the Iliad, 'Striding along and waving a lance that casts a long shadow.' Even when he was dying, he could not resist a joke: 'Woe's me' he said, 'Methinks I'm turning into a god.'

THE TRANSFER OF POWER

Bronze tablet of the 'Lex de Imperio Vespasiani', Capitoline Museum, Rome.

In December 69 a law was passed conferring imperial powers on Vespasian. Part of the text is preserved on a bronze tablet found in the basilica of St John Lateran at Rome during the 14th century.

. . . and that whatever he decides will be in accordance with the advantage of the republic and with the majesty of things divine, human, public, and private, he shall have the right and power so to act and do, just as such right and power were possessed by the deified Augustus and Tiberius Iulius Caesar Augustus and Tiberius Claudius Caesar Augustus Germanicus.

The wording gives Vespasian all the powers formerly invested in Augustus, Tiberius and Claudius. It emphasizes Vespasian's legal succession to the Julio-Claudian dynasty. Significant omissions are the names of Caligula, Nero and Galba, whose memory had been officially condemned. Otho and Vitellius, too, are ignored, presumably because they were usurpers. The law retrospectively validated all actions taken by Vespasian since his proclamation as emperor at Alexandria.

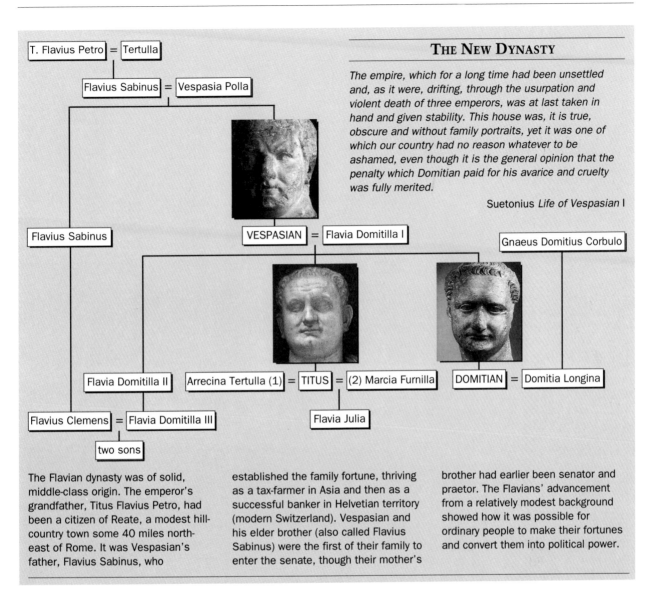

THE NEW DYNASTY

The empire, which for a long time had been unsettled and, as it were, drifting, through the usurpation and violent death of three emperors, was at last taken in hand and given stability. This house was, it is true, obscure and without family portraits, yet it was one of which our country had no reason whatever to be ashamed, even though it is the general opinion that the penalty which Domitian paid for his avarice and cruelty was fully merited.

Suetonius *Life of Vespasian* I

The Flavian dynasty was of solid, middle-class origin. The emperor's grandfather, Titus Flavius Petro, had been a citizen of Reate, a modest hill-country town some 40 miles north-east of Rome. It was Vespasian's father, Flavius Sabinus, who established the family fortune, thriving as a tax-farmer in Asia and then as a successful banker in Helvetian territory (modern Switzerland). Vespasian and his elder brother (also called Flavius Sabinus) were the first of their family to enter the senate, though their mother's brother had earlier been senator and praetor. The Flavians' advancement from a relatively modest background showed how it was possible for ordinary people to make their fortunes and convert them into political power.

His death and reputation

Vespasian's end was in fact relatively peaceful. He was in Campania in 79 when he fell ill. Now a relatively old man of 69, he decided to take the waters at Aquae Cutiliae, a mineral spring in Sabine country, near his birthplace. Suetonius tells us he took the waters too freely, and contracted diarrhoea as well. He continued to attend to state business, studying papers and receiving embassies. Then on 23 June he was hit by a particularly severe attack of diarrhoea and almost fainted. With the memorable last words 'An emperor ought to die standing,' he struggled to his feet, but collapsed and died in the arms of his attendants.

The legacy of Vespasian was a stable government and a restocked treasury. He came to power as a military man, but had the good sense to rule with the co-operation of the senatorial aristocracy. His success can be judged from the fact that there is scant mention of internal unrest

THE COLOSSEUM

Vespasian was without doubt one of Rome's greatest imperial builders. He reconstructed the Capitol, destroyed by fire the day his forces entered Rome, and erected many new temples. His most famous building, however, is the Flavian Amphitheatre, known in later times as the Colosseum, perhaps from the giant statue of Nero that once stood nearby. Completed in 80, the year after Vespasian's death, the Colosseum came to symbolize the power and splendour of imperial Rome. Up to 55,000 spectators could be seated in its terraces (women were confined to the topmost tier of seats). Beneath the arena lay a warren of rooms and cages for wild animals and mechanical devices.

Lavish Hundred-Day Games were held to mark the inauguration of the building in Titus's reign, including a mock naval battle and gladiatorial contests. (*Below*) Mosaic from the Villa Borghese, Rome, showing gladiators, one with a crested helmet, another lying dead beneath his oblong shield.

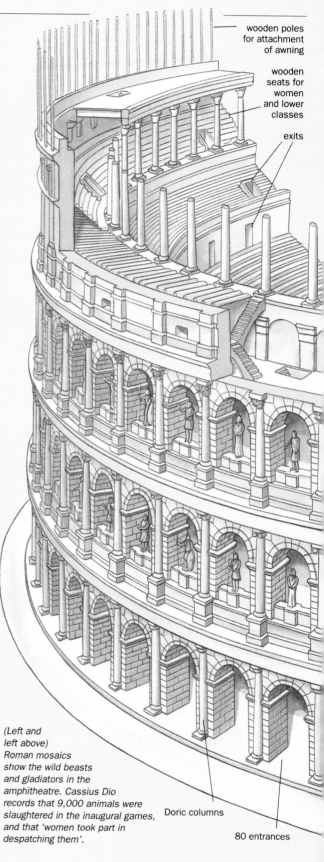

wooden poles for attachment of awning

wooden seats for women and lower classes

exits

(Left and left above) Roman mosaics show the wild beasts and gladiators in the amphitheatre. Cassius Dio records that 9,000 animals were slaughtered in the inaugural games, and that 'women took part in despatching them'.

Doric columns

80 entrances

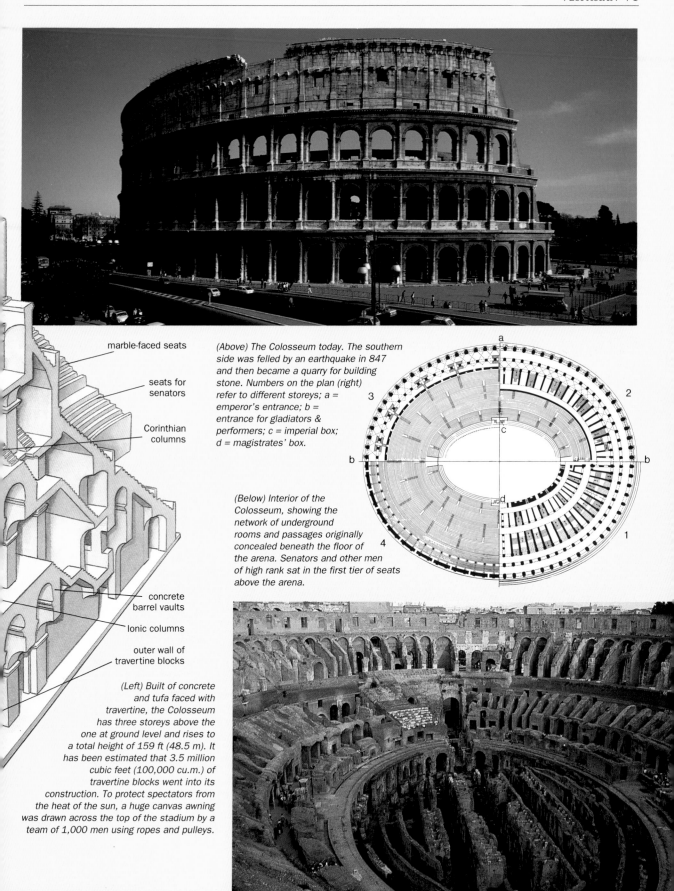

marble-faced seats

seats for senators

Corinthian columns

concrete barrel vaults

Ionic columns

outer wall of travertine blocks

(Above) The Colosseum today. The southern side was felled by an earthquake in 847 and then became a quarry for building stone. Numbers on the plan (right) refer to different storeys; a = emperor's entrance; b = entrance for gladiators & performers; c = imperial box; d = magistrates' box.

(Below) Interior of the Colosseum, showing the network of underground rooms and passages originally concealed beneath the floor of the arena. Senators and other men of high rank sat in the first tier of seats above the arena.

(Left) Built of concrete and tufa faced with travertine, the Colosseum has three storeys above the one at ground level and rises to a total height of 159 ft (48.5 m). It has been estimated that 3.5 million cubic feet (100,000 cu.m.) of travertine blocks went into its construction. To protect spectators from the heat of the sun, a huge canvas awning was drawn across the top of the stadium by a team of 1,000 men using ropes and pulleys.

during his reign, and only a single failed conspiracy against his life. Deified by the senate, his ashes were laid to rest in the Mausoleum of Augustus, alongside those of the Julio-Claudians. The impression we are left with is of a man of firm though limited objectives, conscientious and generally tolerant, not one to harbour a grudge or imagine enemies around every corner. He was, in that sense, one of the good emperors of Rome.

TITUS

Titus, of the same surname as his father, was the delight and darling of the human race; such surpassing ability had he, by nature, art, or good fortune, to win the affections of all men, and that, too, which is no easy task, while he was emperor; for as a private citizen, and even during his father's rule, he did not escape hatred, much less public criticism.

Suetonius *Life of Titus* I

The emperor Titus, the 'darling of mankind', emerges through the writings of the historians as something of an enigma. How could such a cruel and unpopular heir-apparent become such a well-loved emperor? Are we to believe that his benevolence was simply a façade adopted purely for political reasons? Or did he really change character when he became emperor?

Titus was born at Rome on 30 December AD 39, during Caligula's reign. The birth took place 'in a mean house . . . and in a very small dark room besides.' It was not until the accession of Claudius in AD 41 that the family fortunes began to improve. His father Vespasian served with distinction in Claudius's invasion of Britain, and in return, Titus was awarded the rare honour of a court education. He learned to write poetry in Latin and Greek, and even composed Greek tragedies. In addition, Titus studied music, and sang while accompanying himself on the harp. Above all, however, he became a close friend of Claudius's own son Britannicus, and remained so until the latter was poisoned by Nero. It is said that Titus drank from the same cup, and was ill for some while afterwards.

War and politics

Once out of school, Titus embarked on the usual senatorial career, beginning as military tribune in Germany and Britain in 61–63. He then returned to Rome and married Arrecina Tertulla, daughter of a former commander of the praetorian guard. When Arrecina died after only a year or so of marriage Titus took a new wife of much more distinguished family: Marcia Furnilla. This match also lasted only a short time, for Marcia's family was too closely linked to the opposition to Nero. Titus took fright at the failed Pisonian conspiracy of 65 and ruthlessly severed the connection by divorcing his wife. He did not remarry, but his marriages left him with one or possibly two young daughters.

TITUS	
Born 30 December AD 39 at Rome Titus Flavius Vespasianus (as with his father) *On accession of Vespasian* Titus Caesar Vespasianus *Added in September AD 70 after fall of Jerusalem* 'Imperator' *On accession to sole rule 24 June AD 79* Imperator Titus Caesar Vespasianus Augustus *Added after June AD 79* 'Pontifex Maximus' and 'Pater Patriae' Consul I (70), II (72), III (74), IV (75), V (76), VI (77), VII (79), VIII (80) Imperator I (70), II (71), III-IV (72), V (73), VI-VIII (74), IX-XII (76), XIII (77), XIV (78), XV (79), XVI-XVII (81)	Tribunicia potestas, first on 1 July 71, renewed annually *Full titles at death* Imperator Titus Caesar Vespasianus Augustus, Pontifex Maximus, Tribuniciae potestatis XI, Imperator XVII, Consul VIII, Pater Patriae *Wives* (1) Arrecina Tertulla (2) Marcia Furnilla *Children* a daughter Julia (by Arrecina) a daughter (by Marcia Furnilla) *Died at Aquae Cutiliae 13 September AD 81; buried first in Mausoleum of Augustus, later tranferred to the Temple of the Flavian Family*

GAMES AND SPECTACLES

Most that he did was not characterized by anything noteworthy, but in dedicating the hunting-theatre and the baths that bear his name he produced many remarkable spectacles.

Cassius Dio LXVI.25

In his short reign Titus proved himself a great patron of the games. The most lavish of all were the Hundred-Day Games held to mark the inauguration of the Flavian Amphitheatre (Colosseum) in the middle of AD 80:

There was a battle between cranes and also between four elephants; animals both tame and wild were slain to the number of nine thousand; and women (not those of any prominence, however) took part in despatching them. As for the men, several fought in single combat and several groups contended together both in infantry and naval battles. For Titus suddenly filled this same theatre with water and brought in horses and bulls and some other domesticated animals that had been taught to behave in the liquid element just as on land. He also brought in people on ships, who engaged in a sea-fight there.

Titus also distributed gifts to the people during the games: a special machine threw down wooden balls carved with the names of various commodities (food, clothing, slaves, silver vessels) which the lucky recipients could then collect from his attendants. The whole affair was a massive public relations exercise, designed to cheer up the people of Rome after the disastrous fire earlier in AD 80.

Titus's career so far had not been especially distinguished, but the events of the years 66–70 were to change all that. First came his appointment as commander of the Fifteenth Legion 'Apollinaris', to serve under his father in the Jewish War. He became invaluable to his father as a trusted agent and negotiator. When Galba was murdered Titus won over Mucianus, governor of Syria, to the Flavian cause, and worked with him and others to launch Vespasian's bid for power. When Vespasian was proclaimed emperor on 1 July 69, Titus became Caesar. And while Vespasian stayed in Alexandria during the final months of 69, awaiting news of his army's fortunes in Italy, Titus took over command of the Jewish War. In September 70, after a lengthy siege, Titus finally captured Jerusalem, his most significant military achievement.

The unpopular heir

Titus returned to Rome in June 71. He was clearly marked out as Vespasian's heir from the start. He shared no fewer than seven consulships with his father, an unprecedented number for anyone other than the emperor himself. He also held the tribunician power, and was saluted as 'Imperator' no fewer than 14 times during Vespasian's reign. Suetonius describes him as his father's partner and protector, the latter no doubt a reference to his surprising appointment as praetorian commander. The treachery of the praetorians towards Galba no doubt warned Vespasian that he needed to put a trusted colleague in command. There was another reason. Titus used his position as praetorian commander to carry out his father's dirty work, removing political opponents by methods that were barely legal. Suetonius mentions his talent as a forger, and on several occasions he forged incriminating letters to secure a conviction. Titus came to be regarded as callous and cruel, and his underhand activities earned him widespread unpopularity. He also gained the reputation of a libertine, a man who partied late into the night surrounded by troops of catamites and eunuchs.

Worst of all in the eyes of the Roman public, however, was Titus's passion for Queen Berenice, a member of the Judaean royal family. They had become lovers while Titus was in the east, but oriental monarchs were so disliked by the populace that Titus did not call her to Rome until 75. For a short time Titus and Berenice lived together openly in the imperial palace, but such was her unpopularity that Vespasian ordered him to send Berenice back to Judaea. This he did, and refused to have further dealings with her even when she made a second visit to Rome after Vespasian's death.

Titus acted as his father's assistant, taking charge of routine affairs, dictating letters, drafting edicts, and delivering his father's speeches in the senate. It was Vespasian, however, who made all the key decisions.

The good emperor

When Titus succeeded his father on 24 June 79 many were convinced he would turn out to be a second Nero. In fact, during his short reign of 2

Statue of the emperor Titus in the Vatican Museum.

He had a handsome person, in which there was no less dignity than grace, and was uncommonly strong, although he was not tall of stature and had a rather protruding belly.

Suetonius *Life of Titus* III

Extant portraits depict Titus with high forehead, close-set eyes and squarish head shape. The family resemblance to Vespasian is immediately apparent and is not just a matter of stylistic preference. On the other hand it is not easy to distinguish Titus's portraits from those of his younger brother Domitian. For the emperor's portliness we have only Suetonius's word; the imperial sculptors were careful to smooth away any trace of the protruding stomach. Yet Suetonius does not accuse him of gluttony: on the contrary, though as a young man Titus's revels frequently went on until midnight, his banquets are described as pleasant rather than extravagant.

years 2 months and 20 days he gained one of the best reputations of any Roman emperor. His goodness became legendary. A famous story told how on one occasion, 'remembering at dinner that he had done nothing for anybody all that day, he gave utterance to that memorable and praise-worthy remark: "Friends, I have lost a day."' He dismissed his catamites, banished informers, and donned a mask of clemency and constitutional probity.

His generosity was soon put to the test, for on 24 August, exactly two months after his accession, the towns of Pompeii and Herculaneum were wiped out by the eruption of Vesuvius. Titus poured disaster relief into the stricken area and visited it just after the eruption and again the following year. It was while he was away on his second visit that Rome, too, was hit by disaster, the whole area from the Capitol to the Pantheon going up in flames. The trio of calamities was completed by the outbreak of a severe epidemic. It was a wonderful opportunity to win public acclaim, and one which Titus exploited to the full. Work began at once on rebuilding the Temple of Jupiter Optimus Maximus, which had been destroyed by the fire, and lavish games were held later in the year to cheer up the city populace.

The calamities in Rome and Campania did not prevent Titus from attending to the needs of the provinces and the frontiers. The only major military activity was in Britain, where the conquest of Scotland made further progress. Another disturbance was the curious episode of the 'False Nero': a man from Asia Minor called Terentius Maximus, who resembled Nero in voice and appearance, and sang like him to the lyre. He gathered a band of supporters but was soon forced to flee beyond the Euphrates and take refuge with the Parthians.

A sudden death

Titus's end was sudden and unexpected. In summer 81 he set out from Rome for the Sabine hill-country where Vespasian too had often spent the hot months. On the journey he went down with a fever, which was not improved by bathing in the cold spa waters of Aquae Cutiliae. It was probably malaria, though later writers were not content with a story of natural death. They tried to point the finger at Domitian. Even Suetonius reports the rumour that Domitian tried to hasten Titus's death by placing him in a snow-packed chest. Claiming it would help him recover, he then hurried to Rome to seize power while Titus was still alive. All this, however, is part of the later attempt to blacken Domitian's reputation in every way possible, and there is no good reason to suspect that Domitian acted improperly. He certainly ensured that Titus was deified without delay.

Titus left one final legacy: the enigmatic dying words, 'I have made but one mistake.' Nobody knows what he meant, but there has been no shortage of theories. Had he had sex with his brother's wife Domitia? Had he altered Vespasian's will to deny Domitian his rightful inheritance? Did he regret not having killed Domitian for plotting against

From the senate and people of Rome to the deified Titus Vespasianus Augustus, son of the deified Vespasian.

Inscription on the Arch of Titus

Titus did not have time in his short reign to become one of Rome's great imperial builders. His most significant achievement was the completion of the Flavian Amphitheatre to its full height of four storeys. As an addition to the scheme, Titus built new imperial baths just to the south of the amphitheatre and connected the two together by one of the most magnificent stairways of ancient Rome. It was said to his credit that he sometimes used these baths himself, in company with the common people, but little of them survives today, and the stairway has entirely gone. More conspicuous are the three reconstructed columns of the Temple of the Deified Vespasian which Titus began in the Forum. He also launched a massive operation to restore the buildings destroyed in the great fire of AD 80, though the work was not completed until the reign of Domitian. It was under Domitian also that the famous Arch of Titus (*right*) was dedicated by the senate and people of Rome to commemorate his deification and the suppression of the Jewish revolt 10 years earlier.

(*Above*) The Arch of Titus in the Forum. (*Left*) Relief panel on the inside of the archway: Titus rides in triumphal procession after his victory in the Jewish War.

him? Whatever the truth, he died on 13 September 81, aged only 42, in the same villa as his father. The people of Rome mourned him 'as they would have for a loss in their own families'; the senate heaped even greater praise on him than when he was alive. Yet Cassius Dio, for one, wondered whether Titus would still have gone down as a good emperor had he reigned longer. Would the mask have slipped?

Domitian
Imperator Caesar
Domitianus Augustus
81–96

Domitian went bald in early middle age but official portraits, like this one from the Capitoline Museum, Rome, continue to show him with flowing locks of curly hair, carefully brushed forward. So obsessed was he with baldness that he even wrote a book on the subject of hair care. Suetonius tells us that Domitian 'was so sensitive about his baldness, that he regarded it as a personal insult if anyone else was twitted with that defect in jest or in earnest.'

Even Nero forbore to witness the abominations he ordered. Under Domitian more than half our wretchedness consisted in watching and being watched, while our very sighs were scored against us, and the blanched faces of us all were revealed in deadly contrast to that one scowling blush behind which Domitian sheltered against shame.

Tacitus *Agricola* 45

Domitian's reputation suffered badly from being the last of his dynasty. His successors were delighted to believe all kinds of outrageous stories about him; they had after all gained their position by murder. Domitian also paid a high price for ignoring the senate, stripping away the empty formalities which pretended that he ruled in conjunction with them. Instead, Domitian saw the role of emperor as that of an autocratic monarch with absolute power. It was senators, however, who wrote the histories, and their verdict dominates our picture of the reign. The relative peacefulness of his reign, and his conscientious attention to administration, might otherwise have been almost sufficient to place Domitian among the good emperors.

Domitian was born at Rome, in the area known as 'Malum Punicum' (Pomegranate) on 24 October 51. He did not share in the court education

Domitian had this worst quality of all, that he desired to be flattered, and was equally displeased with both sorts of men, those who paid court to him and those who did not – with the former because they seemed to be flattering him and with the latter because they seemed to despise him.

Cassius Dio LXVII.4

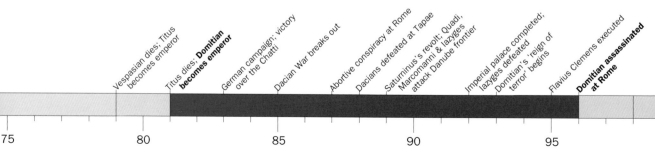

Vespasian dies; Titus becomes emperor

Titus dies; **Domitian becomes emperor**

German campaign; victory over the Chatti

Dacian War breaks out

Abortive conspiracy at Rome

Dacians defeated at Tapae

Saturninus's revolt; Quadi, Marcomanni & Iazyges attack Danube frontier

Imperial palace completed; Iazyges defeated

Domitian's 'reign of terror' begins

Flavius Clemens executed

Domitian assassinated at Rome

75   80   85   90   95

DOMITIAN	
Born 24 October AD *51 at Rome* Titus Flavius Domitianus *On Vespasian's accession* Caesar Domitianus *On accession 14 September 81* Imperator Caesar Domitianus Augustus, Pontifex Maximus, Pater Patriae *Added late 83* Victory title 'Germanicus' Consul I (71), II (73), III (75), IV (76), V (77), VI (79), VII (80), VIII (82), IX (83), X (84), XI (85), XII (86), XIII (87), XIV (88), XV (90), XVI (92), XVII (95) Tribunician power first on accession; renewed annually on anniversary of accession 14 September	Imperator first on accession, then II (82), III-V (83), VI-VII (84), VIII-XI (85), XII-XIV (86), XV-XVII (88), XVIII-XXI (89), XXII-XXIII (92) *Full titles at death* Imperator Caesar Domitianus Augustus Germanicus, Pontifex Maximus, Tribuniciae potestatis XVI, Imperator XXIII, Consul XVII, Pater Patriae *Wife* Domitia Longina *Children* a son (died in childhood) *Murdered in the Imperial Palace at Rome 18 September* AD *96; buried in the Temple of the Flavian Family*

awarded to his brother Titus, and may have been left with his uncle Flavius Sabinus while his father Vespasian was absent from Rome governing Africa and suppressing the Jewish revolt. Domitian was certainly with his uncle in December 69 when the Flavians were besieged by Vitellian forces on the Capitol. He escaped to safety, however, and when the Flavians took control of the city, Domitian became a key representative of the new dynasty until Vespasian himself reached Rome in October 70. Thereafter he was loaded with honours but little real power by his father or his brother. Relations with his brother Titus seem to have been cool, though there is no reason to believe that Domitian intrigued against him, still less that he poisoned him.

Titus was childless when he fell mortally ill in September 81. Whether Domitian had expected to become emperor we do not know. He acted quickly to forestall any opposition, however, and without waiting for Titus to die hurried to the praetorian camp at Rome and had himself proclaimed emperor by the guards. The following day, 14 September, Domitian was formally invested with imperial office by the senate.

The benevolent autocrat

Domitian was an able administrator; whatever his shortcomings as a person he did not neglect the welfare of the empire. According to Suetonius, 'he administered justice scrupulously and conscientiously, frequently holding special sittings on the tribunal in the Forum. He rescinded such decisions of the Hundred Judges as were made from interested motives. . . . He degraded jurors who accepted bribes, together with all their associates. . . . He took such care to exercise restraint over the city officials and the governors of the provinces, that at no time were they more honest or just.'

Domitian also tried to raise standards of public morality. He forbade the castration of males, and punished senators who practised homosexuality. As Pontifex Maximus he condemned to death four of the six Vestal Virgins; three for incest, and a fourth, the Chief Vestal Cornelia, for entertaining a whole string of lovers. The first three were allowed to choose the manner of their death, and their lovers were exiled. Cornelia, however, suffered the traditional penalty of being buried alive, while her lovers were beaten to death in the Forum.

In punishing the Vestals, Domitian was acting entirely within the law, however harsh. In other contexts his peremptory manner was less well judged. The senate, in particular, still felt that it had a part in the government, and that its wishes and advice should be respected by the emperor. For Domitian this was merely empty formality. Chosen senators were indeed called to high office within his administration, but it was the imperial court rather than the senate house which was the centre of power. In fact, provincials played a growing part in the imperial government, and several consulships went to men of Greek descent.

Domitian's autocratic style of government was underlined by his adoption of the titles 'dominus et deus', 'lord and god'. He changed the

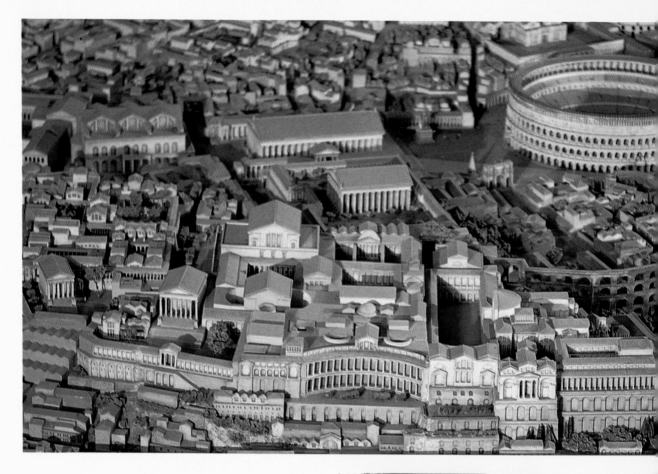

THE NEW PALACE

An edifice august, huge, magnificent not with a hundred columns, but with as many as would support heaven and the gods, were Atlas eased of his burden. . . Libyan mountains and gleaming Ilian stone are rivals there, and much Syenite and Chian and the marble that vies with the grey-green sea; and Luna, also, chosen but to bear the pillars' weight. Far upward travels the view; scarce does the tired vision reach the summit, and you would deem it the golden ceiling of the sky.

Statius *Silvae* IV.2

Thus did the court poet Statius praise Domitian's new imperial palace, and it was indeed one of the most spectacular constructions of the reign. It was decorated with elaborate wall paintings and with coloured stone including granite from Aswan (Syene) in Egypt and marbles from Libya and the Aegean island of Chios, not to mention plain white marble from Luna in Etruria. To provide a site for the palace the whole top of the Palatine Hill had first to be levelled. The buildings themselves were divided into two main groups, the Domus Flavia or official palace, and the Domus Augustana, the private residence of the emperor and his family, with a large garden in the form of a stadium. The architect was Rabirius, and the entire complex covered 440,000 square feet (41,000 sq. m). Though reduced to ruins, much of Rabirius's plan can still be made out today.

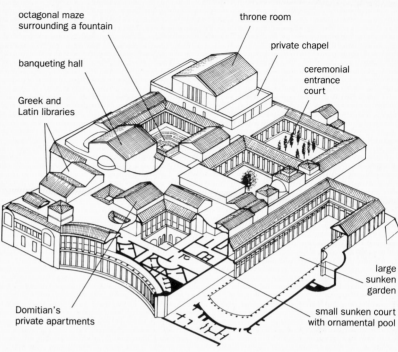

octagonal maze
surrounding a fountain

throne room

private chapel

banqueting hall

ceremonial
entrance
court

Greek and
Latin libraries

large
sunken
garden

Domitian's
private apartments

small sunken court
with ornamental pool

The Palace of Domitian on the Palatine Hill,
(above right) reconstruction drawing and
(above) in the model of imperial Rome from
the Museo della Civilta Romana. The curved
southern façade of the Domus Augustana
provided walkways at two levels with clear
views over the Circus Maximus and the
Aventine Hill beyond. On the right is the
extension of the Aqua Claudia built by
Domitian to bring water to his palace. Directly
below may be seen the new wing added by
Septimius Severus, built out on massive
substructures from the corner of the Palatine
Hill.

(Right) View looking south across the large
sunken garden. The curved southern end
gives this the form of a hippodrome, an
illusion strengthened by rooms at the straight
northern end designed to resemble starting
gates.

(Left) Sunken court with ornamental pool. The
curved and scalloped platforms may once
have supported decorative columns and
plants. Domitian's own private apartments
lay on the left hand side of the court.

Portrait-bust from the Louvre, of the empress Domitia Longina, daughter of Nero's famous general Corbulo. Domitian is said to have divorced her for adultery with Paris, an actor, at some point early in his reign. She was sent into exile, and her lover cut down in the public street. Domitian then took to bed Julia, his niece (the daughter of Titus), and openly cohabited with her; but soon became reconciled with Domitia through the pressure of popular feeling, and married her again. Much of this sounds like malicious fabrication, but Domitia does seem to have been exiled in 83, and is said eventually to have encouraged Domitian's murder.

names of the months September and October to 'Germanicus' and 'Domitianus', after his own name and title. He was brusque and businesslike in instructions to governors and officials, wasting no time on polite platitudes. But he also executed senators who opposed his policy, ignoring the frequent decrees of the senate that it should be unlawful for the emperor to put to death any of his peers. And as the reign progressed and his paranoia grew, Domitian relied more and more on informers and put suspects to the torture, inventing a new form of inquisition, 'inserting fire into their privates.'

Court and courtiers

At the heart of Domitian's government was the imperial palace. He had inherited the official residence on the Palatine from his predecessors, but it fell below his conception of what the emperor's exalted station demanded. Soon after coming to power he embarked on construction of a whole new palace complex, the Domus Augustana, to the south of the old Domus Tiberiana. When not in Rome itself Domitian spent much time at his country residence, the Villa Albana, about 12.5 miles south of Rome along the Via Appia.

The imperial palace was the locus of Domitian's public and private life. It was there that he held official banquets and receptions. It also contained splendid lodgings for the emperor himself and his empress Domitia. He had become infatuated with Domitia Longina at the time Vespasian came to power, while she was still the wife of Aelius Lamia. She divorced Lamia to marry Domitian in the year 70 and bore him a son in 73 who died when he was only two or three years old. Outside his official marriage Domitian gained a reputation for lustful behaviour. He was said to depilate his concubines with his own hand, and referred to sexual intercourse as 'bed-wrestling'. Yet stories of incest with his brother's daughter Julia should be treated with scepticism. So should allegations of pederasty, not to mention claims that he had sold his body to one-eyed Claudius Pollio in his youth, and perhaps to Nerva also.

Domitian was no great lover of literature, but to adorn the imperial court and promote his image he supported Martial and Statius as court poets. They wrote in glowing terms of his regime, his military achievements, and his ambitious building projects. Domitian also patronized public entertainments, introducing novel elements to the games including female combatants and dwarfs. He was in addition something of a philhellene, and founded Greek-style games and literary competitions at Rome. All this was costly, and these drains on the imperial purse were one of the factors which later drove Domitian to confiscations and heavier taxation.

Domitian's wars

One hefty element in the imperial budget was the army. Here Domitian won their undying gratitude by increasing the soldiers' pay from 300 to 400 sesterces. Like many emperors who lacked military achievements

BUILDINGS AND MONUMENTS

He restored many splendid buildings which had been destroyed by fire, among them the Capitolium which had again been burned, but in all cases with the inscription of his own name only, and with no mention of the original builder. . . He erected so many and such huge vaulted passage-ways and arches in the many regions of the city, adorned with chariots and triumphal emblems, that on one of them someone wrote in Greek 'It is enough'.

Suetonius *Life of Domitian* V, XIII

Domitian's building programme at Rome was the greatest undertaken by any emperor since Augustus. He rebuilt many of the structures destroyed in the great fire of Titus's reign, including the Temple of Jupiter Capitolinus. He also undertook a whole series of major new monuments, including an impressive stadium (now the Piazza Navona), the Forum of Nerva (dedicated, as the name suggests, by his successor) and a lavishly decorated dynastic shrine, the Temple Gentis Flaviae (Temple of the Flavian Family). In addition to buildings, Dio tells us that 'almost the whole world (as far as it was under his dominion) was filled with his images and statues constructed of both silver and gold.' Greatest of all was the Equus Domitiani, a massive equestrian statue of Domitian erected in the Forum in 91 in memory of his German and Dacian victories. It too was included in the orgy of destruction visited upon Domitian's statues after his assassination, but excavations have uncovered its massive base, a concrete plinth almost 40 ft (12 m) long and 19 ft (6 m) wide.

The Piazza Navona (above) preserves the form of Domitian's Stadium.

before coming to power, he embarked on a campaign soon after his accession. His target was the Chatti, a German people living beyond the Rhine frontier, and in 83 he awarded himself a triumph at Rome and the victory title 'Germanicus' for his success against them. It did not rank as an impressive victory, however, and earned Domitian more derision than respect.

The more serious warfare of the reign was on the Danube frontier. In 85 the Dacians (from the area of modern Romania) crossed the river and killed the local Roman governor. They were driven back, but the next year an impetuous Roman commander lost his life and army in a punitive strike deep inside Dacia. It was two years before the Romans regained the upper hand with a conclusive victory at Tapae in 88.

THE SECOND PERSECUTION

Many were the victims of Domitian's appalling cruelty. At Rome great numbers of men distinguished by birth and attainments were for no reason at all banished from the country and their property confiscated. Finally, he showed himself the successor of Nero in enmity and hostility to God. He was, in fact, the second to organize persecution against us, though his father Vespasian had had no mischievous designs against us.

Eusebius *Ecclesiastical History* III.17

Besides other taxes, that on the Jews was levied with the utmost rigour, and those were prosecuted who without publicly acknowledging that faith yet lived as Jews, as well as those who concealed their origin and did not pay the tribute levied upon their people.

Suetonius *Life of Domitian* XII

The people 'who lived as Jews without publicly acknowledging that faith' included many Christians. Some of these were recent Jewish converts, and fell foul of Domitian's campaign to levy the special tax on Jews introduced by Vespasian after the destruction of the Temple of Jerusalem. Whether Domitian deliberately set out to persecute Christians is less clear. Christianity was still technically an illegal religion, however, and later tradition held that high-ranking Romans, even members of the imperial family, were condemned for being Christians by Domitian.

Domitian was forced to break off the war and come to terms with the Dacian king Decebalus in 89 in order to fight against the Quadi and Marcomanni on the Upper Danube. Three years later it was the Sarmatian Iazyges who were the main threat, again on the Danube frontier, and Domitian may have been engaged in a further Sarmatian war the year before his death.

None of the wars produced striking or comprehensive victories, though Domitian was successful in holding the Danube frontier against the successive onslaughts. In order to do this he had to rein in expansionist ambitions elsewhere, notably in Britain where Agricola had hoped to complete the conquest of Scotland. This action earned Domitian harsh criticism in many quarters, but it was a sensible rationalization of frontier policy. Furthermore, though he never won the reputation of a great military leader, Domitian himself was present during several of the wars, and may even have taken part in some of the campaigns.

The suspicious tyrant

Domitian was not a happy individual. He suffered from a sense of social inadequacy, and preferred to take a walk after dinner rather than sitting late into the night drinking with his companions. He was also an exceedingly fearful man, who had the palace colonnades lined with white reflective marble so that he could see what was going on behind him.

During his early years, he endeavoured to act with moderation and justice, punishing false informers and treating even persistent calumnies with lenience. The first change came in 85, when financial problems encouraged him to make use of confiscations to boost the imperial coffers. Yet it was Domitian's deepening suspicion and insecurity rather than his need for money which eventually drove him to cruelty and executions. 'He used to say that the lot of princes was most unhappy, since when they had discovered a conspiracy, no one believed them unless they had been killed.' But there is in fact very little evidence of conspiracy either at Rome or in the provinces during the first six years of his reign.

The first sign of unrest is a brief reference to prayers of thanks for the uncovering of a conspiracy against the emperor on 22 September 87. Senior senators were implicated and executed. The next recorded attempt, in January 89, was more in the nature of a military mutiny. The leader was Lucius Antonius Saturninus, governor of Upper Germany; the cause probably dissatisfaction with Domitian's policy of appeasement towards the Germans and the growing importance of the Danube legions. The uprising was quickly stamped out by Lappius Maximus, governor of Lower Germany.

Terror and death

The 'terror' erupted four years later, in the later months of 93, and continued until Domitian's death. Goaded by paranoia and insecurity,

Domitian turned upon senators, knights and imperial officials alike, ordering executions or exile. Tacitus writes of 'the senate house under siege, the senators hedged in by soldiers, and that one fell stroke that sent so many a consular to death, so many a noble lady to exile or flight.' It was a traumatic experience for the younger Pliny, too: 'a time when seven of my friends had been put to death or banished . . . so that I stood amidst the flames of thunderbolts dropping all around me, and there were certain clear indications to make me suppose a like end was awaiting me.'

The reign of terror had exactly the opposite effect to what Domitian had intended, for he did not even spare his personal staff and relations. In 95 he executed his niece's husband, Flavius Clemens, an ex-consul, on a flimsy charge of atheism. Clemens's widow Domitilla was exiled to the tiny island of Pandateria, but her steward Stephanus stayed on at court. It was there that the successful conspiracy was hatched during the summer months of 96. One version of the story claims that the conspirators happened upon a writing tablet on which their names were marked down for death. The conspirators were Domitian's own personal attendants, driven to seek safety in his murder. The leaders were Stephanus and Parthenius, the imperial chamberlain, but they had encouragement from the empress Domitia, who was also in fear of her life, and from the commanders of the praetorian guard. For several days Stephanus went about with his arm in capacious bandages, pretending an injury, while in fact he had a dagger concealed in the folds of cloth. They chose their moment when Domitian was retiring from the court-room for an afternoon rest. Parthenius had already removed the sword which Domitian always kept beneath his pillow. Stephanus told Domitian he had information of a conspiracy against him, but as soon as they were alone he drew his dagger and struck him down. The first blow was not fatal, however, and the two struggled on the floor for some time, 'Domitian trying now to wrest the dagger from his assailant's hands and now to gouge out his eyes with his lacerated fingers.' The emperor was put out of his misery by the other conspirators, who burst into the room and hacked him to death.

Only the army mourned Domitian's death. The general populace was indifferent, but the senate was overjoyed at the news, and delighted that one of their own number, the elderly Nerva, had been chosen as successor. Domitian's body was carried out of the palace he had built, on a common bier, and taken to the suburban estate of Phyllis, the nurse by whom he had been raised. She at least retained some affectionate memories of him. After cremating the corpse, she secretly carried the ashes back to Rome, to the Temple of the Flavian Family (another of Domitian's creations). There she mingled them with the ashes of Julia, his niece. Thus Domitian's body was saved; but his reputation was lost beyond all hope of redemption. Through the writings of Tacitus and Suetonius he became yet another example of the monster in office, a worthy successor to Nero and Caligula.

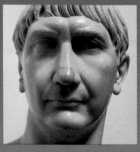

Trajan

Hadrian

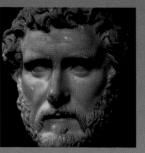

Antoninus Pius

Marcus Aurelius

THE ADOPTIVE EMPERORS AND THE ANTONINE DYNASTY

Nerva
AD 96–98

Trajan
98–117

Hadrian
117–138

Antoninus Pius
138–161

Marcus Aurelius
161–180
and Lucius Verus
161–169

Commodus
180–192

THE CIVIL WAR OF 193

Pertinax
193

Didius Julianus
193

THE SEVERAN DYNASTY

Septimius Severus
193–211

Caracalla
211–217

Geta
211

Macrinus
217–218

Elagabalus
218–222

Alexander Severus
222–235

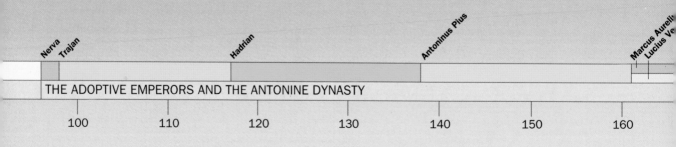

Nerva Trajan — Hadrian — Antoninus Pius — Marcus Aurelius Lucius Verus

THE ADOPTIVE EMPERORS AND THE ANTONINE DYNASTY

100   110   120   130   140   150   160

Septimius Severus

Caracalla

Macrinus

Elagabalus

THE HIGH POINT OF EMPIRE
The Adoptive Emperors and the Antonine Dynasty
AD 96–192
The Severan Dynasty AD 193–235

THE ACCESSION OF TRAJAN marks a new phase in the history of the Roman emperors, since he was the first emperor of non-Italian origin. During the second century the empire came increasingly to be seen not as a system of provinces dependent on Italy, but as a kind of commonwealth. This process was reflected in the polyglot origins of the emperors: Trajan and Hadrian came from Spain, Septimius Severus from Africa, Elagabalus and Alexander Severus from the Levant.

A key feature of the second-century emperors was the nature of the succession. Nerva, Trajan, Hadrian and Antoninus Pius had no surviving sons, and their successors were chosen by adoption. This gave them the chance to select men who had already shown their potential and were not necessarily close relatives. The adoptive emperors gave Rome a period of good stable government lasting for over 80 years.

The first half of the second century was a period of confidence and prosperity, but plague and invasion under Marcus Aurelius, the less than successful reign of his son Commodus, and the civil war of the 190s cast a shadow over the later decades. The Severans introduced a new sense of order, but it was of brief duration, and the murder of Caracalla was followed by a steady decline in imperial authority. By the end of the dynasty the Syrian princes Elagabalus and Alexander Severus were little more than rois fainéants.

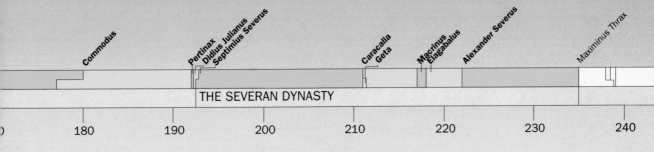

Commodus — Pertinax — Didius Julianus — Septimius Severus — Caracalla — Geta — Macrinus — Elagabalus — Alexander Severus — Maximinus Thrax

THE SEVERAN DYNASTY

180   190   200   210   220   230   240

Nerva
Imperator Nerva Caesar
Augustus
96–98

Trajan
Imperator Caesar Divi
Nervae Filius Nerva
Traianus
98–117

The emperor Nerva is described by
Roman historians as old and feeble in
health, with a tendency to over-
indulgence in wine. Coins and statues
(such as this head now in the Museo
Nazionale at Rome) depict a face with
close-set eyes and a prominent nose.

NERVA

NERVA	
Born 8 November AD *30 at Narnia* Marcus Cocceius Nerva	Tribunician power conferred first on accession, renewed annually
On accession 18 September 96 Imperator Nerva Caesar Augustus	*Full titles at death* Imperator Nerva Caesar Augustus Germanicus, Pontifex Maximus, Tribuniciae potestatis III, Imperator II, Consul IV, Pater Patriae
Conferred by the senate on or soon after accession 'Pater Patriae' *Victory title October 97* 'Germanicus'	
Proclaimed Imperator a second time October 97	*Wives* unknown
Consul I (71), II (90), III (97), IV (98)	*Died of apoplexy at Rome 27 January 98; ashes placed in the Mausoleum of Augustus*

NERVA

*Fourteenth day before the Kalends of October [18 September AD 96]:
Domitian killed. On the same day, Marcus Cocceius Nerva proclaimed
emperor.*

Fasti Ostienses

Thus with characteristic crispness does the calendar of Ostia record the
fall of the Flavian dynasty and the transfer of power to an elderly man
entirely unrelated either by blood or marriage to the emperors whom he
succeeded. Nerva did not seek power so much as have power thrust upon
him. Cassius Dio tells us that he was approached by the conspirators
planning Domitian's murder, and accepted the role of successor to save
his own life, which was under threat from Domitian. The story may well
be an invention, but Nerva's accession was certainly greeted with relief
by many leading figures, tired of Domitian's tyranny.

Marcus Cocceius Nerva was born at Narnia, 50 miles north of Rome,
on 8 November AD 35, the son of a wealthy Roman lawyer. Members of
his family had held high office: his great-grandfather had been consul in
36 BC, and they still moved in courtly circles the following century: his

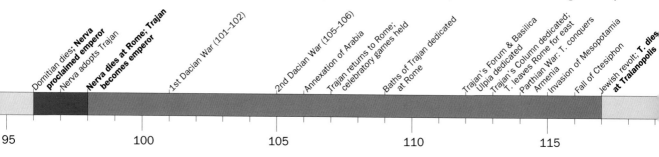

Dedicated by the Senate and People of Rome to the Liberty restored by Imperator Nerva Caesar Augustus in the eight hundred and forty-eighth year since the foundation of the city on the fourteenth day before the Kalends of October (18 September AD 96)

Monumental inscription from Rome

The Forum of Nerva at Rome, built largely by Domitian but completed and named by his successor. Only this small section of the side-walls still stands, but it is enough to illustrate the excellent workmanship. High up between the columns is the figure of the goddess Minerva.

grandfather was in the imperial entourage at the time of Nerva's birth. On his mother's side there was a distant link with the Julio-Claudian family; his aunt was the great-granddaughter of Tiberius.

The young Nerva followed in the footsteps of his father and grandfather, filling a series of official positions. He showed a remarkable ability to ride out the changes in imperial regime, and still achieve high office. He was awarded special honours for helping Nero to suppress the conspiracy of Piso in 65, yet was chosen by the emperor Vespasian to be his colleague as consul in 71. In 90, the emperor Domitian in his turn chose Nerva to serve as consul alongside him. The continued favour shown by this series of emperors suggests Nerva was a respected figure. A darker shade comes from a story reported by Suetonius: Domitian, when a young man, was sexually abused by Nerva, who was 20 years his senior. An idle rumour, or a less exemplary side to Nerva's character?

Murder and mutiny

Nerva was acclaimed emperor by the senate on 18 September 96, as soon as Domitian's murder became known. The assassination unleashed a host of forces held in check during Domitian's tyrannical latter years. Cassius Dio, whose brief account is our main source for Nerva's reign, gives the flavour of the troubled early months. Domitian had been hated by the senate. Once he was dead, popular resentment broke loose in the destruction of his statues and the demolition of his ceremonial arches. Many of Domitian's informers were put to death, and an amnesty was granted to those whom he had sent into exile. There was a general sense of euphoria among the leading families, of liberty and justice restored.

The situation rapidly began to get out of control, and the elderly Nerva had difficulty restoring order. Under Domitian, it was said, nobody had been allowed to do anything; but it was worse under Nerva, when everyone could do whatever they liked. He was already almost 61 when he came to power, an old man by Roman standards, and he is said to have been ill and weak, with a tendency to vomit up his food.

The trouble at Rome was compounded by the opposition of the military. Nerva is portrayed as a benevolent ruler, who allotted land to the urban poor, took an oath not to execute senators, and embarked on a modest programme of public works including the repair of roads and aqueducts. This made him popular in some quarters, but did not placate the army. The army still held dear the memory of his soldiering predecessor, the first emperor to have given them a pay-rise since Augustus.

The military unrest came to a head around the middle of AD 97, when the praetorian guard broke into open mutiny. Casperius Aelianus, commander of the guard, imprisoned Nerva in the imperial palace, demanding the surrender of Petronius and Parthenius, the people responsible for Domitian's death. Nerva resisted these demands with great personal courage, baring his own throat to the soldiers. His brave gesture was in vain for he was helpless to stop the praetorians from seizing their victims. Of the two conspirators, Petronius had the more merciful end. He was killed by a single sword-blow. The unfortunate Parthenius, on the other hand, had his genitals torn off and thrust into his mouth before his throat was cut.

Nerva himself was unharmed in this assault, but his authority was damaged beyond repair. The mutiny of the praetorians brought back memories of the elderly Galba's brief period of rule 30 years before, and the message was clear: an emperor who had lost the support of the army could not expect to live long. As a childless old man, however, Nerva had an effective means of salvation: the adoption as son and successor of someone who would have the support both of the army and the people. Such a man he found in Marcus Ulpius Traianus (Trajan), governor of Upper Germany, a respected individual with legions under his command to safeguard and strengthen imperial authority at Rome. The formal adoption took place towards the end of October AD 97, in a public ceremony on the Capitol.

A peaceful conclusion

The adoption of Trajan may have been a veiled coup d'état, rather than an act of free will, but it enabled the elderly emperor to live out his final months in peace. As a result, Nerva went down in memory as a kindly and amiable man, one who ruled so well that he could claim with sincerity: 'I have done nothing as emperor that would prevent my laying down the imperial office and returning to private life in safety.' Nerva's popu-

Nerva's successor Trajan was responsible for three major extensions of the Roman empire: north of the Danube, where the kingdom of Dacia was conquered in two major wars (101–2 and 105–6); Arabia, where the client kingdom of the Nabataeans was occupied and became a Roman province in 106; and in Armenia and Mesopotamia, where Trajan campaigned from 114 to 116.

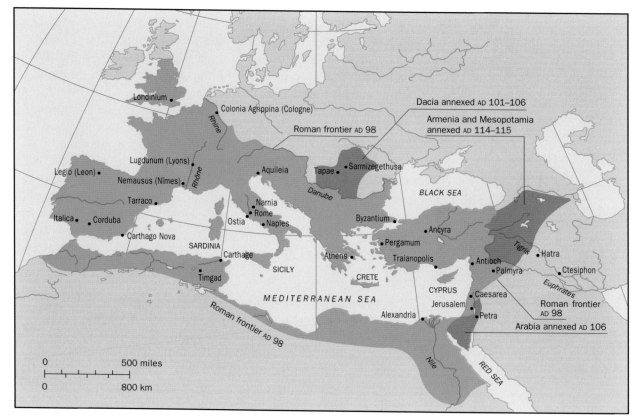

larity with the senate earned him the title 'Pater Patriae' ('Father of his Country') at the very outset of his reign; other emperors had to wait months or years for this honour. For posterity, one of his most memorable acts was the dedication of the Forum at Rome which bears his name, the Forum Nervae (also known as the Forum Transitorium) early in AD 97. But the name hides the fact that the complex was mainly the work of Domitian, and was almost complete by the time Nerva came to power.

Nerva's short, 16-month reign ended with his death on 28 January the following year. During an outburst of anger he was overcome by a fit of sweating. This developed into a fever, and he died shortly afterwards. He was officially deified by the senate, and as a mark of special respect, his ashes were laid in the Mausoleum of Augustus, alongside those of the Julio-Claudian emperors. The day of his burial was marked by an eclipse of the sun.

Although Nerva was popular with the senate, he cannot wholly be absolved from his earlier involvement with Nero and Domitian. Furthermore, the cynical might interpret his reforms, public handouts and remissions of taxes as no more than a desperate attempt to win popular support. But in his choice of Trajan as successor, the gratitude of Nerva's contemporaries proved to be well deserved. For, as Pliny says, 'there is no more certain proof of divinity in a ruler who has chosen his successor than the worthiness of his choice.'

Trajan's Market at Rome. The ground floor openings, originally square-framed doorways of travertine, were for shops; the round-headed windows above lit a curving corridor; and there were further offices and shops (including a large covered market hall) above and behind. This façade was originally hidden behind the curving side-wall of Trajan's Forum, the foundations of which can be seen in the foreground.

Pliny's *Panegyric* tells of Trajan's 'splendid bearing and tall stature, his fine head and noble countenance, to say nothing of the firm strength of his maturity and the premature signs of advancing age with which the gods have seen fit to mark his hair and so enhance his look of majesty'. Born in AD 53, Trajan would in fact have been in his mid 40s at the time of his accession, a mature but not an old man by Roman standards. (*Above*) Bust in the British Museum.

TRAJAN

Born 18 Sept 53 at Italica in Spain	times in 113-117
Marcus Ulpius Traianus	Tribunician power first on adoption
On adoption Oct 97	(October 97),
Caesar Divi Nervae filius Nerva Traianus	renewed 10 December 97, then annually on 10
On accession 28 January 98	December
Imperator Caesar Divi Nervae filius Nerva Traianus Augustus	*Full titles at death* Imperator Caesar Divi Nervae Filius Nerva Traianus Optimus Augustus
Added in 98 'Pater Patriae'	Germanicus Dacicus Parthicus,
Victory titles 'Germanicus' Oct 97, 'Dacicus' 102, 'Parthicus' 114	Pontifex Maximus, Tribuniciae potestatis XXI, Imperator XIII,
Added in August or September 114 'Optimus'	Consul VI, Pater Patriae
Consul six times: AD 91, 98, 100, 101, 103, 112	*Wife* Pompeia Plotina
Proclaimed 'Imperator' on accession, thrice in 101-102, twice in 105-106, seven	*Died at Selinus in Asia Minor after a stroke 7 August 117; buried at base of Trajan's Column*

TRAJAN

His association with the people was marked by affability and his intercourse with the senate by dignity, so that he was loved by all and dreaded by none save the enemy.

Cassius Dio LXVIII.15

Trajan became one of the greatest and most renowned of Roman emperors. His 19 years of rule were distinguished by military exploits which pushed the frontiers of Rome to their widest extent; by a sound paternalism which sought to establish good administration; and by excellent relations with the senate, which healed the breach in the fabric of Roman government opened by Domitian's autocratic rule.

Marcus Ulpius Traianus was born on 18 September, probably in the year AD 53, at Italica near Seville. He was in fact the first emperor of non-Italian origin, though his family was an old-established Umbrian one from northern Italy which had chosen to settle in southern Spain. These were no mere provincials. His father, another Marcus Ulpius Traianus, had a distinguished civil and military career, commanding the Tenth Legion 'Fretensis' during the Jewish War in AD 67–68, consul in around AD 70, and governor of Syria, one of the most important provinces of the Roman empire, soon afterwards. Marcus Ulpius senior was clearly a trusted lieutenant. He had also at some stage served as governor of the Spanish province of Baetica, and towards the end of his life was appointed governor of Asia, the Roman province of western Asia Minor. He died some time before AD 100.

With such a distinguished father, the young Trajan had a head start in life. After serving as military tribune under his father in Syria in the 70s he rose rapidly to become commander of the Seventh Legion 'Gemina' based at Legio (modern Léon) in northern Spain by the late 80s. In January AD 89 he marched his legion to the Rhine to assist the emperor Domitian in suppressing the rebellion of Saturninus, governor of Upper Germany, but arrived too late to take part in the action. Trajan found favour with Domitian and was chosen to serve as praetor in around AD 85 and consul in AD 91. This association with the unpopular Domitian became something of an embarrassment after Domitian's assassination and this phase of Trajan's career is passed over in silence in Pliny's *Panegyric*. The *Panegyric* also makes no reference to Trajan's Spanish origin, so here too was something best left unmentioned.

Nerva's heir

On Nerva's accession in AD 96, Trajan was appointed governor of Upper Germany, and it was there late the following year that he received a handwritten note from the emperor, informing him of his adoption. The use of adoption to establish the imperial succession had been established by Augustus, and the meaning of the action was clear, though whether Trajan had any forewarning of his impending promotion is unknown.

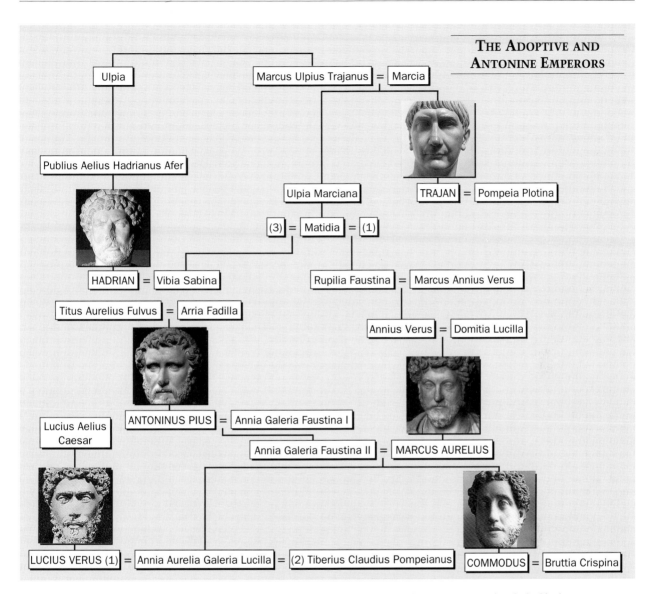

THE ADOPTIVE AND ANTONINE EMPERORS

Ulpia

Marcus Ulpius Trajanus = Marcia

Publius Aelius Hadrianus Afer

Ulpia Marciana

TRAJAN = Pompeia Plotina

(3) = Matidia = (1)

HADRIAN = Vibia Sabina

Rupilia Faustina = Marcus Annius Verus

Titus Aurelius Fulvus = Arria Fadilla

Annius Verus = Domitia Lucilla

Lucius Aelius Caesar

ANTONINUS PIUS = Annia Galeria Faustina I

Annia Galeria Faustina II = MARCUS AURELIUS

LUCIUS VERUS (1) = Annia Aurelia Galeria Lucilla = (2) Tiberius Claudius Pompeianus

COMMODUS = Bruttia Crispina

Friends at Rome may well have been active on his behalf; there is even a story that Trajan did not in fact passively wait on events, but covertly seized power through their assistance. Whatever the truth, the adoption of Trajan was an astute move by the ailing Nerva, who desperately needed a powerful supporter against the troubles pressing on him at Rome. The most serious was the mutiny of the praetorian guard under Casperius Aelianus. Yet Trajan did not hurry back to the capital to restore authority. Instead, he merely sent for the leaders of the mutiny, on the pretext of handing them a special commission. When they arrived at his headquarters in Germany he had them executed.

Such firm action restored confidence and stability in the government. When Nerva died, on 28 January AD 98, Trajan felt no need to start out for Rome to secure his position. Instead, after settling the affairs of his own province, he embarked on a tour of inspection of the Rhine and

TRAJAN'S COLUMN

This impressive stone column, almost 100 ft (30 m) high, was the special contribution of the senate of Rome to Trajan's Forum. It is made from 20 enormous blocks of Carrara marble, carved on the outer face with a spiral frieze depicting, like a cartoon strip, the story of Trajan's two Dacian Wars. The upper parts of the Column were designed to be seen not from ground level but from the galleries of the buildings which originally stood around it. A statue of the emperor himself once stood on the summit; the present statue of St Peter dates only from 1588. The base of the Column is a massive cube containing a number of small rooms, the innermost of which was Trajan's tomb chamber. Cremation was still the customary rite among high-ranking Romans at this period, and two holes drilled in the rear wall of the room may have been intended to hold the funerary urns of Trajan and his wife Plotina.

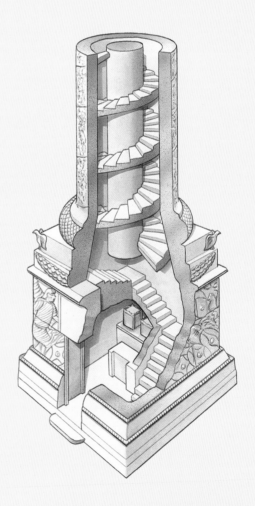

(Above) Cut-away drawing of Trajan's Column showing the spiral stair and the chambers in the column-base.

(Right) The spiral frieze of Trajan's Column depicts scenes from the Dacian Wars. The frieze was carved only when the Column was complete, the sculptors working from the bottom upwards. It has recently been suggested that the carving was added to the Column by Hadrian after Trajan's death. The scenes, however, form part of a single grand pictorial scheme together with those of adjacent buildings of Trajan's Forum, which suggests that the Column frieze was part of Trajan's plan from the beginning.

(Below) Detail from Trajan's Column showing the emperor addressing the troops.

PLINY'S LETTERS

The clearest insight into Trajan's approach to government comes from his official correspondence with the younger Pliny while the latter was serving as governor of Bithynia and Pontus (northern Asia Minor) in AD 110–111. Pliny consulted the emperor on a whole range of administrative matters, and the replies convey an impression of wisdom mixed with firmness. One of the questions concerned the treatment to be meted out to Christians. According to the law of the time, those accused of 'this evil and excessive superstition' were required to acquit themselves of the charge by invoking the gods and making an offering of wine and incense to the emperor's statue. The guilty were liable to execution. Pliny asks Trajan how he should proceed against ex-Christians and people who had been accused of being Christians by an anonymous pamphleteer. In his reply, Trajan directs Pliny to avoid any kind of witch-hunt and to ignore anonymous informers:

My dear Pliny, you have followed the course of action which you should, in investigating the cases of those brought before you accused of being Christians; for it is not possible to establish a fixed rule which would apply to all cases. These people must not be sought out; if they are brought before you and the charge is proved, they must be punished; but any of them who denies he is a Christian and gives visible evidence of that, by praying to our gods, however much he may previously have been suspected, let him be given a pardon for his penitence. The anonymous pamphlets which have been published must have no place in any accusation. For on the one hand they give very bad example, and on the other, they are not the way things should now be done.

Pliny *Letters* X.97

Danube frontiers. The Danube frontier was cause for particular concern, not only because of external threats. Domitian had been popular with the legions, almost one third of which were stationed on the Danube, and Trajan's personal visit was a wise precaution to forestall any trouble from that quarter. He may also already have been planning his Dacian War. Pliny tells us how Trajan stood on the banks of the Danube, but since no enemy presented itself he felt no urge to cross, an action 'demonstrating both courage and moderation'.

Trajan at Rome

Trajan's arrival at Rome in the late summer of 99 was an occasion of great rejoicing. Crowds thronged the streets, rooftops along the way sagged under the weight of spectators. Trajan made his entry on foot, embracing the senators in turn and mingling with the ordinary people. This posture of modesty and approachability was characteristic of his public image during at least the first years of his reign, and helped to ensure popular support. On the other hand, Trajan made no attempt to divest himself of any imperial powers, but remained an absolute ruler. He bore himself towards the senators with dignity and restraint, conduct which stood in sharp contrast to the autocratic manner of Domitian. Yet much of what Trajan was praised for was empty formality: the fact, for example, that on entering and leaving the office of consul he volunteered to swear the customary oath to uphold the law. It was still the emperor who chose the consuls and other officials.

That the new emperor had senatorial approval is clearly evident from Pliny's *Panegyric*. This was a speech delivered during a meeting of the senate on 1 September AD 100, when Pliny took up office as consul and moved a vote of thanks to Trajan. The praises of the emperor are lavish, and prolonged. Indeed, in its expanded published form it would have taken up to six hours to recite. The picture it gives of Trajan is one of powerful machismo, coupled nonetheless with the piety essential to a man of real virtue. For relaxation, we are told, Trajan chose the rigours of the hunt, delighting 'to range the forests, drive wild beasts from their lairs, scale vast mountain heights, and set foot on rocky crags, with none to give a helping hand or show the way; and amidst all this to visit the sacred groves in a spirit of devotion, and present himself to deities there.' The adulation spreads beyond Trajan himself to his wife, the lady Plotina: 'How modest she is in her attire, how moderate in the number of her attendants, how unassuming when she walks abroad.'

Too much of this and the reader tires of the endless superlatives. Yet there is other evidence which shows Trajan as a capable ruler concerned to ensure good government and public welfare. The medical writer Galen almost a century later describes how Trajan restored the road system of Italy, paving those which passed through wet or muddy places, raising some on embankments, building bridges where necessary to carry them across rivers or streams. This is borne out by inscriptions. He also took steps to provide for the poor, especially children, setting up

We know little of Trajan's family. His wife, Pompeia Plotina (*above*), came from Nemausus (Nîmes) in Gaul, where she was born around AD 70. The two were married some time before Trajan's adoption by Nerva, but are not known to have had any children. Cassius Dio tells us of her modest behaviour on Trajan's arrival at Rome: 'When Plotina first entered the palace, she turned round so as to face the stairway and the populace and said: "I enter here such a woman as I would fain be when I depart." And she conducted herself during the entire reign in such manner as to incur no censure.' Plotina nonetheless showed some capacity for intrigue, encouraging Hadrian to marry Trajan's niece against the emperor's wishes. According to another story, she forged documents after Trajan's death to prove that he had adopted Hadrian as his heir. Plotina was awarded the title 'Augusta' in 105, and died in 123.

TRAJAN'S DACIAN CHRONICLES

We know that Trajan wrote his own account of the Dacian Wars, though of this only five words survive: 'inde Berzobim, deinde Aizi processimus' ('We then advanced to Berzobim, and next to Aizi'). It has been argued that since Berzobim and Aizi are only ten miles apart, the account of the war was so detailed it must have been based on Trajan's day-by-day journal. Most of this is unwarranted speculation. On the other hand, Cassius Dio tells us that Trajan was not a man of education, and it is interesting that he should have chosen to write a chronicle of his campaigns. Had it survived, it would have been the literary equivalent of Trajan's Column.

special imperial funds or *alimenta* for their upkeep. The scheme, originally devised by Nerva but first put into effect by Trajan, continued to function for almost 200 years and is one of the most striking examples of paternalism in Roman government.

Trajan was not, however, without flaws. In a short passage, Cassius Dio tells us that Trajan was devoted to boys and to wine. On one occasion, he was enamoured of a pantomime dancer named Pylades. We are assured that neither ever led him into folly or injustice, that he never became drunk, nor did he harm any of the boys he had relations with. Dio also thinks it necessary to excuse Trajan's enjoyment of war. 'And even if he did delight in war, nevertheless he was satisfied when success had been achieved, a most bitter foe overthrown and his countrymen exalted.'

The conquest of Dacia

Warfare was something at which Trajan excelled. Pliny tells us of his popularity with the troops, and of his willingness to bear hardship and danger along with the soldiers under his command. Trajan came to power at a time when Rome's neighbours posed relatively little threat, and the campaigns he conducted may largely reflect his personal fondness for military life. Internal politics, and the need to keep the army employed, no doubt also played a part in the decision to wage no fewer than three major wars during his 19-year reign.

The first and second of these wars were fought against Dacia, a powerful kingdom lying north of the Danube frontier in modern Romania. Domitian had campaigned against them from AD 85 to 89, without securing a decisive outcome, and the Dacian king Decebalus was brazenly flouting the terms of the peace which had been agreed on that occasion. Whether Trajan's expedition was strictly necessary we shall never know. The aim, however, was to forestall further trouble from that quarter by settling accounts with Decebalus once and for all.

Early in AD 101 Trajan left Rome. Leading his troops across the Danube, he struck north into the heart of Dacian territory, defeating the Dacian army near Tapae. This was towards the end of 101. During the following winter, Decebalus attempted a counter-attack across the Danube further downstream, but this was repulsed. The campaign was brought to a successful conclusion the following year, when Trajan's armies advanced further into Dacian territory and camped before the Dacian capital Sarmizegethusa. Decebalus sued for peace, which was granted on somewhat lenient terms. Large tracts of territory north of the Lower Danube were annexed, and when Trajan returned to Rome he celebrated a triumph and was awarded the title 'Dacicus' by the senate.

The settlement did not last, however, and in June AD 105 Trajan once again left Rome to fight against Decebalus. The Dacians in the meantime had not been idle, and already the Roman outposts had fallen. This time the Roman expedition was able to take advantage of the impressive bridge built across the Danube by Trajan's principal architect and engi-

The so-called Taurine Baths near Centumcellae (modern Civitavecchia). These formed part of Trajan's great country villa described in glowing terms by Pliny, who spent several days there advising the emperor in legal hearings.

The harbour of Trajan at Ostia, a hexagonal land-locked basin built to supplement and replace the 'Portus Augusti' begun by Claudius. The harbour was linked to the Tiber by a canal (the 'Fossa Traiani') and warehouses and temples were an integral part of the scheme.

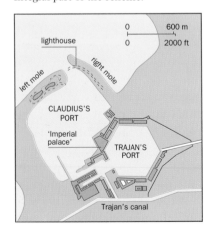

neer, Apollodorus of Damascus. Cassius Dio describes this bridge in admiring terms, maintaining that it surpassed all of Trajan's other achievements. Many allies of Decebalus faded away at Trajan's approach, and despite an attempt to assassinate the emperor, the Roman armies were able once again to advance to Sarmizegethusa. This time there was to be no mercy; Sarmizegethusa was captured and the treasures of the Dacian royal house were carried off to Rome. Decebalus himself was hounded until, in danger of capture, he committed suicide. His severed head was exhibited in Rome on the steps leading up to the Capitol. By the end of AD 106, resistance had been quelled and the entire kingdom of Dacia absorbed as a province of the Roman empire.

The story of the Dacian Wars is told in striking visual narrative by the relief carvings which spiral upwards around Trajan's Column, the vast commemorative pillar erected by order of the senate in Trajan's new imperial Forum at Rome. The reliefs depict in detail the progress of the campaigns, and give valuable information about Roman military equipment and techniques. Above all, however, the Column immortalizes Trajan's own role in the wars. A tall and distinctive figure, he is depicted in many roles – receiving envoys, planning operations, sacrificing to the gods, or receiving the submission of the defeated Dacian forces.

The middle years of the reign, from AD 107 to 113, were an interval of relative peace. On returning from the Dacian War Trajan celebrated another triumph and mounted an extravagant series of public games, in which 10,000 gladiators fought and 11,000 animals were killed. He also devoted some of the vast booty he had won to public works, including a new harbour at Ostia, the port of Rome, and the construction of his own Forum and Market. The Forum of Trajan was dedicated by the emperor on 1 January 112, and Trajan's Column in May the following year.

TRAJAN'S BUILDINGS

But when it comes to public building, you do it on a grand scale. Here stands a colonnade, there a shrine, rising as if by magic, so rapidly as to seem remodelled rather than freshly built. Elsewhere the vast façade of the Circus rivals the beauty of the temples, a fitting place for a nation which has conquered the world.

Pliny *Panegyric* 51

In addition to his military exploits Trajan was also renowned as a great builder. His greatest projects belong to the years following AD 107, when the spoils from the Dacian campaign had restored the imperial finances after the depredations of Domitian's reign. Among his most important projects at Rome were: the Forum Traiani, largest of the imperial fora; Trajan's Market; the Baths of Trajan, on the site of Nero's Golden House; the Naumachia Traiani, an amphitheatre for sea battles; and the Aqua Traiana, last of the great aqueducts of Rome.

In addition to these, Trajan built a new hexagonal harbour at Ostia, since Claudius' earlier harbour proved not to provide sufficient shelter. He also established several colonies for retired Roman soldiers, including Timgad in North Africa, Nijmegen and Xanten in the Rhineland, and Sarmizegethusa in his new province of Dacia. So numerous were Trajan's buildings that centuries later the emperor Constantine called him 'a wall-growing creeper' because of the many inscriptions which bore his name.

The greatest surviving work of Trajan's reign is without doubt the Forum and Market at Rome, but it was the bridge across the Danube which most impressed the historian Cassius Dio: 'Brilliant, indeed, as are his other achievements, yet this surpasses them.' (Dio LXVIII 13)

The eastern campaign

Trajan returned to war in 114, and spent the remaining years of his life campaigning on the empire's eastern frontier. Here the great enemy was the Parthians, rulers of a once powerful empire which had defeated several Roman armies in previous centuries, but was now in decline. The immediate cause of hostilities was Parthian interference in the kingdom of Armenia, a buffer-state lying between the frontiers of Rome and Parthia. The Parthian emperor had succeeded in placing his own nominee on the throne of Armenia, thus upsetting the delicate balance of power on the eastern frontier. Trajan's response was characteristically forthright. He settled the matter of Armenia by advancing in force and changing it from a buffer-kingdom to a Roman province. In AD 115 he extended operations southwards into northern Mesopotamia, and in a spectacular campaign the following year, succeeded in conquering the whole of Mesopotamia, including the Parthian capital at Ctesiphon near modern Baghdad.

For a brief moment Rome had a foothold on the Persian Gulf. But these successes were not to last, and Trajan's final months were marked by a number of reverses. Late in 116 the Mesopotamians launched a rebellion against the occupying Roman forces which was only with difficulty contained. In 117 Trajan's army failed to take the desert city of Hatra. The emperor himself, riding with an escort around the walls, narrowly missed being struck by an arrow which killed one of his bodyguard. Conditions for the besieging force steadily deteriorated, and Trajan was compelled to break off the operation and withdraw. According to Cassius Dio it was at this point that the emperor's health began to fail. At about the same time the Jewish population in Cyrenaica rose in revolt, and the unrest soon spread to Egypt and Cyprus. In Cyrenaica alone, it was claimed that 220,000 non-Jews perished in the uprising. New trouble also threatened on the northern frontier. Leaving the army in Syria, Trajan hurried back to Rome in order to take charge of the crisis.

Cassius Dio tells the end of the tale: already afflicted by some circulatory condition, which Trajan suspected was the result of poison, the emperor suffered a stroke which left him partially paralysed. Finally, 'On coming to Selinus in Cilicia, which we also call Traianopolis, he suddenly expired, after reigning nineteen years, six months and fifteen days.' The date was 9 August AD 117. The body of the emperor was brought back to Rome for burial, and the cremated remains placed in an urn of gold at the base of the Column which bore the record of his Dacian victories.

Trajan's fame as the model ruler lived on down the centuries. He set a standard against which later holders of imperial office were measured. In the fourth century, the senate still prayed that new emperors might be 'More fortunate than Augustus and better than Trajan'. His reputation survived into the Middle Ages, when the poet Dante gave him, alone of pre-Christian emperors, a place in Paradise.

Hadrian
Imperator Caesar Traianus Hadrianus Augustus
117–138

Hadrian was the first Roman emperor to be depicted wearing a beard. This may have been another instance of his love of all things Greek, but the Historia Augusta gives another explanation for the beard: 'He was tall of stature and elegant in appearance; his hair was curled on a comb, and he wore a full beard to cover up the natural blemishes on his face.' Whatever the reason, Hadrian's beard set a fashion which was followed by his immediate successors. (*Right*) Hadrian in military dress; bronze statue found at Beth Shean, Israel, now in the Israel Museum.

HADRIAN	
Born 24 January 76 at Rome	annually on 10 December
Publius Aelius Hadrianus	
Accession 11 August 117 as Trajan's adoptive son	*Full titles at death* Imperator Caesar Traianus Hadrianus Augustus, Pontifex Maximus, Tribuniciae potestatis XXII, Imperator II, Consul III, Pater Patriae
Imperator Caesar Traianus Hadrianus Augustus, Pontifex Maximus	
Added in AD 128 'Pater Patriae'	
Consul I (108),II (118), III (119)	*Wife* Vibia Sabina
Imperator first on accession,then II 135 at termination of the Jewish War Tribunician power first on accession, renewed 10 December 117, then	*Died of illness 10 July 138 at Baiae; buried first at Puteoli, near Baiae, then in the Garden of Domitia, Rome, ashes finally placed in the Mausoleum of Hadrian*

Aelius Hadrianus was more suited to eloquence and the studies of peacetime, and after peace had been restored in the east he returned to Rome. There he began to devote his attention to religious rituals, to laws, to the gymnasia, and to teachers, so much so that he established an institute of liberal arts which was called the Athenaeum.

Aurelius Victor *Book of the Caesars* 14

Thus did the late Roman historian Aurelius Victor characterize the emperor Hadrian: a man of culture and the arts, rather than war. There is indeed some truth in this; Hadrian showed none of that enjoyment of war so conspicuous in Trajan, his predecessor. As a result, he has had a good press in recent times: a pragmatic ruler, who avoided war wherever possible, and concentrated his energies on improving the internal administration of the empire. He gave the Roman world 20 years of good government, and strengthened and stabilized its frontiers. All this is undeniable. Roman historians leave us in no doubt, however, that Hadrian was not without his faults.

Publius Aelius Hadrianus was born on 24 January AD 76, probably at Rome. His family had settled at Italica three centuries before, when this part of Spain was first being opened up to Roman settlers. Hadrian's

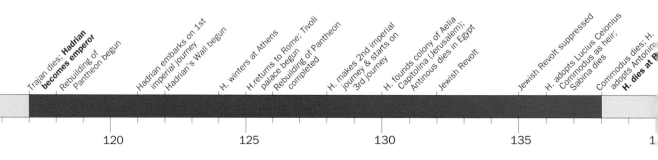

Trajan dies; **Hadrian becomes emperor**
Rebuilding of Pantheon begun
Hadrian embarks on 1st imperial journey
Hadrian's Wall begun
H. winters at Athens
H.returns to Rome; Tivoli palace begun
Rebuilding of Pantheon completed
H. makes 2nd imperial journey & starts on 3rd journey
H. founds colony of Aelia Capitolina (Jerusalem); Antinous dies in Egypt
Jewish Revolt
Jewish Revolt suppressed
H. adopts Lucius Ceionius Commodus as heir, Sabina dies
Commodus dies; H. adopts Antoninus
H. dies at B

120   125   130   135   1

father, Aelius Hadrianus Afer, was a cousin of the emperor Trajan, who was also a native of Italica. Thus as Trajan's career progressed this relatively obscure provincial family found itself increasingly well connected. When Hadrian's father died in AD 86 the boy of 10 became a joint ward of Trajan and of a Roman knight, Acilius Attianus.

Like many wealthy young men before and since, Hadrian is said to have had a misspent youth. Trajan's first attempt to launch him on a military career at the age of 15 was thwarted by his passion for hunting. Servianus, his future brother-in-law, reported Hadrian's life of extravagance to Trajan, who angrily summoned him back to Rome where he could be kept under closer supervision. Hadrian was launched on a new career with his appointment (despite his tender years) as a judge of one of the inheritance courts at Rome, and shortly afterwards we find him serving as an officer of the Second Legion 'Adiutrix' and then the Fifth Legion 'Macedonica' on the Danube. When in AD 97 Trajan, then on the Rhine, was adopted by the emperor Nerva, Hadrian was chosen to convey the army's congratulations to the new imperial heir.

Hadrian's great opportunity came when Nerva died and Trajan became emperor. He was determined to be the first to carry the news of Nerva's death to Trajan and despite the obstacles placed in his way by envious rivals he succeeded in winning the race, travelling the last few stages on foot. Trajan and Hadrian soon became close friends. In the Second Dacian War (AD 105–6) he commanded the First Legion 'Minervia', and on his return was made praetor in AD 106, governor of Lower Pannonia in AD 107, and consul the following year. When Trajan marched against the Parthians in AD 114 Hadrian was once again appointed to a key position, as governor of the important province of Syria. Yet despite these advancements there was no sure sign that Trajan intended him as his successor, and though he had the support of the empress Plotina, his standing at the imperial court was far from firm.

Many Roman emperors travelled, whether for war, inspection or mere curiosity, but none so extensively as Hadrian. His journeys took in practically the whole of the Roman world. Setting out from Rome early in 121, his first itinerary began with a visit to Gaul, the Rhineland and Britain. He then travelled to Spain and Mauretania, before taking ship for Asia Minor, Greece, and the Danube lands. He returned to Rome via Sicily late in 125. In 128 he visited Tunisia (Roman province of Africa) and later the same year he set off on a third journey, visiting the eastern provinces of the empire: Greece (again), Asia Minor, Syria and Judaea, Egypt and Libya, returning to Rome in 133/4. Some memories of these travels were reflected in the buildings of his sumptuous Villa near Tivoli.

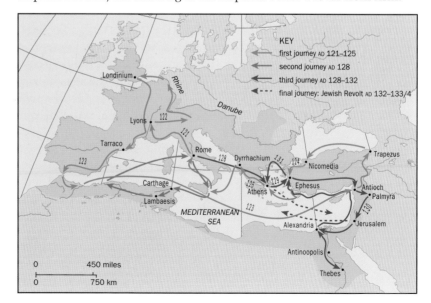

HADRIAN'S FAMILY

Portrait-bust of Vibia Sabina from the Louvre, Paris.

The families of Trajan and Hadrian were already related: Trajan's father had been the brother of Hadrian's grandfather. Family links were further strengthened when Hadrian married Vibia Sabina, granddaughter of Trajan's sister Ulpia Marciana. The match was encouraged by Plotina, Trajan's wife, but does not seem to have been well received by Trajan himself. Plotina was instrumental later in securing Hadrian's rise to power, and one source tells us that she was in love with him. When she died in AD 123, Hadrian honoured her by wearing black for nine days. Of Hadrian's wife Sabina little is known, but relations between the two were not particularly amicable. Two court officials – one the imperial biographer Suetonius – were dismissed for being too familiar with her, and Hadrian declared that he would have sent Sabina away too had he been a private citizen. She died two years before him, in AD 136.

The succession conspiracy

The succession to power when it came is shrouded in mystery. It may be that Trajan did finally resolve to adopt Hadrian as his heir, but if so he left it to the last minute, when he lay on his deathbed in southern Turkey. A plausible tale, which was believed by the historian Dio, held that Trajan had in fact done no such thing. According to this account, Hadrian's accession was engineered by the empress Plotina, who concealed Trajan's death for several days. She used this time to send letters to the senate in Rome, announcing Hadrian's adoption; but these carried her own signature rather than Trajan's, presumably on the excuse that the emperor was too weak to write. Another rumour claimed that Plotina had smuggled someone into Trajan's chamber to impersonate the emperor's voice. Only when Hadrian's succession was finally secure did she announce that Trajan had died.

Hadrian was governor of Syria when news was brought to him of Trajan's death. He immediately set out for Seleucia, where the emperor's body had been brought, and where the cremation was performed; the ashes were then shipped back to Rome for burial at the foot of Trajan's Column. Hadrian himself took a long route back to Rome, settling a military crisis north of the Lower Danube on the way, and abandoning the territory annexed by Trajan in 102.

Hadrian's aim may have been to rule as blamelessly as his distinguished predecessor. If so, he did not begin well. Even before he had arrived in Rome his reputation had been tarnished by the deaths of four distinguished senators. These were all ex-consuls, men of the highest rank, and the incident is known as the 'affair of the four consulars'. The pretext for their deaths was that they were plotting his overthrow; Dio, for one, did not believe this, and gave their wealth and influence as the real reason. What made the whole business particularly unattractive was Hadrian's refusal to accept any responsibility for these executions. The author of the Historia Augusta tells us that in his autobiography, now lost, Hadrian declared that the deaths had been ordered by the senate without his approval. Nevertheless, the matter remained so much in doubt that he swore a public oath that he was not the responsible party. He also wrote to the senate promising not to put any senators to death without proper trial. His strenuous efforts to deflect public criticism did not then and do not now ring entirely true.

A capable ruler

One of Hadrian's first and most significant acts was the abandonment of the eastern territories which Trajan had conquered during his last campaign. Augustus a century before had laid down for his successors the policy that the empire should be kept within the natural borders formed by the Rhine, the Danube and the Euphrates. Trajan had crossed the Euphrates to conquer Armenia and Mesopotamia; Hadrian pulled his forces back again to the Euphrates frontier.

Hadrian soon proved himself an energetic and efficient ruler. Though

HADRIAN'S WALL

Reconstruction of Hadrian's Wall showing turret in the foreground and milecastle beyond

'He then set out for Britain, where he put many things to rights and was the first to build a wall, 80 miles long, which separated the Romans and the barbarians' (Historia Augusta: *Life of Hadrian* XI). The building of Hadrian's Wall was part of the emperor's broader plan to strengthen the Roman frontiers. Hadrian had already ordered the construction of a continuous timber palisade along parts of the German frontier during his visit there in AD 121. The barrier planned during his stay in northern Britain during the summer of the following year was more elaborate and more permanent. It consisted of a stone wall (initially turf and timber in its western third) varying between 8 ft and 10 ft (2.4–3 m) thick, with a series of garrison forts for units of 500 or 1000 men. Some of these were attached to the wall itself; others, mostly pre-existing structures, were a few miles to the rear. Turrets at regular intervals provided look-out posts, and milecastles (spaced approximately one Roman mile apart) housed patrols of men from the garrison forts. The effort involved in building this complex frontier defence was enormous, but it took less than 10 years to complete.

not by nature a military man in Trajan's mould, he tightened discipline in the army and strengthened the frontiers. He continued and expanded Trajan's programme of *alimenta* through which assistance was given to the children of the poor. And he took pains, more than any other Roman emperor before or since, to visit his vast territories in person, and inspect their government for himself. This he did in three extensive journeys, beginning with a visit to Gaul in AD 121 and ending over 10 years later with his return to Rome in AD 133/4. His travels took him from Spain in the west, to Pontus on the Black Sea in the east, and from the Libyan desert in the south, to Britain in the north. One result of his northern journey was the construction of Hadrian's Wall, built to shield the Roman province of Britain against barbarian raids from the north.

Since his younger days Hadrian had had a passion for Greek learning, which had earned him the nickname 'Greekling'. Now, as emperor, he had the opportunity to indulge his tastes on a grand scale. Athens, though by this time in decline, was still a hallowed centre of learning, and Hadrian visited the city on three separate occasions. He was also a great builder, at Athens and at Rome. Characteristically, however, his greatest architectural achievement was the extravagant country mansion which he built for himself near Tivoli, upstream of Rome: a pleasure ground of villas and pavilions extending over 160 acres (65 hectares) of landscaped countryside.

But even his love of the arts was tarnished by wilfulness and jealousy. Setting aside the received opinion, he maintained that Antimachus of Colophon, an obscure fifth-century poet, was preferable to Homer. Hadrian copied the style of Antimachus in poems of his own, and also wrote his own autobiography. In architecture, too, he could be vindictive. The most shocking incident was the persecution of Trajan's architect Apollodorus of Damascus, whose views Hadrian had invited on his own design for a new temple. Open criticism was not something which Hadrian found easy to stomach.

Hadrian's private life

Modern writers have tended to portray Hadrian as a confirmed homosexual. The picture presented by Roman writers is of a man of mixed sexual proclivities. The Historia Augusta criticizes his passion for males and also the adulteries with married women to which he is said to have been addicted. In another place the same writer remarks, 'He ran to excess in the gratification of his desires, and wrote much verse about the subjects of his passion', though to our disappointment he does not give any further details. Certainly Hadrian's relations with his wife Sabina were not close, and there was even a rumour he had tried to poison her.

Roman historians were surprisingly coy on the subject of his homosexuality. The suspicion surfaces most prominently in the story of Antinous, a youth of whom Hadrian became exceedingly, and some said unnaturally, fond. Hadrian took him with him on his visit to Egypt in AD 130, and it was there that Antinous met his untimely and rather myste-

HADRIAN'S BUILDINGS

'In almost every city he constructed some building and gave public games.' (Historia Augusta: *Life of Hadrian* XIX) Ornate temples and theatres are among the most visible legacy of Hadrian's reign. He reserved his greatest efforts for the capital itself, where in addition to new ventures he restored several earlier monuments. The most spectacular were the Pantheon, which he rebuilt, and his own circular Mausoleum, which today forms the base of the Castel Sant'Angelo. The dome of the Pantheon marks one of the high points of Roman architectural achievement, and at 142 ft (43 m) across is larger even than the dome of St Peter's in the Vatican.

These were impressive monuments, but for a mark of Hadrian's personality we must look not to the buildings at Rome but to the luxurious imperial villa which he built near Tivoli, 15 miles inland from the capital at the foot of the Sabine Hills. Work began on this extensive complex of porticoes, pavilions and palaces in AD 125 and was brought to completion some 10 years later. The different parts of the palace were named after famous places which Hadrian had visited on his travels. One group of buildings was called the Accademia, after Plato's school at Athens; another the Canopus, after a famous sanctuary near Alexandria; he even included a Hades and an Elysian Fields. Though now in ruins, Hadrian's Villa still bears witness to the artistic temperament of its imperial creator.

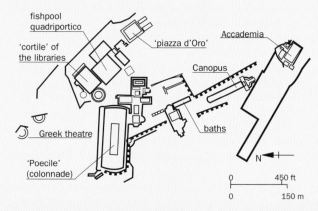

Hadrian's Villa near Tivoli: (right) plan of the complex; (above) looking east across the Poecile, with the Sabine Hills beyond; (below) the Canopus, with ornamental colonnades and statuary; (below, right) colonnaded court with ornamental fishpond.

The Pantheon at Rome (c.118–126), one of Hadrian's greatest buildings in the capital, and a place where he often held court. It purported to be a rebuilding of Agrippa's temple of 27 BC, but was in fact an almost entirely new structure, roofed by an enormous concrete dome. (Below) Cut-away showing the junction of colonnaded porch and circular domed hall; (right) interior, lit only by the single opening in the roof.

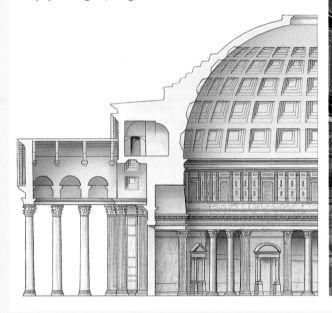

Antinous as an Egyptian; statue from Hadrian's Villa near Tivoli, now in the Vatican Museum.

rious end. In his lost autobiography, Hadrian related the simple story that Antinous had fallen from a boat during a trip on the Nile. Other people saw a more sinister event, in which Antinous offered himself as a sacrifice for Hadrian in some bizarre rite. Whatever the case, Hadrian was deeply grieved by the death of his favourite and founded a city, Antinoopolis, on the spot where he had died. He even identified a new star which he believed embodied Antinous's soul.

The foundation of Antinoopolis drew comment, and even ridicule, but it did not prove as troublesome as Hadrian's attempt to refound Jerusalem. The city had been destroyed after the Jewish revolt of AD 66–74, and had not been officially rebuilt. Hadrian planned to raise a new city on the site, to be called Aelia Capitolina. This was to be a Graeco-Roman city, and part of the plan was the building of a temple to Jupiter Capitolinus on the site of the old Temple of Solomon. The Jews could hardly be expected to tamely accept such a desecration of their holiest place, and in AD 132 they rose in revolt under the leadership of Simon Bar-Kochba. The governor of Britain was dispatched to deal with the rebellion, followed soon afterwards by Hadrian himself. Over half a million rebels were killed, but by the end of AD 135 peace had been restored – or rather reimposed. This was Hadrian's only major war.

The final years

In AD 136 Hadrian, now 60 years old, found himself in failing health. Dio describes his malady as a flow of blood from the nostrils. Fearing death, and in need of support, he chose this moment to appoint a successor. The man he adopted, Lucius Ceionius Commodus, would have been an excellent candidate, if he had not already been showing signs of advanced tuberculosis. Adopted as Lucius Aelius Caesar, he was appointed consul in AD 136 and again the following year, then packed off to learn his trade as governor of Pannonia. All this proved too much, however, and Hadrian's heir consumptive died on 1 January 138. Hadrian had already regretted the bounty he had paid to celebrate the official adoption: 'We have lost the three hundred million sesterces which we have paid out to the army and to the people,' he is said to have complained, 'for we have indeed leaned against a tottering wall, and one which can hardly bear even our weight, much less that of the empire.'

The adoption of Commodus had also led Hadrian into harsh actions against some of his closest supporters. The most serious was the treatment meted out to Lucius Julius Ursus Servianus, a distinguished senator who had governed several provinces and been consul three times. He was also Hadrian's brother-in-law, having married his sister Paulina long before Hadrian became emperor. Suspicious to the last, Hadrian thought that Servianus and his grandson opposed the adoption of Commodus as his heir, and forced both of them to commit suicide. Servianus, in his 90th year, was hardly a serious threat. Furthermore, he maintained his innocence to the end, burning incense and praying to the gods that Hadrian might end his days longing for death but unable to die.

THE EMPEROR AS POET

The emperor Hadrian clearly had literary pretensions; he was interested in poetry and letters, and boasted openly of his knowledge of singing and flute-playing. He also wrote love-poems. Very little of his writing has survived, however, and it is difficult to assess its literary merit. The autobiography which he tried to pass off as the work of one of his retinue has vanished. So too has the Catachannae, which the Historia Augusta describes as 'a very obscure work in imitation of Antimachus'. Whether these writings would have done any good for Hadrian's literary reputation had they survived is open to doubt. Perhaps not, if 'Animula vagula blandula' is anything to go by. Hadrian composed this short poem on his death bed, but the Historia Augusta is less than complimentary: 'He wrote verses such as these, but few that were any better.'

Animula vagula blandula
hospes comesque corporis
quae nunc abibis in loca
pallidula rigida nudula
nec ut soles dabit iocos

'O winsome wandering soul
guest and friend of the body
to what place now are you going,
stern, pale and empty?
– you will be able to joke no more.'

Hadrian's final days were indeed far from happy. His illness grew worse, and left him for long periods in great distress. It was described as a form of dropsy. Hadrian tried to lay his hands on poison or a sword to end his life, but his attendants kept these from him. Eventually he persuaded a barbarian servant called Mastor to plunge a sword into his side; he even marked the exact spot, just below the nipple, with a coloured line. But at the final moment Mastor too drew back and refused to carry out what he had promised. In despair Hadrian handed over the reins of government to Antoninus Pius, his chosen successor, and left Rome for the pleasure resort of Baiae. He died soon afterwards, on 10 July AD 138. But the man who had spent so much of his life travelling was not so soon to find his journey's end. For the great tomb monument which he had begun at Rome – and which forms the base of the Castel Sant' Angelo – was not yet finished, and in the meantime he had to be buried elsewhere. According to one writer he was buried first at Puteoli, near Baiae, on an estate which had once belonged to Cicero. Soon afterwards his remains were transferred to Rome and buried in the Gardens of Domitia, close by the mausoleum. The final move took place the following year, when the ashes of Hadrian and his wife Sabina (who had died in AD 136) were buried together in the completed monument.

Legacy of an emperor

Hadrian died an unpopular man. Dio tries to give a balanced assessment, telling us that he was hated by the people, in spite of his generally excellent reign, on account of the murders committed by him at the beginning and end, since they had been unjustly brought about. Modern writers have often found in him a sympathetic spirit, a man of liberal education and open-minded disposition. But there are too many echoes of Nero and Domitian in his character for this assessment to pass unchallenged. He was, by any standards, a successful ruler, in giving the empire firm frontiers and stable government for over 20 years; yet at a personal level, gifted but somewhat eccentric, the emperor Hadrian was an uncomfortable man to be near.

The Castel Sant'Angelo at Rome, built from the remains of Hadrian's Mausoleum. The central tower is essentially a heightening of Hadrian's original drum. The circular plan followed that of Augustus's Mausoleum, but the internal arrangements were very different. The Pons Aelius (now Ponte Sant'Angelo) in front of the Mausoleum was also part of Hadrian's scheme, though the balustrades and statues were added during the Renaissance.

Antoninus Pius

Imperator Titus Aelius
Caesar Hadrianus Antoninus
Augustus Pius

138–161

Antoninus Pius was the second of the bearded emperors, following the fashion for facial hair established by his predecessor Hadrian. According to one writer, 'He had a stern but comely face, a noble frame, and was becomingly strong.' From another we learn that his tallness caused him difficulty in later life: 'being a tall man, when he was bent by old age he had himself swathed with splints of lime wood bound on his chest in order that he might walk erect.' Portrait-bust from the British Museum.

AN EMPEROR ADMIRED AND REVERED

The most glowing tribute to Antoninus Pius comes in the *Meditations* of his adoptive son and successor Marcus Aurelius: 'He was always equal to an occasion; cheerful, yet long-sighted enough to have all his dispositions unobtrusively perfected down to the last detail. He had an ever-watchful eye to the needs of the Empire, prudently conserving its resources and putting up with the criticisms that resulted. Before his gods he was not superstitious; before his fellow-men he never stooped to bid for popularity or woo the masses, but pursued his own calm and steady way.'

Marcus Aurelius *Meditations* I.16

He was a man of steady and sound morals, which was clearly shown in that his firm character was corrupted neither by unbroken peace nor prolonged idleness, so much that at length the cities were as fortunate as if they had been realms of wisdom.

Aurelius Victor *Book of the Caesars* 15

With Antoninus Pius we come to an emperor who is something of an enigma: a man of even temper, apparently lacking strong ambitions and somewhat self-effacing, whose outstanding qualities were dedication to duty and general rectitude. He ruled the empire for almost a quarter of a century, yet arguably left less of a mark on it than any of his predecessors. Was he able to shelter under the prodigious achievements of his predecessors Trajan and Hadrian? Did he simply have the good fortune to rule when the empire faced no major external threats and was at relative peace? Or do these assessments belittle the real achievement of Antoninus Pius: providing firm government without the ostentatious displays of power so often associated with imperial rule?

Pius may have been considered by Hadrian a safe pair of hands to continue the policies he had formulated. Nevertheless Hadrian's real intentions as regards the succession were perhaps focused not on the

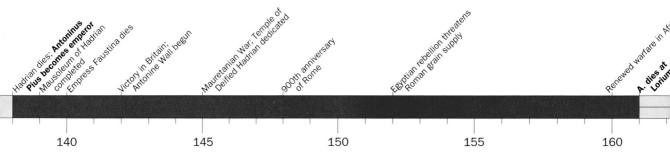

Hadrian dies; **Antoninus Pius becomes emperor**

Mausoleum of Hadrian completed

Empress Faustina dies

Victory in Britain; Antonine Wall begun

Mauretanian War; Temple of Deified Hadrian dedicated

900th anniversary of Rome

Egyptian rebellion threatens Roman grain supply

Renewed warfare in Af[...]

A. dies at Loriu[m]

140   145   150   155   160

ANTONINUS PIUS

Born 19 September 86 at Lanuvium Titus Aurelius Fulvus Boionus Arrius Antoninus *On adoption by Hadrian* Imperator Titus Aelius Caesar Antoninus, the element 'Aelius' derived from Hadrian's family name *On accession 10 July 138* Imperator Caesar Titus Aelius Hadrianus Antoninus Augustus Pontifex Maximus *Added shortly after his accession* 'Pius' *Added in 139* 'Pater Patriae' *After 141* the short form 'Antoninus Augustus Pius PP' generally used on coins. The exception was in 150–151, when Antoninus briefly reverted to a fuller title once again emphasizing his connection with Hadrian 'Imperator Caesar Titus Aelius Hadrianus Antoninus Augustus' *After victory in Britain in 143*	acclaimed emperor a second time Tribunician power first on accession, renewed annually on 10 December Consul I (120), II (139), III (140), IV (145) *Full titles at death* Imperator Caesar Titus Aelius Hadrianus Antoninus Augustus Pius, Pontifex Maximus, Tribuniciae potestatis XXIV, Consul IV, Imperator II, Pater Patriae *Wife* Annia Galeria Faustina (the elder) *Children* two sons: Marcus Aurelius Fulvus Antoninus & Marcus Galerius Aurelius Antoninus; two daughters: Aurelia Fadilla & Annia Galeria Faustina (the younger) *Died of illness at Lorium 7 March 161; body put in the Mausoleum of Hadrian*

51-year-old senator but on his 16-year-old nephew, Marcus Annius Verus, the youth who was to become emperor as Marcus Aurelius. If this was Hadrian's intention, then he chose well in Antoninus Pius as the man to hold the reins while the youth matured. Pius was not markedly ambitious. He had no surviving sons, and his sole surviving daughter, Faustina the younger, ultimately married Marcus Aurelius, thus consolidating the dynastic succession. In addition, Antoninus Pius at 51 was a relatively old man when he was adopted by Hadrian; few could have foretold that he would live to the age of 74, and reign longer than either Trajan or Hadrian; longer indeed than any Roman emperor since Augustus a century and more before.

Antoninus Pius was born Titus Aurelius Fulvus Boionus Arrius Antoninus on 19 September 86, at Lanuvium, 20 miles south of Rome. His family came originally from the city of Nemausus (Nîmes) in southern Gaul, but had long since achieved a leading position at Rome. Antoninus's grandfather had been consul twice, his father, Titus Aurelius Fulvus, once, in AD 89. The young boy was brought up at Lorium, a family estate in southern Etruria, 10 miles west of Rome. The estate retained a special place in his affections, and it was here in later life that he built the palace in which he spent much of his time as emperor. His father died when he was young, and he was brought up first by his paternal grandfather, then by his maternal grandfather. The properties he inherited from both made him one of the richest men at Rome.

He followed the usual career of a distinguished senator, becoming quaestor and praetor, then consul in 120. Fifteen years later, he served as governor of the province of Asia, in western Asia Minor, from summer 135 to 136. Yet his administrative experience was strictly limited, and he had no knowledge at all of military affairs. Indeed, his year as governor of Asia is the only time we know of that he spent outside Italy, either before or after assuming the imperial purple. A sharper contrast with the much-travelled Hadrian is hard to imagine.

Hadrian's heirs

It was on Hadrian's 62nd birthday on 24 January 138 that the emperor announced his wish to adopt Antoninus and thus marked him out as his successor. The formal adoption took place a month later, on 25 February 138. It was in fact a multiple transaction: Hadrian adopted Antoninus, and at the same time Antoninus adopted Marcus Annius Verus, then 16, and the young Lucius Ceionius Commodus, son of that Lucius Ceionius Commodus who had been Hadrian's first choice as heir but had died two months earlier.

When Hadrian died on 10 July 138 the succession of Antoninus went unchallenged. Many of Hadrian's officials were left in post. He quickly gained the affection of the senate as a benign and moderate ruler. Fronto, the leading orator of the time, wrote: 'Antoninus I love, I cherish like the light, like day, like breath, and feel that I am loved by him.' A conflict soon arose, however, when the senate, contrary to previous practice,

ANTONINUS AND SCOTLAND

Relief from Bridgeness on the Antonine Wall showing Roman cavalryman triumphing over fallen barbarians.

He defeated the Britons through his governor Lollius Urbicus and having driven off the barbarians built a second wall, of turf.

Historia Augusta *Life of Pius* V

Hadrian had visited Britain in person and taken a leading role in planning his new frontier defence, Hadrian's Wall; Antoninus, true to form, directed affairs from Rome through his trusted general Lollius Urbicus. Early in the reign, Lollius Urbicus was sent as governor to Britain. By 142 a victory in Britain was proclaimed and Antoninus hailed as 'Imperator', the customary honour after a military success. Hadrian's Wall was abandoned, and the Roman armies pushed northwards to occupy southern Scotland. There across the Forth-Clyde Isthmus, the new wall was built. It was shorter than Hadrian's Wall (40 miles as opposed to 80 miles), and being entirely of turf was a more economical enterprise. The Antonine Wall was nonetheless a major undertaking. Whether it achieved the purpose for which it was built is open to doubt; even before Antoninus died the Roman frontier had been pulled back south to Hadrian's Wall.

refused to confer divine honours on the hated Hadrian. Antoninus finally won this battle of wills, remarking: 'Well, then, I will not govern you either, if he has become base in your eyes, and hostile, and a public foe. For in that case you will, of course, soon annul all his acts, of which my adoption was one.' This was not mere gratitude or piety to Hadrian on Antoninus's part; to have his adoptive father refused divine honours by the senate would have been a serious blow to the prestige of the imperial office, and would have weakened his own legitimacy as ruler.

'Nothing severe'

Antoninus could be astute and determined when necessary, but was also just and compassionate. He introduced new legal rulings to protect slaves against cruelty and indecent abuse. The two treason trials of the reign were handled with due process of law and though both the principals died (one by execution, the other by suicide), every attempt was made to avoid a witch-hunt for co-conspirators. More vivid is the story of the impatient philosopher who, in audience with the emperor, cried, 'Pay attention to me, Caesar.' Antoninus's reply was tart and direct: 'I am paying attention, and I know you well. You are the fellow who is always arranging his hair, cleaning his teeth and polishing his nails, and always smells of myrrh.'

Antoninus Pius was well liked, and appears to have ruled as much by consent as by coercion. We are told that he was strikingly handsome, with an aristocratic countenance, a kindly temperament and a calmness of nature. He was also an accomplished public speaker. Though a rich man even before his accession, he was not noted for excessive displays of wealth or status.

The manner by which Antoninus acquired the sobriquet Pius (meaning 'dutiful' or 'respectful') had early become a matter of hagiography rather than history. The Historia Augusta gives no fewer than five different explanations: 'He was given the name Pius by the senate, either because he supported his frail and elderly father-in-law with his arm when he was attending the senate; . . . or because he reprieved those whom Hadrian in ill-health had ordered killed; or because he decreed great and limitless honours to Hadrian after his death, against the general will; or because, when Hadrian wished to kill himself, he prevented him from doing so by great care and diligence; or because he was truly a most compassionate man by nature and did nothing severe in his time.'

The direction of affairs

Unlike Hadrian, Antoninus Pius ruled the vast Roman empire from the capital, or from his nearby palace at Lorium, never travelling far from Rome during the 23 years of his rule. The Historia Augusta makes a virtue even of this: 'He did not travel on any expeditions, except to visit his own estates and to go to Campania, for, he said, the retinue of a prince, even a frugal one, was a great weight for provincials to bear. And yet he was considered a man of great authority by all peoples for residing

ANTONINUS AND ROME

Antoninus Pius restored and repaired several famous monuments, including the Colosseum, but only two important new projects at Rome can be put to his name: the Temple of the Deified Hadrian in the north of the city and the Temple of Antoninus and Faustina in the Forum. The latter was begun as the Temple of the Deified Faustina after the empress's death in AD 140, but was rededicated in 161, after Antoninus's death. By strange chance, parts of both temples have survived: the Temple of Antoninus and Faustina remodelled as the church of San Lorenzo in Miranda (1602); while 11 enormous columns of the Temple of the Deified Hadrian can be seen built into the wall of the Italian stock exchange.

Temple of Antoninus and Faustina at Rome (above) converted into a church in the 17th century, and (right) in its original form.

(Below) Relief from the Temple of the Deified Hadrian showing crossed shields and spears and personification of the province Hispania.

Antoninus Pius wrote of his affection for his wife, Annia Galeria Faustina (*above*): 'For this is the plain fact: by heaven, I would rather live with her on Gyara than in the palace without her'. (Gyara was an Aegean island to which offenders were exiled.) The Historia Augusta paints a less idyllic picture: 'Many things were said about the great looseness and heedless living of his wife, which with sad spirit he suppressed.' After her death in October or November 140, Faustina was deified by senatorial decree, and a temple and games voted in her honour. Later, Antoninus took one of his wife's former slaves as a concubine, a lady by the name of Galeria Lysistrate. As the emperor's mistress she had considerable influence at court: one commander of the praetorian guard was said to have gained his place through her intervention. Another powerful lady was Domitia Lucilla, mother of Marcus Aurelius and sister of Antoninus's wife Faustina. She was not without ambition. One day, so the story goes, the emperor came upon her worshipping at a shrine to Apollo. Valerius Homullus, the emperor's companion, whispered jocularly to him, 'That woman is praying that your day may end and her son may rule'.
(*Above right*) Apotheosis of Antoninus and Faustina, ascending to heaven on the back of a winged Genius. Base of the Column of Antoninus Pius, now in the Vatican Museum.

in the city, so that in this central location he could receive messengers quickly, wherever they came from.'

Here then was a man content to sit at the centre of the web, pulling strings as required, dispatching governors and generals to solve frontier crises and settle provincial problems. For these were by no means 23 years of untroubled peace. On the contrary, though there was no major war, there is evidence of near continuous fighting and unrest. Early in the reign, perhaps in the quest for military glory, the decision was taken to conquer southern Scotland. Hadrian's Wall was abandoned, and a new frontier defence constructed 40 miles to the north: the so-called Antonine Wall. Soon afterwards there was trouble in Mauretania, then in Germany, and rebellions in Egypt, Judaea and Greece. Still later in the reign there was warfare against the Dacians and Alans who threatened the Danube provinces. Nonetheless, such was the prestige of Roman arms that Antoninus was sometimes able to achieve significant ends by diplomacy alone. A mere letter to Vologaeses king of Parthia was sufficient to dissuade him from attacking Armenia, and Antoninus was accepted as arbiter in disputes by client kings and neighbouring states.

One notable event of the reign was the 900th anniversary of the founding of Rome. This was celebrated in the year 148 in magnificent style.

A peaceful end

Antoninus's final illness when it came was mercifully short, and was attributed by his biographer to over-indulgence in Alpine cheese one

AN IMPERIAL CORRESPONDENT

Little of Antoninus's own writing has survived. Two letters from the emperor are preserved among the correspondence of Marcus Cornelius Fronto, the leading orator of the age. They are friendly in tone, as one might expect of a ruler writing to a trusted courtier who was also tutor to his adoptive sons Marcus Aurelius and Lucius Verus. One of the letters is a reply to Fronto on the occasion of the latter's illness. Fronto had written to explain and be excused his non-appearance at court on the anniversary of Antoninus's accession. The emperor's reply conveys clearly the image of a kindly and benevolent prince: 'Since I have well remarked your evident and sincere goodwill towards me, I have no difficulty in believing from my heart, my dear Fronto, that this day in particular, on which it pleased heaven that I accept this office, is kept special by you with correct and full observance. Accordingly, as was only right, I have pictured you and your vows in my mind.'

evening at dinner. During the night following, he vomited, and by the next day he had developed a fever. The day after, his condition deteriorated further, and he made his final dispositions, handing the reins of power to his adoptive son Marcus Aurelius. Finally, giving the password 'equanimity' to the officer on duty, he turned over as if to sleep, and passed away. This was at the palace he had built at his beloved country estate of Lorium near Rome; the date, 7 March 161.

Due to Antoninus's general popularity, he was deified by the senate without opposition. 'All men vied with one another to give him honour,' we are told. His mortal remains were laid to rest in the Mausoleum of Hadrian, alongside those of his wife, and of two sons who had died over 20 years before. In the brief description of his burial there is something which could easily be overlooked. The text says clearly that his body was laid in the Mausoleum, with magnificent funerary rites. There is no mention of cremation, and it seems that Antoninus Pius was one of the first Roman emperors to adopt the newly fashionable practice of inhumation. The last word must be left to his biographer: 'Almost alone of all emperors he lived entirely unsullied by the blood of either citizen or foe so far as was in his power, and he was justly compared to Numa [a legendary early king of Rome] whose good fortune and tranquillity and religious rites he ever maintained.'

The Antonine Baths at Carthage, begun by Antoninus Pius in 143. One of the largest baths outside Rome, it was lavishly decorated with imported marbles and mosaics, but little survives above basement level.

Marcus Aurelius
Imperator Caesar Marcus Aurelius Antoninus Augustus
161–180

Lucius Verus
Imperator Caesar Lucius Aurelius Verus Augustus
161–169

(*Right*) Official portraits show Marcus in the guise of a bearded philosopher. (*Opposite*) Marcus Aurelius sacrificing; relief panel, possibly from a triumphal arch, now in the Capitoline Museum.

THE PHILOSOPHER PRINCE

He was a solemn child from the very beginning; and as soon as he passed beyond the age when children are brought up under the care of nurses, he was handed over to advanced instructors and attained to a knowledge of philosophy.

Historia Augusta *Life of Marcus* II.1

He studied philosophy with ardour, even as a youth. For when he was twelve years old he adopted the dress and, a little later, the hardiness of a philosopher, pursuing his studies clad in a rough Greek cloak and sleeping on the ground; at his mother's solicitation, however, he reluctantly consented to sleep on a couch strewn with skins.

Historia Augusta *Life of Marcus* II.6

Being forced by the senate to assume the government of the state after the death of the Deified Pius, Marcus made his brother his colleague in the empire, giving him the name Lucius Aurelius Verus Commodus and bestowing on him the titles Caesar and Augustus. They began to rule the state on equal terms, and then it was that the Roman empire first had two emperors, when he shared with another the empire left to him.

Historia Augusta *Life of Marcus* VII

Thus, with one minor inaccuracy (for Verus dropped the name Commodus on his accession), does the imperial biographer describe the joint rule of Marcus Aurelius and Lucius Verus. In the event, it was a partnership which survived only until the latter's death in 169, a period of less than eight years. The device of shared rule, however, was destined to become a regular feature of imperial government in the troubled later centuries of the Roman empire.

The reign of Marcus Aurelius was marked by bitter and near-continuous warfare, first on the eastern, then on the northern frontier, exacerbated by plague, invasion and insurrection. The sequence of calamities is reflected in the bleak stoicism of Marcus's *Meditations*. These, the bedside jottings of a philosopher-king, forced by his imperial destiny to

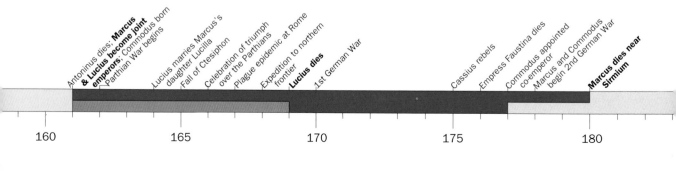

Antoninus dies; **Marcus & Lucius become joint emperors**; Commodus born
Parthian War begins
Lucius marries Marcus's daughter Lucilla
Fall of Ctesiphon
Celebration of triumph over the Parthians
Plague epidemic at Rome
Expedition to northern frontier
Lucius dies
1st German War
Cassius rebels
Empress Faustina dies
Commodus appointed co-emperor
Marcus and Commodus begin 2nd German War
Marcus dies near Sirmium

160   165   170   175   180

MARCUS AURELIUS

Born 26 April 121 at Rome
 Marcus Annius Verus
On adoption
 Marcus Aelius Aurelius Verus
AD 139
 Aurelius Caesar Augusti Pii Filius
On accession 7 March 161
 Imperator Caesar Marcus Aurelius Antoninus Augustus, Pontifex Maximus
Added 166
 'Pater Patriae'
Victory titles
 'Armeniacus' 164
 'Medicus' & 'Parthicus Maximus' 166
 'Germanicus' 172
 'Sarmaticus' 175
Consul I (140), II (145), III (161)
Tribunicia potestas first on 1 December 147, renewed annually on 10 December

Imperator first on accession, then II (163), III (165), IV (166), V (167), VI (171), VII (174), VIII (175), IX (177), X (179)

Full titles at death
 Imperator Caesar Marcus Aurelius Antoninus Augustus Germanicus Sarmaticus, Pontifex Maximus, Tribuniciae potestatis XXXIV, Imperator X, Consul III, Pater Patriae

Wife
 Annia Galeria Faustina (the younger)
Children
 8 sons: 1 Titus Aurelius Antoninus; 2 Titus Aelius Aurelius; 3 Titus Aelius Antoninus; 4 (name unknown); 5 Titus Aurelius Fulvus Antoninus; 6 Lucius Aurelius Commodus; 7 Marcus Annius Verus; 8 Hadrianus; 6 daughters: 1 Domitia Faustina; 2 Annia Aurelia Galeria Lucilla; 3 Annia Aurelia Galeria Faustina; 4 Fadilla; 5 Cornificia; 6 Vibia Aurelia Sabina

Died 17 March 180 near Sirmium; buried in the M. of Hadrian

LUCIUS VERUS

Born 15 December 130 at Rome
 Lucius Ceionius Commodus
On adoption
 Lucius Aelius Aurelius Commodus
On accession 7 March 161
 Imperator Caesar Lucius Aurelius Verus Augustus
Victory titles
 'Armeniacus' 164
 'Parthicus Maximus' 165
 'Medicus' 166
Added 166
 'Pater Patriae'

Consul I (154), II (161), III (167)
Tribunician power first on 7 March 161, renewed annually on 10 December

Imperator first on accession, then II (163), III (165), IV (166), V (167)

Full titles at death
 Imperator Caesar Lucius Aurelius Verus Augustus Armeniacus Parthicus Maximus Medicus, Tribuniciae potestatis VIIII, Imperator V, Consul III, Pater Patriae

Wife
 Annia Aurelia Galeria Lucilla
Children
 A daughter (name unknown)

Died of a stroke Jan/Feb 169 at Altinum; buried in the M. of Hadrian

spend most of his energies campaigning on the Danube, are dominated by thoughts of death and the transitoriness of human experience. Rarely do we get such an insight into an emperor's true character as the glimpse which these writings provide. They are not the work of a happy man, but they testify to a certain grandeur of spirit. Indeed, historians such as Cassius Dio made Marcus Aurelius a model for later generations: 'In addition to possessing all the other virtues, he ruled better than any others who had ever been in any position of power.'

Marcus Aurelius spent a longer apprenticeship than any previous emperor since Tiberius. He was born Marcus Annius Verus into a family originally from Ucubi, near Corduba, in the south Spanish province of Baetica. Their wealth may have derived from olive oil, and they pros-

MEDITATIONS

The first rule is, to keep an untroubled spirit; for all things must bow to Nature's law, and soon enough you must vanish into nothingness, like Hadrian and Augustus. The second is to look things in the face and know them for what they are, remembering that it is your duty to be a good man. Do without flinching what man's nature demands; say what seems to you most just – though with courtesy, modesty, and sincerity.

Marcus Aurelius *Meditations* VIII.5

The most famous legacy of Marcus Aurelius are the writings, originally headed simply 'To myself', but now generally referred to as the *Meditations*. These were written in the later years of the emperor's life, while he was campaigning on the northern frontier. It seems almost as though Marcus wrote them to console himself during the privations of the long war. They show clearly his adherence to the stoic school of ancient philosophy, which subscribed to the principle of virtue, or duty to oneself and to others. The *Meditations* paint a dark picture of life, however, with much musing on the nearness of death and the transitoriness of human existence.

devolved instead upon Tiberius Claudius Pompeianus, a distinguished senator who had married Annia Aurelia Galeria Lucilla, Marcus's eldest surviving daughter and the widow of Lucius Verus. The empress Faustina, however, had entered into conspiracy with Avidius Cassius. It is unlikely that Avidius Cassius had any intention of deposing Marcus Aurelius, but once he had been proclaimed emperor by the troops there was no turning back. At first, things went well for him. He was Alexandrian by birth, and the eastern provinces supported him with enthusiasm. By the beginning of May, Egypt and Alexandria had come over to his side. But there the dream ended, and just as he was setting out for Rome, Avidius Cassius was assassinated by soldiers loyal to Marcus.

Final years

The emperor was careful not to mount a witch-hunt, aware perhaps of Cassius's mistaken motives and the involvement of Faustina. He nonetheless took measures to avoid any future attempt at revolt. Commodus was proclaimed heir-apparent, and Marcus and he set out to tour the rebellious eastern provinces. When they eventually returned to Rome in the autumn of 176, Marcus had been absent from the capital for almost eight years. On 23 December they celebrated a belated triumph for the German victories, which were further commemorated by the Aurelian Column, carved with a spiralling frieze in the manner of Trajan's Column half a century earlier.

But the war in the north was not finished, and on 3 August 178 Marcus and Commodus set out once more for the Danube frontier. The year 179 saw a vigorous campaign against the Quadi, but by 180 Marcus was seriously ill. He had been intermittently unwell for several years with stomach and chest troubles, and cancer is one possibility. Cassius Dio tells us 'it was never his practice to eat during the daytime, unless it was some of the drug called theriac. This drug he took, not so much because he feared anything, as because his stomach and chest were in bad condition; and it is reported that this practice enabled him to endure both this and other maladies.' Theriac contained opium, and the failing Marcus Aurelius may well have been a drug addict.

The final illness lasted only a week. Dying, he berated his friends for their emotion: 'Why do you weep for me, instead of thinking about the plague, and about death which is the common lot of us all?' Marcus Aurelius died near Sirmium, on 17 March 180. The body was buried in the Mausoleum of Hadrian. The senate pronounced deification; and though the northern wars were broken off, and the provinces which he had hoped to establish abandoned, his legacy survived in the *Meditations*, the musings of a stoic prince. The final word may be left to Cassius Dio: 'He did not meet with the good fortune that he deserved, for he was not strong in body and was involved in a multitude of troubles throughout practically his entire reign. But for my part, I admire him all the more for this very reason, that amid unusual and extraordinary difficulties he both survived himself and preserved the empire.'

Commodus
Aurelius Commodus Antoninus Augustus
180–192

In the later years of his reign Commodus identified himself with Hercules, a Greek god famous for his strength, courage and endurance. Commodus called himself the Roman Hercules. He also had statues made portraying him with the lion skin and club (*right*) which were the distinctive trappings of this god. Bust in the Capitoline Museum, Rome.

Our history now descends from a kingdom of gold to one of iron and rust, as affairs did for the Romans of that day.

Cassius Dio LXXII.36

'My father has gone up to heaven and now sits as a companion of the gods. We must concern ourselves with human affairs and govern the world.' Such were the sober and practical words Commodus addressed to the troops on the death of Marcus Aurelius in March 180. The 18-year-old emperor may well have been daunted by the tasks which lay ahead; the rule of Marcus Aurelius would have been a difficult act for anyone to follow. Commodus, however, not only failed to measure up to his father's elevated standard; he went down in history as a positive monster, a megalomaniac who thought himself a god, had the months renamed in his honour, and delighted in nothing better than playing the gladiator in front of the assembled Roman populace.

Commodus was in fact the very first Roman emperor to be born in the purple while his father was reigning. For the previous 80 years, emperors had chosen their successors on grounds of merit more than heredity. The last emperor to have inherited the position from his father was Domitian. The stability of the intervening years shows how well the

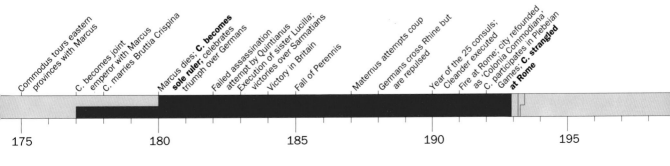

Commodus tours eastern provinces with Marcus

C. becomes joint emperor with Marcus
C. marries Bruttia Crispina

Marcus dies; **C. becomes sole ruler;** celebrates triumph over Germans

Failed assassination attempt by Quintianus
Execution of sister Lucilla; victories over Sarmatians
Victory in Britain

Fall of Perennis

Maternus attempts coup
Germans cross Rhine but are repulsed

Year of the 25 consuls; Cleander executed
Fire at Rome; city refounded as 'Colonia Commodiana'
C. participates in Plebeian Games; **C. strangled at Rome**

175   180   185   190   195

IMPERIAL PERFORMANCE

Various myths arose concerning Commodus's birth and parentage which attempted to explain his curious obsession with gladiators. It was said that his mother, Faustina, had passed some time at the coastal resort of Caieta, choosing lovers from among the sailors and gladiators. She fell in love with one of them, and when her husband Marcus 'reported it to the Chaldaeans, it was their advice that the gladiator should be killed and that Faustina should bathe in his blood

and thus couch with her husband. When this was done, her passion was indeed allayed, but their son Commodus was born a gladiator, not really a prince.'(*Life of Marcus* XIX) The story is hardly credible, but shows just how far people would go to explain the emperor's excessive interest in gladiators.

Commodus performed his most memorable exploits in the arena during the Plebeian Games of November 192. Cassius Dio and Herodian provide vivid eye-witness accounts:

On the first day he killed a hundred bears all by himself, shooting down at them from the railing of the balustrade. . . . On the other days he descended to the arena from his place above and cut down all the domestic animals that approached him. . . . He also killed a tiger, a hippopotamus and an elephant. Having performed these exploits, he would retire, but later, after luncheon, he would fight as a gladiator. The form of contest that he practised and the armour that he used were those of the 'secutores' . . . he held the shield in his right hand and the wooden sword in his left, and indeed took great pride in the fact that he was left-handed.

Cassius Dio LXXIII.18-19

His marksmanship was generally agreed to be astonishing. . . On one occasion he used some arrows with crescent-shaped heads to shoot at Mauretanian ostriches . . . Commodus decapitated the birds at the top of their necks with his arrows, so that they went on running around as though they had not been touched.

Herodian I.15

(Above) Terracotta lamp with scene of fighting gladiators; (below) Gladiators fighting wild animals. Mosaic from Villa Borghese.

COMMODUS	

Born 31 August 161 at Lanuvium
   Lucius Aurelius
   Commodus
 In 166 raised to Caesar
 Joint ruler 177
   Imperator Caesar
   Lucius Aurelius
   Commodus
   Augustus, Pater
   Patriae
 On accession 17 March 180
   Imperator Caesar
   Lucius Aurelius
   Commodus
   Antoninus
   Augustus, Pontifex
   Maximus, Pater
   Patriae'
 In October 180.
   'Lucius' replaced by
   'Marcus'
 Added 182
   'Pius'
 Added 185
   'Felix'
 In 191
   reversion to earlier
   form 'Imperator
   Caesar Lucius
   Aelius Aurelius
   Commodus
   Augustus'
 	
 Victory titles
   Germanicus (15
   October 172),
   Sarmaticus (spring
   175), Germanicus
   Maximus (mid-182),
   Britannicus (late
   184)
	Consul I (177), II
	 (179), III (181),
	 IV (183), V (186),
	 VI (190), VII (192)
	
	 Tribunicia potestas
	 first in late 176 or
	 early 177; then a
	 second time in late
	 177; renewed
	 annually on 10
	 December
	
	 Imperator first in
	 176, then II (177), III
	 (179), IV (180), V
	 (182), VI (183), VII
	 (184), VIII (186)
	
	 Full titles at death
	   Imperator Caesar
	   Lucius Aelius
	   Aurelius Commodus
	   Augustus Pius Felix
	   Sarmaticus
	   Germanicus
	   Maximus
	   Britannicus
	   Invictus, Hercules
	   Romanus, Pontifex
	   Maximus,
	   Tribuniciae
	   potestatis XVIII,
	   Imperator VIII,
	   Consul VII, Pater
	   Patriae
	
	 Wife
	   Bruttia Crispina
	
	 Strangled in the Vectilian Villa at Rome 31 December 192; buried in the M. of Hadrian

procedure of adoption had worked in giving the empire a long period of dynastic peace.

The young heir-apparent

Commodus was born Lucius Aurelius Commodus at Lanuvium, some 14 miles south-east of Rome, on 31 August 161. He was the tenth of Marcus's 14 children, and one of twins, though his twin brother Titus Aurelius Fulvus Antoninus died at the age of four. Commodus became the only son of the imperial couple to survive infancy. The details of his early life are shrouded in the hostile interpretation which later historians strove to put on it. This contrast with the revered Marcus even led to rumours that he was illegitimate, the product of his mother's adultery.

Later tradition also held that Marcus was gravely disappointed in his son. The facts show instead that Commodus was groomed from the start as his father's destined successor. In 166, at the tender age of five, he was given the title Caesar, and in 171 assumed his father's title 'Germanicus'. In 176 he shared in Marcus's triumph at Rome. Commodus was elevated to the status of joint ruler, in 177, with the title Imperator Caesar Lucius Aurelius Commodus Augustus. That same year he served as consul for the first time, under a special dispensation on account of his youth.

Marcus and Commodus fought together on the Danube front in 178 and 179, but the campaign planned for 180 had hardly begun when Marcus died. Commodus chose to break off hostilities and return to Rome rather than continue the war, as his father had wished. Many thought this a shameful decision, but it was not clear that war would ever settle the problems of the northern frontier, even if much of central Europe was made a Roman province. Furthermore, the peace that Commodus secured was on terms highly favourable to Rome, and there was to be no further trouble on this frontier for several decades.

Back in Rome, Commodus began to cut a curious and controversial figure. In the triumphal procession on 22 October 180 he showed great fondness for a certain Saoterus, seating him in the imperial chariot and kissing him from time to time during the proceedings. Saoterus became chamberlain to Commodus, and was the first of a whole series of powerful officials who were effectively to run the empire on his behalf.

The first conspiracy

Commodus's hands-off approach to imperial government gave rise to intrigue and conspiracy, and led to a series of attempts on his life. The first, in the year 182, was instigated by his elder sister Lucilla. The plan was for her nephew, Claudius Pompeianus Quintianus, to lie in wait for Commodus in the entrance to the Colosseum with a dagger concealed in his cloak. When Commodus drew near, Quintianus rushed from his hiding place brandishing the dagger, but rather than stabbing the emperor at once he wasted time crying, 'See! This is what the senate has sent you!' As he was speaking he was seized by the imperial guard and disarmed.

Commodus, though physically unscathed, was deeply shaken by the attempted assassination. He was further alarmed when Saoterus was murdered (probably as part of a separate quarrel) a little later. The reprisals were sharp. Lucilla and Quintianus were executed. So too was Taruttienus Paternus, commander of the praetorian guard, for complicity in Saoterus's death. Commodus had already appointed Tigidius Perennis joint commander with Paternus, and after Paternus's execution Perennis assumed overall control, not only of the imperial guard, but of the government in general. Fearful for his life, Commodus himself shunned any further public appearances, and ordered all messages to be passed to him through Perennis.

The reign of Perennis

While Perennis assumed the reins of power Commodus abandoned himself to a life of luxury and debauchery. He was said to have a harem of 300 concubines and 300 young boys, some bought, some kidnapped, from various walks of life. There were orgies and intercourse with both sexes. Or so it was said; but whatever the case, Commodus gained a serious reputation for depravity.

So matters stood until 185, when Perennis fell from power. There was a story that he had grown over-mighty, and planned to make away with Commodus and install one of his own sons as emperor. A delegation of 1500 disaffected soldiers from the army of Britain travelled to Rome to alert the emperor to his danger. Corrupt government may have been the real reason for the protest, or perhaps the harshness with which Perennis had suppressed a mutiny among the Roman forces in Britain earlier in the year. Either way, the result was the same: Commodus ordered the immediate execution of Perennis and his sons. Control of affairs was handed to the new chamberlain, the notorious Cleander.

A LEFT-HANDED EMPEROR

Commodus was of a striking appearance, with a shapely body and a handsome, manly face; his eyes were burning and flashing; his hair was naturally fair and curly, and when he went out in the sunlight it gleamed with such brilliance that some people thought gold dust was scattered on it before public appearances, though others considered it supernatural and said that a heavenly halo was shining round his head.

Herodian I.7

Commodus (*left*, Louvre, Paris) followed his imperial predecessors in growing a beard. Herodian thought him good-looking, despite his bizarre behaviour. The author of the Historia Augusta painted a less complimentary picture, alleging a dullness of expression 'as is usual with drunkards', and furthermore 'such a conspicuous growth on the groin that the people of Rome could see the swelling through his silken robes.' We are told this growth was 'the subject of many verses'; but whatever its nature the man himself can hardly be blamed for it. It may have caused Commodus acute sexual embarrassment, and could account for the curious story (possibly invented), that 'he kept among his minions certain men named after the private parts of both sexes, and on these he liked to bestow kisses.' A more straightforward feature was his left-handedness. Commodus is one of the very few Roman emperors that we know for certain to have been left-handed.

The Nymphaeum of the Villa of the Quintillii, beside the Via Appia south of Rome. This was confiscated by Commodus from the Quintillii brothers in 182 and rebuilt on a lavish scale. It became one of the emperor's favourite residences.

The rise and fall of Cleander

Cleander had come to Rome as a Phrygian slave, but had risen by degrees to the highest offices in the imperial household. He must have been an able man; but he was also avaricious and unscrupulous, abusing the opportunity which his position afforded to amass a personal fortune. Like Perennis, his power depended on the ability to deliver to Commodus the lifestyle that the emperor desired. Cleander openly sold public offices and military commands, culminating in the appointment of 25 consuls for one particular year. He kept much of the revenue for himself, but was careful to pass on a substantial portion to Commodus.

Around this time a second attempt was made on Commodus's life. The instigator was not a member of the imperial household but a complete outsider, an enterprising army deserter-turned-brigand called Maternus who had been fomenting trouble in Gaul. His plan was to assassinate Commodus during the festival of the Great Goddess at Rome in March 187, but the plot was betrayed and Maternus executed before the festival began. Commodus tightened security still further. 'He surrounded himself with a stronger guard and rarely appeared in public, spending most of his time avoiding legal and imperial business away in the suburban districts or on his imperial estates far from Rome.'

Cleander's downfall came in 190, during a severe shortage of grain at Rome, and may well have been engineered by his enemies. The populace believed that Cleander had used his vast wealth to buy up the available grain and so create an artificial shortage. The real culprit was probably the grain commissioner Papirius Dionysius, who had taken steps to exacerbate a natural shortage and then laid the blame for it on Cleander. The result was a riot in the Circus Maximus. The enraged crowd marched south down the Via Appia towards the Villa of the Quintillii, 4 miles from the city, where Commodus was then staying, and demanded Cleander's execution. Cleander ordered the cavalry to drive the crowds back to Rome, but when they reached the city itself, the soldiers lost the upper hand. They were attacked from the rooftops, and the urban cohorts (the police force of Rome) joined in on the side of the people.

THE FACE OF ROME

Commodus as Hercules, ploughing the boundaries of the new city of Rome. Bronze coin (COS VII PP = AD 192).

The city of Rome was extensively damaged by fire towards the end of Commodus's reign. The fire, which broke out in the year 191, raged for several days and was only checked when rain began to fall. The Temple of Peace, 'the largest and most beautiful building in the city', was destroyed by the fire, along with the Temple of Vesta and adjacent areas. The imperial palace was also affected by the blaze, and many of the official state archives were lost. Commodus may have begun to put repairs and rebuilding in hand during his final months, but the work was completed under Septimius Severus and was credited largely to him.

The Historia Augusta dismisses Commodus's achievements in few words: 'No public works of his are in existence, except the baths which Cleander built in his name. But he inscribed his name on the works of others; this the senate erased.' (*Life of Commodus* XVII). This summary does Commodus somewhat less than justice. The Temple of the Deified Marcus was built during his reign, and the baths which are attributed to Cleander bore the name 'Thermae Commodianae' and may have been built at the emperor's command. They were said to be enormous. We might have a better opinion of Commodus's legacy had either of these buildings survived.

It was only at this point that Commodus learned what was going on. Fearful for his own life, he summoned Cleander and had him executed. The crowd were delighted, abusing the body of the fallen minister and carrying his head around the city on a pole. Commodus himself returned to Rome and was greeted by the cheering populace. He had learned his lesson. No powerful official took the place of Cleander and the emperor himself was left holding centre-stage. The result, however, was not quite the success that the people had hoped.

God and gladiator

It was after the death of Cleander that Commodus began to show signs of megalomania. He may well have been unhinged by the insecurity of continual attempts on his life. He demanded from the senate that they deify him as a living god, sometimes associating himself with Jupiter. His favourite divine persona, however, was Hercules, and he gave orders that he should be called Hercules son of Zeus instead of Commodus son of Marcus, and took to wearing a lion skin and carrying a club on public occasions.

Another grandiose act was to have the months renamed after his various titles: Amazonius, Invictus, Felix, Pius, Lucius, Aelius, Aurelius, Commodus, Augustus, Herculeus, Romanus, Exsuperatorius, 'so superlatively mad had the abandoned wretch become'. 'Exsuperatorius', the supreme, was the title given to Jupiter, while 'Amazonius' identified the emperor with Hercules once again.

A serious fire in 191 provided Commodus with the pretext for yet another megalomaniac act. The fire destroyed the Temple of Peace, which many wealthy Romans had used as a safe deposit for valuables. More ominously, it also destroyed the Temple of Vesta, and the sacred image which was supposed to have been brought from Troy by Aeneas. Large areas of the central city were severely affected, and required major restoration and rebuilding. This gave Commodus the idea of calling himself the second founder of Rome, and he officially renamed the city 'Colonia Commodiana'.

The final years of the reign also saw Commodus increasingly insecure and vengeful towards the senators. While Rome was being refounded and the emperor declared a living god, heads rolled. But the most graphic evidence of Commodus's eccentricity was provided by his exploits in the amphitheatre.

The provision of gladiatorial games was generally recognized as part of an emperor's duty, but Commodus departed from precedent by taking part in the games in person. Gladiators were among the most despised classes of ancient Rome, and many citizens, not only the knights and senators, must truly have been shocked to see their emperor lowering himself to such a level. But since the emperor commanded their attendance, few of the leading citizens could risk staying away, while for the rest, it was a remarkable and unusual spectacle which drew crowds from all over Italy.

IMPERIAL RELATIONS

Commodus was married in 178 at the age of 16 to Bruttia Crispina. Her father, Gaius Bruttius Praesens, had campaigned with Marcus Aurelius in the Danube wars. The wedding was celebrated without excessive ostentation, and shortly afterwards Commodus left Rome for the northern frontier. The relationship ended in tragedy some 10 years later, when Bruttia Crispina was banished to Capri and then executed for adultery. There were no children. Commodus did not restrict his attentions to his wife, but is said to have enjoyed the company of numerous mistresses and concubines. One story credits him with a veritable harem of 300 women, and a like number of young boys. It was the emperor's favourite mistress, Marcia, who eventually procured his death.

The climax was reached in the final months of 192. In the November games, Commodus appeared in the guise of Hercules Venator, 'the hunter', shooting at wild beasts from the safety of a raised walkway, or descending to the floor of the amphitheatre to kill other animals wild and domestic, including a tiger, an elephant and a hippopotamus. He also fought as a gladiator with wooden shield and sword, receiving a million sesterces from the gladiatorial fund for each appearance. What should have been entertainment (albeit of a grisly kind) was coupled with menace, as when he walked up to the seated senators brandishing a severed ostrich head in his left hand and a bloody sword in his right; meaning that he could kill senators, too, just as he had the ostrich.

The November games ran their course, and Commodus turned his attention to another series planned for the beginning of the New Year 193. These were to celebrate the refounding of Rome as Colonia Commodiana, and were to feature the emperor in the guise of Hercules Romanus Conditor ('the Founder of Rome'). There was another element to the scheme: Commodus intended to kill both the consuls elect, then issue forth next day as both gladiator and consul.

A successful coup

In this atmosphere of bloodthirsty megalomania no-one was secure, and those closest to the emperor decided they must act first if they were to save their own lives. The key figures were Eclectus, who had succeeded Cleander as imperial chamberlain, Quintus Aemilius Laetus, commander of the praetorian guard, and Marcia, the emperor's favourite concubine. During the evening of 31 December Marcia secretly gave Commodus poison. He was spending the night at the Vectilian Villa (a school for gladiators near the Colosseum), ready for his star appearance the next day. Feeling drowsy but suspecting nothing, the emperor went to his bedroom to lie down. The assassins waited for Commodus to die, but instead he was violently sick and vomited up the poison. Fearful that he would recover, they sent in a young athlete called Narcissus to finish the job by strangulation.

The emperor's body was handed over to Fabius Cilo, one of the consuls-elect whom Commodus had planned to kill, and was buried during the night. The senate called fiercely for the body to be dug up and dragged about the city like that of a common criminal. 'More savage than Domitian, more foul than Nero. As he did unto others, let it be done unto him.'

In the event, however, Commodus's remains fared rather better than might have been expected. Pertinax removed them to the Mausoleum of Hadrian, and although the name was erased from all official records, Commodus was deified four years later by Septimius Severus. The abiding memory of Commodus was nonetheless one of cruelty and megalomania. A sharp contrast with his respected father, he proved incapable of managing either himself or the power entrusted to him. His death marked the end of the Antonine dynasty.

Pertinax
Imperator Caesar Publius
Helvius Pertinax Augustus
193

Didius Julianus
Imperator Caesar Marcus
Didius Severus Iulianus
Augustus
193

The Historia Augusta describes Pertinax
as 'a stately old man, with a long beard
and hair brushed back. His figure was
somewhat corpulent . . . but his bearing
was regal. He was a man of mediocre
ability in speaking.' Portrait-bust now in
the Vatican Museum.

PERTINAX	
Born 1 August 126 at Alba Pompeia in Liguria *Accession 1 January 193*	*Children* *a son Publius Helvius Pertinax* *a daughter (name unknown)*
Wife *Flavia Titiana*	*Murdered on the Palatine at Rome 28 March 193*

PERTINAX

He failed to comprehend, though a man of wide practical experience, that one cannot with safety reform everything at once, and that the restoration of a state, in particular, requires both time and wisdom.

Cassius Dio LXXIV.10

The death of Commodus plunged Rome into uncertainty, which was soon followed by further bloodshed. Initially, the prospects were good. A new emperor assumed control of the state, without serious opposition, and seemed likely to rule both wisely and well. His untimely death after a mere three months, however, sparked off a fierce civil war. No fewer than four rival claimants struggled for power in the months which fol-

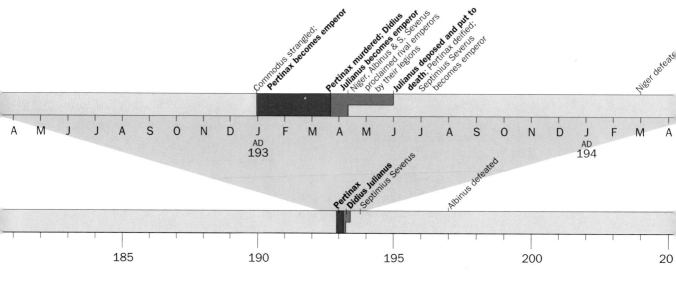

The remarkable story of Pertinax is one of rags to riches, slave to emperor, in the short space of only two generations. His father had been a slave who later prospered in the wool trade. Pertinax was given a proper Classical education and went on to become a teacher himself, but in 161 (at the age of 35) the low pay decided him to opt instead for a military career. He began as commander of a cohort of Gauls stationed in Syria, but soon showed his ability and was promoted to tribune of the VI Legion 'Victrix', stationed at York. Further promotion took Pertinax to the Danube frontier, where he saw vigorous action in Marcus Aurelius's northern wars. He was rewarded by being made a senator, consul (175), governor of the two Moesias, of Dacia, and finally, of Syria (180). He went on to find favour with the emperor Commodus, and was given the crucial task of suppressing the army mutiny which had broken out in Britain. After a short spell as governor of Africa (modern Tunisia), he was appointed urban prefect at Rome (189). It was as urban prefect that he heard the news of Commodus's death on 31 December 192.

lowed. As in the troubled year 69, it was the might of the frontier armies that ultimately dictated the outcome. But four years were to pass before one man again held undisputed sway throughout the whole of the Roman empire.

The night of 31 December 192 was full of drama. The hated Commodus was dead, but Laetus and Eclectus, leaders of the conspiracy, needed time to bring their scheme to full fruition. Accordingly they wrapped the emperor's body in cheap bed-clothes and two of their trusted slaves carried it out of the Vectilian Villa (where Commodus had been spending the night) as laundry, straight past the unsuspecting imperial guards. Laetus and Eclectus then made their way through the streets of Rome to the residence of Publius Helvius Pertinax. The midnight knock on the door caused great alarm in the household, but Laetus and Eclectus at last succeeded in convincing Pertinax that Commodus was dead. That done, they offered him the imperial power.

To be recognized as emperor, however, the support of the praetorian guard was crucial. They were won over by the offer of 12,000 sesterces each. Escorted by soldiers and people, Pertinax then made his way through the still-dark streets to a meeting of the senate. Here a remarkable scene was in progress, with the assembled senators chanting savage denunciations of Commodus. Pertinax, after a symbolic show of reluctance, was confirmed in the imperial power by receiving the title Augustus, along with all the customary powers.

Pertinax made the fatal mistake of trying to change too much too quickly, alienating key constituencies as he did so. He curbed the excesses of the praetorian guard: a popular move, but hardly calculated to endear the emperor to the soldiery. As early as 3 January, they tried to set up one of the senators as a rival emperor, though the individual concerned reported the affair to Pertinax and left the city.

At the same time the imperial freedmen – the ex-slaves who as palace officials ran much of the administration – were accused of embezzlement. Pertinax blamed them publicly for the shortage of funds in the imperial treasury. The senate and people of Rome were delighted, but the combined opposition of both the guards and palace officials placed Pertinax in a position of considerable danger.

There was a serious coup attempt in early March, while Pertinax was at Ostia inspecting the arrangements for the all-important grain shipments. Once again it was the praetorian guard who were behind the move, but this time their candidate was Quintus Sosius Falco, the consul. The plot was betrayed, and though Falco himself was pardoned, several of the soldiers were executed for their part in the conspiracy.

They were more successful a few weeks later. On 28 March Pertinax had cancelled his public engagements for the day and was at the palace when a contingent of 300 soldiers rushed the gates. Neither the guards on duty nor the palace officials sought to resist them, instead egging them on. Pertinax was advised to flee for his life, but in a moment of great courage chose to stay and confront his attackers. He tried to reason with them, 'hoping to overawe them by his appearance or win them over by his words.' But all in vain. While he was speaking, one of the soldiers lunged forward and struck him, shouting 'The soldiers have sent you this sword.' The others joined in, raining blows on the 66-year-old man until he was dead. He had ruled for only 87 days.

DIDIUS JULIANUS

Bearing Pertinax's head aloft on a pole, the soldiers responsible for his death hurried back to the praetorian camp and shut the gates, fearful how the people of Rome would react. With no obvious successor in the wings, however, it was the soldiers themselves who held the key to real power and would decide who should be the next emperor.

This was the background to one of the most bizarre and scandalous episodes in the history of the Roman empire. For not one but two aspiring emperors presented themselves at the praetorian camp, and proceeded to bid for the support of the soldiers in a kind of public auction. No attempt was made to hide the nature of the negotiations: the praetorians stationed heralds on the walls to announce that the position of emperor was up for sale.

First of the rival candidates was Titus Flavius Sulpicianus, the father of Pertinax's wife. The second was Marcus Didius Julianus, a distinguished ex-consul and reputedly a man of considerable means. The bidding went on for some time, but eventually the soldiers' choice fell on Didius Julianus. He not only bid the higher price, but also warned them that if they elected Sulpicianus they might expect revenge at his hands for the murder of Pertinax.

Didius Julianus owed his position entirely to the backing of the praetorian guard. Aware of his vulnerability, and of Pertinax's sudden end, he is said to have 'passed his first night in continual wakefulness, disquieted by such a fate.' He was popular neither with the people of Rome, who openly demonstrated against him, nor with the senate. He soon lost the support of the praetorians, too, unable to honour the lavish promises he had made them.

The death of Pertinax had in fact led three rival candidates to declare themselves, each in command of frontier armies. First to stir was Gaius Pescennius Niger, governor of Syria. He was proclaimed emperor by the four Syrian legions in the middle of April, and made Antioch his temporary capital. Had he at once made a determined move on Rome, the empire would have fallen into his hands. As it was he delayed fatally at Antioch, gathering in further support before embarking on action. In Britain, the governor Decimus Clodius Albinus, with three legions and numerous auxiliary contingents under his command, declared himself in April. But already a more redoubtable candidate had emerged: Lucius Septimius Severus, governor of Upper Pannonia on the middle Danube. A ruthless and astute politician, he soon won the support of the entire Rhine/Danube army, including no fewer than 16 legions.

Marcus Didius Severus Julianus (*above*, Vatican Museum) had a head start in life, being brought up in the household of Domitia Lucilla, the mother of Marcus Aurelius. The contacts he made then must have served him well in his later career. His own father, Quintus Petronius Didius Severus, came from Milan, while his mother's family were Roman provincials of North African origin. After holding a number of minor positions Didius Julianus became commander of the XXII Legion 'Primigenia' in Germany c.172, was consul with Pertinax c.175, and between 172 and 190 served as governor of no fewer than four provinces, including Lower Germany and Africa (modern Tunisia). By the time of Pertinax's murder in March 193, he had become a respected senior senator, and despite some personal unpopularity and the sordid affair of the praetorian auction, he was a natural candidate for emperor.

DIDIUS JULIANUS	
Born 30 January 133 at Milan *Accession 28 March 193*	*Children* *a daughter Didia Clara*
Wife Manlia Scantilla	*Murdered on the Palatine at Rome 1 June 193*

On 9 April, less than a fortnight after Pertinax's death, Severus had himself proclaimed emperor by the legion stationed at his headquarters at Carnuntum, near modern Vienna. He at once prepared to march on Rome, but first reached an agreement with Clodius Albinus, offering him the title 'Caesar' to buy his support.

As Severus's force marched south towards Rome, Didius Julianus did what he could to oppose him. He set the praetorian guard to dig fortifications around Rome (the city had no defences at this time), but they were unused to the work and did everything they could to avoid it. Assassins were despatched to kill Severus, but he was closely guarded and they were unable to penetrate his security. In a last desperate measure, Julianus asked the senate to appoint Septimius Severus as joint ruler. But Severus was nearing the city and had no need to share power.

On 1 June 193, the senate passed a motion sentencing Julianus to death, naming Severus emperor, and bestowing divine honours on Pertinax. The officer sent to carry out the sentence found Julianus 'alone and deserted by everyone' and killed him 'amid a shameful scene of tears'. According to Cassius Dio, Julianus's last words were 'But what evil have I done? Whom have I killed?' His brief taste of power had lasted only 66 days. The body was handed over to his wife and daughter, who buried it in his great-grandfather's tomb, by the fifth milestone on the Via Labica.

Septimius Severus marched on Rome in the summer of 193 and overthrew Didius Julianus. He then had to fight against rivals in the east (Pescennius Niger: 193–4) and west (Clodius Albinus: 196–7) to become undisputed master of the Roman empire.

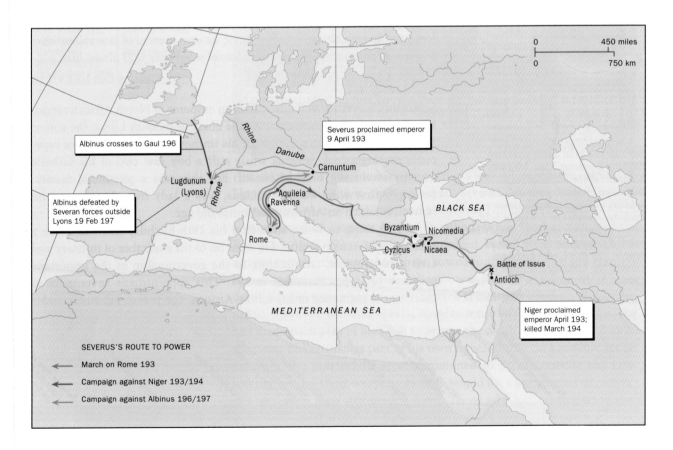

Gaius Pescennius Niger (*above*, Albani Collection, Rome) had a solid but unexceptional military career, and was made consul in 189. In 191, he was appointed governor of Syria. When Pertinax was murdered, Niger was proclaimed emperor by the Syrian legions in April 193, but was killed by Severus less than a year later. Niger seems to have been a man of unusual integrity, though something of a disciplinarian in military matters.

(*Below*) Massive arched substructures are practically all that survives of the new southern wing which Septimius Severus added to the imperial palace on the Palatine.

missed, and warned, on pain of death, not to come within 100 miles of Rome. Their place was taken by men loyal to Severus.

The eastern rival

Once Severus had established his position at Rome his next task was to deal with Pescennius Niger, the governor of Syria who had been acclaimed emperor by the eastern legions. Niger for his part gathered his forces and fortified the passes across the Taurus mountains which protected the northern flank of Syria and his capital city of Antioch. He also sent an army westward to seize Byzantium, the city which controlled the narrow crossing of the Bosphorus. Severus's forces nonetheless crossed from Thrace into Asia Minor and towards the end of 193 won two significant victories over Niger's army, the first near Cyzicus on the shores of the Sea of Marmara, the second at Nicaea, a little way to the east. Despite Niger's preparations, the passes across the Taurus mountains were also forced, and Severus's army advanced into Syria.

The final decisive battle took place in March or April 194 near Issus, on the plain where Alexander the Great had defeated the Persian king Darius III 500 years before. Niger's forces proved no match for the northern legions, and were cut down as they fled. Niger himself took horse towards the south, but was overtaken in the suburbs of Antioch and beheaded. His supporters were ruthlessly punished, and many of them chose to take refuge with the Parthians, Rome's neighbours and traditional enemies to the east, rather than face the ferocity of Severus's retribution. During the summer of 195 Severus led an expedition into northern Mesopotamia in order to punish the Parthians for their support of Niger and his fugitives.

JULIA DOMNA

For all that, he was less careful in his home-life, for he retained his wife Julia even though she was notorious for her adulteries and also guilty of plotting against him.

Historia Augusta *Life of Severus* XVIII

Julia Domna was the remarkable lady whom Severus married as his second wife in 186 or 187. Born around 170, she was the daughter of Julius Bassianus, high priest of the sun god Elagabal at the great sanctuary of Emesa in Syria. It was a match advantageous to both sides: Severus was a rising star in the Roman administration, while Julia and her father were descended from the old ruling dynasty of Emesa. Severus may have been influenced by other factors as well. An intensely superstitious man, he is said to have consulted astrologers when selecting his new bride. The choice fell upon Julia

Portrait of the imperial family: painted wooden panel of C.AD 199 from the Staatliche Museen, Preussischer Kulturbesitz, Berlin; note portrait of Geta erased by Caracalla after his death.

Domna because her horoscope predicted that she would marry a king. Julia bore Severus two sons, Caracalla and Geta. A patroness of writers and philosophers, she gained a reputation for adulterous love-affairs in later years.

She continued to play an important part in public life during the reign of her son Caracalla, but in 217, stricken by cancer and beset by the emperor Macrinus, she starved herself to death.

Like Septimius Severus, Decimus Clodius Albinus was of North African origin, though he came from a family of senatorial rank. We are told he had been 'brought up in the lap of wealth and luxury inherited from his ancestors.' The details of his early career are uncertain, but he held a succession of military posts before becoming consul in 187, governor of Lower Germany in 189, and finally governor of Britain in 191. With its garrison of three legions and a large body of auxiliary troops, Britain was well placed to play a part in the troubled times which followed the murder of Pertinax. Severus at first offered Albinus the title and rank of Caesar to gain his support, but by 196 the two were openly at war. Less cruel than Severus and of better family, Albinus was preferred by many at Rome, but in February 197 he was defeated and killed.

Civil war in the west

The defeat of Niger left Severus with still one serious rival: Clodius Albinus, governor of Britain. Severus had given him the title of 'Caesar' to buy his support – or at least his neutrality – during the war against Niger. But he had no intention of sharing any real power with Albinus. Towards the end of 195 Severus had his eldest son, Septimius Bassianus (better known as Caracalla), renamed Marcus Aurelius Antoninus, in clear reference to the famous Antonine dynasty. At the same time, although only a boy of seven, Caracalla was given the title 'Caesar'. Clodius Albinus was no longer Severus's chosen successor, and formed no part of his future dynastic plans. It was a declaration of war.

During the course of 196 Clodius Albinus crossed over to Gaul with an army of around 40,000 men. The core was formed by the three British legions, and he also had the support of the Seventh Legion 'Gemina' stationed in Spain. Basing himself at Lyons he raised additional forces and came close to capturing the Rhineland with its important forts and garrisons. Severus, by contrast, spent much of the year in Rome, passing new laws and consolidating his hold on power. It was not until January 197 that he set out for the final showdown with his erstwhile colleague.

The decisive battle was fought on 19 February 197, in the outskirts of Lyons. For a while the outcome hung in the balance: Severus was thrown from his horse and tore off his imperial cloak to conceal his identity. But the timely arrival of the cavalry saved the day, and Albinus's

THE MESSAGE IN THE STARS

Septimius Severus was addicted to astrology. He regularly consulted astrologers, and became expert in the interpretation of horoscopes. By this means he even came to know when he would die, though the information was carefully concealed in the astrological decorations of the imperial palace:

He knew this chiefly from the stars under which he had been born, for he had caused them to be painted on the ceilings of the rooms in the palace where he was wont to hold court, so that they were visible to all, with the exception of that portion of the sky which, as astrologers express it, 'observed the hour' when he first saw the light; for this portion he had not depicted in the same way in both rooms.

Cassius Dio LXXVII.11

forces were decisively defeated. Albinus himself fled into Lyons, but was unable to escape and committed suicide. In an act of cruelty typical of the man, Severus laid out the naked body on the ground and rode his horse over it. The head was cut off and sent to Rome, the body thrown into the Rhône along with those of Albinus's wife and sons.

The Parthian War

Back in Rome, Severus took stern measures to root out the supporters of Niger and Albinus. Both had been popular with sections of the senate, and 29 senators were put to death in the purge of 197. Once again, Severus was utterly ruthless. Some called him 'the Punic Sulla', a reference to the notorious proscriptions of the dictator Sulla during the civil wars of the late republic. Severus never became popular with the senate, but relied instead on the support of the army. He improved the soldiers' pay and living conditions, allowing them the right to marry and to live at home with their wives and families rather than in military barracks. Severus also took steps to gain favour with the people of Rome, 'putting on continuous shows of all kinds and slaughtering hundreds of wild animals from all over the world'. Within a matter of months, however, he was off on yet another military campaign.

His enemy this time was the Parthians, who were threatening Roman outposts and client kings in the east. His earlier campaign had been little more than a show of strength. This second expedition was altogether more determined. After crossing into northern Mesopotamia, Severus embarked his army on ships which took them down the Euphrates, before marching them overland to Ctesiphon, the Parthian capital. Resistance was slight, and the city was captured and looted by the Roman forces. The men were killed, the women and children – some 100,000 of them – enslaved, and the Parthian royal treasury emptied of

Septimius Severus waged two wars against the Parthians. The first (195) led to the creation of the new Roman province of Osrhoene; the second (197), a more serious affair, to the sacking of the Parthian capital Ctesiphon and the addition of a second new province, Mesopotamia.

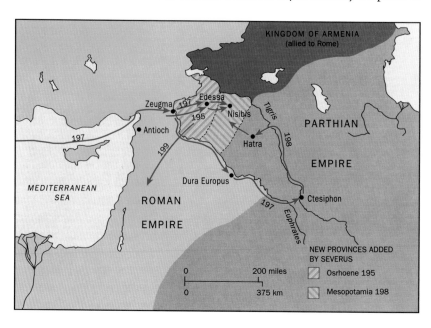

its jewels and valuables. Northern Mesopotamia became once again a Roman province, as it had been in the last years of Trajan.

The capture of Ctesiphon occurred late in 197. Severus remained in the east for five years, the first two of which were spent organizing the new Roman province and seeking (without success) to capture the important caravan city of Hatra. Severus then embarked on a tour of Palestine and Egypt, viewing the embalmed body of Alexander the Great at Alexandria, and journeying up the Nile to visit the pyramids and the temples of Thebes.

The Plautianus affair

Septimius Severus returned to Rome in the summer of 202. A relatively old man by Roman standards, troubled by recurrent illnesses, he had already indicated his plans for the imperial succession, by raising his elder son Caracalla to the rank of Augustus early in 198. Now on their return to Rome he endeavoured to provide him with a wife. This was Publia Fulvia Plautilla, the daughter of Severus's friend Gaius Fulvius Plautianus. Commander of the praetorian guard, Plautianus had been given extensive powers and great wealth by the emperor, and had accompanied Severus on all his campaigns. It was even rumoured that Severus and Plautianus had once been boy-lovers. But he was not well liked. Herodian tells us 'he misused this power to commit all kinds of acts of cruelty and violence in everything he did, making himself one of the most feared prefects of all time.' Rumour even had it that he castrated grown men to serve as eunuch-attendants for his daughter.

Caracalla disliked the marriage, objecting both to his wife and her father. He refused to eat with her or sleep with her, and threatened to kill both her and her father when he came to power. Matters came to a head three years later, on 22 January 205. Accounts differ, but according to one version, Caracalla persuaded three centurions to bring false information against Plautianus. They made their move after the festival of dead ancestors, just before dinner was served, telling the emperor that Plautianus had ordered them and seven other centurions to murder Severus and Caracalla. In Herodian's version, the plot was a real one, by which Plautianus intended to forestall the succession of Caracalla and seize the empire for himself. The man he enlisted to kill the emperor and his son, however, went straight to Severus and Caracalla and told them the tale. Both stories have the same ending: Plautianus was summarily killed, and his body thrown out onto the street. There it lay, to be reviled by the populace. The clear winner was Caracalla, rid at a stroke of both his father-in-law and his wife; she, the daughter of the dead man, was sent into exile on the island of Lipari. But the hatred lived on, and Caracalla had her killed as soon as he came to power.

The final campaign

The death of Plautianus may have neutralized one source of trouble at Rome, but it did nothing to allay the growing antagonism between

SEVERUS THE BUILDER

He restored a very large number of the ancient buildings and inscribed on them his own name, just as if he had erected them in the first place from his own private funds. He also spent a great deal uselessly in repairing other buildings, and in constructing new ones; for instance, he built a temple of huge size to Bacchus and Hercules.

Cassius Dio LXXVII.16

It fell to the emperor Severus to make good the ravages of the great fire of 191 by extensive restorations and repairs. One of the most fascinating by-products of this work was the large-scale map of Rome, carved on 151 marble slabs and fixed to the wall of one of the public buildings near Vespasian's Library of Peace. The map shows details of public and private buildings, including shops, streets and staircases.

Severus's new buildings in Rome were part of a policy to strengthen the image of the new regime. One of the most ambitious has disappeared without trace: the Septizonium, a massive colonnaded façade fronting the south-eastern corner of the Palatine Hill. Severus also made elaborate extensions to the imperial palace on the Palatine Hill, building out on the edge of the hill overlooking the Circus Maximus. The massive vaulted substructures may still be seen today, though the buildings they supported have largely gone.

The most famous monument associated with Septimius Severus today is the triumphal arch in the Forum at Rome erected by the senate in 203 to celebrate his Parthian victories. Scenes from the war are vividly portrayed in four large relief panels, which already show a departure from the classical tradition, and a move towards the conventions of late Roman art.

Cassius Dio had little time for the huge new temple dedicated by Severus to Bacchus and Hercules. These were the Roman equivalents of North African deities Melqart and Shadrapa, and the temple was probably one of the many new buildings which Severus undertook at his birthplace, Lepcis Magna. These included a new artifical harbour, new baths, a forum and basilica, temples, colonnaded streets, and a four-way triumphal arch, all constructed and finished to the highest standard of workmanship. Under the patronage of Severus and Caracalla, Lepcis Magna became the showpiece city of Roman North Africa.

(Left) Relief from the Severan arch at Lepcis Magna (203–4); the emperor and his sons in a chariot. (Below) The Severan basilica at Lepcis Magna, dedicated in 216.

Caracalla and his brother Publius Septimius Geta. Their supporters fed and encouraged this enmity: 'Each of their admirers tugged them in opposite directions, not merely by catering for their desires and low tastes but by being always on the look out for novelties to please their favourite and irritate his brother.' Thus it came as some relief when trouble in Britain obliged Severus to leave Rome and take his sons with him on campaign.

The imperial cortège set out from the capital in the first months of 208. Severus himself was incapacitated by gout, and had to be carried in a litter, but his strength of will would never tolerate resting in any place longer than was necessary. They hastened across Gaul and then took ship for Britain. Severus resolved to settle the recurrent frontier problems of the province once and for all by conquering the whole island. Geta was put in charge of the province and the civil administration of the empire while Severus and Caracalla led the army across Hadrian's Wall into Scotland.

During the years 209 and 210 the expedition achieved some success, pushing far to the north and forcing the natives to come to terms. But Severus was now an old man and increasingly unable to direct affairs in person. Caracalla, on the other hand, had no interest in the British campaign, but saw it merely as an opportunity to win favour from the army. Herodian tells us 'He regarded his father, who was suffering from a drawn-out illness and taking a long time to die, as a troublesome nuisance and tried to persuade his doctors and attendants to do him some mischief while they tended the old man, so as to get rid of him sooner.' There is even a story that Caracalla tried to stab his father in the back while the two were riding ahead of the army. Severus was alerted to the danger by shouts from the people nearest him, and turned in the saddle to see what was amiss. The shouting frightened Caracalla into giving up the attempt.

Septimius Severus finally died at York on 4 February 211, aged 65, leaving unfinished the projected conquest of Scotland. His sons broke off the operation and set sail back to Rome, carrying the cremated ashes of their father in an urn which they laid to rest in the Mausoleum of Hadrian. Soon afterwards, the senate decreed his deification. We may leave the final word to Herodian: 'No one had ever before been so successful in civil wars against rivals or in foreign wars against the barbarians. For eighteen years he ruled, before making way for his young sons to succeed, bequeathing to them greater wealth than any previous emperor and an invincible army.'

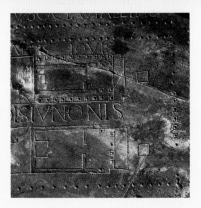

(Top) Arch of Septimius Severus in the Forum at Rome.

(Above) Fragment of the Severan marble plan of Rome, carved on 151 slabs and fixed to a wall near the Library of Peace in the Forum of Vespasian.

(Below) Medusa head, part of the rich sculptural decoration of the Severan Forum at Lepcis Magna.

Caracalla

Imperator Caesar Marcus
Aurelius Severus Antoninus
Pius Augustus
211–217

Geta

Imperator Caesar Publius
Septimius Geta Augustus
211

Macrinus

Marcus Opellius Severus
Macrinus Augustus
217–218

Portraits of Caracalla show a pug-faced individual, with features often set in an angry scowl. The 'rough soldier' image was a reaction against the last statues of Septimius Severus which depicted the emperor as a god-like being. But there is also a hint in Caracalla's portraits of his hero Alexander the Great.

THE EMPEROR'S NEW CLOTHES

He also invented a costume of his own, which was made in a rather foreign fashion out of small pieces of cloth sewed together into a kind of cloak.

Cassius Dio LXXIX.3

The caracallus was a short close-fitting cloak with a hood, of German or Celtic origin. Caracalla lengthened it so that it reached down to the feet, and this new type of cloak came to be so closely associated with him that he took his nick-name from it. Two centuries earlier an emperor had been named after his boots; now one was named after a cloak! By the fourth century the form 'Caracallus' had been replaced by 'Caracalla', the name we customarily use today.

CARACALLA AND GETA

His mode of life was evil and he was more brutal even than his cruel father. He was gluttonous in his use of food and addicted to wine, hated by his household and detested in every camp save that of the praetorian guard; and between him and his brother there was no resemblance whatever.

Historia Augusta *Life of Caracalla* IX

In the popular history books Caracalla goes down as one of the bad emperors of Rome, much given to cruelty and violence. He is another example of the perils of son succeeding father, where there is no guarantee of virtue or ability. But the fact that Caracalla receives a bad press does not in itself make him a bad emperor. He was certainly popular with the army. Geta, by contrast, remains a shadowy figure. His death at his brother's hands gives him the character of a martyr. But would he have proved a better or more virtuous emperor than Caracalla?

Septimius Severus had passed on to his sons the secret of successful rule: 'Agree with each other, give money to the soldiers, and scorn all other men.' The last two precepts were easy enough to follow, but the

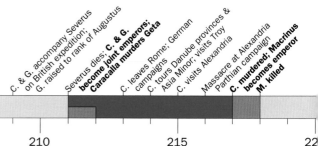

200   205   210   215   22

CARACALLA	
Born 4 April 188 at Lyons	(213)
Lucius Septimius Bassianus	Tribunicia potestas first on 28 January 198, renewed annually on 10 December
In 195 self-adoption into the family of Marcus Aurelius	
Marcus Aurelius Antoninus Caesar	Imperator first on 28 January 198, then II (207), III (September 213)
In January 198 on elevation to rank of Augustus	
Imperator Caesar Marcus Aurelius Antoninus Augustus Proconsul	*Full titles at death* Imperator Caesar Marcus Aurelius Antoninus Pius Felix
Added from 198 'Pius'	Augustus Parthicus Maximus, Britannicus Maximus,
Conferred by senate 199 'Pater Patriae'	Germanicus Maximus, Pontifex Maximus,
From 200 'Pius Felix'	Tribuniciae potestatis XX, Imperator III,
On accession on 4 February 211	Consul IV, Pater Patriae
Imperator Caesar Marcus Aurelius Severus Antoninus Pius Augustus	
Assumed with Severus late 209 or 210	*Wife* Publia Fulvia Plautilla
'Britannicus Maximus'	
Added 213 'Germanicus Maximus'	*Murdered 8 April 217 near Carrhae in Mesopotamia; ashes placed in the Mausoleum of Hadrian, Rome*
Consul I (202), II (205), III (208), IV	

GETA	
Born 7 March 189 at Rome	*Wife* none *Children* none
Accession on 4 February 211	
	Murdered December 211 at Rome

chances of the two brothers, Marcus Aurelius Antoninus (Caracalla) and Publius Septimius Geta, agreeing together appeared slim indeed. They were young men, 23 and 22 years old respectively, but already had a long history of rivalry and bitter mutual hostility. It was hardly surprising, then, that one of Caracalla's first actions after Severus's death was an attempt to gain sole power. Severus himself had probably initially intended power to pass undivided to Caracalla. He had given Caracalla the titles 'Imperator Destinatus' and 'Augustus' as long ago as 198; only in 209 had Geta been raised to the rank of Augustus, even though the two boys were separated in age by just a year. But Geta's claims were supported by their powerful mother, the empress Julia Domna. Caracalla's bid for sole power was thwarted, and it was as joint rulers that the brothers accompanied their father's remains back to Rome.

The murder of Geta

Rome was not big enough to contain comfortably two emperors so implacably opposed to each other. They sought to co-exist in the imperial palace on the Palatine Hill by dividing it into two, each part with its own main entrance, at the same time blocking off all the interconnecting doors and passages. But this in itself was scarcely enough to establish a modus vivendi. Each brother fought against the other to gain support from senators and other important people. Geta built up a following among the literary men of Rome, ensuring a better press than Caracalla, though it is far from clear that as rulers there was much to choose between them. When any official appointment was made, each struggled to have his own man successful. They backed, and were backed by, different factions in the circus games. Their rivalry even affected the outcome of legal proceedings, as the joint Augusti interfered in the administration of justice to secure successful outcomes for their own supporters. Finally, each of the brothers sought to poison the other.

After not many months had passed Caracalla and Geta came to realize that the only peaceful solution available to them was to divide the empire between them. Geta was to have the Asiatic provinces, while Caracalla would be left in possession of Europe and the north-west of Africa. Geta planned to make his new capital at either Antioch or Alexandria. The scheme might have produced a peace. More likely, it would have led to full-scale civil war. In the event it was blocked by Julia Domna, who asked the brothers how, if they were to divide the empire between them, they were planning to divide her, their own mother?

The collapse of this scheme drove Caracalla to a more desperate solution. Geta was carefully guarded by his own supporters, but Caracalla managed to find a moment, late in December, to murder him, when they were both together with Julia Domna. According to one account, Caracalla carried out the deed in person. Geta expired on his mother's breast, allegedly crying 'Mother that didst bear me, mother that didst bear me, help! I am being murdered.' Their joint reign had lasted little more than 10 months.

THE BATHS OF CARACALLA

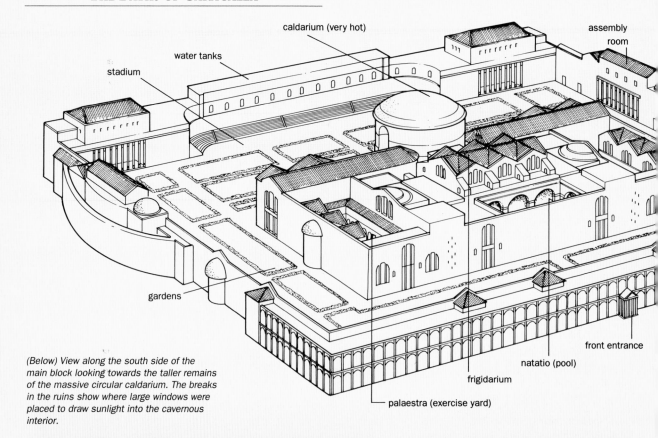

stadium

water tanks

caldarium (very hot)

assembly room

gardens

(Below) View along the south side of the main block looking towards the taller remains of the massive circular caldarium. The breaks in the ruins show where large windows were placed to draw sunlight into the cavernous interior.

palaestra (exercise yard)

frigidarium

natatio (pool)

front entrance

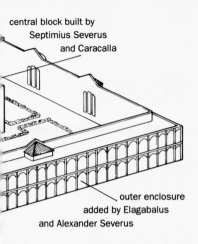

central block built by
Septimius Severus
and Caracalla

outer enclosure
added by Elagabalus
and Alexander Severus

(Above) Reconstruction of the Baths of Caracalla as they would have appeared in the reign of Alexander Severus. (Right) Interior of the frigidarium, the main hall of the Baths.

(Left) Mosaic of an athlete from the Baths of Caracalla. These were not merely bathing establishments but included gymnasia, libraries and lecture halls.

Among the public works which he left at Rome was the notable Bath named after himself, the cella soliaris of which, so the architects declare, cannot be reproduced in the way in which it was built by him. For it is said that the whole vaulting rested on gratings of bronze or copper, placed underneath it, but such is its size, that those who are versed in mechanics declare that it could not have been built in this way.

Historia Augusta *Life of Caracalla* IX

The remains of the Thermae Antoninianae or Baths of Caracalla survive today as one of the most impressive monuments of imperial Rome. It is clear they were already considered a wonder when the *Life of Caracalla* was written, towards the end of the fourth century. The massive structure makes full use of brick and concrete, yet combines both artistry and practicality in its design. The scale is enormous: the circular domed caldarium (hot room) alone is almost as large as the Pantheon, and much taller. The cella soliaris which so impressed the writer of the *Life* is the main hall or frigidarium; its vaulted roof was supported on a grid of iron bars welded together. With mosaic floors, marble veneers on the walls, and mosaics or painted stucco on the vaults, the interior was truly splendid. The Baths, dedicated in 216, must have been many years in building, and may originally have been commissioned by Septimius Severus.

THE YOUNGER AUGUSTUS

The emperor Geta; portrait-bust from Munich.

He (Caracalla) exhibited his hatred for his dead brother by abolishing the observance of his birthday, and he vented his anger upon the stones that had supported his statues, and melted down the coinage that displayed his features.

Cassius Dio LXXVIII.12

Caracalla was able to destroy Geta's coins and memorials but could not prevent him receiving favourable treatment from ancient historians. Geta was born only a year after Caracalla, probably on 7 March 189 at Rome, and is said to have resembled his father, Septimius Severus, in appearance. If the Historia Augusta is to be believed, he was certainly no saint: 'As a youth, he was handsome, brusque in his manners though not disrespectful, incontinent in love, gluttonous, and a lover of food and of wine variously spiced.' Geta also had a reputation for meanness, spending money on clothing and jewellery for himself, but never giving presents to anyone else. He was 20 years old when his father raised him to the rank of Augustus, whereas Caracalla had been Augustus from the age of 9. The decision to make the two brothers joint emperors seems to have been a change of plan late in Severus's reign. It is hard not to sympathize with Caracalla's feelings of resentment and hostility to the new arrangement.

The bloody aftermath

Geta had powerful friends, and Caracalla was aware that his action would lead to widespread opposition. His first move, for his own safety, was to throw himself on the mercy of the praetorian guard, claiming that he had narrowly escaped death at his brother's hands, and had had to kill him in self-defence. The soldiers were suspicious, but were won over by the promise of a large money-gift and a substantial rise in pay. Next day he appeared in the senate house to explain his action, once again claiming that Geta had tried to murder him.

Still insecure in his new position, Caracalla sought safety in a general massacre of his brother's erstwhile supporters. Senators, praetorian commanders, provincial governors, palace servants, soldiers, charioteers and friends were executed without trial or on the most specious charges. They were killed at table, at the public baths, and in the streets. During the early months of 212, some 20,000 people perished in this way. There were public protests at the scale of the executions, but these Caracalla suppressed with the same harshness. Among the dead were Cornificia, elderly daughter of Marcus Aurelius, who was found weeping for Geta, and Publia Fulvia Plautilla, Caracalla's exiled wife.

The slaughter of his brother's supporters in 212 permanently soured relations between emperor and senate, and alienated many other sections of Roman society. The shadow of Geta's murder hung over the rest of Caracalla's reign.

The grand tour

Uncomfortable in the capital, in the early months of 213 Caracalla set out for the German frontier. The young emperor soon became popular with the soldiers, marching alongside them on foot rather than riding in

THE CHILDHOOD OF CARACALLA

He himself in his boyhood was winsome and clever, respectful to his parents and courteous to his parents' friends, beloved by the people, popular with the senate, and well able to further his own interests in winning affection. Never did he seem backward in letters or slow in deeds of kindness, never niggardly in largesse or tardy in forgiving.

Historia Augusta *Life of Caracalla* I

The future emperor Caracalla was born Lucius Septimius Bassianus at Lyons in 188, while his father Septimius Severus was governor of the province of Gallia Lugdunensis (northern France). He was the eldest child of Severus and his second wife Julia Domna; he took his last name from his mother's father, Junius Bassianus, who was high priest in the Syrian city of Emesa. Another son, Geta, followed in 189, but no other brothers or sisters are known. As a child, Caracalla is said to have been intelligent and sensitive, but it is clear that even in his early years, and certainly by the time he reached his teens, Caracalla was caught up in jealous rivalry with his brother Geta.

a carriage, and eating ordinary local food rather than delicacies specially transported from Rome. He was even said to grind his own barley flour. The support of the soldiery was not entirely disinterested, since on assuming sole rule Caracalla had given them a substantial rise in pay: an increase of at least 50 per cent, costing the treasury the enormous sum of 70 million sesterces.

The summer of 213 saw imperial victories over German peoples in both the Agri Decumates and on the Rhineland front. The senate was sufficiently impressed by these to award Caracalla the title 'Germanicus Maximus'. The following year Caracalla and his retinue proceeded eastwards, through Dacia and Thrace into Asia Minor. It was on the march through Thrace, we are told, that 'he suddenly became Alexander and commemorated him afresh in all sorts of ways'. Cassius Dio tells us that Caracalla kept numerous elephants in his entourage, in imitation of Alexander the Great, and persecuted the Aristotelian philosophers because Aristotle was supposed to have had some part in Alexander's death. Statues of Alexander were ordered for Rome and other cities. The hero-worship was carried to extremes; pictures were ordered showing a head with two half faces, one of them Alexander's, the other Caracalla's.

The romantic side of Caracalla's character came out again at Ilium, site of ancient Troy. The emperor visited the ruins of the city and the supposed tomb of Achilles, which he decorated with garlands and flowers. When one of his secretaries happened to die during their stay, Caracalla took advantage of the occasion to stage an elaborate funeral ceremony involving animal sacrifices and a large wooden funeral pyre modelled on the one Homer describes for Achilles' friend Patroclus.

Massacre at Alexandria

The grand tour continued the following year. The winter of 214–215 was spent at Nicomedia in north-west Asia Minor, but by May 215 Caracalla had reached Antioch in Syria. He spent the summer there, then passed on to Alexandria, where he was given a splendid reception by the citizens. The city was the second largest of the empire, with a population of about half a million. It had the further distinction of being the burial place of the emperor's hero Alexander the Great. One of Caracalla's first actions on entering the city was to visit the tomb and lay his purple imperial cloak on the grave, together with the ornaments he was wearing.

The visit to Alexandria which had begun so pleasantly ended in a violent massacre, by Caracalla's men, of unarmed civilians. The immediate provocation that gave rise to this atrocity is unknown, but Caracalla's anger was somehow inflamed, leading to the slaughter of thousands of Alexandrians (p.144).

Caracalla's Parthian War

The main object of Caracalla's visit to the east was a war of conquest against the Parthians. After the massacre at Alexandria he returned to

THE BURDEN OF GUILT

For he was sick not only in body, partly from visible and partly from secret ailments, but in mind as well, suffering from certain distressing visions, and often thought he was being pursued by his father and by his brother, armed with swords.

Cassius Dio LXXVIII.15

(Above) Approach to the Sanctuary of Aesculapius at Pergamum. (Below) Theatre at Alexandria, third century AD.

Caracalla has received an extremely hostile press from most ancient and modern historians. Yet as a child he does not seem to have been exceptionally evil, and his violent actions as emperor seem all to have been tied up with the murder of his brother Geta. The violence which ended their joint rule left an indelible mark on Caracalla's reputation, but was perhaps more the result of insecurity than any natural tendency to cruelty. There is a story that, just before Caracalla died, his father appeared to him in a dream, saying 'As you killed your brother, so I will slay you.' He was clearly happiest away from Rome, in the company of the army. Caracalla also suffered from some medical condition, and vainly sought cures at the shrine of Apollo Grannus (a Celtic god of healing) in Germany, at the Temple of Aesculapius (Greek god of healing) at Pergamum in Asia Minor, and at the Temple of Serapis at Alexandria. But it was guilt and insecurity which caused him most distress, and it was this which lay behind atrocities such as the massacre at Alexandria which occurred during Caracalla's grand tour. The emperor arrived in the city in December 215, and stayed there until March or April the following year. During that time, something happened to inflame his anger against the Alexandrians. It may have been a plot against his life; more likely, the Alexandrians criticized him for the murder of Geta. Whatever the cause, Caracalla's response was breathtaking in its ferocity. Lured by false promises, the young men of the city were rounded up, surrounded by his soldiers, and slaughtered. The killing soon spread to other parts of the city, and thousands perished in the massacre of unarmed civilians. It was one of the bleakest episodes in Alexandria's history, and one of the darkest moments of Caracalla's reign.

Antioch to assemble his forces and take the field. Arrangements for the campaign had begun two years before, when Caracalla was in Asia Minor. Military units were brought up to strength, lines of communication improved, and new mints established to supply coin for the troops. The army which assembled at the Syrian frontier in the early summer of 216 consisted of all or part of no fewer than eight legions, a substantial force.

It was an ideal moment to strike, for since 213 the Parthian empire had been riven by civil war between two rival claimants. One of these, Vologaeses V, held lower Mesopotamia and the capital city of Ctesiphon. The other, Artabanus V, controlled the Iranian plateau beyond. Caracalla took advantage of this division, siding with Artabanus against Vologaeses, and proposing marriage with Artabanus's daughter to cement their alliance. But the plan miscarried. Caracalla marched against the unprepared Artabanus, and Roman forces ravaged the countryside east of the Tigris more or less unhindered.

It was a treacherous victory, but Caracalla was no doubt well satisfied with the outcome. He withdrew to spend the winter at the city of Edessa in northern Mesopotamia, which had become the headquarters of his campaign, and passed the time in hunting and chariot racing, and planning new operations against the Parthians for the following year.

But this was not to be. While he campaigned in the east, intrigue was casting its net around the emperor's life. News of a conspiracy was leaked to Flavius Maternianus, commander of the troops in Rome during Caracalla's absence. He sent warning of the plot to Caracalla, but the letter was diverted to Julia Domna, the emperor's mother, who was in charge of imperial correspondence at Antioch. Suspicion pointed to Marcus Opellius Macrinus, commander of the praetorian guard, as one of the ring-leaders.

It was Julius Martialis, an officer in the imperial bodyguard, who was chosen to carry out the deed. Martialis had a private grievance against Caracalla: Herodian says his brother had been executed a few days earlier on a charge which had not been proved; Cassius Dio, on the other hand, tells us he was angry that Caracalla had refused to promote him to centurion. Whatever the case, Macrinus and Martialis were both included in the party which accompanied Caracalla on 8 April from Edessa to Carrhae. The emperor was suffering at the time from a stomach upset, and ordered a halt while he went to relieve himself. It was an ideal opportunity for Martialis: only a single attendant went with Caracalla, and the rest of the bodyguard turned their backs in respect for the emperor's privacy. Martialis moved forward, as if he had been beckoned, and killed Caracalla with a single sword thrust while he was lowering his breeches.

The assassin immediately took to horse and fled, but one of Caracalla's mounted bodyguard brought him down with a javelin. Macrinus, meanwhile, feigned innocence, lamenting the emperor's death with the rest. The body of Caracalla, hated by many but loved by

The Moorish origin of Macrinus was clear from his appearance. He made a point of cultivating mannerisms which were associated with the memory of Marcus Aurelius, down to dressing his beard in the fashion of Marcus's day. He also wore more jewellery and personal ornaments than was customary among high-ranking Romans of the early third century. Four busts of the emperor survive, though only one (*above*), a bronze discovered near Belgrade in 1969, shows the long beard in the style of Marcus Aurelius.

MACRINUS	
Born 164 at Caesarea in Mauretania Marcus Opellius Macrinus	Tribunicia potestas first on 11 April 217; renewed 10 December 218
On accession 11 April 217 Imperator Marcus Opellius Severus Macrinus Augustus, Pius Felix, Proconsul *Conferred by senate 217 (?June)* 'Pater Patriae'	*Full titles at death* Imperator Marcus Opellius Severus Macrinus Pius Felix Augustus, Pontifex Maximus, Tribuniciae potestatis II, Consul, Pater Patriae, Proconsul
Consular rank in 217, but took up office as consul for first time on 1 January 218. Some inscriptions recognize 'Cos I' for 217 and 'Cos II' for 218; but correct form is 'Cos I' for 218 only.	*Wife* Nonia Celsa *Children* a son Marcus Opellius Diadumenianus *Executed at Archelais in Cappadocia June/July 218*

the army, was duly cremated, and the ashes sent to Julia Domna in Antioch. He was only 29. The urn was conveyed back to Rome, and laid to rest in the Mausoleum of Hadrian. The ashes of Julia Domna followed a few weeks later. Some months later they were deified, mother and son together, by Elagabalus.

So ended the reign of Caracalla, a man driven to cruelty by guilt and insecurity, but not without ability as a ruler nor concern for good government. He was patient and conscientious in the hearing of lawsuits. He also reformed the currency, introducing a new silver coin, the antoninianus. Furthermore, it was Caracalla who in the Antonine Constitution of 212 first extended Roman citizenship to all male free (non-slave) people of the empire. The intention was most likely to widen the obligation for public service and increase imperial revenues, since citizens were liable to pay additional taxes. But by removing the division between Roman and non-Roman, the edict strengthened the concept of the empire as a commonwealth rather than a series of provinces dominated by Italy.

If we seek a lasting reminder of Caracalla's reign, however, it is not the extension of citizenship to which we look, nor even his reputation for cruelty, but to the vast Baths which he built at Rome. Today, even in ruins, they stand as one of the most impressive monuments to Roman power.

MACRINUS

Macrinus was a Moor by birth, from Caesarea, and the son of most obscure parents, so that he was very appropriately likened to the ass that was led up to the palace by the spirit; in particular, one of his ears had been pierced in accordance with the custom followed by most of the Moors. But his integrity threw even this drawback into the shade. As for his attitude towards law and precedent, his knowledge of them was not so accurate as his observance of them was faithful.

Cassius Dio LXXIX.11

The murder of Caracalla on 8 April 217 left the Roman empire without an obvious candidate for the succession. Caracalla had no children, and no heir had been publicly named. The field lay open for the conspirators to put forward their own nominee. Dio and Herodian would have us believe that Caracalla was killed in order to make Macrinus emperor; that the succession was already decided. If so, the conspirators trod very warily, and Macrinus waited three days before seeking the imperial acclamation from the troops, on 11 April 217.

Macrinus was far from being the first provincial to become emperor, but he does have the distinction of being the first non-senator to achieve such high office. Born in 164 at Caesarea, a harbour town on the coast of Mauretania, Macrinus was probably not of such lowly origin as ancient historians would like to suggest; his parents were of equestrian rank,

HEIR TO DEFEAT

The boy himself was beautiful beyond all others, somewhat tall of stature, with golden hair, black eyes and an aquiline nose; his chin was wholly lovely in its modelling, his mouth designed for a kiss, and he was by nature strong and by training graceful.

Historia Augusta *Life of Diadumenianus* III

This flattering description of Diadumenianus seems to forget that he was only nine years old when he was killed. Marcus Opellius Diadumenianus was in fact one of the youngest and most shadowy figures to have carried the title of Roman emperor. He was born in 208, and became heir-apparent with the title of Caesar when Macrinus was declared emperor in April 217. He also took the surname Antoninus, in a bid to give legitimacy to the new regime. In May 218, during the mutiny in support of Elagabalus, Diadumenianus was raised to the rank of Augustus. This was never confirmed by the senate, however, and the titles remained unofficial though they appeared on coins minted at Antioch. When the rebels gained the upper hand Macrinus sent his son for safety to the Parthian court, but Diadumenianus was intercepted and killed at Zeugma.

belonging to the middle class rather than the labouring poor. Macrinus trained as a lawyer, but found his first real opening when he was appointed steward by the powerful Plautianus, commander of the praetorian guard under Septimius Severus. By 212 Macrinus himself was praetorian commander, and he was serving with Caracalla in the east when the opportunity came to seize power.

Macrinus began his reign with some necessary executions, and replaced several provincial governors by men of his own class and choosing. He quickly fell out with Julia Domna, who was at first left in peace at Antioch but could not resist conspiring with the soldiers. She was in fact at an advanced stage of breast cancer and when Macrinus ordered her to leave Antioch, she chose instead to starve herself to death.

The real test, however, was the Parthians. They had been ill-prepared for Caracalla's invasion the previous year, but by the autumn of 217 had mustered a powerful army and were advancing in strength on the Roman position. The two forces met near Nisibis in northern Mesopotamia but in a hard-fought battle neither side gained the upper hand. To win peace Macrinus agreed to pay the Parthians the enormous sum of 200 million sesterces. This humiliating settlement did nothing for Macrinus's standing with the troops; even less so when he began to remove some of the privileges they had received from Caracalla.

It was in these uneasy circumstances that the 'False Antoninus' made his appearance. This was Varius Avitus, better known as Elagabalus, the 14-year-old grandson of Julia Maesa, the sister of Julia Domna. During the night of 15 May 218 a small band of followers smuggled him into the camp of the Third Legion 'Gallica' at Raphanaea, near Emesa. The following morning, the soldiers proclaimed him emperor and rose in open rebellion. They took special encouragement from the rumour that Avitus was really the illegitimate son of Caracalla; for Caracalla, like Commodus before him, was immensely popular with the military. Macrinus tried to strengthen his position by raising his 9-year-old son Diadumenianus to the rank of Augustus. Macrinus used this as a pretext for distributing money to the troops to win back their favour, but it failed to stem the tide of desertions, and Macrinus was forced to flee to Antioch.

On 8 June 218 Macrinus was defeated by rebels outside Antioch, and fled north hoping to rally support at Rome. He shaved his beard and hair in the hope of avoiding detection, but was betrayed and apprehended at Chalcedon while waiting to cross the Bosphorus. At about the same time his son, too, was captured at Zeugma on the Syrian frontier, attempting to escape into Parthia. Macrinus was taken back south under guard, but executed by a centurion at Archelais in Cappadocia. He was 53. The failure to win a clear victory over either the Parthians or the rebels loyal to Elagabalus had critically weakened his position. Above all, however, Macrinus had failed to realize how dangerous it was to tamper with the pay and privileges of the army, and had paid the inevitable price.

Elagabalus
Imperator Marcus Aurelius
Antoninus Pius Felix
Augustus Proconsul
218–222

Alexander Severus
Imperator Caesar Marcus
Aurelius Severus Alexander
Pius Felix Augustus
222–235

Only one contemporary bust of
Elagabalus survives (*right*); this shows a
soft, immature face, with large eyes and
full lips. Capitoline Museum.

ELAGABALUS

He would wear a tunic made wholly of cloth of gold, or one made of purple, or a Persian one studded with jewels, and at such times he would say that he felt oppressed by the weight of his pleasures. He even wore jewels on his shoes, sometimes engraved ones – a practice which aroused the derision of all, as if, forsooth, the engraving of famous artists could be seen on jewels attached to his feet. He wished to wear also a jewelled diadem in order that his beauty might be increased and his face look more like a woman's; and in his own house he did wear one.

Historia Augusta *Life of Elagabalus* XXIII

He was the last of the Antonines, a man so detestable for his life, his character, and his utter depravity that the senate expunged from the records even his name.

Historia Augusta
Life of Elagabalus XVIII

If Commodus and Caracalla were remembered as monsters and tyrants, the man who succeeded Macrinus was truly extraordinary. The bizarre behaviour of the Syrian emperor Elagabalus shocked Roman opinion, not least through his bisexual antics and exotic religious practices. The story of his reign is portrayed in lurid colours by ancient historians, who were by turns perplexed and horrified. It was one thing to have an emperor of provincial origin who had risen through the ranks of a mili-

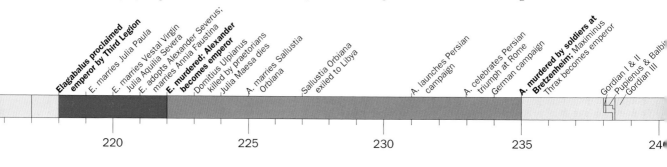

Elagabalus proclaimed emperor by Third Legion
E. marries Julia Paula
E. marries Vestal Virgin Julia Aquilia Severa
E. adopts Alexander Severus; marries Annia Faustina
E. murdered; Alexander becomes emperor
Domitius Ulpianus killed by praetorians
Julia Maesa dies
A. marries Sallustia Orbiana
Sallustia Orbiana exiled to Libya
A. launches Persian campaign
A. celebrates Persian triumph at Rome German campaign
A. murdered by soldiers at Bretzenheim; Maximinus Thrax becomes emperor
Gordian I & II
Pupienus & Balbinus
Gordian III

220   225   230   235   24

ELAGABALUS

Born 203 or 204 at Emesa in Syria
Varius Avitus Bassianus

On accession 16 May 218
Imperator Caesar Marcus Aurelius Antoninus Pius Felix Augustus Proconsul (Identical title to that of Caracalla, whose natural son he claimed to be)

In inscriptions
'Divi Antonini Magni filius, Divi Severi Pii nepos' (son of Caracalla, grandson of Severus)

Added on recognition by the senate and priestly colleges at Rome July 218
'Pater Patriae' and 'Pontifex Maximus'

From 220
'Sacerdos Amplissimus Dei Invicti Solis Elagabali' (high priest of the unconquerable sun god Elagabalus)

Consul I (218), II (219), III (220), IV (222)

Tribunicia potestas first on 16 May 218, renewed annually on 10 December

Full titles at death
Imperator Caesar Divi Antonini Magni filius, Divi Severi Pii nepos, Marcus Aurelius Antoninus Pius Felix Augustus, Sacerdos Amplissimus Dei Invicti Solis Elagabali, Pontifex Maximus, Tribuniciae potestatis V, Consul IV, Pater Patriae

Known from the name of his god as Elagabalus, but never officially; later Latin writers give this (erroneously) as Heliogabalus. By Cassius Dio referred to as Sardanapalus.

Wives
(1) Julia Cornelia Paula
(2) Julia Aquilia Severa
(3) Annia Faustina

Murdered 11 March 222 at the praetorian camp in Rome; body thrown into Tiber

The sacred stone being carried in religious procession; the legend reads 'Sanct Deo Soli', 'to the holy sun god', with 'Elagabal', the name shared by both god and emperor, below.

tary career, as had Pertinax and Septimius Severus; quite another for the Roman world to be ruled by the hereditary priest of an Oriental sun god, a Syrian boy only 14 years old.

Elagabalus was born Varius Avitus Bassianus, the grandson of Julia Maesa, younger sister of the empress Julia Domna. He belonged to the same Emesene family, and was hereditary high priest of the god Elagabal. His father, Sextus Varius Marcellus, another Syrian, had risen to the rank of senator under Caracalla; but his mother put it about that his real father was Caracalla, whose memory the army still held dear. In truth, he was only Caracalla's nephew.

The scheme to make Avitus emperor sprang from Gannys, his mother's lover. It was Gannys who conducted the two under cover of darkness to the camp of the Third Legion 'Gallica' and had him acclaimed emperor by the troops on the morning of 16 May 218. Avitus took the title Marcus Aurelius Antoninus. But it was as Elagabalus, the name of his god, that he came to be known.

The rebels overthrew the troops loyal to Macrinus, the reigning emperor, with surprising ease. Their victory outside Antioch on 8 June 218 led to the immediate recognition of Elagabalus as emperor at Rome and throughout the empire.

The new emperor did not immediately hurry to Rome, but spent some months in the east, first at Antioch, then later at Nicomedia in Asia Minor. One of his actions at Nicomedia was to execute Gannys, the very man who had helped him to power. The reason we are given is that Gannys was forcing him to live 'temperately and prudently'. It is much more likely that his mother's lover was growing too powerful, treating Elagabalus as a mere cipher for his own commands. The emperor had at one stage intended to give Gannys the title of Caesar, and allow him to marry his mother. But it was not so much the emperor who benefited from the demise of Gannys; real power now lay with his mother, Julia Soaemis, and his grandmother, the redoubtable Julia Maesa.

The imperial cortège set off for Rome from Nicomedia in the spring of 219. Apart from the imperial family, it included one other notable component: an inanimate one at that – the famous black stone, cult symbol of the god Elagabalus, brought from the temple at Emesa in Syria, described by Herodian as being 'rounded at the base and coming to a point on the top'. Herodian continues, 'This stone is worshipped as though it were sent from heaven; on it there are some small projecting pieces and markings that are pointed out, which the people would like to believe are a rough picture of the sun, because this is how they see them.' The emperor wished to take his god with him to Rome. When they arrived at the capital, in the summer of 219, the black stone was installed on the Palatine Hill where a great new temple was built to hold it, the so-called Elagaballium.

Elagabalus was deeply devoted to the god whose high-priest he was. Every day at dawn he used to sacrifice large numbers of cattle and sheep at the altars of this temple. The senators and equestrians stood around in

THE TEMPLES OF ELAGABALUS

No public works of his are in existence, save the temple of the god Elagabalus (called by some the Sun, by others Jupiter), the Amphitheatre as restored after its destruction by fire, and the public bath in the Vicus Sulpicius, begun by Antoninus, the son of Severus. This bath, in fact, had been dedicated by Antoninus Caracalla, who had bathed in it himself and opened it to the public, but the portico was left unbuilt, and this was added after his death by this spurious Antoninus, though actually completed by Alexander.

Life of Elagabalus XVII

The emperor Elagabalus was responsible for repairs to the Flavian Amphitheatre (Colosseum), which had been struck by lightning in 217 and seriously damaged. He also began work on the enclosure wall around the Baths of Caracalla and built the Horti Variani, a palace complex which included an amphitheatre, a circus, a bath-building and an audience hall. But his most famous projects were undoubtedly the two temples built for the worship of Elagabalus, one on the Palatine Hill (the Elagaballium), the other on the south-eastern edge of the city.

The Elagaballium, later rededicated to Jupiter Ultor (the Avenger), was an enormous colonnaded structure, some 230 x 130 ft (70 x 40 m), within a rectangular porticoed enclosure. The massive temple platform is still a prominent feature of the north-east corner of the Palatine. The second temple built to the god may have been where the church of Santa Croce in

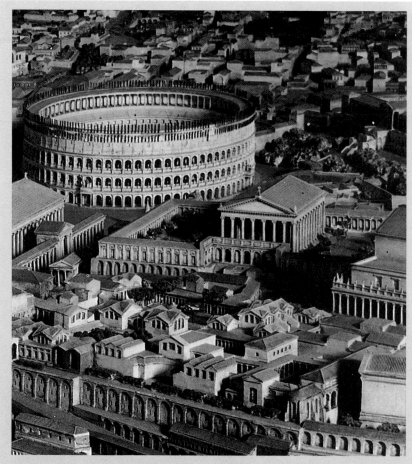

Reconstruction of imperial Rome showing the Temple of Elagabalus in front and to the right of the Colosseum.

Gerusalemme now stands. Contemporaries described it as vast and magnificent, with high towers from which the emperor distributed largesse to the crowds gathered below. Within the temples, however, the religious excesses of Elagabalus went unchecked. Cassius Dio gives us a chilling account of Elagabalus's religious rites, 'I will not describe the barbaric chants which Sardanapalus, together with his mother and grandmother, chanted to Elagabalus, or the secret sacrifices that he offered to him, slaying boys and using charms, in fact actually shutting up alive in the god's temple a lion, a monkey and a snake, and throwing in among them human genitals, and practising other unholy rites, while he invariably wore innumerable amulets.' (Cassius Dio LXXX.11)

attendance, while 'the entrails of the sacrificial victims and spices were carried in golden bowls, not on the heads of household servants or lower-class people, but by military prefects and important officials wearing long tunics in the Phoenician style down to their feet, with long sleeves and a single purple stripe in the middle. They also wore linen shoes of the kind used by local oracle priests in Phoenicia.' (Herodian V.5)

This in itself caused quite a stir at Rome; but that was nothing com-

THE SEXUAL ANTICS OF ELAGABALUS

He had the whole of his body depilated, deeming it the chief enjoyment of life to appear fit and worthy to arouse the lusts of the greatest number. . . . And even at Rome he did nothing but send out agents to search for those who had particularly large organs and bring them to the palace in order that he might enjoy their vigour.

Life of Elagabalus V; VIII

The husband of this 'woman' was Hierocles, a Carian slave, once the favourite of Gordius, from whom he had learned to drive a chariot. . . . Certain other men, too, were frequently honoured by the emperor and became powerful, some because they had joined in his uprising and others because they committed adultery with him. For he wished to have the reputation of committing adultery, so that in this respect, too, he might imitate the most lewd women; and he would often allow himself to be caught in the very act, in consequence of which he used to be violently upbraided by his 'husband' and beaten, so that he had black eyes.

Cassius Dio LXXX.15

He had planned, indeed, to cut off his genitals altogether, but that desire was prompted by his effeminacy; the circumcision which he actually carried out was a part of the priestly requirements of Elagabalus, and he accordingly mutilated many of his companions in like manner.

Cassius Dio LXXX.11

pared with the opposition aroused by his interference with Rome's traditional gods. His great religious initiative, aimed at making Elagabalus the chief and only god, came to a head in the year 220. The eastern god was to take precedence 'even before Jupiter himself', the ruler of the Roman pantheon. He was also to have a wife. First choice was Pallas, the sacred statue (reputedly from Troy) kept hidden in the Temple of Vesta in the Forum, and tended by the Vestal Virgins. As part of this scheme the emperor himself, high-priest of Elagabalus, married one of the Vestals. The plan drew such scandalized opposition, however, that it had to be abandoned, and the place of Pallas as consort of the god Elagabalus was taken by Urania, the moon goddess, also known as Caelestis.

A huge, eastern-style temple of the sun was built on the edge of Rome. Each year at midsummer, the black stone of Elagabalus was brought here from the temple on the Palatine in a grand procession. The stone itself was carried in a chariot drawn by six white horses, the emperor running backwards in front of the chariot, so as not to turn his back on the god.

His aim was to establish a kind of monotheism, wherein the sun-god Elagabalus was the principal deity, and others gods merely its slaves or attendants. As part of this policy of religious syncretism he tried to remove the sacred symbols of several religions to the temple of Elagabalus. Christians and Jews, too, were obliged to worship at this shrine. On the same principle, that all religions are subordinate to the worship of the sun-god, the emperor participated in the rituals of several different religions. According to the *Life of Elagabalus*, 'He kept about him every kind of magician and had them perform daily sacrifices . . . he would examine the children's vitals and torture the victims after the manner of his own native rights.'

Alongside his religious mania, the young emperor also indulged in extravagant sexual practices. He married at least three wives – some sources say as many as five – in the space of three years. In addition to his official wives, Elagabalus 'had intercourse with even more without any legal sanction.'

But it was not his relations with women which so shocked Roman opinion, as his liaisons with men. Homosexuality was not respectable in third-century Rome; and still less so in the bizarre form practised by Elagabalus. For he was not only bisexual but also a transvestite. 'He would go to the taverns by night, wearing a wig, and there ply the trade of a female huckster. He frequented the notorious brothels, drove out the prostitutes, and played the prostitute himself.' This activity culminated in his 'marriage' to a Carian slave called Hierocles, who was even permitted to beat him as if he really were his wife. The scandalous reports go still further: not only did Elagabalus act and dress like a woman; he wished to be physically transformed into one. 'He asked the physicians to contrive a woman's vagina in his body by means of an incision, promising them large sums for doing so.' Another story tells of his delight in a man with peculiarly large private parts, who was however

THE THREE WIVES OF ELAGABALUS

Soon after his arrival in Rome in 219 Elagabalus married Julia Cornelia Paula, a lady of distinguished family who took the imperial title Augusta. By the end of 220 he had divorced her and married Julia Aquilia Severa, a Vestal Virgin. This was a flagrant breach of Roman law and tradition, which held that any Vestal found guilty of sexual intercourse should be buried alive; four had been executed in this way during the reign of Caracalla. Elagabalus defended his marriage on the grounds that he was high priest, and she high priestess, of their respective deities, and god-like children might be expected to spring from their union.

Within a year Aquilia Severa in turn had been deserted by Elagabalus. He now married Annia Faustina, a descendant of Marcus Aurelius and widow of a man the emperor had recently put to death. The marriage took place in July 221, but Elagabalus soon tired of his new wife and set her, too, aside. By the end of the year he had returned to Julia Aquilia Severa, whom he claimed was the only woman he really loved. These ladies bore the title of Augusta and the rank of empress; but over all of them hung the power wielded by the emperor's mother and grandmother.

spared the emperor's further attentions when he failed to perform in bed.

Elagabalus was also criticized for his appointment of men of humble origin to important positions of state. A notable example was Publius Valerius Comazon, appointed commander of the praetorian guard in 218, whose family may have been professional dancers or actors. Such appointments nonetheless provided rich ammunition for critics and scandal-mongers, who made out that cooks, barbers and charioteers were governing the empire. In fact, they were men on whom the emperor and his family could rely; but they did little to strengthen the respectability of the regime.

All this was too much for the soldiery. There were a series of rebellions and uprisings throughout the reign. As early as 218 the Third Legion 'Gallica', stationed in Syria, decided they had had enough of their erstwhile protegé and tried to make Verus, their commander, emperor. The move failed, as did subsequent attempts by the Fourth Legion, by the fleet, and by a shadowy pretender called Seleucus.

By the summer of 221, however, even Elagabalus's close family and supporters were dismayed by his behaviour. In an effort to rescue the regime they persuaded him to adopt his cousin Bassianus Alexianus, a boy of 13, as Caesar, son, and heir. The adoption took place on 26 June. Alexianus, later to become emperor as Alexander Severus, was popular with the praetorian guard. He and Elagabalus became rivals for power, each backed by an ambitious mother: Elagabalus by Julia Soaemias, and Alexander by his mother Julia Mamaea and grandmother Julia Maesa.

Late in 221, Elagabalus tried to have his cousin murdered. No-one would carry out the order, but Elagabalus did not give up his designs on Alexander's life. On 11 March 222, during a visit to the praetorian camp, the emperor became enraged at the open support for Alexander, and his own unpopularity. He ordered immediate arrest and punishment of the offenders, but the soldiers had had enough. They killed Elagabalus in the latrine where he had taken refuge. (Another source says he was being carried to safety in a chest when he was discovered and killed.) His mother perished with him. Their bodies were beheaded and dragged naked around the streets of Rome, until at last the emperor's corpse was thrown into the Tiber, the traditional punishment for convicted criminals.

So perished Elagabalus, after a reign of less than four years. But it is not so much the shortness of his reign which surprises, as that he managed to hold on to power for so long. How was this possible? The answer lies partly in his youth (he was only 18 when he died), and in the fact that real power lay with his female relations, the Syrian princesses Julia Maesa and Julia Soaemias. The emperor's sexual excesses were frowned upon but tolerated by the people and the soldiery, while the princesses managed affairs of state with care and astuteness. Key positions were staffed by supporters of the new regime, including men of humble origin entirely dependent on the backing of the imperial family. It was only when the princesses themselves fell out that a real crisis materialized.

And even then, the result was not a change of regime; merely a change of ruler. For the new emperor Alexander Severus was every bit as Syrian as his cousin Elagabalus.

ALEXANDER SEVERUS

Although he held power no more than thirteen years, he left the state strengthened on every side. From Romulus to Septimius the state had grown steadily in power, but it reached its apogee under the government of Caracalla. It was due to Alexander that it did not immediately decline.

Aurelius Victor *Book of the Caesars* XXIV

With the death of Elagabalus in 222, the imperial mantle passed to his young cousin Alexander Severus, who had already been given the rank of Caesar the previous year. The new reign brought hope of a more orderly government, and indeed the ancient historians regarded Alexander as one of their model emperors. They cannot hide the fact, however, that Alexander was not fully in command of events. Real power lay with his mother, Julia Mamaea, who governed the empire with her advisers. But even she could not control the army, and the reign was bedevilled by military unrest and indiscipline.

The reign began as a joint regency between Mamaea and her own mother, Alexander's grandmother, the redoubtable Julia Maesa. The death of Maesa in 224 gave Mamaea a free hand to extend her own authority. She assumed ever greater powers, which drew resentment from Alexander. He 'was very much upset to see her avarice and absolute obsession with money', and 'deplored her forcible confiscation of some people's inherited property'. By 227 Mamaea was being styled 'Mater Augusti et castrorum et senatus et patriae' (mother of the emperor, the army, the senate and the homeland); later this became the still more grandiloquent 'Mater universi generis humani' (mother of the whole human race).

Despite these high-flown claims, Julia Mamaea had the good sense to govern moderately and with consent, taking care to avoid the pitfalls of the previous reign. She chose 16 senators as councillors and advisers to the emperor, dignified men who commanded respect. The religious excesses of Elagabalus were reversed, and the old gods restored to their sanctuaries. The black stone was sent back to Syria, and the Elagaballium on the Palatine Hill became the Temple of Jupiter Ultor. Mamaea also kept her son's private life in check, preventing the kind of promiscuous behaviour exhibited by Elagabalus.

Mamaea's right-hand man in the early months was Domitius Ulpianus (Ulpian), a distinguished lawyer and writer. Ulpian was appointed commander of the praetorian guard and given wide powers. But while he successfully introduced a number of reforms, he could not control the praetorians. On one occasion they quarrelled with the city

He did not like to be called a Syrian and asserted that his ancestors were Romans, and he had his family-tree depicted, showing that he was descended from the Metelli.

Historia Augusta
Life of Alexander XLIV

Alexander Severus was only 13 when he came to power, and only 26 when he died. Portrait busts show him as boy, teenager, and young adult, and allow us to follow his progress to maturity. The sculptors seem to have emphasized his qualities of quiet spirituality and noble calm, in contrast to the tense religious fanaticism of Elagabalus. Busts of Alexander as a young man, such as this one from the Louvre, adopt a classical stylishness of dignified restraint, in conscious imitation of portraits of the Augustan age, and in reaction against the baroque sculptures with flowing hair of the Antonine emperors.

populace and praetorians and people fought for three days, many on both sides losing their lives. Ulpian's downfall came in 223, or early 224, when the praetorians refused to tolerate his execution of Julius Flavianus and Geminius Chrestus, their other commanders. He was pursued by disgruntled soldiers and assassinated in the imperial palace.

There was further trouble in 225, when Mamaea arranged for Alexander to marry the daughter of a patrician family, a lady with the redoubtable name Gnaea Seia Herennia Sallustia Orba Barbia Orbiana. The result, as Herodian tells us, was not harmonious: 'Wishing to be the only empress, Mamaea was jealous of the title of Augusta going to the girl.' She was also jealous of the girl's father's power: he may even have been elevated to the rank of Caesar. The friction came to a head in 227. Orbiana was thrown out of the imperial palace with such insults that her father took her to refuge with the praetorians. This was a clear act of rebellion; Mamaea had the father executed, and his daughter exiled to North Africa. Alexander, meanwhile, stood feebly by; attached to his wife, but too weak to oppose his mother's wishes.

Military unrest continued during the following years. In 229 Alexander advised the historian Cassius Dio to spend his consulship away from Rome, because he could not guarantee his safety. Indiscipline and insubordination were rife, not only among the praetorians, but also among the legions stationed on the imperial frontiers.

The Persian War

Against this background of smouldering discontent, news of serious trouble arrived from the east. For 300 years, Rome's traditional enemies in the Near East had been the Parthians. Since the second century, however, Parthian power had been in decline, and the Parthian capital

Ctesiphon had been sacked by the Romans on no fewer than three occasions. Septimius Severus had even been able to carve out the new province of Mesopotamia from Parthian territory. All this changed with the resurgence of Persian power in the early third century. The Persian king Ardashir began his reign as a Parthian subject, but in April 224 he defeated his overlord, the Parthian king Artabanus, and in 226 was officially installed as the ruler of a new Persian empire. His own name, Ardashir or Artaxerxes, was a conscious reminder of the links with a glorious Persian past, when the Persian empire had stretched from the Mediterranean to the Indus.

As soon as he had secured his position at home Ardashir turned his attention to the territories recently conquered by the Romans in northern Mesopotamia. In 230 his forces overran the Roman province of Mesopotamia, capturing the important cities of Nisibis and Carrhae. The Romans had been watching events in the east with mounting concern, but the conquest of Mesopotamia seems to have taken them by surprise. With no military experience of his own and with some reluctance, Alexander made preparations for an eastern campaign.

The emperor set out from Rome in the spring of 231, collecting troops along the Danube frontier, and arriving in Antioch in late summer. But Alexander's plans were still bedevilled by unrest among the military, and before the expedition could be launched there was a mutiny by troops of the Legio II 'Traiana', from Egypt, who sought to depose Alexander in favour of a new emperor. Another usurper – or perhaps the same one – took fright and drowned himself in the Euphrates. The uprisings were crushed, but they did not augur well for the future.

The assault on the Persians was launched in 232. Alexander led the main advance to Palmyra and Hatra, while flanking columns struck northwards through Armenia into northern Iran and south along the

JULIA MAMAEA

Completely dominated by his mother, he did exactly as he was told. This was the one thing for which he can be faulted; that he obeyed his mother in matters of which he disapproved because he was over-mild and showed greater respect to her than he should have done.

Herodian VI.1

Julia Mamaea wielded enormous power during her son's reign. Her jealousy was responsible for the exile of Alexander's wife Sallustia Orbiana, but her prominence may have served his reputation well, since criticism of the regime was directed against the emperor's mother rather than the emperor himself. It was tragic, yet fitting in a way, that the two should perish together, the mother clutching the son to her breast. The death of Julia Mamaea marked the end of the dominance of Syrian princesses at Rome which had begun with Julia Domna, wife of Septimius Severus, over 40 years before. Mamaea's unrivalled power was only broken by the outbreak of the Persian War in 231 and Maximinus's uprising in 235. The manipulation of power by the Syrian princesses is one of the most remarkable features of the late Severan period.

Portrait-bust of Julia Mamaea, Louvre, Paris.

ROME RESTORED

He restored the public works of former emperors and built many new ones himself, among them the bath which was called by his own name, adjacent to what had been the Neronian, and also the aqueduct which still has the name Alexandriana.

Historia Augusta
Life of Alexander XXV

Alexander's energies as a builder were divided between the restoration or enlargement of existing monuments and the construction of new ones. The Colosseum, damaged by lightning in 217, was slowly put to rights (though not wholly restored until 238). The enclosure around the Baths of Caracalla, begun by Elagabalus, was completed by Alexander. The emperor also built a splendid Nymphaeum (fountain) and his own bath complex, the Thermae Alexandrinae, but here he cheated somewhat, using the Baths of Nero as the core of the new project. It was a lavish building, nonetheless, standing within a large garden and supplied by its own purpose-built aqueduct. Alexander imposed special taxes to pay for the upkeep of baths throughout the city, and donated oil for lamps so that they could remain open after dark.

Euphrates towards the Persian Gulf. The plan achieved only a qualified success. The northern column was victorious, but for some unknown reason Alexander's own central column did not make much effort to advance into enemy territory, leaving the southern column at the mercy of the main Persian army. By the time Alexander withdrew to Antioch at the end of the summer, both sides had suffered heavy losses. Morale had been damaged, too, and there was no resounding Roman success to report. Alexander himself was accused of cowardice, for not prosecuting his part of the war more resolutely. But the Persians made no further attempts on Roman territory during Alexander's reign.

The German War

Alexander had only recently returned to Rome (where he celebrated a triumph in honour of his Persian 'victory') when news was brought to him of trouble in the west. The Germans had breached the Rhine frontier in several places, destroying forts and overrunning the countryside. Alexander once again prepared for war, drafting troops from the east to meet this new threat.

Alexander mustered his forces along the Rhineland frontier in 234. The army crossed the Rhine into Germany on a pontoon bridge and Alexander sought to buy off the Germans with promises of cash, so as to gain time. This may have been wise policy, but it did not go down well with the legions, who increasingly despised the unsoldierly conduct of their emperor. As Herodian says, 'In their opinion Alexander showed no honourable intention to pursue the war and preferred a life of ease, when he should have marched out to punish the Germans for their previous insolence.' They were also dismayed by Alexander's attempts to reduce military expenditure and limit their pay and bonuses. This combination of circumstances drove them to find a new leader by the name of Gaius Julius Verus Maximinus, a Thracian soldier, who had worked his way up through the ranks.

In March 235 Maximinus was in camp near Mainz, where he had been put in charge of new recruits by Alexander. Herodian gives a dramatic account of what followed. One morning, the troops in training gathered on the exercise ground as usual; but as soon as Maximinus appeared they threw the purple imperial cloak over his shoulders and declared him emperor. He pretended to be surprised, and reluctant to accept the honour, but the whole scene was prearranged and carefully stage-managed. The rebels decided to move quickly against Alexander, who was in camp at Vicus Britannicus (modern Bretzenheim) nearby.

Alexander heard the news before the rebels arrived, but acted neither with wisdom nor fortitude. 'He came rushing out of the imperial tent like a man possessed, weeping and trembling and raving against Maximinus for being unfaithful and ungrateful, recounting all the favours that had been showered upon him.' The soldiers promised to remain faithful to him, but at dawn on the next day, when a cloud of dust in the distance heralded the approach of Maximinus's troops, they

Ardashir's victory over the Parthian king Artabanus V in 224 heralded a resurgence of Persian power, which had been dormant since the fall of the Achaemenids over 500 years before. Persian ambitions caused severe problems for Alexander and his successors during the third century, especially during the reign of Ardashir's son Shapur I (242–272).
(*Right*) Investiture of Ardashir I by the god Hormuzd. Rock relief from Naqsh-i Rustam, Iran.

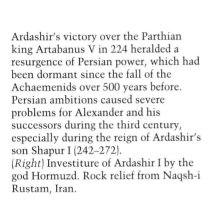

changed their minds and went over to the rebels. The end was quick: 'Trembling and terrified out of his wits, Alexander just managed to get back to his tent. There, the reports say, he waited for his executioner, clinging to his mother and weeping and blaming her for his misfortunes. Maximinus was hailed with the title of Augustus by the whole army, and sent a tribune with some centurions to kill Alexander. They burst into the tent and slaughtered the emperor, his mother, and all those thought to be his friends or favourites.' (Herodian VI.9)

If the Historia Augusta is correct, Alexander's body was brought back to Rome for burial in a splendid tomb. A cenotaph in his memory was also erected in Gaul. This must have been after some delay, however, since Alexander was officially condemned by his immediate successor, Maximinus, and his name erased from inscriptions. It was three years later, in 238, that he was deified by the senate, and a college of priests, the sodales Alexandrini, appointed to administer his cult.

Alexander Severus reigned, in name at least, for 13 years, over three times as long as the colourful Elagabalus. Yet he remains a shadowy and enigmatic character. Herodian, our major source for the reign, describes him with a kind of double vision. On the one hand, we are told his accession marked a change from the high-handed tyranny of Elagabalus to an aristocratic type of government approved by both people and senate. There is special praise for the years before the outbreak of the Persian War, during which Alexander is said to have reigned without cause for complaint. The Historia Augusta goes even further, describing him as 'the best of emperors'. Yet most sources agree that he was weak, and far too much under his mother's thumb. Furthermore, he showed little competence in military affairs, and failed to be generous to the army. It was this in the end that sealed his fate.

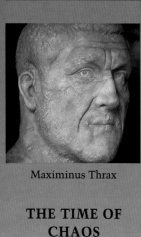

Maximinus Thrax

Pupienus

Philip the Arab

Decius

THE TIME OF CHAOS

Maximinus Thrax
AD 235–238

Gordian I
238

Gordian II
238

Pupienus and Balbinus
238

Gordian III
238–244

Philip the Arab
244–249

Decius
249–251

Trebonianus Gallus
251–253

Aemilius Aemilianus
253

Valerian
253–260

Gallienus
253–268

Claudius II
268–270

Quintillus
270

Aurelian
270–275

Tacitus
275–276

Florianus
276

Probus
276–282

Carus
282–283

Numerian
283–284

Carinus
283–285

The Gallic Empire

Postumus
260–269

Laelianus
269

Marius
269

Victorinus
268–271

Tetricus
271–274

THE EMPIRE RESTORED

Diocletian
284–305

Maximian
286–305,
307–308

Constantius I
305–306

Galerius
305–311

Severus II
306–307

Maxentius
306–312

Maximinus Daia
310–313

Constantine
307–337

Licinius
308–324

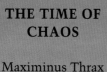

Alexander Severus — Maximinus Thrax — Gordian I & II — Pupienus & Balbinus — Gordian III — Philip the Arab — Decius — Trebonianus Gallus — Aemilius Aemilianus — Valerian — Gallienus — THE GALLIC EMPIRE — Claudius II — Quintillus — Aurelian — Tacitus — Florianus — Probus — Carus — Carinus — Numerian — Diocletian — Maximian

THE TIME OF CHAOS — THE EMPI

220   230   240   250   260   270   280   29

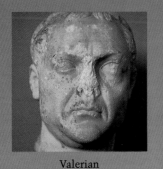
Valerian

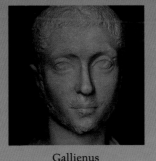
Gallienus

Probus

Constantine

CRISIS AND RENEWAL
The Time of Chaos AD 235–285
The Empire Restored AD 284–337

THE 50 YEARS following the murder of Alexander Severus were one of the lowest points in the history of the Roman empire. There were new threats and pressures on the frontiers, and new problems and divisions at home. The second-century emperors had been men of high standing at Rome; those of the third were increasingly chosen from the army, and were often of humble origin.

The troubled times led to a succession of short-reign emperors who frequently met a violent death, many of them murdered by their own troops. By the middle of the third century the Roman empire was fighting for its life, beset by a resurgent Persia in the east and by Alemanni and Goths on the Rhine and the Danube. Decius in 251 became the first Roman emperor to fall in battle against a foreign enemy, and Valerian in 260 the first and only one to be captured and die in captivity abroad. Yet despite these reverses the emperors fought back, and Aurelian and Probus recovered both lost territory and prestige.

A further turning point was reached in 284, with the accession of Diocletian. His comprehensive reform of the imperial administration led to a new concept of emperor and the division of power among a college of four, two Augusti and two Caesars. The imperial college fell apart soon after his retirement, but the new structures of government proved effective and resilient. The final transformation was left to Constantine, who in the early fourth century abandoned the old gods of Rome and made Christianity the official religion of the Roman empire.

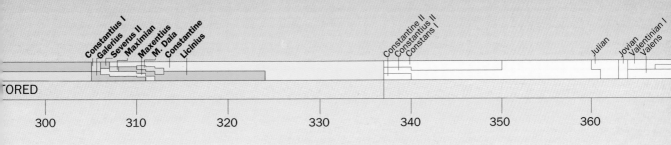

Constantius I
Galerius
Severus II
Maximian
Maxentius
M. Daia
Constantine
Licinius

Constantine II
Constantius II
Constans I

Julian

Jovian
Valentinian I
Valens

TORED

300   310   320   330   340   350   360

Maximinus Thrax
Imperator Caesar Gaius
Iulius Verus Maximinus Pius
Felix Invictus Augustus
Augustus
235–238

Gordian I & II
Imperator Caesar Marcus
Antonius Gordianus
Sempronianus Romanus
Africanus (both)
238

Pupienus & Balbinus
Imperator Caesar Marcus
Clodius Pupienus Maximus
Augustus
Imperator Caesar Decius
Caelius Calvinus Balbinus Pius
Felix Augustus
238

Gordian III
Imperator Caesar Marcus
Antonius Gordianus Pius Felix
Augustus
238–244

Maximinus was probably the biggest man ever to hold the office of Roman emperor. The Historia Augusta has it that he was 8 ft 6 in (2.6 m) tall, and so strong that he could pull laden carts unaided! The size of his footwear was also legendary, and the expression 'Maximinus's boot' came to be used in popular parlance for any tall or lanky individual. Surviving portrait busts, such as this one from the Louvre, show Maximinus as a heavily-muscled man with powerful jaw and close-cropped hair, the image of a seasoned soldier. Not for him the meditative, spiritual pose favoured by Alexander Severus.

MAXIMINUS THRAX	
Born 172 or 173 in Thrace or Moesia	*Children* a son Gaius Julius Verus Maximinus
Accession February or March 235	*Murdered by the troops at Aquileia April 238*
Wife Caecilia Paulina	

MAXIMINUS THRAX

For Gaius Iulius Maximinus, commander of Trebellica, was the first of the ordinary soldiers who, though almost illiterate, seized power with the votes of the legions.

Aurelius Victor *Book of the Caesars* 25

The accession of Maximinus, surnamed 'Thrax' (Thracian), represents a further stage in the development of the imperial office, and was a sign of

Gordian III born at Rome — Maximinus commander of recruits on Rhine frontier; Alexander Severus killed; **Maximinus made emperor** M. campaigns in Dacia & Sarmatia (236–237) — **Gordian I & II proclaimed joint emperors: die (Jan); Pupienus & Balbinus joint emperors: M. killed; Gordian III P. & B. killed; Gordian III sole emperor (May 238)** — Persian campaign; Timesitheus dies **Gordian III killed near Circesium;** Philip becomes emperor

225 230 235 240 245

GORDIAN I

Born 158 or 159 place unknown	Antonius Gordianus II, 2nd son name unknown, a daughter Maecia Faustina
Accession early January 238 in Africa	
Wife Fabia Orestilla	Committed suicide late January 238 at Carthage
Children two sons: Marcus	

GORDIAN II

Born c. 192 place unknown	Killed in the defence of Carthage late January 238
Accession early January 238 in Africa	

PUPIENUS

Born c. 164 place unknown	Clodius Pupienus Pulcher Maximus & Marcus Pupienus Africanus, a daughter Pupiena Sextia Paulina Cethegilla
Accession (with Balbinus) early February 238	
Wife name unknown	Murdered by the praetorians at Rome early May 238
Children two sons: Titus	

BALBINUS

Date and place of birth unknown	Wife and children unknown
Accession (with Pupienus) early February 238	Murdered by the praetorians at Rome early May 238

GORDIAN III

Born 20 January 225 at Rome Marcus Antonius Gordianus	renewed annually on 10 December Imperator first on accession, II (239), III (240), IV (241), V & VI (242), VII (243)
Accession to Caesar March 238 Marcus Antonius Gordianus Nobilissimus Caesar, Princeps Iuventutis	Full titles at death Imperator Caesar Marcus Antonius Gordianus Pius Felix Augustus, Pontifex Maximus, Tribuniciae potestatis VII, Imperator VII, Pater Patriae, Consul II, Proconsul
On accession May 238 Imperator Caesar Marcus Antonius Gordianus Pius Felix Augustus, Pontifex Maximus, Pater Patriae, Proconsul	
Consul I (239), II (241)	Wife Tranquillina
Tribunicia potestas first on accession,	Murdered near Circesium in Mesopotamia February 244

things to come. For Maximinus was of less distinguished origin than any of his predecessors: a common soldier, who had risen through the ranks of the Roman army. Furthermore, though born a Roman citizen, he came from Thrace (probably in fact from that part falling within the Roman province of Moesia). This was one of the less respectable parts of the empire, and Maximinus was referred to by several Roman writers as a barbarian. On the other hand, he showed real military ability, strengthened the Rhine and Danube frontiers, and gained the support of the Roman army. The animosity of the senate towards him arose partly from class-prejudice, and partly from the heavy financial contributions which he had to raise to finance his expensive military operations. It was not helped by the fact that he spent his entire three-year reign with the army, never once visiting Rome.

Maximinus's military career began with enlistment in a Thracian auxiliary unit. This would have been around 190. By 232 he was playing a leading role in Alexander Severus's Mesopotamian expedition, and again in the German campaign of 234 when he was placed in charge of new recruits.

Maximinus was acclaimed emperor by the army near Mainz in March 235. His accession was recognized and ratified by the senate – not without reservations – a few days later. Almost immediately a conspiracy arose against him, instigated by a group of prominent senators with the assistance of elements in the army. Maximinus was about to campaign against the Germans and had built a new pontoon bridge across the Rhine. The conspirators planned to wait until he was in enemy territory then cut the bridge of boats, leaving him stranded on the farther shore. As it was, the plot was discovered and those responsible were arrested and executed without trial. A second plot soon afterwards, led by Titus Quartinus, backed by Osrhoenian archers from Syria, was equally swiftly suppressed.

Maximinus eventually crossed the Rhine bridge in the summer of 235, and spent the rest of the year fighting the Germans in the Taunus and Württemberg area. His active participation in military engagements contrasted strongly with Alexander's rather timid approach, and Maximinus was awarded the title 'Germanicus Maximus' for his efforts. He then switched his attention to the Danube frontier, where he waged campaigns against the Dacians and Sarmatians during the two following years.

These military operations met with significant success, but were enormously costly, and Maximinus soon became unpopular with the propertied classes of Rome and the provinces for his confiscations and extortion. While these measures were limited to the rich, the stability of the state was not threatened; but Maximinus went further, taking money from the funds for the poor and the corn dole to finance his expeditions. The frontiers were secured, but by the beginning of 238, the combined weight of the emperor's financial exactions began to generate serious resistance.

Portrait bust, thought to be of Gordian II, from the Capitoline Museum, Rome.

THE ELDERLY PATRICIAN

In height he was characteristically Roman. He was becomingly grey, with an impressive face, more ruddy than fair. His face was fairly broad, his eyes, his countenance, and his brow such as to command respect. His body was somewhat stocky. In character he was temperate and restrained; there is nothing that you can say he ever did passionately, immoderately or excessively.

Life of the Gordians VI.1

The elder Gordian was said to be 80 years old when he was proclaimed emperor in 238. A wealthy man, he was fond of literature, and wrote an account in verse of the lives of Antoninus Pius and Marcus Aurelius, the Antoniniad, in 30 books. High office came to him only late in life: governor of Lower Britain in 216, consul under either Caracalla or Elagabalus, and governor of Africa in 237. His three weeks of imperial fame in January 238 have left no identifiable portraits of either him or his son and co-ruler Gordian II. Both were condemned by Maximinus but deified soon afterwards by the senate under Pupienus and Balbinus.

GORDIAN I & II

Although Gordian declined the offer on the grounds of his old age, he was actually ambitious for power and not reluctant to accept it, partly because he preferred to accept the future danger to the present one, and partly because, being now an extremely old man, he did not find the prospect of a possible death while holding imperial honours such a terrible thing.

Herodian VII.5

The reaction when it came was centred not in Rome or Italy but in the wealthy North African province of Africa Proconsularis (roughly equivalent to modern Tunisia), where the fiscal procurator had shown himself particularly zealous on Maximinus's behalf. Popular feeling against the imperial administration ran high, both among peasant farmers and the rich landowners. It was a group of young aristocrats who in January 238 organized this seething resentment into a plan of action. They ordered their tenants and retainers to gather at Thysdrus (modern El Djem) where the procurator was supervising the revenues from the olive harvest. Choosing a suitable moment the young aristocrats went up to the man and killed him. They then approached the governor of the province, who was also in Thysdrus at the time, and obliged him to don the imperial purple.

The governor in question was Marcus Antonius Gordianus Sempronianus, an old man of 80. Gordian accepted the title of Augustus with some reluctance, but returned from Thysdrus to Carthage, the capital of the province, with all the trappings of imperial office. From there he sent messages to his friends in Rome, where the senate hastened to recognize him as emperor: he was after all one of their own number, a distinguished ex-consul claiming descent from Trajan and the Gracchi, and much preferable in their eyes to the low-born Maximinus. They gave both the aged Gordian and his 46-year-old son (Gordian II) the title

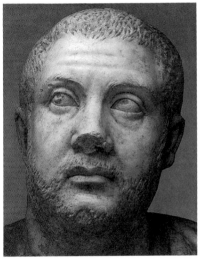

of Augustus, and set about rousing the provinces in support of the pair.

News of these events in Rome reached Maximinus at Sirmium near Belgrade some 10 days later. He at once assembled his army and advanced on Rome, the Pannonian legions leading the way. Meanwhile, however, the Gordian revolt had not gone as planned. The province of Africa Proconsularis where Gordian held sway was bordered on the west by Numidia, whose governor Capellianus nurtured a long-standing grudge against the Gordians. He also controlled the forces of the Third Legion 'Augusta', the only legionary unit in the region, and a substantial body of frontier troops. With these at his back he marched on Carthage and easily overwhelmed the local militias which sought to defend the city. The younger Gordian was killed in the fighting, and when his father heard the news he withdrew into a private room, took off his belt and hanged himself. It was late January; their joint reign had lasted only 20 days.

PUPIENUS & BALBINUS

The untimely end of the Gordian rebellion placed the senate at Rome in great jeopardy. Buoyed up by hopes of victory, they had made their support for the Gordians all too clear, and could expect no mercy from Maximinus when he and his army reached Rome. In this predicament the senators decided to stake all on a desperate gamble. Meeting together in the Temple of Jupiter Optimus Maximus on the Capitol, they determined to defy Maximinus and elect two of their own members as joint emperors, in an arrangement reminiscent of the consuls under the old republic.

The choice fell upon a distinguished pair of ex-consuls, Decius Caelius Calvinus Balbinus and Marcus Clodius Pupienus Maximus. Both were men of advanced years, perhaps in their 70s, who had led distinguished careers, and together they combined much civil and military experience. The senate also appointed a Council of Twenty, the *vigintiviri*, to assist the new emperors in the defence of Italy.

The first obstacle to the senatorial scheme came from the city populace. A crowd had gathered while Pupienus and Balbinus were being elected, and when they heard that the senate had chosen two patricians – men whom the ordinary people held in no great regard – they refused to let the emperors leave the Capitol, but showered the imperial cortège with stones and sticks. They demanded that the new emperor be drawn from the family of the Gordians, who had a strong following among the poorer people of the city. The emperors had no option but to compromise. Accordingly they sent for the 13-year-old grandson of the elder Gordian (his daughter's son) and appointed him Caesar.

The new regime took control of affairs at Rome in the early days of February 238. Maximinus had by this time reached the borders of Italy, and Pupienus gathered what forces he could and set out to oppose him. Maximinus crossed the Alps and was surprised and angry to find that the

In portraits, Pupienus (*top*, Capitoline Museum) is represented as a dour military man, with a long gaunt face, full beard, and hair close-cropped in the military manner. Balbinus, on the other hand is shown relaxed and meditative. One of the finest surviving portraits of Balbinus is found in the reclining figures of him and his wife from the lid of his marble sarcophagus (*above*), which was discovered in fragments near the Via Appia.

(*Left*) Amphitheatre at Thysdrus (modern El Djem in Tunisia), built early in the third century AD from the profits of the olive groves. The Gordian rebellion began at Thysdrus, and the town was severely punished when it collapsed.

Portrait bust of the teenage emperor Gordian III.

city of Aquileia, on the Adriatic coast of northern Italy, closed its gates against him, and refused all offers of an amnesty. A siege was begun, but the defenders fought bravely, and the Council of Twenty blockaded the roads, preventing supplies from reaching the besiegers. One picturesque rumour says that the women of Aquileia sacrificed their hair to make bow strings for the defenders. The Italian divisions in Maximinus's army soon began to tire of this fruitless warfare against their own countrymen. Around the middle of April a plot was formed between soldiers of the praetorian guard (from Rome) and the Second Legion 'Parthica' (whose regular base was in Latium). Making their way to the emperor's tent, they tore down his portrait and killed him. With him perished his 23-year-old son, Gaius Julius Verus Maximus, who had been raised to the rank of Caesar some two years before.

The assassins took the heads of Maximinus and his son to Ravenna, where Pupienus was mustering troops, and then on to Rome. Pupienus disbanded the forces of both sides, sending the legions back to their provinces and taking only the praetorians with him to Rome, together with a guard of German soldiers specially loyal to himself. He arrived back at Rome to an enthusiastic welcome.

But already the two emperors had begun to fall out. Balbinus thought he should take precedence, since he had the more distinguished background; Pupienus, on the other hand, had had a respected military career, and his name comes first in all the inscriptions. These dangerous divisions were particularly ill-timed since the praetorians had never come fully to terms with the new regime and disliked serving under emperors chosen by the senate. At the beginning of May a group of praetorians rushed the palace, seized the two elderly men, and dragged them naked through the streets of Rome. Pupienus and Balbinus were beaten up and mutilated, their hair and eyebrows torn out, and were finally murdered in the praetorian camp. They had reigned a mere 99 days. In their place, the praetorians proclaimed Gordian III emperor of Rome.

GORDIAN III

This was the end of Maximus and Balbinus, a death that was undeserved and desecrated for two respected and distinguished old men, who had come to power through their high birth and by their own merits. Gordian, aged about thirteen, was saluted as emperor and took over the Roman empire.

Herodian VIII.8

With the death of Pupienus and Balbinus we enter upon a confused period of Roman history where we no longer have the testimony of contemporaries such as Cassius Dio and Herodian as our guide but must rely instead on summary accounts compiled during the fourth century and on the highly unreliable and heavily embroidered biographies in the Historia Augusta.

THE YOUNGEST GORDIAN

He was a merry, light-hearted lad, handsome, winning, agreeable to everyone, merry in his life, eminent in letters; in nothing, indeed, save in his age was he unqualified for empire.

Historia Augusta
Life of the Gordians XXXIII

Gordian III was the son not of Gordian II but of the daughter of Gordian I. He was only 13 when he was proclaimed emperor, and only 19 when he died. The outbreak of the Persian War and his premature demise prevented him from carrying out a number of building projects he had planned at Rome, including colonnades on the edges of the Campus Martius and summer baths which were to bear his name. His portraits show a return towards the idealizing style of Alexander Severus, in contrast to the stern realism espoused by Maximinus.

Gordian III's murder by Philip the Arab is only one of the versions of his death. The Persians claimed that they had won a great victory over the Romans at Meshike north-west of Ctesiphon, and that Gordian was killed in the battle.

Gordian III was only 13 years old when the revolt of the praetorians in May 238 raised him to sole emperor. He was not a particular favourite of the soldiers, but he did have the backing of a powerful faction among the senate and people of Rome. Others must have held the reins of power for the young emperor during his earliest years. There is mention of his mother in one source, but true power soon came to rest with Gaius Furius Sabinius Aquila Timesitheus, a conscientious official whom Gordian appointed commander of the praetorian guard. The bond was further strengthened when Gordian married his daughter, Furia Sabinia Tranquillina, early in 241.

Given the events of the previous years it was hardly to be expected that the young Gordian should live out his reign in peace. The first challenge came in 240, when Marcus Asinius Sabinianus, governor of Africa, had himself proclaimed emperor at Carthage. The rebellion was efficiently suppressed by the governor of neighbouring Mauretania. More serious trouble was brewing in the east, however, where in 240 the Persians under crown prince Shapur I succeeded in capturing the desert city of Hatra – a prize which had escaped previous attempts by both Trajan and Septimius Severus.

In 241 Shapur began the anticipated assault on Roman territory and Timesitheus made arrangements for a major eastern expedition. At first all went well. A preliminary operation on the lower Danube pushed back the Goths who had crossed the river and restored the frontier. The Roman forces then proceeded to Syria, where during the course of 243 they defeated the Persians at Rhesaina in northern Mesopotamia and recovered control of Carrhae and Nisibis. But in the midst of the campaign, Timesitheus fell ill and died. He was replaced as praetorian commander by Marcus Iulius Philippus, known as Philip the Arab.

With the death of Timesitheus the heart seems to have gone out of the campaign. Philip used his position not to further the expedition but to undermine Gordian's position and foment mutiny among the troops. Supply difficulties and military reverses were blamed on the young emperor's incompetence, and Philip cleverly manipulated the situation to have himself appointed regent. Gordian, now 19 years old, found his position increasingly intolerable, and in camp near Circesium he called upon the soldiers to choose between himself and Philip. The gamble failed: the soldiers voted for Philip, and Gordian was killed. A monument was raised to him near the spot where he died, on the banks of the Euphrates some 20 miles from Circesium. His remains, however, were brought back for burial to Rome, where the senate proclaimed his deification.

Gordian III cuts a rather sad picture, even among the sorry gallery of third-century emperors. Orphaned in childhood, he seems never to have tasted real power, and the death of his able protector Timesitheus left him at the mercy of whatever factions the army gave ear to. His vain appeal on the hustings to the loyalty of the troops, against the treachery of Philip the Arab, remains the most vivid image of his reign.

Philip the Arab
Imperator Caesar Marcus
Iulius Phillipus Pius Felix
Invictus Augustus
244–249

Decius
Imperator Caesar Gaius
Messius Quintus Traianus
Decius Pius Felix Invictus
Augustus
249–251

Trebonianus Gallus
Imperator Caesar Gaius
Vibius Trebonianus Gallus
Pius Felix Invictus Augustus
253

Aemilius Aemilianus
Imperator Caesar Marcus
Aemilius Aemilianus Pius
Felix Invictus Augustus
253

This famous portrait-bust of Philip the Arab in the Vatican Museum shows the return to a more severe style after the idealized statues of Gordian III and the senatorial dignity of Pupienus. No descriptions of Philip survive, but the bust itself conveys an impression of vivid realism.

PHILIP THE ARAB	
Born c. 204 at Philippopolis in Arabia	Children a son Marcus Julius Phillipus (Junior)
Accession February 244 in Mesopotamia	Killed in battle at Beroea in Macedonia September/October 249
Wife Marcia Otacilia Severa	

PHILIP THE ARAB

The two Philips, son and father, seized power after Gordian had been killed, brought the army back safely and set out for Italy from Sicily. During their reign the thousandth anniversary of the city of Rome was celebrated with games and shows of great magnificence. Both were then killed by the army.

Eutropius *Breviarium* IX. 3

The years 244 to 260 are the most confused and sketchy in the whole history of the Roman empire. No fewer than 16 men were given or

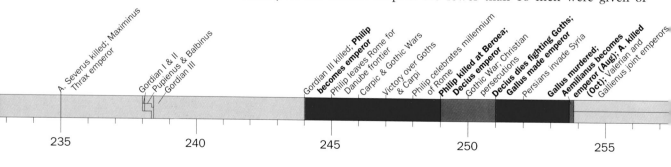

A CHRISTIAN EMPEROR?

Philip made his son Philip his colleague in rule, and was the first of all the Roman emperors who was a Christian.

Jerome *Chronici Canones*

Philip the Arab was a conscientious ruler who governed with the consent, or at least the acquiescence, of the senate. He took steps to stamp out male prostitution, and was tolerant towards the Christians. Later tradition held that Philip himself was a Christian, and had on one occasion done penance in order to be admitted into church to attend an Easter service. The fact that Philip had his father deified suggests that claims for his Christianity are in fact ill-founded, the result of wishful thinking rather than firm evidence. This is borne out by the spectacular pagan games (including gladiatorial shows) which Philip mounted to celebrate the 1000th anniversary of the foundation of Rome; these were hardly the work of a devout early Christian.

claimed the title of Augustus, and none of them died an entirely natural death. Some were killed in battle, others were murdered by their own supporters, and at least one died of plague. The period ends with the Roman empire at its nadir, and a Roman emperor dying in slavery among the Persians.

The first of these short-lived emperors was Philip the Arab, native of a small town in the region known as Trachonitis, in south-western Syria. He had risen through the ranks to become praetorian commander under Gordian III, succeeding the trusty Timesitheus when the latter died towards the end of 243. Later accounts tell us that Philip used his position to undermine Gordian's standing with the troops, eventually manipulating events so that the army chose him as emperor, in preference to Gordian. This was during the Persian campaign, while the army was in camp at Circesium on the Euphrates. The story has it that Philip was loth at first to kill Gordian, but eventually realized that his own reign could never be secure if Gordian was still alive. Perhaps Philip was the beneficiary of a general military uprising, rather than the callous traitor who single-handedly overthrew his master. But, either way, his accession was secured by the murder of the young Gordian.

Philip became emperor early in 244, between January and March. His first concern was to consolidate his hold on power by returning to Rome, and in order to do this he quickly agreed peace terms with the Persian king Shapur. These terms were widely held dishonourable to the Romans: Philip agreed to make a down-payment of 500,000 denarii, in addition to an annual indemnity. Once this was settled, Philip placed his brother Gaius Julius Priscus in overall charge of the eastern provinces and returned to Rome. There he announced that Gordian had died of illness, and organized a state funeral and divine honours for his predecessor.

Little is known of events during the next three years, but Philip seems to have spent much of his time fighting against the Carpi on the Danube frontier. He had made his young son Caesar on his accession in 244, though the lad was then only five or six years old; in July or August of 247 he raised him to the rank of Augustus. Shortly afterwards he celebrated a triumph at Rome for his victories over the Carpi. Philip also built a reservoir at Rome to relieve a chronic water shortage in the western part of the city. But the most famous event at Rome during his reign was the celebration of the 1000th anniversary of the founding of the city, marked by a magnificent series of games from 21 to 23 April 248.

At around the same time as Philip was celebrating the anniversary of Rome there was an uprising on the Danube frontier, where the legions of Moesia and Pannonia declared their commander Tiberius Claudius Marinus Pacatianus emperor. Coins bearing his name and the legend 'Victory of the emperors' suggest he sought some accommodation with Philip, but if so it was in vain since within a short time he was killed by the soldiers. This same year a second uprising broke out in the east, where the harsh rule and financial exactions of Priscus were spreading disaffection; here one Iotapianus was proclaimed emperor in a rebellion which was not finally stamped out until the summer of 249. Two other abortive rebellions during Philip's reign are known from coins alone: one led by Silbannacus on the Rhine, the other by Sponsianus on the Danube.

It was in a move to ensure the loyalty of the Danube legions and repel an incursion by the Goths that Philip in 249 despatched a respected senator, Quintus Decius Valerinus, to be governor of the provinces of Moesia and Pannonia. This was a dangerous and perhaps foolhardy appointment, since it placed several legions under the command of one man. Furthermore, these were legions that had already shown they wished for a change of emperor. The outcome should have been foreseen: Decius was successful against the Goths, but was then coaxed by the soldiers into accepting the imperial nomination himself. Decius and his legions marched on Rome, and in September or October 249 the two sides confronted each other at Beroea in Macedonia. Philip was defeated and killed in the battle; as soon as the news reached Rome, his son too was murdered in the camp of the praetorian guard.

DECIUS

The Decii, while pursuing the barbarians across the Danube, died through treachery at Abrittus after reigning two years. But very many report that the son had fallen in battle while pressing an attack too boldly; that the father however, had strenuously asserted that the loss of one soldier seemed to him too little to matter. And so he resumed the

THE BURDEN OF EMPIRE

Decius was therefore clothed in purple and forced to undertake the government, despite his reluctance and unwillingness.

Zosimus *New History* I.22

Though originating from one of the Danube provinces, Decius was a staunch upholder of the old Roman order, and married Herennia Etruscilla, a member of the Italian aristocracy. A marble head from Rome conveys an impression of anxiety and weariness, as of a man shouldering heavy responsibilities. Decius's death in battle has been taken as evidence of military incompetence, but one tradition holds that he was betrayed by his successor Trebonianus Gallus, who was in secret alliance with the Goths.

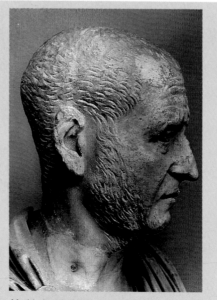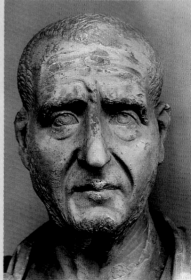

Marble head of the emperor Decius, from the Capitoline Museum, Rome.

The Goths, a powerful Germanic people, first appear on the scene as enemies of Rome in the 230s. Later tradition placed their ancestral homeland in southern Sweden, but by the early third century AD they had moved south to settle the lands north of the Black Sea. In 238 they crossed the Danube to raid the Balkan provinces of the Roman empire, and from 248 launched a sustained series of attacks, culminating in the defeat and death of the emperor Decius in 251. In 256 and again in 267 they ravaged north-west Asia Minor. They were eventually brought to heel by Claudius 'Gothicus' a few years later, and subsequently they split into two parts, the Ostrogoths remaining in the Black Sea region, the Visigoths occupying the abandoned Roman province of Dacia. But this was not the last the Romans were to hear of the Goths: for it was the Visigoths led by Alaric who sacked Rome in the fateful year 410.

The Gothic invasions were however only one of the Germanic peoples who breached the Roman frontier in the middle decades of the third century. In the west a major Germanic confederation known as the Alemanni raided Gaul and Italy (and were joined by a Frankish warband which sacked Tarraco in Spain). Sarmatians and Juthungi, too, had to be fought off on several occasions.

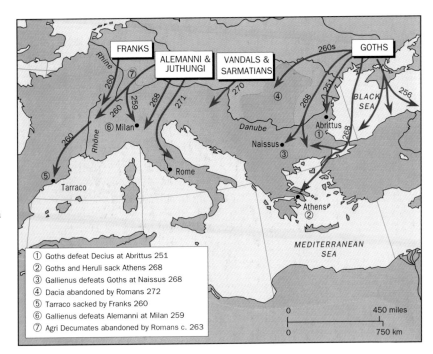

① Goths defeat Decius at Abrittus 251
② Goths and Heruli sack Athens 268
③ Gallienus defeats Goths at Naissus 268
④ Dacia abandoned by Romans 272
⑤ Tarraco sacked by Franks 260
⑥ Gallienus defeats Alemanni at Milan 259
⑦ Agri Decumates abandoned by Romans c. 263

war and died in a similar manner while fighting vigorously.

Aurelius Victor *Book of the Caesars* 29

The emperor who replaced Philip the Arab, Quintus Decius Valerinus, was the first of a long and distinguished line of Roman emperors to come from the Balkans. He had been born at Budalia, near Sirmium, in around 190. Far from being a military upstart in the fashion of Maximinus or Philip, Decius was a distinguished senator who had served as consul in 232 and had been governor of Moesia and Lower Germany immediately afterwards, governor of Hispania Tarraconensis 235–8, and urban prefect at Rome during the early reign of Philip the Arab.

After Philip's death at Beroea in late 249, Decius proceeded south to Rome and stayed there for several months, consolidating his hold on power. He adopted the surname 'Traianus' in memory of one of the greatest Roman emperors of the previous century. He also undertook a number of building projects in the capital, including the Thermae Decianae or Baths of Decius on the Aventine, completed in 252 and still surviving in the 16th century to be planned by Palladio. Alongside his work on new buildings Decius also repaired the Colosseum, which had been struck by lightning again.

In 250 the emperor embarked on a campaign against the Goths, who had once again crossed the Danube and were ravaging the province of Thrace. They had allied themselves with the governor of Thrace, Titus Julius Priscus, who declared himself emperor in opposition to Decius, but was killed soon afterwards. The war against the Goths continued in 251, when Decius, campaigning on the Lower Danube, received news of yet another would-be usurper. This was Iulius Valens Licinianus, at

DECIUS

Born c. 190 at Budalia near Sirmium	Herrenius Decius & Gaius Valens Hostilianus
Accession September/October 249	*Killed in battle against the Goths at Abrittus in Moesia June 251*
Wife Herannia Etruscilla	
Children two sons: Quintus	

Rome, who had support among the senate and people of the capital. By the end of March, however, Valens too was dead. But Decius was not destined to survive the year. He had had some success against the Goths and was endeavouring to cut off their retreat at Abrittus, just south of the Lower Danube, in June 251 when his army fell into a trap. Decius was killed, the first emperor to die in battle against a foreign enemy. With him perished his elder son Quintus Herennius Etruscus Messius Decius who had been raised to the rank of Caesar the previous year.

It was a glorious end to a short but honourable reign. For later generations, however, Decius was a villain rather than a hero, because of his persecution of the Christians. The background is clouded by uncertainty over the allegation in the History of Eusebius of Caesarea that Philip the Arab had himself been a Christian. If that were true, then Decius's persecution could be seen as a reaction against the previous regime. The persecution of 249–51 arose directly from an imperial edict obliging all citizens of the empire to make pagan sacrifice for the emperor's well-being by a specified date. Those who did not do so risked torture and execution. The edict was not aimed specifically against Christians; it did not single them out for particular attention, but was conceived as an oath of allegiance to the emperor and the Roman state. A number of Christians refused to sacrifice and were killed, among them Pope Fabianus at Rome. Anti-Christian feeling led to pogroms at Carthage and Alexandria. But already by the second year of Decius's reign the ferocity of the persecution had eased off, and the earlier tradition of religious tolerance had begun to reassert itself. Brief though it was, however, the Christian church did not easily forget the reign of Decius, that 'fierce tyrant'.

TREBONIANUS GALLUS	
Born c. 206 Perugia	Volusianus and a daughter Vibia Galla
Accession June 251	
	Murdered by his own soldiers at Interamna August 253
Wife	
Afinia Gemina Baebiana	
Children	
a son Gaius Vibius	

TREBONIANUS GALLUS

Since those in power were quite unable to defend the empire and were concerned only for Rome, the Goths, Borani, Urugundi, and Carpi immediately plundered the cities of Europe.

Zosimus *New History* I.26

On the death of Decius and his son in battle against the Goths in June 251 the defeated Roman army chose Gaius Vibius Trebonianus Gallus as emperor. Gallus was an Italian, born in Perugia in around 206. He was a senator, had served as consul, and as governor of Upper Moesia from 250 had played a leading role in Decius's Danube wars. There were those who claimed that Gallus had been privy to the trap laid by the Goths in which Decius was killed, though this is probably later invention. Indeed, whether through his own wishes or under pressure from the troops he adopted Decius's surviving younger son Gaius Valens Hostilianus Messius Quintus, whom Decius had left at Rome. Hostilianus, too young to rule in his own name, was proclaimed joint emperor, while Gallus's son Gaius Vibius Volusianus was given the rank of Caesar.

Head of colossal bronze statue, possibly of Trebonianus Gallus, found near the Lateran at Rome; now in the Metropolitan Museum, New York.

It was to prove a troubled reign, beset by the Goths, the Persians and the plague. Eager to make his appearance at Rome, Gallus made peace with the Goths, allowing them to retain the booty and Roman captives they had taken, and agreeing to pay them an annual tribute. He returned to Rome, where he found the city in the grip of the plague. One of the early casualties was his adopted son Hostilianus, who died in around July of 251. In his place, Gallus raised his own son Volusianus to the rank of emperor.

Gallus won the affections of the people of Rome by taking steps to ensure proper burial for even the poorest victims of the plague. But this disaster was coupled with serious setbacks on both the northern and eastern frontiers. In the east, the Persian king Shapur I in 252 launched a new expedition against the Roman provinces. At Barbalissos (modern Qal'at Balis) he defeated the eastern legions and overran the entire province of Syria. Antioch, third city of the Roman world and capital of Syria, fell to the Persians the following year. Meanwhile on the lower Danube the Goths had soon broken their agreement with Gallus and were once again ravaging Roman territory. They were defeated by Aemilius Aemilianus, governor of Upper Moesia, who was at once proclaimed emperor by the legions he had led to victory.

Gallus and his son hurriedly mustered their troops to meet the expected invasion of Italy, but were taken by surprise at the speed of Aemilianus's approach. They had reached Interamna (modern Terni), 50 miles north of Rome, when the pair of them were murdered by the soldiers. The date was August 253; Gallus had reigned just over two years.

AEMILIUS AEMILIANUS	
Born c. 207 at Jerba in Africa	Supera
	Children none known
Accession August 253	
	Murdered by his own soldiers near Spoleto October 253
Wife Gaia Cornelia	

AEMILIUS AEMILIANUS

Aemilianus came from an extremely insignificant family, his reign was even more insignificant, and he was slain in the third month.

Eutropius *Breviarium ab Urbe Condita* IX.6

Thus power passed briefly to Marcus Aemilius Aemilianus. The new emperor was about the same age as Gallus, having been born in around 207. He too was a senator and ex-consul, though he came not from Italy but from the island of Jerba off the coast of southern Tunisia. Aemilianus is said to have ruled with moderation and with the support of the senate, presenting himself as their general rather than their overlord. But he failed to retain the support of the troops when a new contender appeared on the scene. Publius Licinius Valerianus had been entrusted by Gallus with the raising of troops for a campaign on the Upper Danube. When he learned of Gallus's murder he had himself proclaimed emperor, and marched on Italy with the forces he had assembled. In a re-run of events three months earlier, direct confrontation was avoided when Aemilianus was killed by his own army near Spoleto in October 253, after a reign of only 88 days. The place where he died was known ever afterwards as the Pons Sanguinarius, the Bridge of Blood.

Valerian
Imperator Caesar Publius
Licinius Valerianus Pius Felix
Invictus Augustus
253–260

Gallienus
Imperator Caesar Publius
Licinius Egnatius Gallienus
Pius Felix Invictus Augustus
253–268

Claudius II
Imperator Caesar Marcus
Aurelius Claudius Pius Felix
Invictus Augustus
268–270

Quintillus
Imperator Caesar Marcus
Aurelius Claudius Quintillus
Invictus Pius Felix Augustus
270

Aurelian
Imperator Caesar Lucius
Domitius Aurelianus Pius
Felix Invictus Augustus
270–275

THE GALLIC EMPIRE

Postumus
Imperator Caesar Marcus
Cassianius Latinius Postumus
Pius Felix Invictus Augustus
260–269

Laelianus
Imperator Caesar Gaius
Ulpius Cornelius Laelianus
Pius Felix Augustus
269

Marius
Imperator Caesar Marcus
Aurelieus Marius Pius Felix
Augustus
269

Victorinus
Imperator Caesar Marcus
Piavonius Victorinus Pius Felix
Invictus Augustus
269–271

Tetricus
Imperator Caesar Gaius Pius
Esuvius Tetricus Pius Felix
Invictus Augustus
271–274

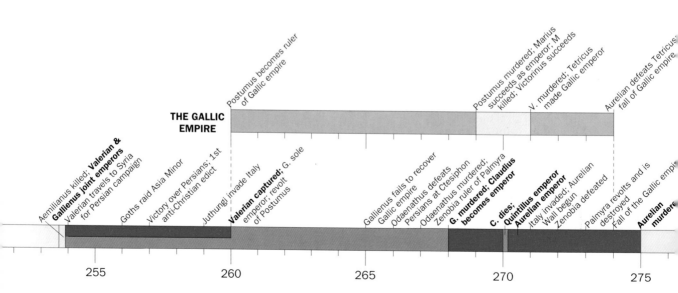

<table>
<tr><td colspan="2" align="center">VALERIAN</td></tr>
<tr><td>Born c. 195 place unknown</td><td>Licinius Egnatius Gallienus and Publius Licinius Valerianus</td></tr>
<tr><td>Accession October 253</td><td rowspan="2">Captured by the Persians June 260; died in captivity (date unknown)</td></tr>
<tr><td>Wife
Egnatia Mariniana</td></tr>
<tr><td>Children
two sons: Publius</td><td></td></tr>
</table>

This is all that is worthy of being known about Valerian, whose life, praiseworthy for sixty years long, finally rose to such glory, that after holding all honours and offices with great distinction he was chosen emperor, not, as often happens, in a riotous assemblage of the people or by the shouting of soldiers, but solely by right of his services, and, as it were, by the single voice of the entire world.

Historia Augusta *Life of Valerian* V

The emperor Valerian was born in about 195, a scion of the distinguished Licinia family of Etruria. Little certain is known of his background, though he served as consul in the 230s and became a leading supporter of the Gordian rebellion in 238. He held high office under later emperors, being entrusted with a major military command by Gallus just before the latter's death. Valerian's reputation as emperor is overshadowed by the ignominy of his end. His seven years in the east failed to halt the Persian advance, but he did achieve some temporary successes and disaster struck only when his army was ravaged by plague. The date of Valerian's death is uncertain; his capture by the Persians can probably be dated to June 260, and he may still have been alive two years later.
(*Below*) Fourth-century cameo showing Shapur's victory over Valerian. Now in the Bibliothèque Nationale, Paris.

VALERIAN

With the death of Aemilianus, Publius Licinius Valerianus became undisputed ruler of the Roman world. He made his way to Rome and set about the awesome task of bringing order to the empire. For the civil wars of 253 had exacerbated the already fragile situation on both the northern and eastern frontiers, by drawing away troops to fight battles in Italy. Valerian was at least an emperor whom the senate could accept without reservation – an ex-consul from one of the most distinguished old Roman families – and they had no difficulty in elevating his elder son Publius Licinius Egnatius Gallienus to joint rule almost immediately on their arrival in the capital in October 253. Valerian himself was 58; his son 40; the plan was to make use of their combined abilities by entrusting Gallienus with the defence of the west while Valerian took charge in the east.

Valerian's first priority was to restore the situation in Syria, where many leading cities, including Antioch, had been sacked during the Persian invasion of Shapur I. The emperor arrived in Antioch (already probably abandoned by Persian forces) in 254, and spent his remaining years in the east. One of his first acts was to suppress the rebellion of Uranius Antoninus, priest-king of Emesa, who had defeated the Persian force attacking his city and declared himself emperor on the strength of this success. Valerian was rewarded for his work in restoring some measure of order to the eastern provinces by the titles 'Restorer of the Orient' and 'Restorer of the Human Race'.

Valerian campaigned against the Persians during the following years, though little is known of the details. A victory in 257 was commemorated on coins and considered sufficient to justify the title 'Restorer of the World'. Meanwhile Gallienus was winning victories against the Germans in the west. But, alas, the run of successes did not continue. In the early summer of 260 Valerian's army, facing a renewed Persian onslaught, was decimated by plague and besieged by the Persians at Edessa. The emperor attempted to extricate his forces by negotiation, but foolishly acceded to Shapur's demands to come before him in person, accompanied by only a small retinue. When they arrived the ruthless Shapur seized the entire party, which included not only Valerian but also the praetorian commander and other high-ranking officials and senators. Valerian was never released, and ended his days as a slave. Though now a relatively old man, he was forced to crouch down so that Shapur could step on his back when mounting his horse. When at length he died, his skin was removed, dyed with vermilion, and placed in a Persian temple where it could be shown in later years to visiting Roman delegations as a dire warning.

For early Christian writers, this ignominious end was clear evidence of the wrath of God, for Valerian, like Decius before him, was a noted persecutor of Christians. Decius, however, had legislated only against those who refused to make the pagan oath of

He went out in public adorned with the radiate crown, and at Rome – where the emperors always appeared in the toga – he appeared in a purple cloak with jewelled and golden clasps.

Historia Augusta *Life of Gallienus* XVI

The Historia Augusta suggests that Gallienus's reign marked a further step towards the portrayal of the emperor as an absolute monarch, arrayed in public with imperial cloak and crown. The man himself, however, was both an able military commander and a cultured poet. He kept strict control over the army, punishing indiscipline with great severity, but was careful also to woo its allegiance. Gallienus minted special gold coins known as 'multipla' for the soldiers' pay in place of the increasingly debased silver coinage.

(*Above*) Portrait bust of the emperor Gallienus now in the Staatliche Museen, Berlin.

GALLIENUS	
Born c. 213 place unknown	Valerianus, Licinius Saloninus and Licinius Egnatius Marinianus
Accession October 253 (jointly with Valerian); sole rule from June 260	
	Murdered in camp outside Milan September 268, buried in a tomb on the Via Appia
Wife Cornelia Salonina	
Children three sons: Licinius	

loyalty. Valerian, by contrast, aimed his twin edicts of 257 and 258 specifically against Christians, and the church hierarchy and knights and senators in particular, in a systematic attempt to eradicate Christianity from the upper echelons of Roman society. It can be seen as a reaction to the successive calamities which afflicted the empire at this time: war, famine, and above all the plague. Valerian's reign was the most troubled and unhappy since the foundation of the Roman empire, and his capture by the Persians came close to bringing the whole edifice to its knees.

GALLIENUS

Gallienus, although he had been made Augustus as quite a young man, at first governed the empire successfully, afterwards appropriately, but at the end disastrously.

Eutropius *Breviarium* IX.8

The capture of Valerian led to a crisis in the empire which his son Gallienus – now sole emperor – needed all his determination and courage to overcome. Gallienus gets a bad press in many of the sources; after an initial period of action he is said to have abandoned himself to luxury and to have become besotted with Pipa, daughter of the Germanic chieftain Attalus. The truth is far different, and shows us an embattled emperor struggling valiantly to maintain his own position and restore a measure of order to the shattered empire. Furthermore, Gallienus showed himself a patron of the arts, and revoked the anti-Christian edicts of his father Valerian, introducing a period of religious toleration which lasted for over 40 years.

Previous decades had shown that the dangers facing the peace and unity of the empire were twofold: external invasion and internal division. Gallienus had to face both in extreme measure. At least seven others claimed the imperial power during the troubled years 260–262, not to mention the dynasty of Palmyrene rulers who assumed control of the eastern provinces. The Historia Augusta calls the reign of Gallienus the period of the twenty pretenders, and though the number is inflated, it captures the spirit of the times well enough.

Publius Licinius Egnatius Gallienus was around 40 years old when his father Valerian became emperor in 253. He himself was named Caesar at the same time, but within a month he had been raised to the rank of Augustus and joint ruler. The following year, when his father left Rome to counter the Persian menace, he handed to Gallienus responsibility for the western provinces. The two never met again.

The troubled years 254–262

While Valerian campaigned in the east, Gallienus sought to defend the Rhine and Danube frontiers against attacks by the Germans. From 254 to 256 he concentrated on the Danube, then when that frontier was

SOLDIER AND POET

Gallienus's interest in poetry, literature and the arts comes as something of a surprise in a period of plague, civil war and foreign invasion. The literary side of his character showed itself in numerous poems and speeches, including the following lines composed for a family wedding:

*Ite, agiter, o pueri, pariter sudate medullis
omnibus inter vos, non murmura vestra columbae,
brachia non hederae, non vincant oscula conchae.
Ludite: sed vigiles nolite extinguere lychnos.
Omnia nocte vident, nil cras meminere lucernae.*

'Come now, my children, grow heated together in deep-seated passion
Never, indeed, may the doves outdo your billings and cooings,
Never the ivy your arms, or the clinging of sea-shells your kisses.
Enjoy yourselves: but don't turn out the watchful lamps.
At night they see everything, but oil lamps remember nothing tomorrow.'

Even the acidulous Historia Augusta concedes that his literary accomplishments made him 'illustrious among both the poets and the rhetoricians of his own time'. Gallienus also gave support to Plotinus, the last great pagan philosopher, and encouraged a new style of sculpture which harked back to the classicism of the Augustan age.

secure he moved west to the Rhine. That his efforts met with success can be seen from the fact that he was granted the title of 'Germanicus Maximus' five times between 255 and 258, and 'Dacicus Maximus' in 257; German victories were also recorded on the coins. In 258 he returned to the Danube frontier. There his eldest son, the younger Valerian, who had been given the rank of Caesar two years before, died early in 258. Gallienus was probably still operating on the middle Danube when trouble broke out once again further west. In 259 the Juthungi crossed the Upper Danube and descended upon Italy. They advanced towards Rome, but were turned back by a hastily assembled army, and then intercepted by Gallienus who hurried back to Italy and decisively defeated them at Milan. The following spring they were defeated again near Augsburg and thousands of Italian captives freed.

By the autumn of 260, Valerian's capture had become general knowledge and to many it seemed that with Gallienus so weakened the imperial power was there for the taking. One of the first to take advantage of the situation was Ingenuus, governor of Pannonia and Moesia. He was proclaimed emperor at Sirmium by the troops left under his command, but was defeated soon afterwards at Mursa (modern Osijek) in Pannonia by Gallienus's general Aureolus. Ingenuus fled from the battlefield but was killed by his own supporters. The banner of rebellion in the Danube provinces was then taken up by Regalianus, but was quickly stamped out again by prompt action from Gallienus.

Late in 260 a more serious uprising broke out in the eastern provinces, where Fulvius Iunius Macrianus and his younger brother Fulvius Iunius Quietus were proclaimed joint emperors. They made Antioch their capital and won widespread recognition in Syria, Egypt and Asia Minor. Macrianus and his father (also Macrianus) marched against Gallienus but were defeated and killed in the Balkans by Aureolus in 261. Quietus, who had remained in Syria, was murdered by the people of Emesa, the city where he had taken refuge, at the instigation of Odaenathus, ruler of Palmyra, acting on the orders of Gallienus. Thus ended the rebellion of the Macriani. But Gallienus's troubles were not over, since the following year Aureolus rose in revolt. He was induced to make peace with his master Gallienus, and the threat of yet another civil war receded, but Aureolus's ambitions were yet to play a part in the final act of Gallienus's reign.

The revolt of Postumus

Gallienus managed to retain control of the Danube army despite these vicissitudes, but he was less successful with the Rhine army and the eastern provinces. While one group of Alemanni invaded Italy in the summer of 260, another party ravaged Gaul, and a Frankish war-band struck as far west as Spain, destroying the city of Tarragona. Gallienus could provide no immediate assistance to the terrified provincials, nor could Saloninus, his second son, whom he had left in control at Colonia Agrippina. It was in these circumstances that Marcus Cassianus

THE GALLIC EMPIRE

The revolt of Postumus, governor of Lower Germany, in the autumn of 260 led to the creation of a Gallic empire which survived as a separate state for almost 15 years. The core of this breakaway empire was formed by the three provinces of Gaul (Lugdunensis, Aquitania and Narbonensis) plus the two Germanies with their powerful frontier forces. By 261, Britain and Spain had also gone over to Postumus. The Gallic empire won support from the people of these regions by concentrating on the defence of the Rhine frontier; neither Postumus nor any of his successors made an attempt to march on Rome. Instead, they recognized the distinctive personality of the western Roman provinces and sought to make this a source of strength. A measure of their success is shown by the way the Gallic empire survived the death of its founder, Postumus; there were in all four Gallic emperors and at least one pretender, before the breakaway realm was reabsorbed into the central Roman empire by Aurelian.

POSTUMUS

Proclaimed emperor by the Rhine legions early in the autumn of 260, after Valerian's capture by the Persians, Postumus was himself of Gallic origin (probably a Batavian), though his age and birthplace are unknown. He set the seal on his rebellion by the capture and execution of Gallienus's son Saloninus at Colonia Agrippina. When it became clear that Postumus had no immediate intention of marching on Rome, Gallienus decided to leave him in peace until he had settled matters on the Danube front. Postumus used this four-year breathing-space to reorganize the administration of his empire, restoring the defences of the Rhine frontier and repairing the damage done by the Frankish and Alemannic invasions of 260. By 265, however, Gallienus had determined to win back the western provinces and with Aureolus commanding the cavalry he marched against Postumus. The expedition achieved some initial success but was abandoned when Gallienus was wounded in the back during a siege. Postumus continued in power for a further four years, outlasting his opponent Gallienus. He took no advantage of Aureolus's defection in 268, refusing to lead his troops into Italy to support the rebel. The failure to seize such a golden opportunity may well have alienated some of Postumus's key supporters, however, and it was probably this which led to his murder early the following year, during the revolt of Laelianus.

LAELIANUS

In February 269 Postumus was at Trier (capital of the Gallic empire) when news came of the rebellion of Laelianus at Mainz. As governor of Upper Germany (under Postumus), Laelianus would have had two legions at his disposal, as against the two legions in Lower Germany which remained loyal to Postumus, not to mention the more distant armies of Spain and Britain. Laelianus's support seems rapidly to have withered, however, and within a couple of months Postumus had defeated the usurper and retaken Mainz. The fate of Laelianus is not recorded, but Postumus himself perished in the aftermath, for he refused to allow his soldiers to pillage the city, and was murdered by them for his refusal.

MARIUS

The man who succeeded Postumus was an unlikely choice for emperor. Marius is said to have been a blacksmith by profession, and was probably only a common soldier at the time of his elevation to power. Some sources give the length of his reign as a mere two days, but the quantity of coins issued in his name makes it likely that he survived at least two or three months. He was strangled as a result of a private quarrel in the summer or autumn of 269.

VICTORINUS

The death of Marius was followed by a two-day interregnum. Power then passed to Victorinus, an able military man who had risen to high office under Postumus and had come perhaps to be regarded as his natural successor. By the middle of 269, however, the fortunes of the Gallic empire were on the wane. Spain refused to recognize Victorinus, and an expeditionary force sent by Claudius II seized control of Gallic territory east of the Rhône. This in turn encouraged the Aedui of central Gaul to rise in revolt against Victorinus. The revolt was finally suppressed in the autumn of 270, when Victorinus succeeded in capturing the city of Autun after a seven-month siege. He might then have been relatively secure, had not his persistent seduction of other men's wives – amounting perhaps to rape – built up smouldering resentment among his entourage. At last he went too far. Early in 271 Victorinus was killed after propositioning the wife of one of his officials.

TETRICUS

The sudden death of Victorinus once again plunged the Gallic

Mosaic floor from the house at Trier owned by Victorinus before he became Gallic emperor. The inscription reads 'Marcus Piaonius Victorinus, tribune of the praetorian guard, restored this at his own expense.' The house it belonged to was large and luxurious, as befitted an officer of his status.

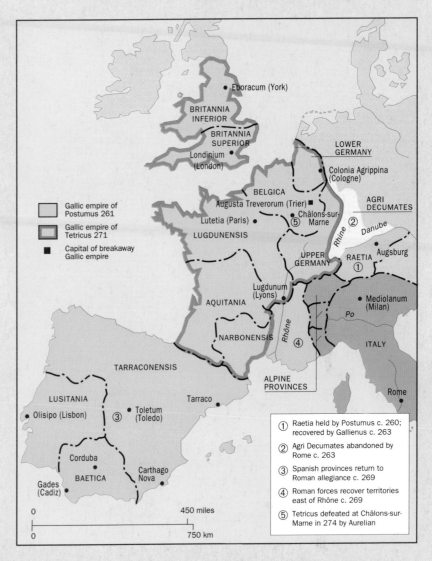

The Gallic empire established by Postumus in 260 survived as a separate state for almost 15 years. The core was formed by the three provinces of Gaul (Lugdunensis, Aquitania and Narbonensis) plus the two Germanies with their powerful frontier forces. By 261, Britain and Spain had also gone over to Postumus, and even Raetia was briefly in his control. Raetia was recovered by Gallienus in c.263, but serious decline set in only after Postumus' murder in 269. In that year the Spanish provinces seceded and the lands east of the Rhône were recaptured by Claudius II. At last in 274 the final Gallic emperor, Tetricus, was defeated by Aurelian at Châlons-sur-Marne and the provinces of Gaul, Britain and Germany were reabsorbed into the Roman empire.

Map labels:

- Eboracum (York)
- BRITANNIA INFERIOR
- BRITANNIA SUPERIOR
- Londinium (London)
- LOWER GERMANY
- Colonia Agrippina (Cologne)
- BELGICA
- Augusta Treverorum (Trier)
- AGRI DECUMATES
- Châlons-sur-Marne
- Lutetia (Paris)
- LUGDUNENSIS
- Rhine
- Danube
- UPPER GERMANY
- RAETIA
- Augsburg
- Lugdunum (Lyons)
- AQUITANIA
- Mediolanum (Milan)
- Po
- NARBONENSIS
- Rhône
- ITALY
- TARRACONENSIS
- ALPINE PROVINCES
- Rome
- LUSITANIA
- Tarraco
- Olisipo (Lisbon)
- Toletum (Toledo)
- Corduba
- Carthago Nova
- Gades (Cadiz)
- BAETICA

Legend:

- Gallic empire of Postumus 261
- Gallic empire of Tetricus 271
- Capital of breakaway Gallic empire

① Raetia held by Postumus c. 260; recovered by Gallienus c. 263
② Agri Decumates abandoned by Rome c. 263
③ Spanish provinces return to Roman allegiance c. 269
④ Roman forces recover territories east of Rhône c. 269
⑤ Tetricus defeated at Châlons-sur-Marne in 274 by Aurelian

0 — 450 miles
0 — 750 km

empire into uncertainty, for there was no natural successor waiting in the wings. The situation was taken in hand by Victoria, mother of Victorinus. This wealthy lady bought the allegiance of the legions with a substantial bribe, and with their support conferred the office of emperor on Tetricus, governor of Aquitania. He was a member of one of the leading families of Gaul, possibly even related to Victoria, and apparently a popular choice.

Tetricus was installed as emperor at Bordeaux in the spring of 271, and then set out for Trier, the imperial capital. Before reaching Trier he took steps to defeat a Germanic invasion, and he fought against the Germans again the following year. There is little doubt that the new emperor was an accomplished and respected military commander. In the spring or summer of 273 he made his son, also called Tetricus, formally heir-apparent, with the rank of Caesar. Father and son were together at Trier early in 274, when Aurelian marched against them. The forces of the Gallic empire took the field to oppose him, but in a hard-fought

battle at Châlons-sur-Marne Aurelian's army gained the upper hand. Tetricus and his son surrendered, and the breakaway provinces of Britain, Gaul and the two Germanies were reunited with the rest of the Roman empire.

The end of the story had a curious twist, for several writers tell us that Tetricus had reached a secret understanding with Aurelian before the battle, and surrendered as soon as the fighting began. It is even said that Tetricus invited Aurelian to invade, beseeching him to rescue him from his political difficulties. Still more surprising is it to find that Aurelian did not execute Tetricus, or even imprison him, but gave him a senior administrative position in southern Italy (governor of Lucania), where he lived into old age. His son, too, was pardoned, and confirmed in his senatorial rank, and many of the high officials who had served under Tetricus were allowed to continue their careers in other parts of the empire. Aurelian's policy was clearly one of pacification rather than repression, and the western provinces were welcomed rather than cajoled back into the fold.

A SHORT-LIVED DYNASTY

Little is known of Gallienus's family beyond the names of his wife and three sons, all of whom died prematurely. Salonina, appointed Augusta and 'Mater castrorum' (mother of the army) in 254, was probably murdered along with Gallienus in 268. At the same time their youngest son Marinianus, only three years old, is thought to have been killed at Rome by order of the senate, along with Gallienus's brother Publius Licinius Valerianus. Their two older sons were already dead: the eldest perished in Illyricum in 258, probably from natural causes; the second son, Saloninus, was murdered by the Gallic usurper Postumus at Colonia Agrippina in 260. In addition to his official family Gallienus had also 'married' or taken as concubine a certain Pipa, daughter of Attalus, king of the Marcommani. This arrangement was part of a treaty by which Gallienus ceded Roman territory to Attalus in return for his assistance against other Germanic invaders.

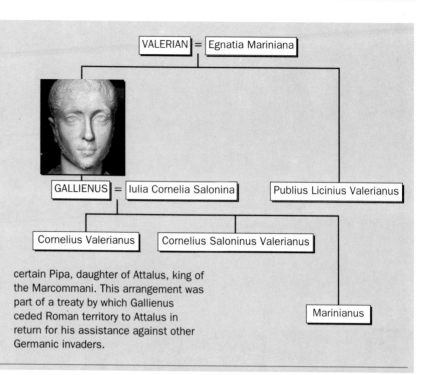

Latinius Postumus, the governor of Lower Germany, defeated one of the raiding parties and made a bid for power on the strength of this success. He was proclaimed emperor by the soldiers, and marched to Colonia Agrippina, where Saloninus, though still a young boy, had recently been made Augustus. Postumus laid siege to the city and refused to desist until Saloninus and his guardian Silvanus were handed over to him. Once they were in his power he immediately put them to death.

Postumus cleared the western provinces of the empire of foreign invaders and re-established the Rhine frontier. By the end of 261 he was recognized as emperor in Gaul, Britain and Spain. He made it plain to Gallienus that he was satisfied with these territories and had no intention of attacking Rome. Initially, indeed, Gallienus could do little about the breakaway provinces. Once some measure of order had been restored to the rest of the empire, however, Gallienus made his preparations and marched against Postumus in the spring of 265. Gallienus advanced deep into Gaul, but was unable to bring matters to a decisive conclusion. Postumus avoided a pitched battle, and Gallienus himself had to break off the campaign when he was wounded in the back by an arrow while besieging Postumus in a city where he had taken refuge. Postumus was left in undisturbed possession of his Gallic empire throughout the remaining years of Gallienus's rule.

The Palmyrene alliance

While Gallienus was dealing with pretenders on the Danube and secessionists in Gaul, events in the east had taken an unexpected turn. The capture of Valerian gave the Persian king Shapur a second chance to

THE AGE OF PRETENDERS

Now let us pass on to the twenty pretenders, who arose in the time of Gallienus because of contempt for the evil prince.

Historia Augusta *Life of Gallienus* XXI

The author of the Historia Augusta speaks here of 20 rival emperors, and confusingly devotes the following book to the Thirty Tyrants who appeared during the reigns of Valerian and Gallienus. The blame is laid largely on the shoulders of Gallienus, described here as an 'evil prince' and given no praise for his efforts to restore order to the empire. Twenty pretenders is in any case an exaggeration; the serious contenders numbered only seven:

Ingenuus: governor of Pannonia and Moesia, acclaimed emperor by the soldiers at Sirmium after the capture of Valerian in the summer of 260.

Defeated in battle at Mursa the same year by Gallienus's general Aureolus and killed during flight.

Regalianus: acclaimed emperor by the remnants of Ingenuus's forces in Moesia after the latter's defeat in 260. Victory over the Sarmatians was followed by defeat by Gallienus; after which Regalianus was killed by his own soldiers (260 or early 261).

Macrianus: acclaimed emperor by the soldiers in Syria in 260, together with his younger brother Quietus. Marched against Rome but defeated and killed in battle in Illyricum by Aureolus in spring of 261.

Quietus: acclaimed emperor with Macrianus in 260. Took refuge at Emesa after the latter's defeat in 261 but besieged by Odaenathus of Palmyra and killed by the Emesenes.

Mussius Aemilianus: governor of Egypt, acclaimed emperor after the downfall of Macrianus and Quietus in 261. Defeated by Gallienus's general Theodotus early in 262 and executed.

Aureolus: commander of Gallienus's forces in victories over Ingenuus in 260 and Macrianus in 261; rebelled in 262 but was reconciled with Gallienus. Cavalry commander in campaign against Postumus in 265; stationed at Milan to defend Alpine passes against Postumus in 268 but defected and declared himself emperor a second time in August 268. Killed at Milan by the soldiers of Claudius II the following month.

Postumus: governor of Lower Germany, acclaimed emperor in 260; by 261, ruler of Gaul, Britain and Spain. Successfully resisted attack by Gallienus in 265, but was murdered by his own soldiers at Mainz in 269.

overrun the eastern provinces of the Roman empire, as he had done seven years before. Antioch fell to the Persians once again, and there was widespread killing and destruction. But the Persian invasion did not end in victory, nor were they able to take permanent possession of any of the territories they ravaged. The first check to their ambitions came from Ballista, whom Valerian had appointed commander of the praetorian guard. Rallying the Roman forces, Ballista defeated the Persians in Cilicia and captured Shapur's harem. The Persians hastily withdrew across the Euphrates, but were then attacked by Odaenathus of Palmyra, who acting as an ally of Rome reoccupied the province of Mesopotamia.

The following year, 261, Odaenathus performed another important service for Gallienus, suppressing the rebellion of Quietus at Emesa. Quietus had risen in support of his father and brother, the two Macriani, who had staged a bid for power in the Balkans. Gallienus rewarded Odaenathus with the titles 'Ruler of the Romans' and 'Governor of the East'. Odaenathus neither claimed nor was given the rank of joint-Augustus, but it was clear where real power in the eastern provinces now lay. Odaenathus's finest hour came in 266 when, still fighting against the Persians, he advanced deep into Mesopotamia and defeated the Persians at Ctesiphon. The following year he extended his field of interest still further, advancing into northern Asia Minor to check a Gothic invasion. It was on his return from this success, in the autumn of 267, that he fell victim to a domestic quarrel and was murdered. Some placed the blame for this at the door of Gallienus, fearful of the enormous power of his Palmyrene ally. If so, the move was a failure. The Palmyrenes easily defeated the Roman general whom Gallienus sent

PALMYRA

The oasis-city of Palmyra in the desert country between Syria and Mesopotamia rose to wealth and prominence as an important trading emporium in the first century BC. Early the following century it fell within the sphere of Roman control, but the city retained some measure of autonomy and in the troubled decades of the mid-third century, Palmyra emerged as a major power in its own right. Control of the city passed to Septimius Odaenathus, leader of the most powerful of the four Palmyrene tribes. Odaenathus became the uncrowned king of Palmyra and was invested by Gallienus with authority over the eastern provinces of the empire, campaigning successfully against the Persians until his murder in 267. He was succeeded by his wife, the famous Zenobia, and their son Vaballathus, who ruled Palmyra until they were captured by the emperor Aurelian in 272. The city itself was sacked by the Romans the following year and thereafter declined into obscurity.

(Left) Temple of Bel at Palmyra in Syria, dedicated in AD 32. View across the vast rectangular precinct towards the shrine itself, a tall rectangular colonnaded structure. The architecture follows Graeco-Roman models, but details such as the pointed cornice are distincively eastern.

(Right) The Palmyrene empire at its greatest extent, and Aurelian's campaign of 272.

(Bottom left) Colonnaded street, one of the most striking features of Palmyra today, begun in the first century, added to in the second and third, the final section left incomplete at Zenobia's fall. Brackets half way up held statues of Palmyrene notables.

(Below) Theatre at Palmyra, second century AD, showing screen wall at back of the stage with the richly carved detail typical of Palmyrene architecture.

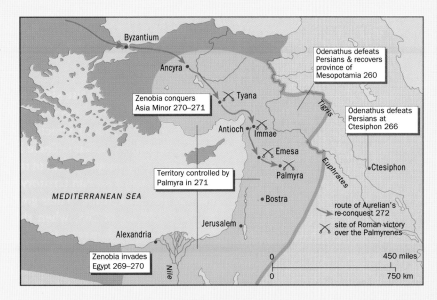

Byzantium

Ancyra

Zenobia conquers
Asia Minor 270–271

Tyana

Antioch

Immae

Odenathus defeats
Persians & recovers
province of
Mesopotamia 260

Odenathus defeats
Persians at
Ctesiphon 266

Tigris

Emesa

Palmyra

Ctesiphon

Euphrates

Territory controlled by
Palmyra in 271

MEDITERRANEAN SEA

Bostra

route of Aurelian's
re-conquest 272

Jerusalem

site of Roman victory
over the Palmyrenes

Alexandria

Nile

Zenobia invades
Egypt 269–270

0   450 miles

0   750 km

ZENOBIA

Her face was dark and of a swarthy hue, her eyes were black and powerful beyond the usual wont . . . and her beauty incredible.

The Thirty Tyrants XXX

Zenobia was the second wife of Odaenathus of Palmyra who became virtual ruler of the eastern provinces of the empire following Valerian's capture by the Persians in 260. In Palmyrene inscriptions she is named Bat-Zabbai, daughter of Al-Zabba, which means (perhaps in reference to her mother) 'one with beautiful long hair'. When Odaenathus was killed in 267, Zenobia took control of affairs as regent for her young son Vaballathus. She was renowned for her intellect and for her chastity. No shrinking violet, she loved hunting, and would sit drinking with her generals and with foreign emissaries. She inherited Odaenathus's position as ruler of the east, with the acquiescence first of Gallienus and then of Claudius II. Not content with this, she broke with Rome in 270, invading Egypt and spreading her power across most of Asia Minor. Early in 272 she had her son Vaballathus (then only in his teens) proclaimed emperor, with the full Roman titles: 'Imperator Caesar Lucius Iulius Aurelius Septimius Vaballathus Athenodorus Pius Felix Invictus Augustus'. Zenobia became 'Augusta'. Within a few months, however, she had been defeated by Aurelian and taken prisoner. Her ultimate fate is uncertain, but according to one story she was the star exhibit at Aurelian's triumph at Rome in autumn 274, and lived out the rest of her days in honourable confinement in a villa at Tivoli.

against them the following year, and control of the east passed to the redoubtable Zenobia, widow of Odaenathus, and their young son Vaballathus.

The Gothic War and the siege of Milan

The Gothic invasion of 268 was the last great catastrophe of Gallienus's reign. It was this, indeed, which prevented him taking any further action against Postumus in Gaul. There had been continual pressure from the Goths and other peoples north of the Danube frontier earlier in the reign: they had attacked Roman territory in 256 and again in 262–3, and in 267 had ravaged Asia Minor. Their greatest assault, however, was launched at the beginning of 268, when they staged a massive invasion of the Balkans in which they were joined by another Germanic people from the Black Sea region, the Heruli. Gallienus advanced against them, and though he was too late to prevent the sacking of Athens, defeated the invaders in a great battle at Naissus.

Gallienus was prevented from following up his victory at the Naissus by news of a serious rebellion at Milan. He had left the cavalry commander Aureolus in charge there, to head off any attack on Italy by Postumus while Gallienus was occupied with events in the Balkans. Early in 268, however, Aureolus defected to Postumus, and by the summer had declared himself emperor. Leaving the conduct of the Gothic War to his generals, Gallienus returned to Italy in September 268, defeated Aureolus at Pontirolo and laid siege to him at Milan. Before Gallienus could bring the affair to a successful conclusion, however, he fell victim to a conspiracy among his officers. One night after dark a messenger arrived with false information that the enemy were attacking. Disturbed by the news, Gallienus hurried from his tent without his usual bodyguard. Unprotected, he was struck down by the commander of his Dalmatian cavalry, the new mobile striking force which he himself had created as part of his army reforms.

Thus perished one of the most maligned and heroic of Roman emperors. Gallienus was buried not in a grand imperial mausoleum but in a tomb on the Via Appia, nine miles south of Rome. His successor Claudius secured him divine honours from the senate, but could not prevent a number of his inscriptions being defaced. For Gallienus had lost the goodwill of the senators by barring them from military office. There were good reasons for this. Many senators had shown their disloyalty by supporting Postumus, Regalianus or Macrianus. At the same time, fewer and fewer senators had the requisite military experience for positions of high command, choosing increasingly to follow a safer civil career rather than a dangerous military one. Be that as it may, Gallienus's policy encouraged feelings of resentment among the senators, who responded by making Gallienus himself the scapegoat for the troubles of his reign. The prejudice was passed down to later historians, who have hardly a good word to say for Gallienus's 15-year struggle to hold the ailing empire together.

CLAUDIUS II	
Born 10 May 214 in Illyricum	Wife and children unknown
Accession September 268	Died of plague at Sirmium August 270

CLAUDIUS II

It would be too long to set forth all the many honours that this man earned; one thing, however, I must not omit, namely, that both the senate and people held him in such affection both before his rule and during his rule and after his rule that it is generally agreed among all that neither Trajan nor any of the Antonines nor any other emperor was so beloved.

Historia Augusta *Life of the Deified Claudius* XVIII

The man who succeeded Gallienus, the emperor Claudius II 'Gothicus', became something of a hero-figure to later historians. This arises in part from the legend surrounding his death, in part from his supposed kinship with the later emperor Constantine, and in part is simply in contrast to the hostile press given to Gallienus. Despite the desire to believe well of Claudius – a desire which has been followed by modern historians – there is surprisingly little to mark him out for special mention. He deserves credit nonetheless for continuing the work of consolidation which was begun by Gallienus and completed by his successor, the emperor Aurelian.

The future emperor Claudius was born on or around 10 May 214, probably in the Dardania district of Illyricum. He was the first in a distinguished line of Illyrian emperors which extended well into the following century. Before his elevation to Augustus, Claudius had held important military commands under Valerian and Gallienus, and was regarded by the army as the natural choice for emperor when Gallienus was murdered in September 268. His accession seems also to have been welcomed by the senate and to have been popular with the people of Rome.

When Gallienus was killed at Milan, by the commander of the Dalmatian cavalry, Claudius was in command of a military reserve at Ticinum (modern Pavia), 20 miles away. He immediately took command of operations against Aureolus; Milan surrendered, and Aureolus was executed. No action was taken against the murderers of Gallienus, however, perhaps because Claudius himself had been involved in the conspiracy. Be that as it may, Claudius persuaded the senate to deify his predecessor, and ordered a stop to the murder of Gallienus's supporters at Rome.

Having settled affairs in Milan, Claudius marched north to confront the Alemanni, who had once again invaded Roman territory, crossing the Alps to threaten Italy itself. In late autumn of 268 he inflicted a crushing defeat on the invaders in the vicinity of Lake Garda. He spent the following winter in Rome, before setting out northwards to finish off the Gothic campaign begun by Gallienus the previous year. Claudius campaigned successfully against them in 269, receiving the title 'Gothicus Maximus'. In 270, however, the Goths won a partial victory at Mount Haemus in Thrace, and it was only the outbreak of severe plague

THE MUCH-PRAISED CLAUDIUS

Now Claudius himself was noted for the gravity of his character, and noted, too, for his matchless life and a singular purity; he was tall of stature, with flashing eyes and a broad, full face, and so strong were his fingers that often by a blow of his fist he would dash out the teeth of a horse or a mule.

Historia Augusta *Life of the Deified Claudius* XIII

The exploits of Claudius's fists do not arouse the admiration of the modern reader in the way the fourth-century biographer intended. His biography is indeed a thinly-veiled panegyric, stimulated more by the supposed kinship between Claudius and Constantine (emperor 306–37; claimed to be Claudius's great-grandson) than on specific attributes of Claudius himself. There is nevertheless no reason to doubt that Claudius was an effective ruler who might have achieved great things had he not died of plague after a reign of only two years. The senate is said to have honoured him with a golden statue, 10 ft (3 m) tall, in front of the Temple of Jupiter on the Capitol, though this story may well be a later invention.

THE STUFF OF LEGENDS

Claudius's sudden death after only a short reign must have been a bitter blow to the many factions in the army and the senate who regarded Claudius as a model emperor. The story grew up that Claudius had knowingly accepted death for the good of the state. Before leaving Rome for the Gothic War, the emperor had ordered the Sibylline books to be consulted, and learned from them that victory could be gained only through the death of the head of state. Hero to the last, Claudius did not shirk his duties but set out against the Goths in full knowledge of his prophesied end.

among them soon afterwards which finally gave the Romans the upper hand. Claudius did not live to enjoy the fruits of his success, for the same plague which had devastated the Goths carried him off, too, at Sirmium, in August 270.

So much for Claudius's victories on the northern frontier; what of the eastern and western provinces which still lay outside central control? Here, gains in the west were counterbalanced by more serious losses in the east. In 269, Claudius sent an expeditionary force to recover southern Gaul east of the Rhône from the Gallic emperor Victorinus. At about the same time, Spain threw off the Gallic allegiance and returned to Rome. Preoccupied with the Goths, however, Claudius made no attempt to follow up these successes and take back the rest of Gaul. Furthermore, the situation in the east was much more urgent. Zenobia, widow of Odaenathus, had broken with Claudius in 269, advancing her power as far as Ankara in the west. The following year she invaded the province of Egypt, defeating the Roman garrison and cutting off the corn supply on which the city of Rome had depended since the time of Augustus. Before he could do anything about this situation, Claudius had succumbed to plague.

The first serious threat to the city of Rome came in the reign of Aurelian. In 271 the Juthungi and Marcomanni invaded northern Italy and defeated the imperial army at Placentia, advancing into central Italy. They were turned back, but Aurelian recognized the need to protect the city against further attacks by building a defensive wall. The work was undertaken with some urgency, and existing monuments were incorporated into the circuit wherever possible. Construction was of concrete faced with brick; only the gateways were built of stone, and even the brick was largely re-used. As built by Aurelian and completed under Probus the city wall was 13 ft (4 m) thick at the base and 21 ft (6.4 m) high, with projecting rectangular towers at intervals of roughly 100 Roman feet (97 ft). There were 18 major gates, and the whole circuit measured over 12 miles in length. It marked the end of more than 300 years of Rome as an open city, defended only by the power of the legions. (*Right*) The Porta Appia (now Porta San Sebastiano) in the Aurelian Wall at Rome. The wall itself was doubled in height by Maxentius (306–312) and this gate along with others was extensively remodelled by Honorius in 403.

QUINTILLUS	
Date & place of birth unknown	Children two offspring, names unknown
Accession August 270	Committed suicide at Aquileia September 270
Wife name unknown	

QUINTILLUS

Popular with the senate and the people of Rome, Claudius was deified without opposition. Power passed briefly to his younger brother Quintillus, who became emperor in September 270. He had been left at Aquileia and entrusted with the defence of northern Italy while Claudius was dealing with the Goths. His reign, however, lasted a couple of months, at most, perhaps as little as 17 days. For the Danube legions on whose support he had counted quickly declared in favour of Aurelian, commander of the cavalry; whereupon Quintillus, despairing of success, called for a doctor to open his veins and took his own life, without having stirred from Aquileia.

AURELIAN	
Born 9 September 214 in Moesia	Murdered by the praetorian guard at Coenofrurium September/October 275, buried in Coenofrurium
Accession August 270	
Wife Ulpia Severina	
Children a daughter, name unknown	

AURELIAN

For after the misfortune of Valerian and the evil ways of Gallienus our commonwealth did indeed under Claudius's rule begin to breathe once more, but Aurelian it was who won victories throughout the enitre world and restored it again to its former state.

Historia Augusta *Life of the Deified Aurelian* XLI

Aurelian was with the army on the Danube frontier in August 270 when Claudius died. One of his most trusted generals and commander of the effective cavalry arm established by Gallienus, Aurelian was an obvious choice as successor. He had already been involved in one imperial coup; for it was he who is credited with the idea of the night-alarm which drew Gallienus from his tent before Milan and gave the assassins their opportunity. On that occasion, Aurelian's claims to the succession were laid aside in favour of the more-widely respected Claudius. Now, two years later, after the death's of Claudius and his brother Quintillus, Aurelian's route to the purple was at last clear.

Aurelian spent the winter in Rome, but the following year he rejoined the army on the Danube, where Claudius had been preparing for operations against new Germanic invaders, the Vandals. The campaign of 271 was indecisive but the Vandals, reinforced by Sarmatians, were driven back across the Danube and sued for peace. News then arrived that other Germans, the Juthungi and Marcomanni, had invaded northern Italy. Aurelian was defeated by them in a first encounter, and the invaders were able to advance as far as Piacenza before being turned back in two major battles. The invasion had one lasting and visible effect; for Aurelian decided that the city of Rome, unwalled since the beginning of the imperial period, should be given a circuit of defences to protect it against any future Germanic invasions. The famous Aurelian Wall, begun in 271, was eventually completed by his successor Probus.

Despite his northern victories, Aurelian's rule was challenged by a number of rivals during 271 and early 272: Domitianus in the Balkans, Septimius in Dalmatia, and a certain Urbanus. These have come down

RESTITUTOR ORBIS

Now Aurelian, indeed, is placed by many among neither the good nor the evil emperors for the reason that he lacked the quality of mercy, that foremost dower of an emperor.

Historia Augusta *Life of the Deified Aurelian* XLIV

Lucius Domitius Aurelianus, the future emperor Aurelian, was born probably on 9 September 214 in the province of Moesia (later Dacia Ripensis) in the northern Balkans. His father was the tenant farmer of a wealthy senator Aurelius, after whom the family were named. Aurelian chose a military career and rose through the ranks, serving with distinction on the Danube frontier under Gallienus and Claudius. When Claudius died of plague he was commander of the cavalry, the same key post which Claudius had held when he succeeded Gallienus. Aurelian as emperor showed himself an energetic and able commander, but gained a reputation for severity. It was said, for instance, that he killed his sister's son (others say her daughter) without any good reason, and for this he was judged a prince who was necessary rather than good. Yet he spared the lives of both Tetricus and Zenobia, kept strict discipline in the army, and took steps to stamp out extortion and corruption among his officials.

He was also concerned to create a more distant dignity for the imperial office, styling himself 'deus et dominus', 'god and lord'.

to us simply as names, and their uprisings must have been quickly suppressed.

The defeat of Zenobia

The defeat of the Juthungi and Marcomanni left Aurelian free to deal with the secessionist eastern and western provinces of the empire. In the spring of 272 he led his army eastwards, first crossing the Danube to inflict a final crushing defeat on the Goths, then organizing the abandonment and evacuation of the province of Dacia to stabilize the northern frontier. He was now ready to confront the Palmyrene ruler Zenobia who controlled all the territory between Egypt and Asia Minor. The first battle was fought at Immae, 26 miles east of Antioch. By careful strategy Aurelian neutralized the threat posed by the Palmyrene heavy cavalry and gained a complete victory. Antioch fell the following day, and Zenobia and her forces retreated south to Emesa. Here a second battle was fought, in which again Aurelian defeated the Palmyrenes. During this battle the club-wielding auxiliaries from Palestine made a particularly significant impact on Palmyrene heavy armour.

This second defeat left Zenobia no option but to retreat to her capital, the oasis-city of Palmyra, and to make a final stand. Her hope was that Aurelian would find it impossible to supply his army for a long-running siege in severe desert conditions. She soon found that she was mistaken, however, and it was the Palmyrene defenders who began to run short of food during the siege. In this extremity Zenobia resolved to seek assistance from the Persians, and set off in person for the Euphrates frontier riding a fast camel. Aurelian sent horsemen in pursuit who managed to capture her just as she was about to cross the river. Palmyra surrendered, though the city itself was spared, and the eastern provinces were taken back peacefully into the Roman empire. As for Zenobia, there are two accounts of her end. One says she died on the journey back to Rome, where she was to have been paraded in Aurelian's triumph the following year. The other maintains she appeared in the triumph and was then installed in a villa at Tivoli, near Rome, where she died not long afterwards.

The ambitions of the Palmyrenes were not over, however, and shortly after Aurelian left the region they again rose in revolt. The Roman garrison of 600 archers was slaughtered, and a man named Septimius Antiochus had himself proclaimed emperor. He may have been a younger son of the former Palmyrene ruler Odaenathus, but whatever his origin his reign proved to be very short-lived. Aurelian was campaigning against the Carpi on the Danube in the spring of 273 when news was brought to him concerning the rebellion. The emperor hurried back to Syria, taking the Palmyrenes completely by surprise, and easily captured the city. After this second rebellion Aurelian was to show no clemency; Palmyra was systematically sacked and looted by his troops. The once spectacular oasis-city never regained her former glory.

The empire restored

The following year saw Aurelian on the war path once again, this time with the intention of suppressing the Gallic empire in the west. His forces won a resounding victory at the battle of Châlons-sur-Marne in the summer of 274, and the last Gallic emperor, Tetricus, surrendered. His life was spared; he was taken to Rome to appear along with Zenobia in the magnificent triumph celebrated by Aurelian later that year, but was subsequently given an administrative position in southern Italy, and allowed to live out his days in peace.

The autumn of 274 saw the Roman empire finally re-united, and Aurelian could with some justice assume the title 'Restitutor Orbis', 'Restorer of the World'. Other problems remained to be solved, however, including the crisis in the imperial currency. The quality of the silver coinage had declined sharply since 268, undermining confidence in the money economy itself. Aurelian endeavoured to rectify matters by buying in the old debased currency and issuing new reformed coins with higher silver content. This may have been the move which triggered a serious revolt by the moneyers at Rome (either now or earlier in the reign), led by Felicissimus, controller of the mint. Accused perhaps of embezzling the silver and debasing the coins for their own profit, the rebels took refuge on the Caelian Hill, and in the fighting which followed as many as 7000 soldiers were killed.

The year 274 also saw the dedication of the new temple to the Sun which Aurelian built in the northern part of Rome, near the Mausoleum of Augustus. The temple contained extravagant fittings, which included jewel-encrusted robes and other materials stripped from the Temple of Bel at Palmyra. The cult of Sol Invictus (the Unconquered Sun) was popular in the Roman army and in the eastern provinces, and Aurelian may have built the temple not only through a sense of personal devotion but also as a common focus for the disparate peoples of the empire.

In 275 Aurelian set out for the northern frontier once again, defeating another incursion by the Juthungi. He then travelled eastwards, gathering an army together for a new war against the Persians. In September or October of that year he was at Coenofrurium near Perinthus, preparing to cross the Bosphorus, when he was murdered. The instigator of the deed was Eros, his private secretary, the perpetrators members of the praetorian guard. The motives are unclear, though one source lays the blame on Aurelian's growing tendency to cruelty; it may have arisen from a private grievance, or perhaps from the severity with which he punished any extortion by his officials.

Whatever the reason for his murder, Aurelian died beloved of the army he had led to victory on so many occasions, and was buried by them at Coenofrurium with great ceremony. He was deified by the senate soon afterwards, and few indeed had deserved the honour as much as Aurelian. Though he had reigned only five years, they had been years full of achievement. Above all, he had restored the integrity of the Roman empire, now once again a unified realm for the first time in 15 years.

Tacitus
Imperator Caesar Marcus
Claudius Tacitus Pius Felix
Augustus
275–276

Florianus
Imperator Caesar Marcus
Annius Florianus Pius Felix
Augustus
276

Probus
Imperator Caesar Marcus
Aurelius Probus Pius Felix
Invictus Augustus
276–282

Carus
Imperator Caesar Marcus
Aurelius Carus Pius Felix
Invictus Augustus
282–283

Numerian
Imperator Caesar Marcus
Aurelius Numerianus Pius
Felix Augustus
283–284

Carinus
Imperator Caesar Marcus
Aurelius Carinus Pius Felix
Invictus Augustus
283–285

Portrait-bust from the Louvre, Paris,
thought to represent the emperor
Tacitus. The Historia Augusta describes
him as frugal and temperate in his
habits, a respected elderly senator fond
of lettuce and country produce. In
reality he was probably just another
general brought out of retirement by the
military.

TACITUS

*It was a noble achievement that he obtained the imperial power with
such glory to himself, but by reason of the shortness of his reign he
peformed no great exploit.*

Historia Augusta *Life of Tacitus* XIII

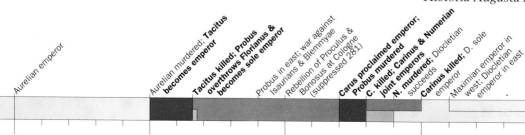

Aurelian emperor

Aurelian murdered; **Tacitus
becomes emperor**

**Tacitus killed; Probus
overthrows Florianus &
becomes sole emperor**

Probus in east; war against
Isaurians & Blemmyae

Rebellion of Proculus &
Bonosus at Cologne
(suppressed 281)

**Carus proclaimed emperor;
Probus murdered**

**C. killed; Carinus & Numerian
joint emperors**

N. murdered; Diocletian
succeeds

Carinus killed; D. sole
emperor

Maximian emperor in
west; Diocletian
emperor in east

270   275   280   285   290

TACITUS	
Born c. 200 in the Danube provinces	*Children several sons, names unknown*
Accession November/December 275	*Murdered at Tyana in Cappadocia July 276*
Wife name unknown	

The remarkable fact about the emperor Tacitus was the way in which he came to power, or rather the myth which surrounded his accession. For when Aurelian was murdered in September 275, there was nobody ready to take on the mantle of emperor, no designated successor waiting in the wings. In the normal run of events, we might have expected one of the leading military men – the praetorian commander, for example – to have taken advantage of the opportunity and seized power for himself. What the ancient historians tell us, however, is a very different story: that the soldiers who were with Aurelian when he died wrote to the senate at Rome, asking it to nominate one of its own members as emperor. According to this account, the senate at first mistrusted the soldiers' offer, suspecting that it was some kind of trap; but when it became clear that the soldiers were in earnest, they elected their leading member, the elderly Marcus Claudius Tacitus, to don the purple and govern the empire.

That, at least, is the conventional story: an interregnum of six or eight weeks, while senate and army discussed how best to proceed. Given the circumstances of the time, it is perhaps easier to believe that Tacitus was the army's own choice. He may indeed have been an elderly general, brought out of retirement in Italy by his former colleagues to take over the reins of power. We are told he was 75 at the time, that his birthplace was Interamna (modern Terni) in Umbria, and that when he became emperor he was a wealthy senator with a personal fortune of 280 million sesterces. Most if not all of this is fiction. His true birthplace was probably one of the Danube provinces, and in reality he was simply another of the long line of military emperors drawn from that region who dominated Rome during the third century. He had become consul only in his latter years, in 273, and he did not come from an especially old or distinguished family. The relationship he claimed with the famous historian Tacitus was false, despite the coincidence of names and the many copies of the latter's works he ordered for the libraries of Rome.

Tacitus was installed as emperor late in 275. Early the following year he set out to join the army in Thrace, probably the same that Aurelian had assembled for the projected Persian offensive. Tacitus advanced into Asia Minor leading his forces to victory over the Heruli in the spring of 276, and being rewarded with the title 'Gothicus Maximus'. He did not long outlive this success, however, for in July of that year he was murdered at Tyana in Cappadocia (southern Turkey), while preparing to return to Europe, after a reign of only six months.

The emperor Tacitus comes down to us as a man of temperate lifestyle with a particular fondness for glassware, a dislike of ostentation, and sharp eyesight even into old age. A senatorial favourite, he gets a good press from the senatorial historians Aurelius Victor and the author of the Historia Augusta. He was even given the title 'Restitutor Rei Publicae' (Restorer of the Republic) on coins. But the true character of his short reign may have been less flattering. The stated reason for his murder was discontent caused by the exactions of his relative

Maximinus in Syria, and it may be that Tacitus had difficulty in controlling and restraining the actions of his subordinates. And as we have seen, the portrayal of Tacitus as an elderly civilian chosen by the senate owes more to myth and to wishful thinking than to the military autocracy and realpolitik of the age.

FLORIANUS

FLORIANUS	
Date and place of birth unknown	unknown
Accession July 276	Murdered by his own soldiers at Tarsus September 276
Wife and children	

Florianus, who had succeeded Tacitus, was in power for two months and twenty days and did nothing worth remembering.

Eutropius *Breviarium* IX.16

At the death of Tacitus power passed to the praetorian commander Marcus Annius Florianus, who was quickly recognized by the senate and by the majority of the provinces. Little is known of his earlier career, but he is said by some to have been half-brother to Tacitus, sharing the same mother. The new emperor at once embarked on further actions against the Heruli, and within a matter of weeks had brought them to the brink of defeat. All might indeed have been well had not Egypt, Syria and the eastern provinces declared for a rival emperor: Marcus Aurelius Probus, commander on the eastern frontier. Breaking off the Heruli campaign, Florianus marched south to face the pretender, pitching camp at Tarsus, near the border of rebel Syria.

Florianus had much the larger force at his disposal and for a time it must have seemed that Probus could only lose. But summer heat and the ravages of disease hit Florianus's European units particularly hard, and the loyalty of his troops began to evaporate. Indecisive skirmishing was followed by a military coup, in which Probus's soldiers talked Florianus's men into deposing their emperor in favour of their own nominee. When Florianus attempted to regain the initiative he was killed, after a reign of only 88 days. A marble statue 30 ft (9 m) tall was erected in his memory at Interamna, with another for his predecessor Tacitus. Their deaths brought the tally of murdered emperors to three within a single year; the imperial government was once again on the brink of crisis.

PROBUS

He was an ardent, energetic and fair man, one who could equal Aurelian in military reputation but surpass him by virtue of his gracious nature.

Eutropius *Breviarium* IX.17

With the murder of Florianus in September 276 power passed to his rival Marcus Aurelius Probus. The new emperor was a military man, a native of Sirmium near the Danube frontier (or possibly of Siscia (modern Sisak) 170 miles to the west). Nothing certain is known of his family or

PROBUS	
Born 19 August 232 at Sirmium Marcus Aurelius Probus	Consul I (277), II (278), III (279), IV (281), V (282)
On accession July 276 Imperator Caesar Marcus Aurelius Probus Pius Felix Invictus Augustus, Pontifex Maximus, Pater Patriae, Proconsul	*Full titles at death* Imperator Caesar Marcus Aurelius Probus Pius Felix Augustus Pontifex Maximus, Gothicus Maximus, Germanicus Maximus, Persicus Maximus, Tribuniciae potestatis VII, Consul V, Pater Patriae, Proconsul
Added 277 'Gothicus' *Added 279* 'Gothicus Maximus', 'Germanicus Maximus', 'Parthicus' or 'Persicus Maximus'	*Wife and children unknown*
Tribunician power first in summer 276; renewed annually each summer	*Murdered by his own soldiers near Sirmium late September 282, buried near Sirmium*

background, but by the time of his accession, aged about 44 years old, he had gained a considerable reputation in the army. His skill in warfare and military training was said to equal the famous Aurelian's. This was to prove fortunate, since practically the whole of Probus's reign was spent opposing foreign invaders and imperial pretenders.

The most pressing concern at the time of Probus's accession was the widespread destruction of Gaul and the Rhineland provinces by invasions of Franks in the north and Germanic peoples (including Vandals and Burgundians) in the centre and south. It was the greatest disaster to strike this part of the Roman world since its absorption into the empire some three centuries before. Probus spent two years (277–278) defeating each of these invaders in turn and restoring the Roman frontier on the Rhine and Upper Danube. In 279 he turned his attention eastwards, defeating the Getae on the Lower Danube before crossing to Asia Minor, where bands of robbers led by Lydius the Isaurian were terrorizing Pamphylia and Lycia. The rebel headquarters surrendered to Probus's forces after a lengthy siege and Lydius was killed in the fighting. Next came suppression of a rebellion in Upper Egypt, led by a Nubian people, the Blemmyae.

By the autumn of 279 Probus must have felt that he had consolidated his hold over the eastern and western provinces. He even assumed the title 'Persicus Maximus' for some unspecified successes against the Persians. Alas, this confidence was soon to prove ill-founded, and his final years were overshadowed by a series of internal insurrections. The first of these broke out in 280, when Bonosus and Proculus proclaimed themselves joint emperors at Cologne. They won considerable support in the western provinces of the empire, and it took Probus several months to bring the situation under control. The rebels were eventually defeated near Cologne; Bonosus committed suicide, while Proculus was

THE FATAL ERROR

Here lies Probus, the Emperor, a man of probity indeed, the conqueror of all barbarian nations, the conqueror, too, of pretenders.

Historia Augusta *Life of Probus* XXI

The tomb inscription recorded by the Historia Augusta may well be fictitious, but the pun on the name ('probus' being Latin for probity or virtue) illustrates the high regard in which Probus was held during the fourth century. He was remembered for public works, setting the soldiers to drain marshes on the Nile and the Danube, building temples and bridges in Egypt, and completing the great

defensive wall around the city of Rome which Aurelian had begun. Probus also promoted the development of viticulture in Gaul and the Danube provinces, using military labour to plant new vineyards which he then entrusted to local farmers. Probus's aim was to rebuild the prosperity of provinces which had suffered extensive damage from wars and invasions during the previous decades. This policy overlooked one vital fact: the soldiers did not share the emperor's enthusiasm for rural reconstruction, and forcing them to do these tasks may have been the fatal error which led to Probus's downfall.

Possible portrait-bust of Probus from the Capitoline Museum, Rome.

either killed in battle, or fled to the Franks, who delivered him up to Probus for execution. Another rebellion by the governor of Britain was quickly suppressed by Probus's agents. More menacing was the eastern revolt led by Iulius Saturninus, the Moorish governor of Syria, who styled himself 'Imperator Caesar Iulius Saturninus Augustus'. Probus was preparing to deal with the rebellion in person when news came that Saturninus had been killed by his own troops.

Probus celebrated his German victories with a triumph held at Rome towards the end of 281. We are told this was accompanied by lavish spectacles involving wild animals and gladiators in their hundreds. For one wild beast hunt the Circus Maximus was planted with mature trees set within earth-filled timber caissons so as to resemble a forest. On another day, spectators in the Colosseum witnessed the slaughter of 200 lions, 200 leopards and 300 bears. Captive Germans, Isaurians and Nubians who had been paraded in Probus's triumphal procession were then finished off in a series of bloody gladiatorial contests.

The following spring Probus set off once again for the east, intending to campaign against the Persians. His departure proved too much of a temptation to Marcus Aurelius Carus, commander of the praetorian guard. Around the beginning of September 282, with the support of the armies of Raetia and Noricum (along the Upper Danube), Carus had himself proclaimed emperor. The soldiers whom Probus sent ahead to suppress the uprising joined forces with the usurper. When news of their defection reached the rest of Probus's army, they too decided to change sides: they turned on the emperor and murdered him in a look-out tower where he had fled for refuge, not far from Sirmium. Probus was buried nearby, under a large mounded tomb according to one account, but his memory was condemned and his name erased from inscriptions. Official propaganda, however, did not prevent him becoming a hero to fourth-century historians such as Eutropius, Aurelius Victor and the author of the Historia Augusta. They leave us yet again with the picture of an able and industrious emperor, cut off in his prime by the fickleness of the soldiery and the bad faith of his subordinates.

CARUS	
Born c. 224 at Narbo in Gaul	Aurelius Carinus & Marcus Aurelius Numerius Numerianus; a daughter Aurelia Paulina
Accession September 282	
Wife name unknown	
Children two sons: Marcus	Killed by lightning near Ctesiphon July/August 283

CARUS

Let us pass on to Carus, a mediocre man, so to speak, but one to be ranked with the good rather than the evil princes, yet a better ruler by far, had he not left Carinus to be his heir.

Historia Augusta *Life of Carus, Carinus and Numerian* III

The murder of Probus by his own soldiers in September 282 ensured a smooth transfer of power to the new ruler, Marcus Aurelius Carus. It was at Sirmium and as commander of the praetorian guard that Carus was proclaimed emperor in opposition to Probus at the beginning of that month, and Carus was probably still at Sirmium when Probus marched against him and met his death. Carus clearly enjoyed widespread support among the army and its commanders in his bid for supreme power. He probably belonged to that same officer corps which had governed the empire for the previous 40 years. Yet Carus differed from his predecessors in the geography of his origin, coming not from the heavily militarized Danube provinces but from the sleepy town of Narbo on the Mediterranean coast of Gaul. He had been born there around 224, and was hence some six years older than Probus; indeed, at the age of 58, he was approaching the end of his career when the opportunity for a coup d'état presented itself.

With power in his grasp Carus travelled to Rome accompanied by his sons Marcus Aurelius Carinus and Marcus Aurelius Numerius Numerianus. There both sons were given the rank of Caesar, and the elder of the two, Carinus, became consul with his father on 1 January 283. Carinus was then entrusted with the government and defence of the western provinces while Carus himself and his younger son Numerian took charge of affairs in the east.

In the spring of 283 Carus and Numerian fought successfully against Sarmatians and Quadi on the Danube. Their main object, however, was to embark on the war against Persia which Probus had been planning at the time of his death. This seems to have been a military adventure rather than a strategic necessity; Persia was no longer the menace it had been in the days of Shapur I. The Roman invasion force advanced through Mesopotamia, defeating the Persians and capturing Ctesiphon, the capital, and the adjacent city of Coche which the Persian king Ardashir had founded some 50 years before. Despite these remarkable gains, the expeditionary force got no further. For Carus was in camp on the banks of the Tigris, some say in his tent, when he was killed by a bolt of lightning. Or so we are told. The story seems hardly credible, and many have suggested that the 'lightning' was wielded by the hand of Aper, the praetorian commander, or by Diocletian, commander of the imperial bodyguard. But for these conjectures we have no evidence.

NUMERIAN

The sudden death of Carus in July or August 283 placed command of the Persian expedition in the hands of his younger son, Numerian. He was no mere teenager, but a mature man of around 30, yet his father had entrusted him with substantially less power and responsibility than his elder brother Carinus. He had kept Numerian by his side as a mere Caesar while Carinus governed the western provinces as joint Augustus. Numerian had indeed won considerable acclaim for his poetry, but there may have been legitimate doubt about his ability to rule.

In the event, Numerian's shortcomings as emperor were given little opportunity to manifest themselves. During the Mesopotamian campaign he had contracted a serious eye infection which left him partially blind. The capture of Ctesiphon had brought the Persian campaign to a successful climax, and on Carus's death Numerian had no difficulty in

NUMERIAN	
Born c. 253 place unknown	*Murdered near Nicomedia November 284*
Accession July/August 283	
Wife name unknown	

ordering a Roman withdrawal. The winter of 283 was spent in Syria, then the following year the imperial cortège continued on its way across Asia Minor towards the Bosphorus. Incapacitated and travelling in a closed litter, Numerian at last proved easy prey for his father-in-law, the unscrupulous praetorian commander Lucius Flavius Aper. Or so it was alleged. For some time, the murder remained undetected; the litter daily took its place in the order of march, until the smell of putrefaction could no longer be concealed.

The army had reached Nicomedia when the crime was revealed, in November 284. Aper was hauled before a full military assembly and accused of the murder, with hardly a chance to defend himself. The troops acclaimed Diocletian, commander of the bodyguard, as emperor in place of Numerian. His first action was to dispose of Aper; some sources say he killed the man himself, there on the platform in full view of the army. The whole process looks suspiciously stage-managed, and it does not need a confirmed cynic to suspect that Diocletian was behind the death of Numerian too. It must have seemed to contemporaries like just another stage in the blood-stained imperial succession. Yet it was Diocletian who was to reform the Roman empire and reign for over 20 years, longer than any emperor since Antoninus Pius a century and a half before.

CARINUS

It would be too long to tell more, even if I should desire to do so, about his excesses.

Historia Augusta Life of Carus, Carinus and Numerian XVIII

The death of Numerian left his elder brother Carinus still in control of the western provinces. Born around 250, Carinus had been promoted to the position of joint Augustus by his father Carus in the spring of 283. At about that time he led a successful campaign against the Germans on the Rhine, and in autumn 283 won a victory over the Quadi on the Danube front. Carinus celebrated a triumph for these victories early in 284, and became consul a second time, jointly with Numerian, from 1 January. It was Carinus's private life, and in particular his voracious bisexual appetite, that gave cause for criticism: or so we are told. The author of the Historia Augusta excels himself in recounting a series of scandalous tales: how he was a constant corrupter of youth; how by marrying and divorcing he accumulated a total of nine wives; and how he filled the palace with actors, harlots and pimps. In fact only one official wife is known, a lady by the name of Magnia Urbica, and much of this scandal can be set aside as false propaganda, spread by Diocletian to justify his usurpation. The story of Carinus's end, however, shows that there was some truth in the allegation of sexual misconduct.

During the course of 284 Carinus campaigned in Britain, winning the title 'Britannicus Maximus' for his achievements. It was after his broth-

THE EVIL CARINUS

Portrait-bust of the emperor Carinus from the Capitoline Museum, Rome.

He put to death very many innocent men on false charges, seduced the wives of nobles, and even ruined those of his school fellows who had taunted him at school, even with trivial banter.

Eutropius *Breviarium* IX.19

The emperor Carinus comes across in the ancient sources as a cruel and vindictive ruler who forced himself on the wives of leading citizens and debauched a number of young men also. The Historia Augusta paints Carinus in very grim colours indeed, 'He was left by his father as Caesar in Gaul and Italy and in Illyricum, Spain, Britain and Africa . . . and he exercised there a Caesar's powers, but with the permission to perform all the duties of an Augustus. Then he defiled himself by unwonted vices and inordinate depravity, he set aside all the best among his friends and retained or picked out all the vilest, and he appointed as city prefect one of his doorkeepers, a baser act than which no one can conceive or relate. He slew the prefect of the guard whom he found in office and put in his place Matronianus one of his clerks and an old procurer, whom he had always kept with him as accomplice and assistant in debaucheries and lusts. . . . By marrying and divorcing he took nine wives in all, and he put away some even while they were pregnant. . . . He granted favours most of all to the base, and always invited them to banquets. At one of his banquets he often served one hundred pounds of birds, one hundred of fish, and one thousand of meat of different kinds, and he lavished on his guests vast quantities of wine. He swam about among apples and melons and strewed his banqueting-halls and bedrooms with roses from Milan. The baths which he used were as cold as the air of rooms that are under the ground, and his plunge-baths were always cooled by means of snow. Once, when he came in the winter to a certain place in which the spring water was very tepid . . . and he had bathed in it . . . he shouted to the bath attendants, it is said. "This is water for a woman that you have given me."' Despite these judgments we must balance the fact that he successfully governed the western provinces for over two years and that much of his evil reputation came from the propaganda machine of his rival Diocletian. On the other hand, there is no reason to suppose that Carinus in power was a model of decency and self-control.

CARINUS	
Born c. 250 place unknown	*Children* a son Nigrinianus
Accession spring 283	*Murdered during battle at the River Margus (Morava) summer 285*
Wife Magnia Urbica	

er's death in August or September of that year that the reign descended into crisis. The first problem was the rise of a pretender in northern Italy, who styled himself 'Imperator Caesar Marcus Aurelius Sabinus Iulianus Pius Felix Augustus'. Carinus marched against Julianus and defeated him near Verona (some sources say in Illyricum) at the beginning of 285. This left Carinus free to deal with the real threat: the advance of Diocletian and the army of the east. In late summer the forces of Diocletian and Carinus met in battle on the River Margus (Morava), near modern Belgrade. Carinus had the larger army and was gaining the upper hand – may even have won the battle – when his past misdeeds caught up with him. A number of Carinus's officers bore grudges against the emperor for seducing or molesting their wives. One of these men, fearful of what the future would hold if Carinus were victorious, struck him down in the hour of success.

Thus did Diocletian snatch victory from the jaws of defeat. Carinus's forces went over to him without opposition. The empress Magnia Urbica (wife of Carinus) perished at about the same time as her husband; her memory, together with that of Carus, Numerian and Carinus himself, was officially condemned, and their inscriptions erased. The dynasty founded by Carus had lasted only three years. Its demise brought an end to 50 years of struggle and crisis for the Roman empire; for the accession of Diocletian marked the dawn of a new era.

Diocletian
Imperator Caesar Gaius
Aurelius Valerius
Diocletianus Pius Felix
Invictus Augustus
284–305

Maximian
Imperator Caesar Marcus
Aurelius Valerius
Maximianus Pius Felix
Invictus Augustus
286–310

Portrait-bust of Diocletian found at
Nicomedia, his eastern capital. The
diadem is typical of the new regal image
which Diocletian sought to present.

DIOCLETIAN AND MAXIMIAN

*Diocletian was an author of crimes and a deviser of evil; he ruined
everything and could not even keep his hands from God. In his greed
and anxiety he turned the world upside down. He appointed three men
to share his rule, dividing the world into four parts and multiplying the
armies, since each of the four strove to have a far larger number of
troops than previous emperors had had when they were governing the
state alone.*

Lactantius *On the Deaths of the Persecutors* 7

With this mixture of falsehood and exaggeration does the Christian
polemicist Lactantius describe the character and reign of the emperor
Diocletian. Yet even Lactantius is forced to admit that Diocletian's
accession on 20 November 284 marked the beginning of a new era in the
history of the Roman empire. The successive crises of the previous 50
years had shown all too well the deficiencies of the imperial administration. Despite the prestige and achievements of Aurelian and Probus it
was left to Diocletian to introduce effective measures to counter these
defects. The most important change was the division of imperial author-

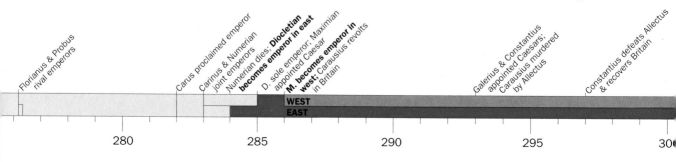

Florianus & Probus
rival emperors

Carus proclaimed emperor

Carinus & Numerian
joint emperors

Numerian dies; **Diocletian
becomes emperor in east**

D. sole emperor; Maximian
appointed Caesar

**M. becomes emperor in
west;** Carausius revolts
in Britain

Galerius & Constantius
appointed Caesars;
Carausius murdered
by Allectus

Constantius defeats Allectus
& recovers Britain

WEST
EAST

280   285   290   295   300

DIOCLETIAN

Born 22 December 245 in Dalmatia (Split?)
Diocles (full name unknown)

On accession 20 November 284
Imperator Caesar Gaius Aurelius Valerius Diocletianus Pius Felix Invictus Augustus, Pontifex Maximus, Pater Patriae, Proconsul
Added 286
'Jovius'

Victory titles
Germanicus Maximus (285), Germanicus Maximus II (287), III (287), IV (288), V (293), VI (301); Sarmaticus Maximus (285), Sarmaticus Maximus II (289), III (294), IV (300); Persicus Maximus (295), Persicus Maximus II (298); Britannicus Maximus (297), Carpicus Maximus (297), Armenicus Maximus (298), Medicus Maximus (298), Adiabenicus Maximus (298) Imperator I (284), II (285), renewed annually until XXI (304)

Consul I (284), II (285), III (287), IV

(290), V (293), VI (296), VII (299), VIII (303), IX (304), X (308)

Tribunicia potestas, first on accession, then renewed annually on 10 December.

Full titles on abdication
Imperator Caesar Gaius Valerius Diocletianus Pius Felix Invictus Augustus, Pontifex Maximus, Germanicus Maximus VI, Sarmaticus Maximus IIII, Persicus Maximus II, Britannicus Maximus, Carpicus Maximus, Armenicus Maximus, Medicus Maximus, Adiabenicus Maximus, Tribuniciae potestatis XXII, Consul X, Imperator XXI, Pater Patriae, Proconsul

Wife
Prisca
Children
a daughter Galeria Valeria

Died (suicide?) 3 December 311 at Split

ity among a small group of brother-emperors, first two, then the four to whom Lactantius refers. These were entrusted with the defence of different frontiers and helped prevent the rise of rebels and pretenders. The effectiveness of this policy is shown by the fact that Diocletian reigned for over 20 years and abdicated to pass his old age in retirement. In the eyes of Lactantius, any positive achievements were completely overshadowed by Diocletian's savage persecution of the Christians.

Diocletian was born on 22 December in around the year 245 in Dalmatia, probably near Spalato (Split) where he later chose to spend his final years. He was of humble origin, perhaps the son of a scribe or maybe even a freedman (former slave) of a wealthy senator. Opting for an army career, he rose through the ranks to become part of the élite corps of Illyrian army officers which dominated the army and the empire during the middle decades of the third century. During the 270s Diocles (as he was then known) served as commander in Moesia, on the middle Danube. He accompanied Carus on the Persian expedition of 283 as commander of the 'protectores domestici' or household cavalry, a key section of the imperial bodyguard, and retained this position under Numerian. We can only speculate what part he may have played in the murder of Numerian; if guilty, he successfully transferred the blame to Aper, the praetorian commander. Aper was an extremely ambitious man, but at the army assembly of November 284 outside Nicomedia, Diocles outmanoeuvred him and it was he who was proclaimed emperor by the troops.

The elevation of Maximian

The defeat of Carinus at the battle of the River Margus ten months later gave Diocletian undisputed control of the whole empire. Much to everyone's surprise, he sought reconciliation with Carinus's supporters, rather than revenge, and retained many of them in key positions in his own administration. Two months later, in November 285, he surprised everyone again by bestowing on one of his most trusted colleagues the title of Caesar, with control of the western provinces. The intention was to give Diocletian himself a free hand to deal with the problems of the Danube frontier, untroubled by the threat of invasions across the Rhine. Though he was a mature married man of 40 with a daughter probably now in her teens, Diocletian lacked a son on whom he could rely, and had perforce to seek the support of one of his generals. He chose well. Maximian, the new Caesar, was another Illyrian army officer, some five years his junior. The son of shopkeepers near Sirmium, he, like

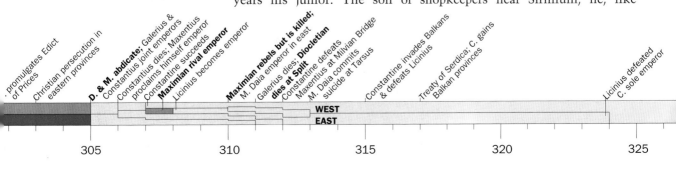

MAXIMIAN	
Born 21 July c.250 near Sirmium Maximianus (full name unknown) *On appointment as Caesar in 285* Aurelius Valerius Maximianus Nobilissimus Caesar *On accession 1 April 286* Imperator Caesar Marcus Aurelius Valerius Maximianus Pius Felix Invictus Augustus, Pontifex Maximus, Pater Patriae, Proconsul *Adopted 286* 'Herculius', but not generally as part of the complete titulature Consul I (287), II (288), III (290), IV (293), V (297), VI (299), VII (303), VIII (304), IX (307) The remainder of his titles are the same as those of Diocletian, save that, as he came to power a year after Diocletian, the numbers of imperial acclamations, tribunician powers, and victory titles 'Germanicus Maximus' and 'Sarmaticus Maximus' are each one fewer	*Full titles on abdication* Imperator Caesar Marcus Aurelius Valerius Maximianus Pius Felix Invictus Augustus, Pontifex Maximus, Herculius, Germanicus Maximus V, Sarmaticus Maximus III, Persicus Maximus II, Britannicus Maximus, Carpicus Maximus, Armenicus Maximus, Medicus Maximus, Adiabenicus Maximus, Tribuniciae potestatis XXI, Consul IX, Imperator XX, Pater Patriae, Proconsul *After abdication in May 305, Diocletian and Maximian became 'Seniores Augusti' (senior emperors) and 'Patres imperatorum et Caesarum' (fathers of the emperors and Caesars)* *Wife* Eutropia *Children* a son Marcus Valerius Maxentius a daughter Fausta a step-daughter Theodora *Murdered (or committed suicide) at Marseilles July 310*

Diocletian, had risen through the ranks to serve with distinction in the Mesopotamian campaign of 283–4. He proved himself a loyal and able colleague to Diocletian, and what could easily have developed into bitter rivalry remained a relationship of mutual trust.

Maximian never forgot that Diocletian was the senior emperor, even when he was raised to the rank of Augustus on 1 April 286. Diocletian retained a veto on all major policy issues, and Maximian respected the wisdom and judgment of his fellow-emperor. They shared the consulship in 287, and imperial propaganda likened their respective roles to that of the gods, with Diocletian as Jove, the senior, paternal figure, and Maximian as Hercules, his agent in ridding the world of evils. Diocletian adopted the title Jovius, Maximian the title Herculius. They proclaimed themselves the sons respectively of these two gods, and named their divine birthday as 21 July 287. This divine parentage was designed to inspire respect and to distance the rulers of the world from ordinary mortals.

From joint rule to tetrarchy

Diocletian spent five seasons 286–290 campaigning on the Danube and on the eastern frontier. Already in 285 he had fought against the Sarmatians; in 289 he did so again. The year 287 was devoted to the eastern frontier and a show of strength against the Persians. Maximian, meanwhile, was engaged in similar operations in the west. In 286 he suppressed the Bagaudae, powerful robber-bands of displaced peasants who were wreaking havoc in parts of Gaul. One of their leaders, Amandus, even had the audacity to assume the imperial title. Having dealt with the Bagaudae, Maximian turned his attention to the Rhine frontier. In 288 the two emperors mounted a combined operation against the Alemanni in which Maximian advanced across the Rhine and Diocletian across the Upper Danube.

The story of these years was not altogether one of unbroken success, for late in 286 serious trouble developed when Carausius, commander of the Roman North Sea fleet, seized control of Britain and pronounced himself emperor. Maximian attempted to unseat the British pretender in 289, but his forces were turned back, probably with heavy losses, by Carausius's powerful navy.

Despite the Carausian setback, the years 285–290 had amply demonstrated the effectiveness of Diocletian's experiment of joint emperors. The only serious difficulty was the question of the succession. In appointing Maximian as Caesar in 285 Diocletian had marked him out as his chosen successor. As time went by, however, Diocletian became anxious to have some more formal arrangement for an orderly succession. Furthermore, he saw the wisdom of preserving the device of joint emperors which he had established. The solution was for himself and Maximian each to appoint a junior ruler or Caesar, who would succeed automatically when he and Maximian died or retired. Accordingly on 1 March 293, Maximian adopted his praetorian commander Julius

THE FAMILY OF DIOCLETIAN

Diocletian chose his colleagues on the basis of loyalty and ability rather than blood ties, but arranged marriages were used to bind together the families of the tetrarchs. Nothing is known of the family background of Diocletian's own wife, Prisca. It seems, however, that when Diocletian retired to Split, Prisca stayed on with her daughter Valeria and son-in-law Galerius at Thessalonica. When Galerius died, Valeria refused to marry the new emperor Maximinus Daia, and mother and daughter fled to exile in Syria. They were put to death there in 314 on the orders of Licinius. Galerius's illegitimate son Candidianus, whom Valeria had adopted, died by the same hand the previous year. The fate of their legitimate daughter, Valeria Maximilla, is unrecorded; she may well have perished after her husband Maxentius's death at the Battle of Milvian Bridge in 313. Their son Valerius Romulus had already predeceased them in 309, and no other children are known.

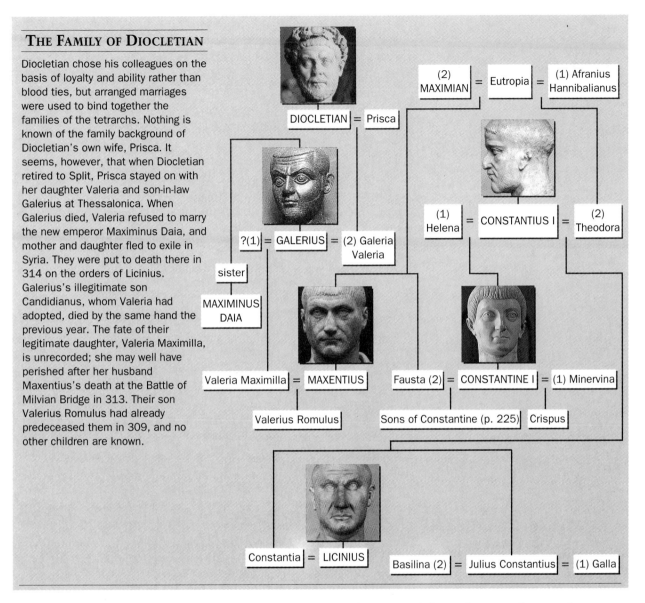

Constantius as son and Caesar, while on the same day Diocletian conferred the corresponding position on Galerius Maximianus at Nicomedia. Constantius had already married Maximian's stepdaughter Theodora some four years previous; the dynastic arrangements were completed by the marriage of Galerius with Diocletian's daughter Valeria in June 293.

Victories in east and west (293–298)

There was trouble in North Africa, where a Berber confederation known as the Quinquegentiani ('five peoples') had broken through the imperial frontier. There was the still outstanding problem of the breakaway empire of Carausius. And in the east, there was a new threat from Persia, where the warlike Narses had overthrown the four-month reign of

CARAUSIUS AND THE SAXON SHORE

The success of Carausius's revolt owed much to his reputation as a military commander, though to bolster his legitimacy he adopted the evocative names 'Marcus Aurelius'. His full official titulature became 'Imperator Caesar Marcus Aurelius Mausaeus Carausius Pius Felix Invictus Augustus', together with the traditional titles 'Pontifex Maximus' and 'Pater Patriae'. He made skilful use of imagery and propaganda to present himself as joint ruler alongside Diocletian and Maximian; coins show three imperial busts with the explanatory legend 'Carausius and his brothers'. Attempts to reconquer the breakaway province were made more difficult by the existence of powerful fortresses constructed during the third century to guard vulnerable landing places on the southern and eastern shores of Britain. These so-called Saxon shore forts were intended as protection against Germanic sea-borne raiders but would have been equally effective against invasion from the Continent.

Burgh Castle, Suffolk, one of the new Saxon shore forts of the late third century.

Bahram III in 293. In 296 the Persians seized control of Armenia from the Roman client-king Tiridates and began to advance towards the Syrian capital Antioch. Galerius advanced against him but suffered a heavy defeat on the plains of northern Mesopotamia between Carrhae and Callicinum. Poor judgment was largely responsible for this reverse, and Galerius was publicly humiliated by Diocletian for his rashness in attacking the Persians with an inferior force.

Narses's victory had serious repercussions in Egypt, where it encouraged a shadowy pretender called Lucius Domitius Domitianus to declare himself emperor. When he died (or was killed) after only four or five months, in December 297, his place was taken by the equally obscure Aurelius Achilleus. Order was only restored when Achilleus was defeated and killed by Diocletian at Alexandria early in 298. The uprising was a warning of the danger lying in wait ready to exploit any weakening of the central power.

Worsted by Narses in 297, Galerius did not make the same mistake a second time. Within months, with reinforcements from the Danube armies, he launched a surprise attack on the Persians in Armenia. The Roman victory was total; Narses fled the field but his wives, sisters and children were captured, together with many Persian noblemen. The treaty which followed was highly favourable to the Romans, who gained control over new territories along the Upper Tigris. The peace which it established lasted for 40 years.

While Diocletian and Galerius were fighting in the east, Constantius and Maximian were bringing the breakaway British empire to heel. The task fell mainly to Constantius. He began in the summer of 293 by recapturing the territories along the southern side of the Channel, including the major naval base at Gesoriacum (Boulogne). Carausius barely survived the setback; later in the same year he was murdered by Allectus, his treasurer, in a palace coup.

Constantius did not immediately carry the campaign to Britain itself, but spent three years making careful preparations, in particular by enlarging his fleet. The great invasion launched in 297 was a two-pronged affair. Constantius with one part of his fleet cruised off the coast of Kent, while his praetorian commander landed another force near Winchester and marched towards London. Allectus, caught off balance by these diversionary tactics, marched hurriedly west to meet the invasion but was defeated and killed near Farnham. After 10 years of separation Britain was restored to the Roman empire once more.

Victory in Britain and the east removed the greatest threats to the stability of the Roman empire, but did not end the almost constant need for military action on one front or another. Maximian crossed to North Africa to quell the troublesome Quinquegentiani. Galerius campaigned against Carpi and Sarmatians on the Danube. Constantius won victories over the Alemanni on the Rhine. But the major military crisis was over, and the key innovations of Diocletian's final years were all in the realm of internal or domestic affairs.

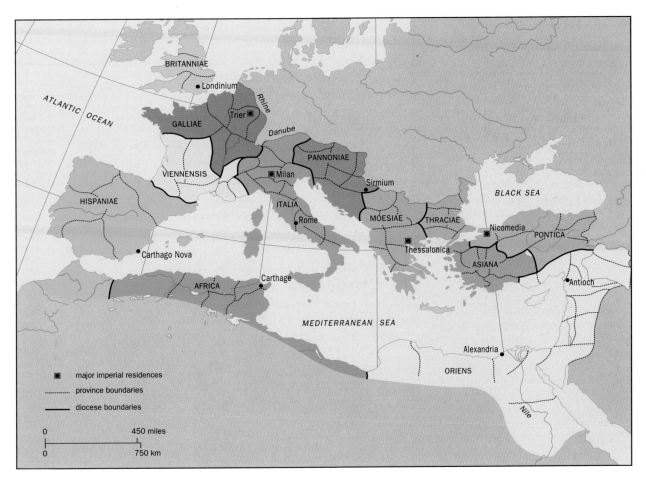

Diocletian reorganized the provincial structure of the empire, creating a system of smaller provinces grouped into twelve larger administrative units called dioceses. At the same time civil and military power were separated, so that governors of provinces and dioceses had no military authority and army commands cross-cut provincial boundaries. Rome was abandoned as a major imperial residence, and new centres established nearer the troubled frontiers, at Trier and Milan in the west, Thessalonica and Nicomedia in the east.

The new empire

Diocletian's greatest legacy to the Roman empire was his comprehensive reorganization of the imperial administration. A two-tier system was developed, with provinces grouped together into twelve large 'dioceses' governed by 'vicars'. Provincial governors and vicars held no military responsibility. The army was given a separate command structure which cross-cut provincial boundaries, the aim being to make rebellion and insurrection well-nigh impossible. The new system worked well, and Diocletian won further praise for the introduction of impartial laws and regulations, for the safeguarding of tax-payers and for the promotion of a better class of men to run the empire.

The main losers under the new provincial structure were the inhabitants of Italy. This (save for the immediate vicinity of Rome) lost the tax-free status it had hitherto enjoyed, and was divided up in a similar way to ordinary provinces. The senate, too, lost much of its power, and though Diocletian did rebuild the senate house when it burned down in 285, senators were steadily squeezed out of provincial administration. By the end of Diocletian's reign senators were permitted to govern only two of the provinces allocated to them by Augustus, and those much reduced in size.

LORD AND MASTER

He was a very industrious and capable emperor, and the one who was first to introduce in the Roman empire a practice more in keeping with royal usage than with Roman liberty, since he gave orders that he should be revered with prostration, though before him all emperors were simply greeted. He had his clothing and shoes decorated with gems, whereas previously the emperor's insignia comprised only the purple robe, and the rest of his dress was ordinary.

Eutropius *Breviarium* IX.26

Diocletian greatly elaborated court ceremonial and set himself apart from ordinary life. The objective was not only to shore up his dignity – fragile though that may have been – but to give himself a god-like aura which induced respect and brought greater security by making assassination seem like sacrilege. Public appearances were carefully stage-managed, and anyone approaching the imperial presence had to perform *adoratio*, kneeling to kiss the hem of the emperor's robe. Diocletian went still further, pronouncing himself the son of Jove, and celebrating a divine birthday each year on 21 July, though he stopped short of claiming to be a living god. These innovations were not restricted to Diocletian alone: the same exalted status and divine parentage were adopted by Maximian, Constantius and Galerius. This was all very far from the public image of the early emperors, who portrayed themselves simply as first among equals.

The decline of the senate corresponded with a decline in the importance of Rome itself, which had ceased to be a major imperial residence by the later third century. It was simply too distant from the critical frontier regions. Diocletian visited the city only once for certain, in November-December of 303. Imperial government was in any case peripatetic by nature; the centre of power was wherever the emperor happened to be at the time. Nonetheless, under the tetrarchs, favoured residences did take on the trappings of imperial capitals: Milan and Trier in the west, Thessalonica and Nicomedia in the east.

Administrative reform was only a part of the battle which Diocletian had to win if he was to hand on a healthy and prosperous empire to his successors. There was also the urgent problem of finance and inflation. Diocletian comprehensively overhauled the tax system and endeavoured to halt inflation by issuing new coins of higher quality. When this measure failed, he issued an Edict of Maximum Prices which sought to fix the maximum prices at which goods and services could be bought and sold. It is a source of fascinating information on wages and prices at the time, but was unenforceable, and prices continued to rise throughout the remainder of the reign.

The Great Persecution

Most emperors of the third century had promoted the worship of the sun as a unifying theme, a cult which few of their subjects would have difficulty in accepting. Diocletian instead went back to the traditional Roman gods such as Jove and Hercules. This was to have dire consequences for the Christians, who by now formed a large minority group within the army and the imperial administration. The first blow fell in 297 or 298, when Diocletian issued an order requiring all soldiers and administrators to sacrifice to the gods; those who refused were forced to quit the service. So matters stood for six years. Then on 24 February 303, an edict was issued ordering the destruction of churches and scriptures throughout the empire, and the punishment of leading Christians. Further edicts later that same year ordered the arrest and imprisonment of the entire Christian clergy; they were to be released only after they had sacrificed to the traditional gods. In April 304, a final edict commanded all Christians, clergy and laity alike, to offer sacrifice, on pain of death.

The anti-Christian measures were enforced to varying degrees in different parts of the empire. The western provinces, which were under the control of Maximian and Constantius, were scarcely affected. In the east, however, Diocletian and Galerius presided over persecution on a grand scale, as Christians who refused to recant were tortured and killed. Christian writers placed the blame squarely at the door of Galerius, who they described as, 'more evil than all the evil men who have ever lived.' They claimed that at Nicomedia during the winter of 302–3 Galerius argued long and hard for an anti-Christian campaign, and that after some hesitation Diocletian reluctantly agreed. It is difficult nevertheless to

A UNITY OF PURPOSE

Diocletian and his fellow tertrarchs in military dress, a porphyry statue-group looted from Byzantium during the Fourth Crusade (1204) and built into the corner of St Mark's Basilica at Venice.

The tetrarchy established by Diocletian was composed of military men from the Balkan provinces. Their unity of purpose is conveyed by statue-groups, where all four rulers are portrayed in identical manner. Their loyalty to Diocletian was really quite remarkable considering the civil unrest of the previous 50 years. The Christian Lactantius explains the cooperation between Diocletian and Maximian by asserting that both were greedy and unscrupulous; only that Diocletian was more hesitant. Non-Christian writers, on the other hand, praise Diocletian's wisdom and foresight, 'a very industrious and capable emperor', one who affected a certain pomp and ceremony but ultimately 'acted like a parent'. Maximian, by contrast, is described as 'openly brutal and by nature ungracious', a man possessed by 'sick desires'. We must not forget, however, that it was the firm loyalty of Maximian which enabled Diocletian to carry through his reforms. The two Caesars, too, dutifully carried out the tasks entrusted to them: it was Galerius who fought the Persian War in 297–8, and Constantius who reconquered Britain in 297. Stresses there must have been, but it is the solidarity of the tetrarchs which is their most remarkable feature.

completely absolve Diocletian from responsibility for the Great Persecution with its lurid tales of beatings, burnings and Christians thrown to the lions.

The final years

By the time the last anti-Christian edict was issued, in April 304, Diocletian was already in poor health. He had been in Rome in November 303 for a grand triumphal celebration and other festivities marking the beginning of his 20th year of rule. In December he left for Ravenna, and it was during the journey that he became ill and had to be carried in a litter. He struggled on through the following summer, but in December collapsed in his palace at Nicomedia. Contrary to expectation he did not die, but the illness persuaded him to take the extraordinary step of abdicating and retiring to spend his last years in the magnificent palace he had built for himself at Spalato (Split), on the Adriatic coast.

In order for the plan to work it was essential for Maximian, too, to abdicate. Rather remarkably, Diocletian managed to persuade him, and the two senior emperors gave up office simultaneously on 1 May 305, Diocletian at Nicomedia, Maximian at Milan. Constantius and Galerius became the new senior emperors, while Maximinus Daia and Severus were appointed to take their place as junior colleagues and Caesars. The tetrarchy was thus maintained, while Diocletian retired to Split and Maximian to southern Italy.

Events were to show that Maximian had not lost the taste for power, and was easily tempted to re-enter the fray the following year. For Diocletian, however, the retirement was final. He made only one further appearance in public life, attending the conference of the emperors at Carnuntum on the Danube in November 308. There Diocletian rejected the invitation to resume his position with the words 'If only you could see the cabbages we have planted at Salonae with our hands, you would never again judge that a tempting prospect.'

Diocletian died at Split, probably on 3 December 311. Lactantius claims that he starved himself to death. It is certainly clear that, despite the cabbages, Diocletian's final months were clouded by disappointment. During the summer of 311 his wife and daughter were expelled from the palace at Nicomedia and sent into exile by Maximinus Daia. Later in the year, many of his statues were destroyed by Constantine as part of a purge directed against Maximian. The retirement may have become a bitter pill, as Diocletian saw his prestige evaporate and his achievements called into question. But in the eyes of historians, it was this that set Diocletian most clearly apart from all other emperors who had held power at Rome: 'Diocletian . . . showed exceptional character inasmuch as he alone of all emperors since the establishment of the Roman empire retired of his own accord from such an eminent position to private life and ordinary citizenship. He experienced, therefore, what no one else has since the creation of man, namely that although he had died as a private citizen, he was nevertheless enrolled among the gods.'

BUILDINGS OF THE NEW EMPIRE

Diocletian had a limitless passion for building, which led to an equally limitless scouring of the provinces to raise workers, craftsmen, waggons, and whatever is necessary for building operations. Here he built basilicas, there a circus, a mint, an arms factory, here he built a house for his wife, there one for his daughter.

Lactantius *On the Deaths of the Persecutors* 7

Diocletian's reforms placed heavy demands on the imperial budget, not least in the construction of suitably splendid palaces for himself and his imperial colleagues. Virtually nothing remains of his own palace at Nicomedia, nor that of Maximian at Milan. Much better preserved is the great walled palace which he built for his retirement at Spalato (Split), near the town of Salonae, on the Dalmatian coast. This had the outward appearance of a military camp, designed on a rectangular plan with projecting towers at the corners and gates in the middle of each side. Within were reception rooms, residential quarters, and the hexagonal mausoleum in which Diocletian himself was eventually buried. Diocletian's fame as a builder rests also on the great Baths constructed at Rome between 298 and 306. The frigidarium was larger even than that of the Baths of Caracalla. Despite the name, the dedicatory inscription makes clear that the Baths of Diocletian were mainly the work not of Diocletian but of his co-ruler Maximian.

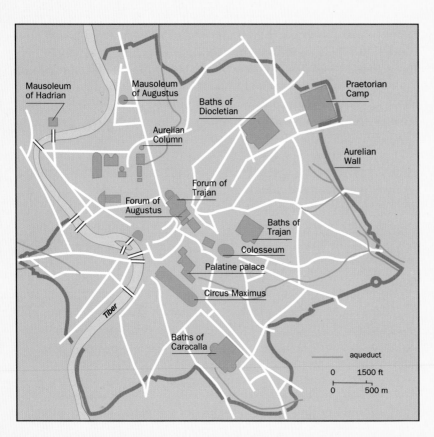

(Above) Diocletian's palace at Spalato (Split) was both fortress and palace combined. Colonnaded streets divided the interior into rectangular blocks of buildings, those in the northern part of the palace each arranged around an open court. The most important buildings were in the south, approached by a ceremonial way from the central cross-roads. This led to a raised vestibule and entrance hall, the principal entrance to Diocletian's private apartments which were ranged along the seaward side of the palace. To the north-east of these lay the mausoleum, an octagonal structure enclosing a domed circular burial chamber. It is ironic that this, the burial place of one of the most notorious persecutors of Christians, should now be a Christian cathedral.

(Left) By the end of the third century, Rome was no longer a major centre of government, but its prestige and tradition ensured that emperors continued to build within it. Diocletian and Maximian restored the Forum Romanum after a major fire in 283, rebuilding the senate house, though largely on earlier lines. Their greatest undertaking was however an entirely new construction, the Baths of Diocletian in the north of the city.

(Top) The north gate of the palace at Split, with remains of one of the flanking towers on the left. Despite their decorative arcades and statue-niches, these gates conformed to latest Roman military design. In each case there was both an outer and an inner gate, the outer flanked by imposing polygonal towers and closed by double doors which could be further protected by lowering a portcullis. The inner gate, too, had heavy doors. These were no mere ceremonial entrances, but serious defensive works.

(Above) The Baths of Diocletian at Rome. The brick-faced exterior was originally covered with stucco carved to resemble large marble blocks. So large was the demand for bricks for this enormous project that it seems the entire brick industry of Rome was reorganized and transferred to imperial control in order to meet it.

(Left) Reconstruction of the interior of the Baths of Diocletian at Rome, looking from the tepidarium (warm room, the main hall of the baths) towards the frigidarium (cold room). The basic structure of the tepidarium survives today in the church of Santa Maria degli Angeli. Note the extensive use of coloured marbles, painted stucco and statues; the interiors of these great imperial bath buildings were as striking for their decoration as for their size.

Constantius I
Imperator Caesar Gaius
Flavius Valerius Constantius
Augustus
305–306

Galerius
Imperator Caesar Galerius
Valerius Maximianus Pius
Felix Invictus Augustus
305–311

Severus II
Imperator Severus Pius Felix
Augustus
306–307

Maxentius
Marcus Aurelius Valerius
Maxentius Pius Felix Invictus
Augustus
306–312

Maximinus Daia
Imperator Caesar Galerius
Valerius Maximinus Pius Felix
Augustus
310–313

Galerius 'was tall in stature, and the vast expanse of his flesh was spread and bloated to a horrifying size. His words, his actions, and his appearance made him a source of alarm and terror to all.' This is the picture of a monster rather than a human being. The non-Christian Eutropius gives a different account, of 'a man who was both honourable in character and outstanding in military matters.' The portrait busts depict a determined military man with the close-cropped hair typical of the times. (*Above*) Porphyry bust of a tetrarch, possibly Galerius, from Athribis, Egypt, late third/early fourth century, now in the Cairo Museum.

Throughout the ten-year period of the persecution, their plotting and campaigning against each other continued without intermission. The seas were unnavigable, and wherever people sailed from they could not avoid being subjected to outrages of every sort. . . . Then again the manufacture of shields and breastplates, and the preparation of javelins, spears, and other munitions of war, not to mention warships and naval

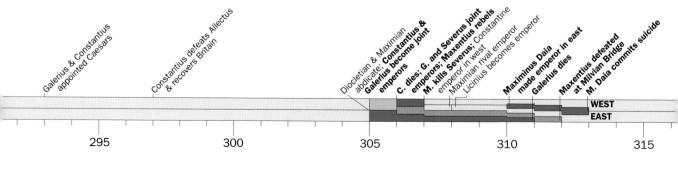

CONSTANTIUS I

Born 31 March c. 250 in Illyricum	Gaius Flavius Valerius Constantinus (Constantine) two sons by Theodora: Flavius Dalmatius and Flavius Julius Constantius
Appointed Caesar 1 March 293	
Accession to Augustus 1 May 305	
Wives 1) Helena 2) Theodora	Died of illness at York 25 July 306
Children one son by Helena:	

GALERIUS

Born c. 260 at Romulianum near Serdica	2) Galeria Valeria
Appointed Caesar 1 March 293	Children a daughter by his first wife: Valeria Maximilla a son Candidianus by an unknown concubine
Accession to Augustus 1 May 305	
Wives 1) name unknown	Died of illness at Serdica May 311

SEVERUS II

Born in Illyricum (date unknown)	Children a son Severus
Appointed Caesar 1 May 305	Forced to abdicate March/April 307; murder or suicide near Rome 16 September 307
Accession to Augustus August 306	
Wife name unknown	

MAXENTIUS

Born probably in Syria c. 283	Children two sons: Valerius Romulus, 2nd son name unknown
Accession to Augustus 28 October 306	Drowned at the Milvian Bridge 28 October 312
Wife Valeria Maximilla	

MAXIMINUS DAIA

Born 20 November 270 in Illyricum	Children a daughter name unknown
Appointed Caesar 1 May 305	Committed suicide at Tarsus July/August 313
Accession to Augustus 1 May 310	
Wife name unknown	

equipment, went on apace everywhere, and no one could look for anything but an enemy attack any day.

Eusebius *Ecclesiastical History* VIII.15

The eight years 305–313 were dominated by civil wars of a rather curious kind, in which some protagonists were striving for sole rule, others merely seeking to secure a place, as Caesar or Augustus, within the system of government established by Diocletian. The curious mixture of individual ambition and joint action led to a complex pattern of intrigue, alliance and open warfare. We find a vivid interpretation of the age in the writings of Christian apologists, who distort the merits and characters of the rival emperors to suit their own ends.

The tetrarchy renewed

The abdication of Diocletian and Maximian left Constantius and Galerius the new senior rulers of the Roman world. The official ceremonies took place at Milan and Nicomedia on the same day, 1 May 305, and each was provided with the support of a junior colleague: Severus in the west, Maximinus, surnamed Daia, in the east. The tetrarchic system of government was thus maintained. We may suspect that Diocletian was behind the new arrangement; but Galerius clearly had a major hand in selecting the new Caesars. Both were already connected with him, Maximinus being Galerius's son-in-law, and Severus a close friend of many years standing.

At first sight, the new men were much like their colleagues: military men of humble origin from the Balkan provinces. Neither gets a particularly good write-up from either pagan or Christian historians. Severus is described as 'ignoble in origin and habits'. Maximinus Daia does little better. Pagan writers call him 'of rustic origin and upbringing, but a cultivator of philosophers and men of letters, quiet in character, rather greedy for wine.' To the Christians, however, he was anathema, a persecutor every bit as determined as Galerius, forger of the anti-Christian 'Acts of Pilate', a textbook tyrant unbridled in his lusts, and a fierce promoter of the old religion to boot.

A more serious error made by Galerius and Diocletian was to underestimate the strength of family ties. For both Maximian and Constantius had ambitious sons who had been passed over in the new appointments. Maxentius, son of Maximian, was in his early 20s; and Constantine, son of Constantius, was then about 30 years old. Events soon showed that these men would seize by force what they were not given voluntarily.

The accession of Constantine

Constantine was serving under Diocletian as a high-ranking staff officer when the new Caesars were announced. Disappointed to be passed over, he was given leave to join his father Constantius in the west, which he did at Boulogne, where the latter was preparing to cross to Britain to campaign against the Picts.

Portrait bust of Maxentius, now in the Museo Torlonia, Rome.

The Pictish expedition of 305 was a success, and by the end of the summer Constantius had won the title 'Britannicus Maximus' for the second time. This victory could not hide the increasingly precarious nature of Constantius's position. Although he was senior emperor in the west, the hostile Galerius not only controlled the east but had also succeeded in installing his own nominee, Severus, as Caesar in the west. Constantius was also in poor health; the nickname 'Chlorus' (the pale) suggests he may have been suffering from leukaemia. When he died, Severus would expect to become senior emperor in the west, and another of Galerius's nominees might become the new western Caesar.

If this was the plan, it was thwarted by the strength of support for Constantius and his son. When Constantius died at York on 25 July 306, his army did not wait for instructions from Galerius, but immediately proclaimed Constantine 'Augustus', and senior emperor in the west in succession to his father. Indeed, Constantine resolutely maintained that he had been appointed Augustus by Constantius on his deathbed.

Faced with this fait accompli, there was little that Galerius could do to remove Constantine. But he could seek to demote him. Thus when messengers came from Constantine announcing his accession, Galerius

MAXENTIUS AT ROME

During his six years at Rome, the usurper Maxentius showed himself an energetic builder. Just south of the city, beside the Via Appia, he laid out a palace complex similar to that of Galerius at Thessalonica. The main feature was an enormous circus or hippodrome, capable of accommodating 15,000 spectators. Adjacent to this was Maxentius's mausoleum, a circular domed building set within a rectangular colonnaded enclosure. Much more impressive, is the enormous basilica which Maxentius built on the northern side of the Forum. Known as the Basilica Nova or Basilica of Constantine (for it was completed by Constantine after Maxentius's death), it was a gigantic hall, similar to the main hall (frigidarium) of an imperial bath complex. Today it stands as a gaunt, semi-ruined torso of brick-faced concrete, but originally it was finished within with marble veneers on the walls and moulded stucco, painted and gilded, on the ceiling. It was the largest vaulted building ever attempted by Roman architects.

Detail of the Basilica Nova at Rome, built largely by Maxentius but completed by Constantine c.313.

He was an outstanding man and exceptionally gracious who showed concern for the wealth of provincials and private individuals instead of simply pursuing the interests of the treasury. . . . He was not only loved but also revered by the Gauls, especially because through his government they had escaped the mistrusted prudence of Diocletian and the bloodthirsty rashness of Maximian.

Eutropius *Breviarium* X.1

The emperor Constantius (*above*, Ny Carlsberg Glyptotek, Copenhagen) was given a eulogistic treatment by Christian historians such as Lactantius and Eusebius. But he also receives praise from pagan writers such as Eutropius. Constantius won particular gratitude for shielding the Christians of the provinces under his control from the excesses of Diocletian's anti-Christian edicts. This was no mere peace-loving administrator, however, but a seasoned general who won a succession of hard-fought victories on the Rhine frontier. He married twice: first in around 270 to a Bithynian lady called Helena; then in the 280s to Theodora, daughter of the emperor Maximian. Constantius and Theodora had six children, but far and away the most famous of Constantius's offspring was the son born of his marriage to Helena: the future emperor Constantine. Opponents of Constantine claimed that Helena and Constantius were never truly married, but that she was merely his concubine. The case cannot be proved, but marriage is plausible, probably while he was serving with Aurelian in the east during the war against Zenobia.

sent back a purple robe with official recognition of Constantine as Caesar, not Augustus. Meanwhile Severus was raised to the rank of Augustus and senior emperor in the west.

The revolt of Maxentius

Thus did matters stand, with the tetrarchy of two Augusti and two Caesars still officially in place, when news of a fresh complication arrived from Italy. Maxentius, son of Maximian, also disappointed in being passed over in 305, had taken up residence in a villa on the Via Labicana, six miles from Rome. There he lost no time in plotting his own advancement. This was made all the easier by the fact that the citizens of Rome and Italy were aggrieved that their homeland was increasingly looked upon as just another province. Northern Italy had already lost its tax-free status under Diocletian. Maxentius's opportunity came when Galerius foolishly decided to extend taxation to peninsular Italy and the city of Rome itself. With the support of the people, and the remnants of the praetorian guard, Maxentius was proclaimed emperor at Rome on 28 October 306.

Maxentius played his cards carefully, hoping to gain official recognition from Galerius without further bloodshed. When that was refused, he proclaimed himself Augustus, in April 307, with control over not only most of Italy but also Sicily, Corsica and Sardinia, and the wealthy provinces of North Africa.

It was a remarkable coup, though with few regular troops at his disposal, and a hostile Severus at Milan in the north, Maxentius's position was far from secure. To bolster it, he made the fateful move of sending a purple robe to his father Maximian, inviting him to come to his aid and assume the rank of emperor for a second time. Eager for action, Maximian hurried from retirement in southern Italy to join his son. They made an alliance with Constantine, who henceforth was recognized as Augustus throughout his own and Maxentius's territories. Galerius meanwhile instructed Severus to crush Maxentius, who had too few troops to risk a decisive battle. Severus arrived before the walls of Rome but there his army deserted him, seduced by Maxentius's bribes. Severus himself fled to Ravenna but was captured, forced to abdicate, and killed, at Tres Tabernae near Rome, on 16 September 307.

The conference of Carnuntum

Determined not to accept Maxentius as a legitimate emperor, Galerius himself invaded Italy that same month. He fared little better than Severus. His troops likewise proved unreliable in the face of Maxentius's bribes, and only with difficulty did he extricate himself from Italy. But though Maxentius's position was strengthened by these victories, and by the marriage of his sister Fausta to Constantine, his regime did not escape serious crisis. In April 308 Maximian tried to usurp his son's position at Rome, and when that attempt failed he fled to refuge with his new son-in-law Constantine in Gaul. Faced with a multiplication of

THE ROMAN USURPER

It is incredible how joyfully and delightedly the senate and people exulted at his death for he (Maxentius) had oppressed them so much that on one occasion he permitted the praetorians to massacre the common people and was the first, through a most reprehensible edict issued under the pretext of obligatory state taxation, to compel the senators and farmers to contribute money for him to squander.

Aurelius Victor *Book of the Caesars* 40

Maxentius, son of Diocletian's co-emperor Maximian, emerges from the writings of Roman historians as another of the monsters of the age. His real ability may be judged from the fact that he seized power in Italy in 306 and held on to it for six years, despite determined attempts by Severus and Galerius to unseat him. Like his father, however, Maxentius came to be branded as a sexual tyrant: 'He would take respectable married women away from their husbands, insult and grossly dishonour them, and send them back to their husbands; and he took care not to victimize unknown or obscure persons, but to make the most outstanding of the senior members of the Roman senate the chief recipients of his besotted attention' (Eusebius VIII.13). It is difficult to say whether this contains a grain of truth, or is to be set aside merely as hostile propaganda.

emperors, Galerius and Maximian coaxed Diocletian briefly out of retirement in November 308 for an imperial conference at Carnuntum near Vienna. The result was the establishment of a new official tetrarchy. Licinius, another Illyrian army officer and friend of Galerius, was appointed Augustus in the west, in place of Severus. Constantine was confirmed in the position of Caesar. And Maximian was forced to relinquish his resumed imperial titles.

This still left Maxentius in control of Italy and Africa, and one of Licinius's primary tasks was to re-establish central control over these regions. Based at Sirmium, he made minor inroads in the extreme northeast during the course of 309. These were much less than might have been expected, however, since in that year Maxentius was distracted by a rebellion in his North African territories. The leader of the uprising was Valerius Alexander, who had been vicar (governor) of the diocese of Africa since 303. Styling himself 'Imperator Caesar Lucius Domitius Alexander Pius Felix Invictus Augustus', he held out against Maxentius for almost 18 months, but was captured and killed by a small army led by Maxentius's praetorian commander Rufius Volusianus late in 309.

Meanwhile, Maximian had not given up his ambitions in the west. For two years he resided at Constantine's court as a trusted adviser and father-in-law, then in 310 decided to have a final go at imperial power. While Constantine was embroiled in a campaign against the Franks, Maximian hurried to Arles, proclaimed himself emperor for the third time, and announced that Constantine was dead.

It was a foolish move. Constantine hurried south to confront the usurper, who by this time had fled from Arles to the more easily defensible Marseilles. The citizens of Marseilles refused to take his side, however, and opened the gates to Constantine. Maximian was captured, and soon afterwards it was given out that he had hanged himself. His demise had one positive result – reconciliation with his son. For Maxentius had his father deified by decree of the senate.

The death of Galerius

The suicide of Maximian removed one of the foremost persecutors of the Christians, but two others remained in power in the east: Galerius and Maximinus Daia. Maximinus's fortune was on the rise; he was elevated to Augustus on 1 May 310. Galerius, meanwhile, was in decline, already suffering from the frightful cancer which was soon to kill him. Christian apologists saw in Galerius's illness clear evidence of the wrath of God. By April 311 even Galerius himself became convinced of this. On his deathbed, on 30 April, he at last passed an edict rescinding the anti-Christian measures he had instigated eight years before. In the words of Eusebius, 'he pulled himself together, and after first making open confession to the God of the universe he called his court officials and ordered them to lose no time in stopping the persecution of Christians, and by an imperial law and decree to stimulate the building of churches and the performance of the customary rites, with the addition of prayers

Galerius made Thessalonica his capital and during the 18 years of his reign, from appointment as Caesar in 293 to death in 311, he endowed the city with a series of splendid new buildings and monuments: a palace and hippodrome; a triumphal arch; and a great domed mausoleum. These were built within a new imperial quarter laid out on the eastern edge of the earlier city. The four-way triumphal arch, commemorating Galerius's victory over the Persians in 298, stood astride the Via Egnatia and formed the link between the palace to the south of the road and the mausoleum to the north. The mausoleum was a great rotunda, with a curious two-centred dome; it survives as the church of Agios Giorgios (*right*). Decorated with marble veneer and colourful mosaics, the interior must have been an impressive sight. In the event, however, Galerius chose not to be buried here, but at his birthplace of Romulianum near Serdica.

THE TERRIBLE FATE OF GALERIUS

Without warning, suppurative inflammation broke out round the middle of his genitals, then a deep-seated fistular ulcer: these ate their way incurably into his inmost bowels. From them came a teeming indescribable mass of worms, and a sickening smell was given off; for the whole of his hulking body, thanks to over-eating, had been transformed even before his illness into a huge lump of flabby fat, which then decomposed and presented those who came near with a revolting and horrifying sight. Of the doctors, some were unable to endure the overpowering and extraordinary stench, and were executed on the spot; others, unable to be of any assistance now that the entire mass had swollen and deteriorated beyond hope of recovery, were put to death without mercy.

Eusebius *Ecclesiastical History* VIII.16

for the emperor's majesty.' It was too late to save Galerius, who died a few days later.

The death of Galerius led to a contest between Licinius and Maximinus Daia for control of the east. Maximinus advanced through Asia Minor, winning support by promising exemptions from Galerius's stern taxation. Licinius led his army east to confront the rival, but the two emperors came to terms without fighting. Licinius retained control over the Balkans, while Maximinus held Asia Minor and the eastern provinces. It was an inequitable division, and one which gave Maximinus a free hand to resume the anti-Christian persecution which Galerius had halted only six months before.

The Milvian Bridge

In 312 Constantine crossed the Alps with a small army and defeated Maxentius's forces at Turin and Verona. Having secured northern Italy he then advanced on Rome. The popularity of Maxentius's rule was clearly in decline by this time. It may be that stories of his financial exactions and his pursuit of other men's wives contain some basis of truth. His popularity at Rome had never recovered from the riots three years earlier in which thousands of citizens were killed by his own guards. Maxentius also displayed an ambivalent attitude towards the Christians. On his accession he had proclaimed a policy of toleration, but it was only in July 311 that he ordered church property which had been confiscated during the persecution to be restored. It was too little, too late.

When Constantine's army appeared outside the walls of Rome in the autumn of 312 Maxentius no longer had the full support of the city

ANOTHER TEXTBOOK TYRANT

But Daia, who had only recently been picked up from looking after cattle in the forests, had at once become a guardsman, then an officer of the guard, soon afterwards a tribune, and then the next day a Caesar, and he now received the east to crush and trample underfoot. . . . He would squander money too on anything, without discrimination or limit. . . . He would also take away people's goods while they were still alive or give them to any of his own followers who sought other people's property.

But his capital vice, in which he surpassed all who have ever lived, was his appetite for seduction. . . . By the end, he had introduced the practice of allowing no one to marry a wife without his permission, so that he himself could sample every marriage in advance. . . . He was not able to keep his hands off the Augusta whom he had recently called his mother [Valeria, daughter of Diocletian and widow of Galerius]. . . The woman was still dressed in black, as the mourning period was not yet completed, when Maximinus sent envoys to her demanding her hand in marriage; he said he would divorce his own wife if Valeria agreed to his request. She gave a frank reply . . . . His lust turned to anger and rage. He at once outlawed the woman, seized her goods, deprived her of her retinue, killed her eunuchs under torture, and sent her, along with her mother, into exile.

Lactantius *On the Deaths of the Persecutors* 19, 37-39

populace. Rather than suffer the uncertainties of a prolonged siege, Maxentius decided to risk all in a crucial battle. The two armies met just beyond the Milvian Bridge, to the west of Rome, and Constantine's army, carrying Christian standards before them, won a decisive victory. As Maxentius's troops fled back across the Milvian Bridge into Rome, the structure gave way beneath them. Maxentius died trying to swim to safety. The date was 28 October 312; Maxentius had been in power six years to the very day.

The end of persecution

Constantine's victory in the west precipitated a final showdown between Licinius and Maximinus Daia in the east. Early in 313, Licinius had married Constantine's half-sister Constantia. Meanwhile, Maximinus Daia crossed the Bosphorus into Europe and seized Byzantium and Heraclea. Licinius marched against the invader, and battle was joined on the plain of the River Ergenus, near Hadrianopolis in Thrace, on 30 April. Licinius had a much smaller force at his disposal – only some 30,000 men as against Maximinus's 70,000 – but by superior tactics he was able to gain the upper hand. Once again the army of God prevailed against the army of paganism; for Licinius like Constantine fought under the banner of the cross, while Maximinus had vowed to eradicate Christianity if the gods granted him victory.

Maximinus fled the battlefield dressed as a slave. Stopping only to collect his family and a few close associates, he hurried across Asia Minor, hoping to hold the Taurus passes against his pursuers. The forts he built proved little obstacle to Licinius's troops, however, and by midsummer he was under close siege by land and sea at Tarsus. Death was the only way out, but he chose an unfortunate means: a poison which proved slow-acting, drove him mad with pain and took four days to kill. 'Thus amid groans which he uttered as if he were being burnt, he breathed out his guilty spirit in a death of detestable horror.'

Licinius chose to celebrate his victory with a far-from-Christian bloodbath. First to be executed was Candidianus, illegitimate son of Galerius. Next was Severianus, son of the emperor Severus. Maximinus Daia's son and daughter, eight and seven years old respectively, were likewise put to death, and their mother thrown into the River Orontes and drowned. Finally Valeria, daughter of Diocletian and widow of Galerius, was discovered in disguise at Thessalonica; she too was arrested and killed. The persecution of Christians was over, but it was hardly an auspicious opening to a new age.

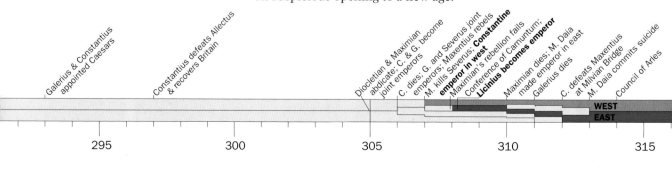

Constantine

Imperator Caesar Flavius
Constantinus Pius Felix
Invictus Augustus

307–337

Licinius

Imperator Caesar Gaius
Valerius Licianus Licinius
Pius Felix Invictus Augustus

308–324

Colossal head of Constantine found in
1486 in the western apse of the Basilica
Nova at Rome. It was originally part of
an enormous seated statue.

CONSTANTINE AND LICINIUS

*When men commend my services, which owe their origin to the inspira-
tion of Heaven, do they not clearly establish the truth that God is the
cause of the exploits I have performed? Assuredly they do, for it belongs
to God to do whatever is best, and to man, to perform the commands of
God.*

Constantine *To the Assembly of the Saints* 26

The reign of the emperor Constantine marks a turning point in the history of the Roman empire no less than that of Diocletian. For it was
Constantine who made Christianity the official religion of the empire,
and founded the new imperial capital of Constantinople. He also
restored the concept of sole rule after the divided administration of the
tetrarchy. The character of the man is more difficult to assess. Much of
the truth lies veiled behind the highly partisan eulogies of Eusebius and
other Christian writers. There is certainly no reason to doubt that
Constantine was a man of sincere religious conviction. But he was also
an able propagandist, a gifted military commander, and an unscrupulous
and determined manipulator.

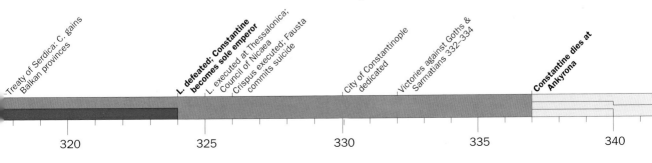

Treaty of Serdica: C. gains
Balkan provinces

L. defeated; Constantine
becomes sole emperor

L. executed at Thessalonica;
Council of Nicaea

Crispus executed; Fausta
commits suicide

City of Constantinople
dedicated

Victories against Goths &
Sarmatians 332–334

Constantine dies at
Ankyrona

320   325   330   335   340

CONSTANTINE	
Born 27 February 272 or 273 at Naissus Gaius Flavius Valerius Constantinus *Acknowledged as Caesar in 306* Flavius Valerius Constantinus Nobilissimus Caesar *In 307* Imperator Caesar Constantinus Pius Felix Invictus Augustus, Pontifex Maximus, Pater Patriae, Proconsul *Added from 312* 'Maximus' *From 324* 'Victor' in place of 'Invictus' *Victory titles* Germanicus Maximus I (307), II (308), III (314), IV (328); Sarmaticus Maximus I (323), II (334); Gothicus Maximus I (328), II (332); Dacicus Maximus (336) Consul I (307), II (312), III (313), IV (315), V (319), VI (320), VII (326), VIII (329) Tribunicia potestas first in 306; then II December 306–summer 307; III summer 307–December 307; thereafter renewed annually on 10 December. Imperator: first on accession, then II & III (307), IV (308);	thereafter renewed annually in July of each year until XXXII (July 336–May 337) *Full titles at death* Imperator Caesar Flavius Constantinus Maximus Pius Felix Victor Augustus, Pontifex Maximus, Germanicus Maximus IV, Sarmaticus Maximus II, Gothicus Maximus II, Dacicus Maximus, Tribuniciae potestatis XXXIII, Imperator XXXII, Consul VIII, Pater Patriae, Proconsul *Wives* 1) Minervina 2) Fausta *Children* a son by Minervina: Gaius Flavius Julius Crispus three sons by Fausta: Flavius Claudius Constantinus (Constantine II), Flavius Julius Constantius (Constantius II) and Flavius Julius Constans two daughters by Fausta: Constantia and Helena *Died of illness at Ankyrona near Nicomedia 22 May 337; buried in the Church of the Holy Apostles, Constantinople*

LICINIUS	
Born c. 265 in the province of Dacia Nova *Accession 11 November 308* *Wife* Constantia	*Children* a son Valerius Licinianus Licinius *Abdicated 19 December 324; executed at Thessalonica early 325*

Constantine and Licinius

The death of Maximinus Daia at Tarsus in the summer of 313 left control of the Roman empire in the hands of two men: Constantine holding the western provinces including Italy and North Africa, Licinius those of the Balkans and the east. Licinius had come to power in 308, at the conference of Carnuntum, as the nominee of Galerius. He was indeed an old friend of Galerius, and had shared his tent on campaign. A little older than Constantine (he was born around 265, as compared with Constantine's 272 or 273), Licinius was appointed over Constantine's head as Augustus in the west, to replace the unfortunate Severus. His inability to remove Maxentius from Italy meant however that his centre of power remained in the Balkans.

The years of co-operation between Constantine and Licinius were those of an uneasy truce rather than true friendship. Their political alliance was cemented in 313 when Licinius married Constantine's half-sister Constantia at Milan. Two factors stood against the chances of a successful sharing of power. First, Constantine had already decided by 313 to make Christianity a key part of his policies; Licinius went along with this but seems never to have been a keen supporter. Secondly, and more crucially, Constantine was determined to tolerate a rival for only so long as was absolutely necessary.

The breach came in 316, and was entirely the fault of Constantine, despite attempts by Christian historians to lay the blame on Licinius. In July or August 315 Licinius and Constantia (Constantine's half-sister) had a son, Licinius the younger, who would naturally be expected to become Caesar in due course. Hoping to steal a march on his rival, Constantine proposed to Licinius that Constantine's brother-in-law Bassianus, husband of his half-sister Anastasia, should be appointed Caesar with authority over Italy. Licinius refused, and in the autumn of 316 Constantine invaded the Balkans, seeking to win over at least the province of Pannonia, and to dispose of Licinius altogether if that proved possible.

At first, all went extremely well for Constantine. At the Battle of Cibalae on 8 October, he defeated Licinius's much larger army. Licinius fled east to Serdica, where he proclaimed Valens, commander of the Danube frontier forces, his colleague in power, with the title 'Imperator Caesar Aurelius Valerius Valens Pius Felix Augustus'. Valens assembled a new army, and a second great battle was fought near Hadrianopolis in Thrace, at a place called Campus Ardiensis. This time the outcome was less clear, and Constantine was forced to come to terms. Valens was executed, and Licinius was compelled to cede most of the Balkan provinces to Constantine. The treaty was officially confirmed at Serdica on 1 March 317, and sealed by a dynastic arrangement. Constantine's sons Crispus and Constantinus were proclaimed Caesars, together with Licinius the younger. None of the three was yet old enough to have an effective share in power: Crispus was in his teens, and the others were mere infants.

He had been honoured with sovereign power in time of prosperity; he had ranked next after the Emperor Constantine, and had become brother-in-law and kinsman of the most exalted person living; yet he turned his back on the examples of good men and emulated the wickedness and criminal folly of the evil tyrants; and he chose to follow the same path as those whose life he had with his own eyes seen ending in calamity, rather than remain on terms of friendship and esteem with his superior.

Eusebius *Ecclesiastical History* X.8

Licinius gets a poor write-up from Christian historians such as Eusebius, but much of this is propaganda. What was his true character? The pagan sources are not especially complimentary; one describes his only virtue as 'frugality, and that, to be sure, of merely a rustic nature'. Yet Licinius patronized pagan philosophers and exercised toleration towards his Christian subjects. Toleration only faltered when he found proof that certain bishops had been conspiring with Constantine behind his back. It is striking to see the change in Christian attitudes over the years. In 313, they praised Licinius for freeing the eastern provinces from the persecutions of Maximinus Daia. By 324, they were reviling him as the arch enemy of their great hero Constantine. It is hard to believe he was as black as they chose to paint him. (*Above*) Portrait-bust of Licinius now in the Museo Chiaramonti at the Vatican.

The final showdown

Over the next six years, Licinius remained tolerant of Christianity, though he also maintained close links with pagan writers and philosophers. Constantine meanwhile presented himself as the champion of Christians everywhere. As a result, Licinius gradually came to suspect that Christians in his service were fifth columnists sympathetic to Constantine. The mistake was to take action against them, for this provided Constantine with just the pretext he needed for a further and final war. Licinius was not a savage persecutor in the mould of Galerius or Maximinus Daia, but he did dismiss Christians from the imperial bureaucracy and the army. Eventually he found cause to suspect certain bishops of open disloyalty, and had them executed and their churches destroyed.

In 324, Constantine gathered a great army and fleet and moved against Licinius. The two armies converged on Hadrianopolis, where on 3 July 324 Constantine won a decisive victory. Licinius fled across the Bosphorus and once again appointed a co-ruler to assist him: the commander of his bodyguard, Martius Martinianus, who assumed the title 'Imperator Caesar Martius Martinianus Pius Felix Augustus'. The respite was short, for Constantine ferried his own army across the Bosphorus and defeated Licinius again at Chrysopolis on 18 September 324.

A few days later Licinius and Martinianus surrendered to Constantine at Nicomedia on the understanding that their lives would be spared. Constantine sent Licinius to Thessalonica to live as a private citizen, 'but not long after broke his oath, as was his custom, and had him hanged.' That was in the spring of 325. With him died his son, the younger Licinius, a boy of nine. Later the same year Martinianus met a similar fate in Cappadocia.

Domestic difficulties

The victory at Chrysopolis left Constantine undisputed master of the Roman world. Up to this point he had been prudent and merciful, branding his opponents as tyrants but seeking popular acclaim for his own conduct. After Chrysopolis, however, contemporaries noticed a change: 'At last he no longer needed to conceal his natural malignity but acted in accordance with his unlimited power.' That much was evident in the treatment of Licinius, but worse followed in 326, when he was instrumental in the deaths of both his own son and his wife.

The son was Crispus, offspring of Constantine and his first wife Minervina. Born around the year 300, he had played a leading role in the war against Licinius. Constantine rewarded him with control of the western provinces, and Crispus took up residence at Trier. The two were reunited at Pola in Istria in May 326, and it was there that Crispus was executed for adultery. One version of the story says that Constantine's wife Fausta was in love with her stepson and accused him of adultery when he rejected her. Certainly Constantine had passed a severe edict

THE VISION OF CONSTANTINE

Constantine was converted to Christianity by seeing a vision of a cross shortly before the Battle at the Milvian Bridge.

He said that about noon, when the day was already beginning to decline, he saw with his own eyes the trophy of a cross of light in the heavens, above the sun, and bearing the inscription 'Conquer by this.' At this sight he himself was struck with amazement, and his whole army also, which followed him on this expedition, and witnessed the miracle. He said, moreover, that he doubted within himself what the import of this apparition could be. And while he continued to ponder and reason on its meaning, night came suddenly on; then in his sleep the Christ of God appeared to him with the same sign which he had seen in the heavens, and commanded him to make a likeness of that sign which he had seen in the heavens, and to use it as a likeness in all engagements with his enemies.

Eusebius *Life of Constantine* I.27-28

THE IMPERIAL PRESENCE

Eusebius gives a glowing account of Constantine's physical and mental characteristics.

For no-one was comparable to him for grace and beauty of person, or height of stature; and he so far surpassed his compeers in personal strength as to be a terror to them. He was, however, even more conspicuous for the excellence of his mental qualities than for his superior physical endowments; being gifted in the first place with a sound judgment, and having also reaped the advantages of a liberal education.

Eusebius *Life of Constantine* I.19

against sexual misconduct the previous month, and Crispus may have fallen foul of that. But there is more than a suspicion of intrigue, since Fausta could well have wished Crispus out of the way to make way for her own sons. A little later, Constantine arrived in Rome to be confronted by his mother Helena, who convinced him that Fausta had falsely procured Crispus's death. Fausta retired to a bath, where she had the temperature raised until she suffocated in the steam and died.

Constantine and Christianity

The historian Zosimus tells us that Constantine was wracked by guilt after the deaths of Crispus and Fausta, and turned to Christianity for forgiveness. The truth is that Constantine had already adopted the new faith in 312, when he had seen a vision of the cross in the sky shortly before his victory at the Milvian Bridge. Yet there is clear evidence that Constantine did not at once exclude worship of the old gods. Imagery of the sun-cult continues to appear on his coinage up to the year 320. It is likely that until 312 Constantine was a regular worshipper of the sun-god as supreme deity, like Aurelian and other soldier-emperors before him. The concept of a nebulous supreme deity lying behind the traditional religion was not too far removed from the Christian notion of a single omnipotent god. When the conviction came to him, the transition to Christianity was easy to make.

Though a committed Christian from 312, Constantine trod warily in imposing the new official religion on the empire. In 313 he and Licinius extended restoration of church property to the Christians of the eastern provinces, but there was no attempt to limit or forbid the worship of the old gods. Constantine's own commitment to Christianity was made clear by his involvement in theological disputes such as the Donatist schism which was dividing the Church in Africa. Western bishops were summoned to a special council at Arles in 314 to settle the dispute. Constantine himself attended the meeting as a layman and then sought to enforce the council's decision by ordering the confiscation of Donatist churches. The measure was repealed in 321, but not before Constantine had shown that he too could persecute Christians if they were of the wrong kind.

The defeat of Licinius gave Constantine a much freer hand to promote his new religious policy. Soon after 324, pagan sacrifice was forbidden, and imperial officials were dispatched throughout the eastern provinces to seek out and confiscate the treasures of pagan temples. Some of the proceeds from this immense confiscation were used for the building of splendid new churches, not least in the Holy Places of Bethlehem and Jerusalem. At about the same time, gladiatorial contests were forbidden, and Constantine passed severe laws against sexual immorality and prohibited ritual prostitution.

Constantine did not exclude pagan officials from the imperial entourage, but throughout his later years bishops played a prominent role in court politics. On one occasion Eusebius even compared

Constantine presents a model of the city of Constantinople to the Virgin Mary; 10th-century mosaic over the south doorway of Haghia Sophia in modern Istanbul. Constantine's foundation of the new city of Constantinople was one of the most significant achievements of his reign. The site he chose was that of Byzantium, a Greek city founded many centuries before. It stood in a strategic location on the point of a promontory projecting into the Bosphorus at the main crossing place from Europe to Asia. Furthermore to one side of the city lay the excellent natural harbour of the inlet known as the Golden Horn. The city Constantine founded was over four times the size of the Byzantium it replaced. His hopes for its success are shown by the fact that he diverted the grain supplies of Egypt from Rome to the new city, and established a corn dole for the citizens. He even established a senate. In many ways Constantine was consciously copying the old Rome, but in one important respect Constantinople was an entirely new concept. It was planned as a Christian capital, a counterbalance to pagan Rome, and much effort went into the building of churches and basilicas. Little of Constantine's work is visible today, since the city was extensively rebuilt during the centuries when it served as the capital of the Byzantine and Ottoman empires.

Constantine and his bishops to the Apostles surrounding Christ in paradise! At the same time, Constantine himself took a leading role in affairs of the Church. In 325 he summoned western and eastern bishops to attend the Council of Nicaea, where Arianism was condemned as heresy and Christian orthodoxy defined in the Creed. On Good Friday 325 he had delivered a long theological address *To the Assembly of the Saints* to an audience gathered probably at Antioch. Yet throughout these years he continued to style himself 'Pontifex Maximus', and it was only on his deathbed in 337 that he took the final step of receiving Christian baptism.

Running the empire

Constantine was an active and able administrator. He established a body of 'Comites' (Companions), divided into three ranks, who owed a special allegiance to the emperor and were employed on a range of government duties. He also continued the lofty court ceremonial established by Diocletian, in which the emperor was portrayed as sacrosanct, removed from ordinary mortals. Constantine took to wearing a bejewelled diadem as the visible symbol of his exalted rank.

In military matters, Constantine's main innovation was his division of the army into *ripenses* (frontier troops) and *comitatenses* (central field army). The latter, stationed some way behind the frontier, was ready to be deployed as need arose without weakening the frontier defences, and built on the arrangements made by earlier emperors since Gallienus. Contemporaries were sceptical of the new arrangement, feeling that troops should be placed on the frontier where the threat to security was greatest, but it could not be denied that the central field army served Constantine well both during the civil wars of his early years and the frontier campaigns of the 320s and 330s.

For the most part, Constantine's administration comes across in the sources as neither good nor bad. Some found his laws too severe. Others praised him for rooting out fiscal abuses. His popularity with the Christian minority ensured him a basic level of support almost regardless of what he did. When it came to taxation, however, even the Christians joined in the complaint. Constantine's particular innovation was a tax paid in gold and silver known as the *chrysargyron*, which was levied every four years on city-dwellers throughout the empire. 'The result was that as each fourth year came round when this tax had to be paid, weeping and wailing were heard throughout the city, because beatings and torture were in store for those who could not pay owing to extreme poverty. Indeed, mothers sold their children and fathers prostituted their daughters under compulsion to pay the exactors of the *chrysargyron*.' How far Constantine raised the overall level of taxation it is difficult to say. The confiscation of pagan temple treasures may have gone some way to off-setting the worst effects. But there does seem to have been a decisive shift in the burden of taxation from countryside to city.

New capital and old

In his early years as emperor in the west Constantine had resided mainly at Trier. A series of impressive buildings, including the 'Kaiserthermen' or Imperial Baths and a great basilica, testify to his efforts to turn this city into a capital befitting his vast ambitions. In 316 he transferred the centre of his activities to the Balkan provinces recently seized from Licinius, making Serdica (modern Sofia) and then Sirmium (near Belgrade) his principal base. The momentous change came on 8 November 324 when Constantine, after his final victory over Licinius, founded an entirely new capital on the site of the existing city of Byzantium. This involved an enormous building programme, greater even than Diocletian's work at Nicomedia, but within six years the new city was ready for dedication as Constantinople.

The foundation of Constantinople marked a further stage in the decline in importance of Rome and Italy, and the western provinces in general. But Constantine did not entirely neglect the old capital. He completed the Basilica Nova begun by Maxentius, and was responsible for the last of the great imperial bath buildings, the Baths of Constantine. Furthermore, two of his closest relatives were buried in specially-built mausolea at Rome: his mother Helena at Tor Pignattara on the Via Praenestina (the sarcophagus can be seen in the Vatican Museum), and his daughter Constantina in what is now the church of Santa Costanza. However, Constantine effectively demoted the city from its status as imperial capital by disbanding the praetorian guard. During the last 20 years of his reign he paid only one brief visit to Rome. The future lay elsewhere.

On his father's death in 306 Constantine held only the western provinces of Britain, Spain, Gaul and the Germanies. In 312 he invaded Italy and defeated Maxentius at Turin and Verona, then at the Battle of the Milvian Bridge. This gave Constantine Italy and North Africa, but he agreed to share power with Licinius, leaving the latter in control of the eastern provinces. As early as 316, however, Constantine attacked Licinius and seized the Balkans (except for Thrace), then in a final campaign in 324 he defeated and captured Licinius and reunited the whole empire under the rule of one man.

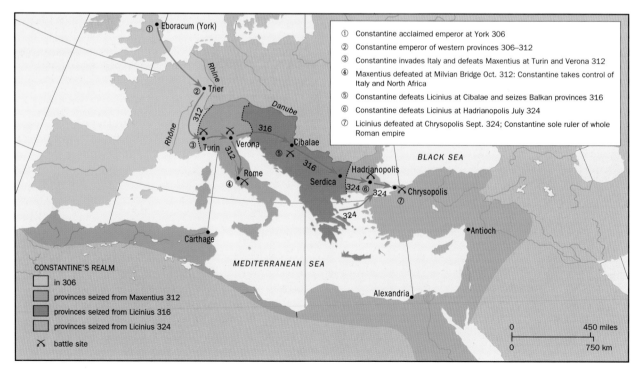

① Constantine acclaimed emperor at York 306
② Constantine emperor of western provinces 306–312
③ Constantine invades Italy and defeats Maxentius at Turin and Verona 312
④ Maxentius defeated at Milvian Bridge Oct. 312: Constantine takes control of Italy and North Africa
⑤ Constantine defeats Licinius at Cibalae and seizes Balkan provinces 316
⑥ Constantine defeats Licinius at Hadrianopolis July 324
⑦ Licinius defeated at Chrysopolis Sept. 324; Constantine sole ruler of whole Roman empire

CONSTANTINE'S REALM
in 306
provinces seized from Maxentius 312
provinces seized from Licinius 316
provinces seized from Licinius 324
✗ battle site

0 450 miles
0 750 km

CONSTANTINE AND ROME

Constantine's victory over Maxentius in 312 made him master of Rome, and he set out to underline his legitimacy by a programme of new building in the old capital. Maxentius had strengthened his support in the city by presenting himself as a Roman emperor with Roman interests at heart – not a distant ruler in one of the new imperial capitals of Trier or Nicomedia. Constantine was keen to show he was just as good a Roman as his predecessor. One of the most famous buildings named after him at Rome is the Arch of Constantine, a usurped second-century monument. Constantine also completed Maxentius's massive basilica in the Forum Romanum. It was here, in the western apse, that the well-known colossal head was found in the 15th century (p.213). Constantine also built some baths (though much smaller than those of Diocletian), and a number of Christian churches. Furthermore, while he was still only emperor of the west (before his victory over Licinius in 324) he made plans to be buried at Rome. The evidence survives in the form of a massive porphyry sarcophagus, now in the Vatican, and in the ruins of the circular Tor Pignattara mausoleum beside the Via Labicana. Both were ultimately used by his mother Helena, and Constantine himself was buried at Constantinople.

(Above) The Arch of Constantine near the Colosseum commemorates his victory over Maxentius, and the inscription records its dedication by the senate and people of Rome in 315. It has long been recognized that many of the decorative panels date to an earlier period, however, and new research suggests that the arch itself may have been built not for Constantine but for Hadrian. Constantine simply replaced the top storey (including the inscription) and added his own frieze half way up.

(Left) Porphyry sarcophagus from Tor Pignattara, thought to have been intended for Constantine himself, but in fact used by his mother Helena. The scenes of battle between Romans and barbarians, though wonderfully executed, are strangely out of place in the tomb of such a reputedly saintly lady. A matching sarcophagus decorated with vine scrolls and putti may have been made for Constantine's wife, the empress Fausta, but was found in their daughter Constantia's mausoleum, now the church of Santa Costanza.

THE CHURCHES OF CONSTANTINE

Constantine became a great builder of Christian churches, both at Rome and Constantinople, and at other key places in the empire. At Rome, he donated the imperial palace of the Lateran to the bishop of Rome as his official residence, and built the cathedral of Saint John Lateran on an adjacent plot. On the slopes of the Vatican hill Constantine created a huge terrace on which the Basilica of Saint Peter was constructed. This was replaced by the present building in the 16th century, and little of the original St Peter's, or the original church of Saint John Lateran, have survived. In Constantinople his greatest religious building was the Church of the Holy Apostles, which he intended as his own mausoleum. It was there that he was buried in 337, but once again, almost nothing survives. In the Holy Land, Constantine's religious building was inspired by the visit of his mother Helena in 326–7. Helena made careful enquiries into the location of events in the Gospels, and succeeded in discovering the site of the crucifixion and the tomb of Christ at Jerusalem, and the stable in which he had been born at Bethlehem. At Jerusalem, she ordered diggings on the site of the crucifixion, and reputedly found three wooden crosses; a handy miracle revealed which of these was the True Cross of Christ. It was on this spot, extending to cover the tomb as well, that Constantine built the original Church of the Holy Sepulchre. Of this, again, almost nothing survives, though it was depicted in mosaic in the church of Santa Pudenziana at Rome.

(Above) Fourth-century mosaics in the church of Santa Costanza at Rome, burial place of Constantine's daughter Constantina.
(Left) Reconstruction of Constantine's basilica of St Peter's at Rome.

The later campaigns

Ever eager for military glory, Constantine fought a series of major wars in his later years. In the autumn of 328, accompanied by his eldest surviving son Constantine, he fought successfully against the Alemanni on the Rhine. Late in 332, he waged a large-scale campaign against the Goths on the Danube, starving them into submission and the acceptance of Roman suzerainty. Constantine had rebuilt Trajan's famous Danube bridge a few years before, and now used it to good effect. Two

CONSTANTINE'S LAWS

He enacted many laws, some good and equitable but most of them superfluous and a few severe.

Eutropius *Breviarium* X.8

Constantine was not one of the great law-makers of ancient Rome, and many of his edicts display a tendency towards undue severity. Under his laws, many professions were made into hereditary castes, with no freedom for sons to choose a different career from their fathers. Peasant farmers were tied to the land even more firmly than they had been under Diocletian. Corruption and extortion were ruthlessly punished. Many of Constantine's laws directly reflect the practice or morality of Christianity. It became illegal, for example, for Jews to own Christian slaves, according to Eusebius 'on the ground that it could not be right that those whom the Saviour had ransomed should be subjected to the yoke of slavery by a people who had slain the prophets and the Lord himself.' Some of his fiercest legislation, however, was reserved for crimes of a sexual nature. Rapists were to be burned alive. If a girl willingly eloped with her lover, she too was to be burned alive, and any nurse who assisted the elopement was to have molten lead poured down her throat. Parents who concealed the fact that their daughters had been seduced were to be deported. Even girls who were violently raped away from home were punished, on the grounds that they should have stayed safely at home. This unreasonable legislation suggests that Constantine suffered from some kind of sexual hang-up.

years later it was the turn of the Sarmatians, and by 336 Constantine could claim to have recaptured many of the Dacian territories conquered by Trajan. The fact that they were lost again after his death did not detract from the brief gust of military glory.

By 336 Constantine, however, was an old man of 63 or 64, and he had to look to the future. His plans for the succession rested on the three surviving sons of his marriage to Fausta, and the son of his half-brother Flavius Dalmatius. By this time he had effectively divided the empire between the four of them. Constantine (II), took the west, Constantius the east and Constans Italy and the Upper Danube. The fourth Caesar, Flavius Dalmatius junior, was installed on 18 September 335 and given command of Greece and the Lower Danube. Constantine clearly expected his heirs to govern the empire as a tetrarchy, the very system which he himself had striven to overthrow. It was an imprudent arrangement, and one of his less lasting achievements.

Baptism and death

Constantine's last and greatest campaign was to be the conquest of Persia. He planned to christianize the Persians, and en route to be baptized (like Jesus) in the River Jordan. As a preliminary to this ambitious undertaking, he installed his nephew Hannibalianus as 'King of Armenia and adjacent regions'. More significantly, Hannibalianus was also styled 'King of kings', the title borne by the Persian king whom he was evidently intended to replace. Nothing came of this grand scheme, however, since shortly after Easter 337, Constantine fell terminally ill. Knowing himself near death, he was baptized by Eusebius, bishop of Nicomedia (not the famous historian), at the imperial villa of Ankyrona.

Constantine died at Ankyrona on Whit Sunday (22 May) 337. His body was taken under guard to the Church of the Holy Apostles at Constantinople, which he had built as his own mausoleum. Within the church were 12 false sarcophagi, one for each of the apostles. Constantine's own sarcophagus was placed in the middle as the thirteenth. It was more an imperial statement of divine pretentions, in the old style, than the humble resting place of a recent Christian convert.

When news of Constantine's burial reached Rome, the citizens were outraged that he had chosen to be buried at his new capital rather than in their own city. This did not prevent the senate from officially deifying the deceased Constantine, in a final act of religious incongruity. Thus did the first Christian emperor of Rome join the ranks of his pagan predecessors. But much had changed, and the death of Constantine marks a very real turning point in the history of the empire. The city of Rome had lost its pre-eminence, the old gods had gone, civic values and political life had been transformed. There was a new army, new provincial administration, new policies and strategies of power, new styles and fashions in art and literature. The theocratic-autocratic state left by Constantine was still the Roman empire, but it was a far cry from the imperial order established by Augustus some 350 years before.

THE HEIRS OF CONSTANTINE	THE HOUSE OF VALENTINIAN	THE THEODOSIAN DYNASTY	THE LAST WESTERN EMPERORS
Constantine II AD 337–340	*East*	Theodosius I 379–395	Petronius Maximus 455
Constans I 337–350	Valens 364–378	*East*	Avitus 455–456
Constantius II 337–361	*West*	Arcadius 395–408	Majorian 457–461
Julian 360–363	Valentinian I 364–375	Theodosius II 408–450	Severus III 461–465
Jovian 363–364	Gratian 367–383	*West*	Anthemius 467–472
	Valentinian II 375–392	Honorius 395–423	Olybrius 472
	Eugenius (usurper) 392–394	Johannes (usurper) 423–425	Glycerius 473–474
		Valentinian III 425–455	Julius Nepos 474–475
			Romulus Augustulus 475–476

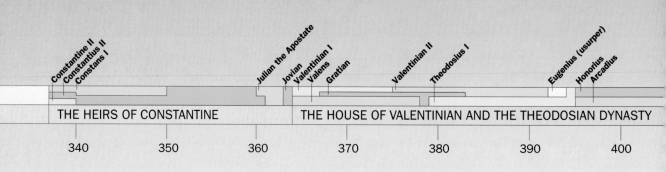

Constantius II

Julian

Arcadius

Valentinian III
or Honorius

THE LAST EMPERORS

The Heirs of Constantine AD 337–364
The House of Valentinian AD 364–378
The Theodosian Dynasty AD 379–455
The Last Western Emperors AD 455–476

T HE REIGN OF CONSTANTINE was one of the high points in the history
of the Roman empire, but his death was followed by 15 years of
squabbling for power among his sons. Christianity was now the privileged state religion, but paganism took on renewed vigour during the
brief reign of Julian, the so-called Apostate emperor who attempted to
turn back the clock and give the old gods pride of place once again. His
failure served to show that Christianity was here to stay.

Julian's murder made way for a new imperial dynasty founded by
Valentinian I. The division of empire into east and west was now an
accepted feature of the government, but in 378 a major disaster occurred
when the eastern emperor Valens was defeated and killed by the Goths
at Hadrianopolis.

The emperor Theodosius restored order in the east and founded yet
another imperial dynasty. His successors in the west, however, steadily
lost control of Britain, Gaul, Spain and North Africa to Germanic
invaders during the first half of the fifth century. By the late 450s the
western emperor no longer held supreme power even in Italy. The last
of them all, Romulus Augustulus, did not expire in a blaze of glory but
simply abdicated and withdrew to comfortable retirement in Campania.

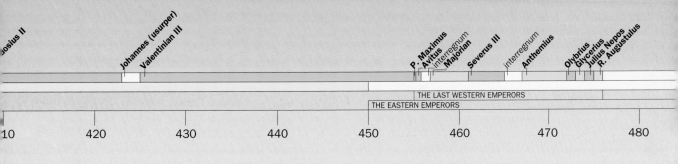

EPILOGUE: THE LAST EMPERORS

The Heirs of Constantine

Head of Constantius II, Capitoline Museum, Rome.

Statue of Julian the Apostate, Louvre, Paris.

Constantine II
337–340

Constans I
337–350

Constantius II
337–361

Julian
360–363

Jovian
363–364

The emperor Constantine died on 22 May 337 leaving three adult sons, Constantine II, Constantius II and Constans, who took the title of Augusti on 9 September. The intervening months had seen a mutiny at Constantinople in which other contenders for power, notably Constantine's nephews Dalmatius and Hannibalianus, had been killed. The three sons divided the empire between them, the eldest, Constantine, taking Britain, Gaul and Spain, the middle brother Constans the rest of the European provinces, while Constantius ruled the east. Notionally Constantine II had a measure of authority over the whole empire, but in practice the three ruled as independent monarchs.

This situation lasted less than three years, for in spring 340 Constantine II attempted to exert his authority over Constans and invaded Italy. He was defeated and killed at Aquileia, leaving Constans in control of the whole European sector. Then in January 350 Constans fell victim to a palace conspiracy and was succeeded by his army chief Magnentius. Constantius II, who had spent much time fighting the Persians in the east, refused to accept the new western ruler and defeated Magnentius at Mursa in the Balkans in September 351 and at Lyons two years later. This left the empire once again in the hands of a single emperor, though one who was judged vain and stupid by contemporary

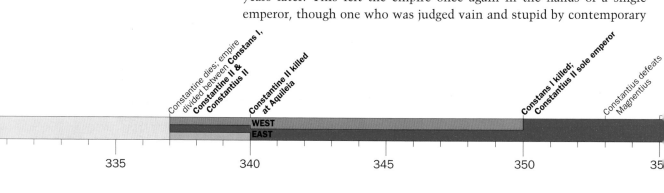

Constantine dies; empire divided between Constans I, **Constantine II & Constantius II**

Constantine II killed at Aquileia

Constans I killed; Constantius II sole emperor

Constantius defeats Magnentius

WEST
EAST

335   340   345   350   35

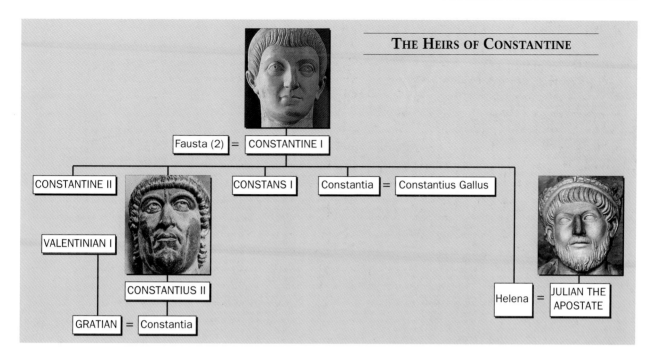

THE HEIRS OF CONSTANTINE

Fausta (2) = CONSTANTINE I

- CONSTANTINE II
- VALENTINIAN I
  - CONSTANTIUS II
    - GRATIAN = Constantia
- CONSTANS I
- Constantia = Constantius Gallus
- Helena = JULIAN THE APOSTATE

historians, and heavily under the influence of his eunuchs.

Constantius soon decided that undivided rule was impractical, and chose a colleague to share his power. This was Flavius Iulianus (Julian), Constantius's half-cousin, who in 355 was recalled from studying at Athens to take command of Gaul and the troubled Rhine frontier. He gained considerable success, both in military security and in reforming and reducing taxation. Julian's popularity with troops and civilians was such that Constantius felt threatened by it and in 360 decided to reduce Julian's power. In response, the army proclaimed Julian Augustus in the west. Constantius refused to recognize the elevation, however, and was on his way to suppress his junior colleague when he died in November 361.

Julian is one of the most famous late Roman emperors. His reign is described in detail by the historian Ammianus Marcellinus, and he left in addition a considerable body of writings of his own. Julian's fame stems particularly from his endeavour to turn back the clock and reinstate the traditional religion of Rome in place of Christianity. Christianity continued to be tolerated, but lost its special status. He won the title 'Apostate' for his pains. He also made a number of important administrative reforms which reduced the burgeoning cost of impe-

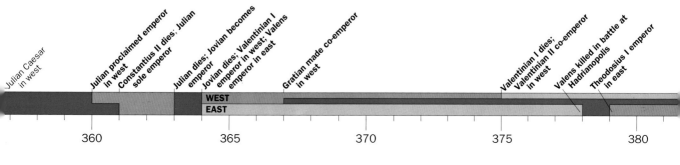

Julian Caesar in west

Julian proclaimed emperor in west

Constantius II dies; Julian sole emperor

Julian dies; Jovian becomes emperor

Jovian dies; Valentinian I emperor in west; Valens emperor in east

Gratian made co-emperor in west

Valentinian I dies; Valentinian II co-emperor in west

Valens killed in battle at Hadrianopolis

Theodosius I emperor in east

WEST
EAST

360   365   370   375   380

rial administration and lightened the enormous burden of taxes on ordinary civilians.

Julian met his end in suspicious circumstances in Mesopotamia, where he had launched a massive invasion in March 363. At first, all went well: the expedition defeated the Persians in front of Ctesiphon, their winter capital. Rather than capture the city, however, the Romans decided to withdraw northwards and join up with reinforcements. It was on this journey that Julian was wounded in a skirmish. Rumour had it that a disenchanted Christian rather than a Persian struck the blow, but whatever the cause Julian died shortly afterwards. In this hour of crisis, deep inside enemy territory, the army chose one of the senior generals, Jovian, as Julian's successor. He made terms with the Persians, withdrew to Asia Minor, and was on his way to Constantinople in February 364 when he was poisoned by the fumes from a brazier in his tent.

The House of Valentinian

Julian was the last surviving male relative of Constantine, and his death marked the end of a dynasty. The demise of Jovian again left no natural successor, and the generals and civil officials met in conclave to name a Pannonian officer of humble origin, Valentinian I, as the new emperor. A month later, in March 364, Valentinian appointed his younger brother Valens joint Augustus, with the arrangement that he (Valentinian) would rule Illyricum and the western provinces while Valens took the rest of the Balkans and the east.

Both were fiercely pro-Christian and anti-intellectual, and chose fellow-Pannonians as their officers and ministers. The traditional aristocracy was ignored. Valentinian spent most of his reign campaigning against the Alemanni on the Upper Rhine, then in 375 moved to Illyricum to counter an invasion by the Quadi and Sarmatians. While giving audience to a deputation from the invaders he became so incensed that he suffered a stroke and died. His eldest son Gratian, then 16 years old, became emperor in his place, but proved to be more pious than practical. Gratian's younger half-brother, Valentinian II, was appointed co-emperor a few days later, but as he was only four years old he remained a junior partner.

Through poor judgment, Gratian slowly lost the support of the military, and in 383 the army of Britain proclaimed their own commander, Magnus Maximus, emperor. Gratian was captured and killed at Lyons in August 383, leaving Magnus Maximus in control of the provinces north of the Alps. When in 387 he invaded Italy, however, he was defeated and

East:

Valens
364–378

West:

Valentinian I
364–375

Gratian
367–383

Valentinian II
375–392

Eugenius (usurper)
392–394

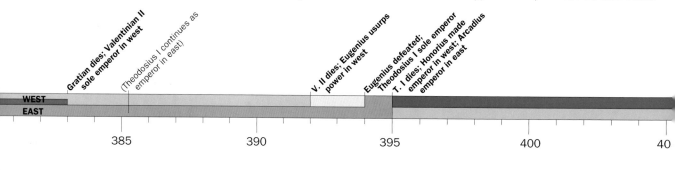

Gratian dies; Valentinian II sole emperor in west

(Theodosius I continues as emperor in east)

V. II dies; Eugenius usurps power in west

Eugenius defeated; Theodosius I sole emperor

T. I dies; Honorius made emperor in west; Arcadius emperor in east

WEST
EAST

385   390   395   400   40

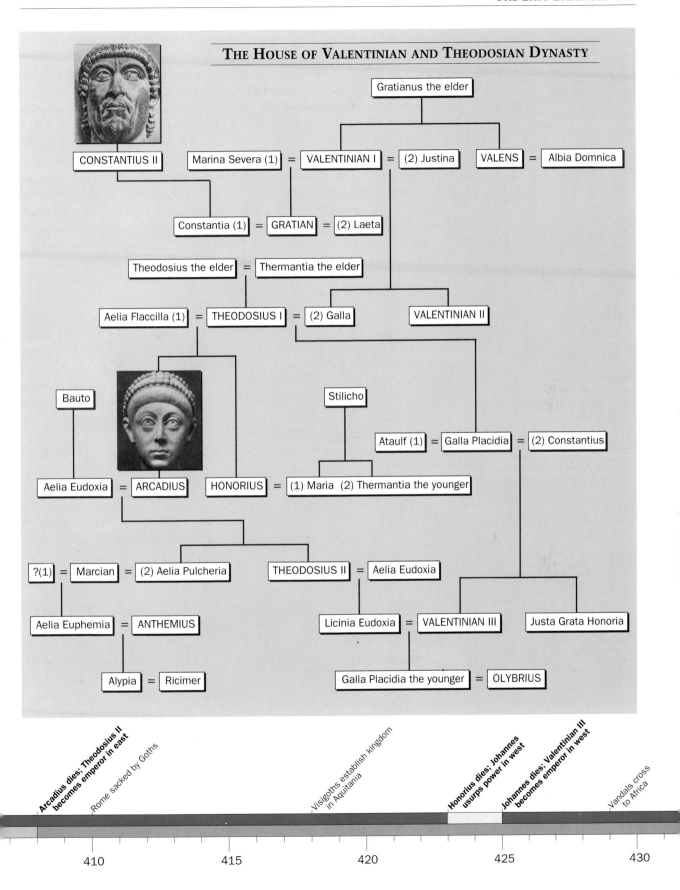

THE HOUSE OF VALENTINIAN AND THEODOSIAN DYNASTY

Gratianus the elder

CONSTANTIUS II | Marina Severa (1) = VALENTINIAN I = (2) Justina | VALENS = Albia Domnica

Constantia (1) = GRATIAN = (2) Laeta

Theodosius the elder = Thermantia the elder

Aelia Flaccilla (1) = THEODOSIUS I = (2) Galla | VALENTINIAN II

Bauto

Stilicho

Ataulf (1) = Galla Placidia = (2) Constantius

Aelia Eudoxia = ARCADIUS | HONORIUS = (1) Maria (2) Thermantia the younger

?(1) = Marcian = (2) Aelia Pulcheria | THEODOSIUS II = Aelia Eudoxia

Aelia Euphemia = ANTHEMIUS | Licinia Eudoxia = VALENTINIAN III | Justa Grata Honoria

Alypia = Ricimer | Galla Placidia the younger = OLYBRIUS

Arcadius dies; Theodosius II becomes emperor in east

Rome sacked by Goths

Visigoths establish kingdom in Aquitania

Honorius dies; Johannes usurps power in west

Johannes dies; Valentinian III becomes emperor in west

Vandals cross to Africa

410   415   420   425   430

Statue of Valentinian II from Aphrodisias, Turkey. Istanbul Archaeological Museum.

killed the following year. The main beneficiary was Valentinian II, now 19 years old, but he in turn was killed by Arbogast, his army commander, in May 392. With his death the luckless House of Valentinian came to an end. Arbogast briefly had Eugenius, a former teacher of rhetoric, elevated as emperor in the west, but their forces were defeated by the eastern emperor in 394.

Valens had perished many years earlier. His civil administration won some praise, but he badly mismanaged his policy toward the Goths, who had been expelled from their South Russian kingdoms by the advance of the Huns from the east. Valens allowed the Visigoths to cross the frontier and settle in Thrace, but local Roman officials drove them to rebellion through their avarice and extortion. The Visigoths were joined by their erstwhile neighbours the Ostrogoths, and the combined army inflicted a crushing defeat on the Romans at Hadrianopolis on 9 August

The *missorium* of Theodosius I, found near Merida in Spain. This large silver dish shows Theodosius (his head framed by a nimbus) enthroned between Arcadius and Valentinian II. Beside them stand Germanic soldiers with their oval shields. The inscription around the edge commemorates the tenth anniversary of his reign (AD 388).

(Valentinian III continues as emperor in west)

(Theodosius II continues as emperor in east)

Carthage falls to Vandals

Theodosius II dies

Attila the Hun defeated at B. of Catalaunian Fields

Valentinian III dies; P. Maximus emperor Avitus emperor

WEST
EAST

EASTERN EMPERORS

435   440   445   450   455

Theodosius I
379–395

East:

Arcadius
395–408

Theodosius II
408–450

West:

Honorius
395–423

Johannes (usurper)
423–425

Valentinian III
425–455

Ivory plaque showing the emperor Honorius. The nimbus around his head carries the dedication 'To our Lord Honorius the Eternal Emperor'.

378. Valens himself was killed along with most of his high command and enormous numbers of troops.

The Theodosian Dynasty

When Valens was killed at Hadrianopolis it fell to the then western emperor Gratian to take measures for the defence of the east. This he did by appointing Flavius Theodosius, a Spanish officer, as emperor for the eastern provinces on 19 January 379. Theodosius proved a redoubtable figure in both civil and military affairs, and came to be called 'the Great'. He was particularly noted as a law-giver and an ardent defender of Christianity. In 391 he at long last brought to completion the official espousal of Christianity by forbidding pagan worship, whether public or private, and closing all pagan temples. Yet he himself ran foul of the religion in 390 when he was excommunicated by Ambrose bishop of Milan for ordering the massacre of the citizens of Thessalonica who had murdered his army commander. Only when he had done penance was he allowed back into the fold.

Theodosius settled the military situation in the east by a four-year war against the Goths ending in a peace treaty in 382. This set a dubious precedent by allowing the Visigoths to settle on lands within the empire under the authority of their own king rather than any imperial official, and the right to fight in the Roman army as allies rather than regular units. Theodosius may have hoped to establish firmer control once the immediate crisis had passed, but the opportunity never came. Indeed the most conspicuous military operations of Theodosius's reign were in the west. It was he who led the army to Italy which defeated Magnus Maximus in 388, and in a second campaign in 394 overthrew Eugenius and Arbogast, murderer of Valentinian II.

When Theodosius died at Milan in 395 he left the eastern empire to his eldest son Arcadius, 17 years old, and the west to his second son Honorius, then only 10. Honorius's reign was dominated by Germanic incursions. In 401 the Visigoths whom Theodosius had settled in Thrace moved westward under Alaric their king and raided northern Italy. They were driven back by Stilicho, Honorius's army commander, but other Germanic peoples entered Italy in 405, and in December 406, Vandals, Sueves and Alans crossed the frozen Rhine to ravage Gaul. Four years later, in 410, the unthinkable happened, when Alaric entered Italy once again and sacked Rome. The imperial court had by now established itself at Ravenna, a near-impregnable city on the Adriatic, but the fall of Rome was nonetheless a milestone in the dissolution of the western empire.

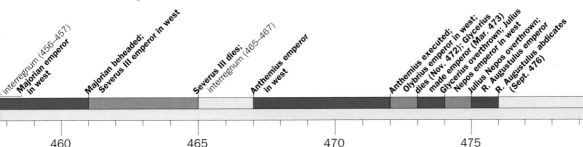

interregnum (456–457) Majorian emperor in west

Majorian beheaded; Severus III emperor in west

Severus III dies; interregnum (465–467)

Anthemius emperor in west

Anthemius executed; Olybrius emperor in west; Olybrius dies (Nov. 472); Glycerius made emperor (Mar. 473)

Glycerius overthrown; Julius Nepos emperor in west

Julius Nepos overthrown; R. Augustulus emperor

R. Augustulus abdicates (Sept. 476)

460   465   470   475   480

From 410 until his death in 423 Honorius did what he could to salvage the situation, but imperial control over the western provinces was irreparably weakened. A series of pretenders rose and fell – Constantine III in Gaul and Britain, Maximus in Spain, Attalus in Italy – and through the work of his general Constantius, Honorius did succeed in reasserting a measure of control over the Burgundians and Visigoths who were now settled within the empire, though Spain was still troubled by Vandals, Alans and Sueves.

In the east, meanwhile, Arcadius died in 408 at the age of only 31, leaving his seven-year-old son Theodosius II to succeed him. Theodosius reigned for over 40 years, though real power was in the hands of his sister Pulcheria and his wife Aelia Eudoxia. Pulcheria eventually won the upper hand and in 433 Eudoxia was disgraced and retired to Jerusalem to devote her life to works of piety and charity. Theodosius's own name is linked to two particular achievements: the Theodosian Code, a systematic compilation of imperial laws from the reign of Constantine onwards; and the Theodosian Walls built to protect Constantinople in these increasingly troubled times. In the military sphere, the main problem of Theodosius's reign was pressure from the Huns who were now

The fall of the western Roman empire owed its immediate cause to invasions by Germanic peoples from the north. The Visigoths had already crossed into the Balkans in 375, and began an attack on Italy in 402. Eight years later they sacked Rome. The year 410 henceforth became a key date in Roman history, but, for the western provinces as a whole, the incursion of Vandals, Alans and Sueves in 406 was no less significant. They, like the Goths, came in search of land as well as plunder, and by the end of the fifth century almost all of the western empire was under Germanic control.

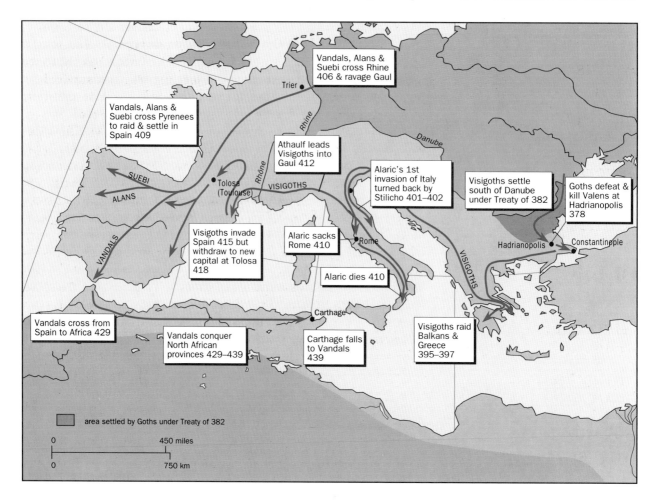

Vandals, Alans & Suebi cross Rhine 406 & ravage Gaul

Trier

Rhine

Danube

Vandals, Alans & Suebi cross Pyrenees to raid & settle in Spain 409

Athaulf leads Visigoths into Gaul 412

Alaric's 1st invasion of Italy turned back by Stilicho 401–402

Visigoths settle south of Danube under Treaty of 382

Goths defeat & kill Valens at Hadrianopolis 378

SUEBI

Tolosa (Toulouse)

Rhône

VISIGOTHS

ALANS

Visigoths invade Spain 415 but withdraw to new capital at Tolosa 418

Alaric sacks Rome 410

Rome

Hadrianopolis

Constantinople

VANDALS

Alaric dies 410

VISIGOTHS

Vandals cross from Spain to Africa 429

Carthage

Vandals conquer North African provinces 429–439

Carthage falls to Vandals 439

Visigoths raid Balkans & Greece 395–397

area settled by Goths under Treaty of 382

0   450 miles

0   750 km

THE LAST EMPERORS 231

Gold medallion of the empress Galla Placidia (392–450), daughter of Theodosius I.

Petronius Maximus
455

Avitus
455–456

Majorian
457–461

Severus III
461–465

Anthemius
467–472

Olybrius
472

Glycerius
473–474

Julius Nepos
474–475

Romulus Augustulus
475–476

established just north of the Danube frontier. The Balkan provinces were devastated by continual raids, until in 450 the Hunnic leader Attila decided to turn his attention to the west.

In the west the death of Honorius in 423 had been followed by a disputed succession. Theodosius toyed with the idea of governing the west himself, but was eventually persuaded to support the claim of Valentinian III, nephew of Honorius, and Valentinian's redoubtable mother Galla Placidia. In May 425 Theodosius's forces installed Valentinian at Ravenna, where the usurper Johannes was killed. Valentinian was only six years old, however, and real power was in the hands of Galla Placidia and the general Aetius. Throughout the 430s and 440s Aetius struggled to restore order in Gaul, achieving some success with only meagre resources. His greatest achievement, however, was the battle fought on the Catalunian Fields in 451, which forced Attila and the Huns to withdraw from Gaul. As Aetius's power grew, Valentinian became increasingly afraid, and eventually lured him to a meeting and had him executed. Valentinian did not long survive the deed, but was himself assassinated by two of Aetius's officers in March 455.

The Last Western Emperors
The assassination of Valentinian III and the death of Theodosius II (injured by falling from his horse) five years earlier brought the Theodosian dynasty to an end. It also marked the point where the histories of the eastern and western empire diverged. The east survived for another 1000 years, in the form of the Byzantine empire. In the west, however, the imperial line had little more than 20 years to run.

Valentinian III was succeeded by Petronius Maximus, a wealthy senator and leading member of the Italian aristocracy. His riches had bought him the support of the troops, but he was killed just 11 weeks later while trying to flee Rome in the face of a Vandal attack. The Vandals had crossed to North Africa in 429 and established a strong kingdom from which they were able to raid the Italian peninsula. In June 455 they captured Rome and spent two weeks sacking the city, leading the empress Licinia Eudoxia (Valentinian's widow) and her two daughters away into captivity.

The next emperor was proclaimed not in Italy but in Gaul. This was Avitus, the friend and nominee of the Visigothic king Theoderic II, who was proclaimed emperor in July 455 at Tolosa (modern Toulouse), where Theoderic had established his court. The following year, however, the Suevian army commander Ricimer rebelled at Ravenna. Avitus marched against him but was captured in battle at Placentia (modern Piacenza) in October 456. Ricimer neutralized him by making him bishop of Placentia, but Avitus was soon forced to flee back to Gaul and died shortly afterwards.

Avitus's overthrow and murder was followed by an 18-month interregnum while Ricimer made futile attempts to win recognition for his chosen successor Majorian from the eastern emperor Leo I (457–474).

Sixth-century Germanic medallion showing a cavalryman.

Majorian, a distinguished senator, was officially installed in December 457. Ricimer at length became troubled by Majorian's growing power and decided to overthrow him. Majorian was returning from Gaul in August 461 when he was captured by Ricimer, tortured and beheaded. Ricimer then installed a harmless senator, Libius Severus, as the emperor Severus III.

The authority of Ricimer and his puppet-emperor now barely extended beyond the Italian peninsula, and even there they were harassed by Vandal raids from North Africa. Thus when Severus died in November 465 Ricimer reopened negotiations with the eastern emperor Leo in an effort to gain military assistance. The price of Leo's support was the appointment of his own nominee Anthemius as western emperor. Anthemius was proclaimed emperor in Italy in April 467, but his great expedition against the Vandals was a complete disaster and in July 472 Ricimer marched on Rome, captured Anthemius and put him to death.

Ricimer appointed a Roman noble Olybrius to succeed Anthemius, but Ricimer himself died in August 472 and Olybrius in November. Effective power passed to a Burgundian prince, Gundobad, who in March 473 nominated Glycerius his puppet-emperor. The demise of Anthemius had antagonized the eastern emperor, however, and in June 474 Zeno I (474–491) despatched a new candidate, Julius Nepos, to Italy with a small army. Glycerius fled, Julius Nepos became emperor, but a year later he too was overthrown by his army commander Orestes. In place of Julius Nepos, Orestes installed his son, Romulus Augustulus ('the little Augustus'). But neither Orestes nor Augustulus had any real power. That lay with the Germanic mercenaries who now dominated the Roman armies. In the summer of 476 they staged the final coup-d'état, demanding one third of the land of Italy for themselves. When Orestes refused their demand he was killed and his son deposed.

On 4 September 476 the 16-year-old Romulus Augustulus abdicated imperial office and retired to the Gulf of Naples with a pension. Historians do not even bother to record when he died. The senate of Rome sent to Zeno, telling him he was now emperor of west as well as east, but it was Odoacer, leader of the Germanic mercenaries, who became king of Italy. Gaul was already in the hands of Franks, Burgundians and Visigoths. Visigoths and Sueves divided Spain between them, the Vandals controlled North Africa, and Roman Britain was well en route to becoming Anglo-Saxon England. The empire of Rome in the west survived only as a memory.

Romulus Augustulus was the last in the unbroken line of emperors who ruled Rome. This only became clear with the passage of time, when no further emperors were appointed in the west to serve as figureheads for Germanic army chiefs. In the east, indeed, emperors, today known as Byzantine, continued to rule until the fall of Constantinople in 1453. It is a mistake, then, to regard 476 as a sharp historical break. In the history of the emperors, however, the abdication of Romulus Augustulus was the final act in the demise of a once-great office.

SELECT BIBLIOGRAPHY

Individual ancient sources

Aulus Gellius *The Attic Nights of Aulus Gellius* trans. J. C. Rolfe vol. III (Loeb ed.) London & New York 1928

Aurelius Victor *Livre des Césars* trans. P. Dufraigne. Paris: Les Belles Lettres, 1975

Aurelius Victor *Liber De Caesaribus*, trans. H.W. Bird. Liverpool: Liverpool UP, 1994

Cassius Dio *Roman History* Books LI-LX (complete), Books LXI-LXXX (epitome), trans. E. Cary (Loeb ed.), vols 6-9, 1917, 1924, 1925, 1927. Cambridge, MA: Harvard UP

Constantine *The Oration of the Emperor Constantine which he addressed "To the Assembly of the Saints"* trans. E.C. Richardson, in *A Select Library of Nicene and Post-Nicene Fathers of the Christian Church, Volume I: Eusebius* eds. H. Wace & P. Schaff. Oxford: Parker & Co., 1890

Epitome de Caesaribus ed. F. Pichlmayr, revised R. Gruendel. Berlin: Teubner, 1970

Eusebius *History of the Church.*, trans. G.A. Williamson revised A. Louth. Harmondsworth & New York: Penguin, 1989

Eusebius *The Life of Constantine* trans. E.C. Richardson, in *A Select Library of Nicene and Post-Nicene Fathers of the Christian Church, Volume I: Eusebius* eds. H. Wace & P. Schaff. Oxford: Parker & Co., 1890

Eusebius *The Oration of Eusebius Pamphili in praise of the Emperor Constantine, pronounced on the thirtieth anniversary of his reign* trans. E.C. Richardson, in *A Select Library of Nicene and Post-Nicene Fathers of the Christian Church, Volume I: Eusebius* eds. H. Wace & P. Schaff. Oxford: Parker & Co., 1890

Eutropius *Breviarium ab Urbe Condita* trans. H.W. Bird. Liverpool: Liverpool UP, 1993

Herodian *History of the Empire from the Time of Marcus Aurelius*, trans. C.R. Whittaker (Loeb ed.), 2 vols, 1969 & 1970. Cambridge, MA: Harvard UP

Historia Augusta (lives of Hadrian, Aelius, Marcus Antoninus , Verus, Avidius Cassius, Commodus Antoninus, Pertinax, Didius Julianus, Severus, Pescennius Niger, Clodius Albinus, Antoninus Caracalla, Antoninus Geta, Opellius Macrinus, Antoninus Diadumenianus, Antoninus Elagabalus, Severus Alexander, The Two Maximini, The Three Gordians , Maximus and Balbinus, The Two Valerians,The Two Gallieni, The Thirty Tyrants, The Deified Claudius, The Deified Aurelian, Tacitus, Probus, Firmus, Saturninus,

Proculus, and Bonosus, Carus, Carinus and Numerian):
1) *Lives of the Later Caesars (The First Part of the Augustan History, with newly composed Lives of Nerva and Trajan)*, trans. A. Birley. Harmondsworth & New York: Penguin, 1976
2) *Scriptores Historiae Augustae,* trans. D. Magie (Loeb ed.), 3 vols, 1921, 1924, 1932. Cambridge, MA: Harvard UP

Jerome *Chronici Canones* ed. J.N. Fotheringham. London: Milford, 1923

Josephus *The Jewish War* trans. G.A. Williamson. Harmondsworth & New York: Penguin, 1984

Juvenal *The Sixteen Satires*, trans. P. Green. Harmondsworth & New York: Penguin, 1974

Lactantius *De Mortibus Persecutorum*, trans. J.L. Creed. Oxford: Clarendon Press, 1984

Marcus Aurelius *Meditations*, trans. M. Staniforth. Harmondsworth & New York: Penguin, 1964

Marcus Cornelius Fronto *Epistulae* trans. C.R. Haines (Loeb ed.), 2 vols, 1919 & 1920. Cambridge, MA: Harvard UP

Martial *Epigrams* trans. D.R. Shackleton Bailey (Loeb ed.), 3 vols, 1993. Cambridge, MA: Harvard UP

Panégyriques Latins, trans. with commentary E. Galletier. 2 vols 1949 & 1952. Paris: Les Belles Lettres

Pliny *Letters & Panegyricus* trans. B. Radice (Loeb ed.), 1969. Cambridge, MA: Harvard UP

Plutarch 'Galba' and 'Otho' in *Plutarch's Lives* trans. B. Perrin (Loeb ed.) Vol. IX, 1926. Cambridge, MA: Harvard UP

Res Gestae Divi Augusti. The Achievements of the Divine Augustus eds. P.A. Brunt & J.M. Moore. Oxford & New York: Oxford UP, 1967

Seneca *Apocolocyntosis* trans. P.T. Eden. Cambridge & New York: Cambridge UP, 1984

Seneca *Moral Essays* trans. J. W. Basore vol. I (Loeb ed.), 1928. London & New York

Statius *Silvae* trans. J.H. Mozley (Loeb ed.),1928. Cambridge, MA: Harvard UP

Suetonius *(Lives of The Deified Augustus, Tiberius, Gaius Caligula, The Deified Claudius, Nero, Galba, Otho and Vitellius, The Deified Vespasian, The Deified Titus, Domitian)*
1) Suetonius *Lives of the Caesars* trans. J.C. Rolfe (Loeb ed.), 2 vols 1913 & 1914. Cambridge, MA: Harvard UP
2) Suetonius *The Twelve Caesars* trans. R. Graves revised M. Grant. Harmondsworth & New York: Penguin, 1989

Tacitus *On Britain and Germany* trans. H. Mattingly. Harmondsworth: Penguin, 1948

Tacitus *Agricola* trans. M. Hutton revised R.M. Ogilvie (Loeb ed.), 1970. Cambridge, MA: Harvard UP

Tacitus *Annals* trans. J. Jackson (Loeb ed.), 3 vols 1934 & 1937. Cambridge, MA: Harvard UP

Tacitus *Histories* trans. C.H. Moore (Loeb ed.), 2 vols, 1925 &1931. Cambridge, MA: Harvard UP

Velleius Paterculus *Roman History* trans. F.W. Shipley (Loeb ed.), 1924. Cambridge, MA: Harvard UP

Zosimus *New History* trans. R.T. Ridley. Sydney: Australian Association for Byzantine Studies, 1982

Anthologies

Dessau, H., 1892. *Inscriptiones Latinae Selectae*. Vol. I. Berlin: Weidmann

Dodgeon, M.H., & Lieu, S.N.C., 1991. *The Roman Eastern Frontier and the Persian Wars AD 226-363. A Documentary History*. London: Routledge

Sherk, R.K., 1988. *The Roman Empire: Augustus to Hadrian. Translated Documents of Greece and Rome 6.* Cambridge & New York: Cambridge UP

Smallwood, E.M., 1966. *Documents Illustrating the Principates of Nerva, Trajan and Hadrian*. Cambridge & New York: Cambridge UP

Modern references

Barnes, T.D., 1981. *Constantine and Eusebius*. Cambridge MA: Harvard UP

Barnes, T.D., 1982. *The New Empire of Diocletian and Constantine*. Cambridge MA: Harvard UP

Barrett, A.A., 1989. *Caligula. The Corruption of Power*. London: Batsford

Benario, H.W., 1980. *A Commentary on the Vita Hadriani in the Historia Augusta. American Classical Studies 7*. Chico, CA: Scholars Press

Birley, A., 1987. *Marcus Aurelius. A Biography*. London: Batsford

Birley, A., 1988. *Septimius Severus. The African Emperor*. London: Batsford; New Haven: Yale UP 1989

Brauer, G.C., 1975. *The Age of the Soldier-Emperors*. Park Ridge, NJ: Noyes Press

Breeze, D.J., & Dobson, B., 1987. *Hadrian's Wall*. 3rd ed. Harmondsworth: Penguin Books

Browning, I., 1979. *Palmyra*. London: Chatto & Windus; Park Ridge, NJ: Noyes 1980

Carter, J.M., 1970. *The Battle of Actium*. London: Hamish Hamilton

Carter, J.M., 1982. *Suetonius: Divus Augustus*. Bristol: Bristol Classical Press

Cary, M. & Scullard, H.H., 1975. *A History of Rome*. London: Macmillan; New York: St Martin's Press 1976

Champlin, E., 1980. *Fronto and Antonine Rome*. Cambridge, MA: Harvard UP

Claridge, A., 1993. Hadrian's Column of Trajan. *Journal of Roman Archaeology* 6, 5-22

Coarelli, F., 1985. *Italia Centrale. (Guide Archeologice Laterza)* Rome: Editori Laterza

Cook, S.A., Adcock, F.E., Charlesworth, M.P., & Baynes, N.H. (eds) 1936. *The Cambridge Ancient History, Vol. XI: The Imperial Peace* AD 70-192.

Cambridge: Cambridge UP

Cook, S.A., Adcock, F.E., Charlesworth, M.P., & Baynes, N.H. (eds) 1939. *The Cambridge Ancient History, Vol. XII: The Imperial Crisis and Recovery AD 193-324*. Cambridge: Cambridge UP

Cornell, T., & Matthews, J., 1982. *Atlas of the Roman World*. Oxford: Phaidon; New York: Facts on File

Daltrop, G., Hausmann, U., & Wegner, M., 1966. *Das Römische Herrscherbild. Die Flavier. Vespasian, Titus, Domitian, Nerva, Julia Titi, Domitilla, Domitia*. Berlin: Mann

Drinkwater, J.F., 1987. *The Gallic Empire. Separatism and Continuity in the North-Western Provinces of the Roman Empire AD 260-274*. (Historia Einzelschrift 52) Stuttgart: Steiner

Elsner, J., & Masters, J., (eds) 1994. *Reflections of Nero*. London: Duckworth; Chapel Hill, NC: U of North Carolina Press

Foss, C., 1990. *Roman Historical Coins*. London: Seaby; North Pomfret, VT: Trafalgar

Fossier, R., ed., 1989. *The Cambridge Illustrated History of the Middle Ages, I: 350-950*. Cambridge & New York: Cambridge UP

Garzetti, A., 1974. *From Tiberius to the Antonines*. London: Methuen

Grant, M., 1993. *The Emperor Constantine* London: Weidenfeld & Nicolson (*Constantine the Great*. New York: Macmillan 1994)

Griffin, M.T., 1984. *Nero: the End of a Dynasty*. London: Batsford; New Haven: Yale UP 1985

Halfmann, H., 1986. *Itinera Principum. Geschichte und Typologie der Kaiserreisen im Römischen Reich*. Stuttgart: Steiner

Hannestad, N., 1988. *Roman Art and Imperial Policy*. Aarhus: Aarhus University Press

Heintze, H. von, 1968. Galba. *Römische Mitteilungen* 75, 149-53

Jones, A.H.M., 1964. *The Later Roman Empire, 284-602: A Social, Economic and Administrative Survey*. Oxford: Blackwell

Jones, B.W., 1984. *The Emperor Titus*. London: Croom Helm

Jones, B.W., 1992. *The Emperor Domitian*. London: Routledge

Kienast, D., 1990. *Römische Kaisertabelle*. Darmstadt: Darmstadt Wissenschaftliche Buchgesellschaft

Lanciani, R., 1897. *The Ruins and Excavations of Ancient Rome*. London: Macmillan

Lane Fox, R., 1986. *Pagans and Christians* Harmondsworth: Penguin; San Francisco: Harper 1988

Le Blois, L., 1976. *The Policy of the Emperor Gallienus*. Leiden: Brill

Lepper, F., 1948. *Trajan's Parthian War*. London: Oxford UP

Lepper, F., & Frere S., 1988. *Trajan's Column*. Gloucester: Alan Sutton

Levick, B., 1990. *Claudius*. London: Batsford; New Haven: Yale UP

Lindsay, H., 1993. *Suetonius: Caligula*.

Bristol: Bristol Classical Press

Ling, R., 1991. *Roman Painting*. Cambridge & New York: Cambridge UP

L'Orange, H.P., 1984. *Das Römische Herrscherbild. Das Spätantike Herrscherbild von Diokletian bis zu den Konstantin-Söhnen*. Berlin: Mann

Macdermot, B.C., 1954. Roman emperors on the Sassanian reliefs. *Journal of Roman Studies* 44, 76-80

Maiuri, A., 1956. *Capri: Storia e Monumenti*. Rome : Liberia dello Stato

Mattingly, H., 1953. The Reign of Macrinus, in *Studies Presented to David Moore Robinson, Vol. II*, edited by George E Mylonas & Doris Raymond. Saint Louis, Missouri: Washington University

Mattingly, H., & Sydenham, E.A., *et al.*, 1923-84. *The Roman Imperial Coinage, Vols. I-VII*. London: Spink

Millar, F., 1992. *The Emperor in the Roman World*. 2nd ed. London: Duckworth; Ithaca, NY: Cornell UP

Mottershead, J., 1986. *Suetonius: Claudius*. Bristol: Bristol Classical Press

Murison, C., 1992. *Suetonius: Galba, Otho, Vitellius*. Bristol: Bristol Classical Press

Packer, J.E., 1994. Trajan's Forum again: the Column and the Temple of Trajan in the master plan attributed to Apollodorus. *Journal of Roman Archaeology* 7, 163-182

Perowne, S., 1960. *Hadrian*. London: Hodder & Stoughton; Westport, CT: Greenwood 1976

Pohlsander, H.A., 1980. Philip the Arab and Christianity. *Historia* 29, 463-473

Polverini, L., 1975. Da Aureliano a Diocleziano, in *Aufstieg und Niedergang der Römischen Welt*, Band II, ed. H. Temporini. Berlin: De Gruyter, 1013-1035

Raaflaub, K.A., & Toher, M., (eds) 1990. *Between Republic and Empire. Interpretations of Augustus and His Principate*. Berkeley & Los Angeles: University of California Press

Raven, S., 1993. *Rome in Africa*. 3rd ed. London & New York: Routledge

Richardson, L., 1992. *A New Topographical Dictionary of Ancient Rome*. Baltimore: Johns Hopkins UP

Rossi, L., 1971. *Trajan's Column and the Dacian Wars*. London: Thames & Hudson

Salway, P., 1993. *The Oxford Illustrated History of Roman Britain*. Oxford & New York: Oxford UP

Scarre, C., 1995. *The Penguin Historical Atlas of Ancient Rome*. Harmondsworth & New York: Penguin

Scullard, H.H., 1982. *From the Gracchi to Nero. A History of Rome 133 BC to AD 68*. 5th ed. London & New York: Routledge

Shotter, D., 1991. *Augustus Caesar*. London & New York: Routledge

Shotter, D., 1992. *Tiberius Caesar*. London & New York: Routledge

Simon, E., 1986. *Augustus: Kunst and Leben in Rome um die Zeitwende*. Munich

Sordi, M., 1988. *The Christians and the Roman Empire*. London: Routledge; Norman, OK: U of Oklahoma Press 1986

Stoneman, R., 1992. *Palmyra and its Empire. Zenobia's Revolt against Rome*. Ann Arbor: U of Michigan Press

Strong, D., 1988. *Roman Art*. Revised ed. Harmondsworth & New York: Penguin

Syme, R., 1939. *The Roman Revolution*. Oxford: Oxford UP

Syme, R., 1968. *Ammianus and the Historia Augusta*. Oxford: Clarendon Press

Syme, R., 1971. *Emperors and Biography. Studies in the Historia Augusta*. Oxford: Oxford UP

Syme, R., 1983. The Son of the Emperor Macrinus, in *Historia Augusta Papers*. Oxford: Clarendon Press, 46-62

Todd, M., 1987. *The Northern Barbarians 100BC-AD300*. Revised ed. Oxford & Cambridge, MA: Blackwell

Traupman, J.C., 1956. *The Life and Reign of Commodus*. Ann Arbor: University Microfilms

Walden, C., 1990. The tetrarchic image. *Oxford Journal of Archaeology* 9, 221-235

Ward-Perkins, J.B., 1981. *Roman Imperial Architecture*. Harmondsworth: Penguin

Warmington, B.H., 1977. *Suetonius: Nero*. Bristol: Bristol Classical Press

Wegner, M., 1971. *Das Römische Herrscherbild. Macrinus bis Balbinus*. Berlin: Mann

Wegner, M., 1979. *Das Römische Herrscherbild. Gordianus III bis Carinus*. Berlin: Mann

Wellesley, K., 1989. *The Long Year AD 69*. Bristol: Bristol Classical Press

Wiedemann, T., 1989. *The Julio-Claudian Emperors*. Bristol: Bristol Classical Press

Wigger, H.B., 1971. *Das Römische Herrscherbild. Caracalla, Geta, Plautilla*. Berlin: Mann

Wightman, E.M., 1970. *Roman Trier and the Treveri*. London: Hart-Davis

Wilkes, J.J., 1986. *Diocletian's Palace, Split. Residence of a retired Roman Emperor*. Sheffield: Department of Ancient History and Classical Archaeology

Williams, S., 1985. *Diocletian and the Roman Recovery*. London: Batsford; New York: Routledge

Williams, S., & Friell, G., 1994. *Theodosius: The Empire at Bay*. London: Batsford

Wiseman, T.P., 1991. *Flavius Josephus: Death of an Emperor*. Exeter: University of Exeter Press

Wood, S., 1986. *Roman Portrait Sculpture 217-260 AD. The Transformation of an Artistic Tradition*. Leiden: E.J Brill

York, J.M., 1972. The image of Philip the Arab. *Historia* 21, 320-332

Zanker, P., 1988. *The Power of Images in the Age of Augustus*. Ann Arbor: University of Michigan Press

Zosso, F., & Zingg, C., 1994. *Les Empereurs Romains 27 av.J.-C.-476 ap.J.-C.* Paris: Errance

ILLUSTRATION AND TEXT CREDITS

Sources of illustrations

a = above, c = centre, b = bottom, l = left, r = right.

The following abbreviations are used to identify sources and locate illustrations: BM – courtesy of the Trustees of the British Museum; CS – Chris Scarre; DAI – Deutsches Archaeologisches Institut, Rome; JGR – John G. Ross; MD – Michael Duigan; PAC – Peter A. Clayton; PW – Philip Winton (illustrator); RW – Professor Roger Wilson.

1 Kunsthistorisches Museum, Vienna. **2** JGR. **5a–b** BM; Ny Carlsberg Glyptotek, Copenhagen; BM; Michael Vickers. **6** Archaeological Museum, Ankara. **7**l&r MD. **8** I Musei Vaticani. **9a** PAC; c BM; b Kunsthistoriches Museum, Vienna. **10–11** ML Design. **14**l–r MD. **15**l–r MD. **16** BM. **18** ML Design. **19a** RW; b CS. **20a** I Musei Vaticani; b Museo Nazionale delle Terme, Rome, Photo Alinari. **21** Kon Penningkabinett, The Hague. **22a**r PW; bl CS. **23a**r CS; b PW. **25** RW. **26a–b** I Musei Vaticani; MD; MD; MD; MD. **28a** MD; b Courtesy Museum of Fine Arts, Boston. **30** ©. Photo RMN. **31** © Bibliothèque Nationale de France, Paris. **32** ML Design. **33** Fototeca Unione. **34** PW. **35** I Musei Capitolini, Rome, Photo Alinari. **36** Musée du Louvre. **37a** BM; c George Taylor. **38** BM. **39** BM. **40** Museo delle Navi, Nemi. **42a**r MD; bl The Royal Collection © Her Majesty the Queen. **44** © Bibliothèque Nationale de France, Paris. **45a** Annick Petersen; b New York University Excavations at Aphrodisias. **46** Fototeca Unione. **47a** Museo Torlonia, Rome, Photo DAI; c George Taylor; b Braun & Hogenberg *Civitas Orbis Terrarum* . **49** Scala. **50** BM. **51** BM. **52a** UDF; a Photothèque; b Annick Petersen. **53a**r PAC; b Annick Petersen. **54** Staatliche Museen zu Berlin. **56** BM. **56** ML Design. **57** Hirmer. **58** I Musei Capitolini, Rome, Photo Alinari. **61** MD. **62** ML Design. **63** Galleria degli Uffizi, Florence, Photo Alinari. **64** Ny Carlsberg Glyptotek, Copenhagen. **65** ML Design. **66a** Zev Radovan; b ML Design. **67** RW. **68** I Musei Capitolini, Rome, Photo DAI. **69a** MD; cl CS; cr Palazzo dei Conservatori, Rome, Photo DAI. **70a** Scala; b Scala; r PW. **71a** JGR; c After Bannister Fletcher; b PAC. **74** CS. **75a** CS; b MD. **76** Palazzo dei Conservatori, Rome, Photo DAI. **78a** JGR; b CS. **79a** PW; b CS. **80** MD. **81** RW. **84**l–r MD; MD; JGR; JGR. **85**l–r JGR; MD; courtesy of City Museum, Belgrade; JGR. **86** Museo Nazionale delle Terme, Rome, Photo DAI. **87** CS. **88** ML Design. **89** CS. **90** BM. **91a–b** MD; MD; JGR; JGR; Cleveland Museum of Art, The J.H.Wade Collection; Musée du Louvre. **92**l CS; r PW. **93a**&b RW. **95** I Musei Capitolini, Rome, Photo DAI. **96a** CS; b ML Design. **98** Zev Radovan. **99** ML Design. **100** MD. **101** PW. **102a**&b CS; c ML Design. **103a**l PW; ar Scala; br CS. **104** I Musei Vaticani, Photo Alinari. **105** PAC. **106** MD. **108** National Museums of Scotland. **109a** Fototeca Unione; c PW; b Fototeca Unione. **110a**l JGR; ar I Musei Vaticani, Photo Alinari. **111** CS. **112** MD. **113** Scala. **114** Cleveland Museum of Art, The J.H.Wade Collection. **115** I Musei Capitolini, Rome, Photo DAI. **116** PAC. **117** a Colin Ridler; b RW. **119** I Musei Capitolini, Rome, Photo Alinari. **120a** PAC; b Scala. **122** RW. **123** CS. **124** Hirmer. **126** I Musei Vaticani, Photo Alinari. **127** BM. **128** I Musei Vaticani, Photo

Alinari. **129** ML Design. **130** BM. **131a** JGR; cl MD; bl JGR; br © Photo RMN. **132a** JGR; b CS. **133** © Bildarchiv Preußischer Kulturbesitz, 1994, Staatliche Museen zu Berlin. **134** ML Design. **136a** RW; b PAC. **137a** JGR; c Direzione dei I Musei Capitolini, Rome; b RW. **138** Staatliche Museen zu Berlin. **140a** PW; b CS. **141a** George Taylor after G.A. Blouet *Restoration des Thermes d'Antonin Caracalla à Rome*, 1828 ; b George Taylor. **142** MD. **144a**&b CS. **146** courtesy City Museum, Belgrade. **148** JGR. **149** BM. **150** Museo Della Civiltà Romana, Rome. **154** © Photo RMN. **155** MD. **157** Oriental Institute, University of Chicago. **158**l–r JGR; JGR; CS; JGR. **159**l–r Michael Roaf; JGR; RW; MD. **160** Musée du Louvre. **162a**l I Musei Capitolini, Rome, Photo DAI; br CS. **163a**&b I Musei Capitolini, Rome, Photo DAI. **164** I Musei Vaticani, Photo DAI. **166** CS. **168**l&r I Musei Capitolini, Rome, Photo DAI. **169** ML Design. **171** Metropolitan Museum of Art, The Rogers Fund, 1905. **173** © Bibliothèque Nationale de France, Paris. **174** Staatliche Museen zu Berlin. **176** Landesmuseum Trier. **177** ML Design. **178** JGR. **180** CS. **181a** ML Design; b CS. **182** BM. **184** CS. **188** Musée du Louvre. **191** JGR. **195** I Musei Capitolini, Rome, Photo DAI. **196** Hirmer. **199a–b** Michael Vickers; Cairo Museum, Photo DAI; Museo Torlonia, Rome, Photo DAI; Ny Carlsberg Glyptotek, Copenhagen; MD; I Musei Vaticani, Photo DAI. **200** CS. **201** ML Design. **203** Hirmer. **204b** ML Design. **205a**l Ernest Hébrard; ar RW; cr CS; bl Alan Sorrel. **206** Cairo Museum, Photo DAI. **208a**r Museo Torlonia, Rome, Photo DAI; b MD. **209** Ny Carlsberg Glyptotek, Copenhagen. **211** Hirmer. **213** Hirmer. **215** I Musei Vaticani, Photo DAI. **217** Ian Mackenzie-Kerr. **218** ML Design. **219a** CS; b Scala. **220a** Hirmer; b After Krautheimer *Early Christian and Byzantine Architecture*, 1965. **223**l–r JGR; © Photo RMN; Archaeological Museum, Istanbul; © Photo RMN. **224**l&r Hirmer. **225a** MD; bl Palazzo dei Conservatori, Rome; r Hirmer. **227a** JGR; b Archaeological Museum, Istanbul, Photo DAI Istanbul. **228** al Archaeological Museum Istanbul; b Accademia de la Historia, Madrid. **229** Aosta Cathedral. **230** ML Design. **231** © Bibliothèque Nationale de France, Paris. **232** After Simons *Barbarian Europe*, 1968.

Coin drawings by Philip Winton, after George Stevenson *A Dictionary of Roman Coins* London 1889, and various sources.

Sources of quotations

The quotations used in this book are taken from the following sources:

Loeb Classical Library:

Aulus Gellius *The Attic Nights of Aulus Gellius* trans. J. C. Rolfe vol. III 1928. Cambridge, MA: Harvard UP (extract used on p. 25).

Cassius Dio *Roman History* Books LI–LX (complete), Books LXI–LXXX (epitome), trans. E. Cary, vols., 6–9, 1917, 1924, 1925, 1927. Cambridge, MA: Harvard UP (extracts used on pp. 73, 76, 90, 95, 97, 118, 119, 120, 126, 134, 136, 138, 142, 130, 144, 150, 151).

Herodian *History of the Empire from the Time of Marcus Aurelius*, trans. C. R. Whittaker, 2 vols., 1969, 1970. Cambridge, MA: Harvard UP (extracts used on pp.120, 122, 130, 150, 155, 156, 157, 162, 164).

Pliny *Letters and Panegyricus* trans. B. Radice 1969. Cambridge, MA: Harvard UP (extracts used on pp. 90, 94, 97).

Scriptores Historiae Augustae (lives of Hadrian, Aelius, Marcus Antoninus, Verus, Avidius Cassius, Commodus Antoninus, Pertinax, Didius Julianus, Severus, Pescennius Niger, Clodius Albinus, Antoninus Caracalla, Antoninus Geta, Opellius Macrinus, Antoninus Diadumenianus, Antoninus Elagabalus, Severus Alexander, The Two

Maximini, The Three Gordians, Maximus and Balbinus, The Two Valerians, The Two Gallieni, The Thirty Tyrants, The Deified Claudius, The Deified Aurelian, Tacitus, Probus, Firmus, Saturninus, Proculus and Bonosus, Carus, Carinus and Numerian) trans. D. Magie, 3 vols., 1921, 1924, 1932. Cambridge, MA: Harvard UP (extracts used on pp. 101, 102, 104, 108, 110. 111, 112, 114, 120, 124, 133, 138, 141, 143, 147, 148, 150, 151, 154, 156, 162, 165, 173, 174, 179, 182, 183, 185, 186, 188, 191, 192, 195).

Seneca *Moral Essays* trans. J. W. Basore vol. I 1928. Cambridge, MA: Harvard UP (extract used on p. 54).

Statius *Silvae* trans. J. H. Mozley, 1928. Cambridge MA: Harvard UP (extract used on p.78).

Suetonius (*Lives of the Deified Augustus, Tiberius, Gaius Caligula, The Deified Claudius, Nero, Galba, Otho and Vitellius, The Deified Vespasian, The Deified Titus, Domitian*) trans. J. C. Rolfe, 2 vols., 1913, 1914. Cambridge, MA: Harvard UP (extracts used on pp. 16, 19, 21, 22, 28, 31, 34, 36, 38, 40, 41, 42, 46, 50, 61, 62, 69, 72, 74, 81, 82).

Tacitus *Annals* trans. J. Jackson, 3 vols., 1934, 1937. Cambridge, MA: Harvard UP (extracts used on pp. 21, 32, 37, 44, 52, 55, 57).

Tacitus *Histories* trans. C. H. Moore, 2 vols., 1925, 1931. Cambridge, MA: Harvard UP (extracts used on pp. 49, 58, 60, 61, 63, 64).

Velleius Paterculus *Roman History* trans. F. W. Shipley, 1924. Cambridge, MA: Harvard UP (extracts used on pp. 18, 33).

Other sources:

Aurelius Victor *Liber De Caesaribus* trans. H. W. Bird. Liverpool: Liverpool UP, 1994 (extracts used on pp. 50, 168, 210).

Constantine *The Oration of the Emperor Constantine which he addressed 'To the Assembly of Saints'* trans. E. C. Richardson, in *A Select Library of Nicene and Post-Nicene Fathers of the Christian Church, Volume 1: Eusebius* eds. H. Wace and P. Schaff. Oxford: Parker and Co., 1890, 561–580 (extract used on p.213).

Eusebius *History of the Church* trans. G. A. Williamson, revised A. Louth, 1989. Harmondsworth: Penguin (extracts used on pp. 82, 206, 210, 215).

Eutropius *Breviarium ab Urbe Condita* trans. H. W. Bird. Liverpool: Liverpool UP 1993 (extracts used on pp. 166, 171, 174, 190, 195, 202, 203, 206, 209, 221).

Lactantius *De Mortibus Persecutorum* ed. and trans. J. L. Creed. Oxford: Clarendon Press, 1984 (extracts used on pp. 196, 204, 206, 212).

Marcus Aurelius *Meditations* trans. M. Staniforth. Harmondsworth: Penguin 1964 (extracts used on pp. 106, 114, 118).

Res Gestae Divi Augusti. The Achievements of the Divine Augustus eds. P. A. Brunt and J. M. Moore. Oxford: Oxford UP 1967 (extract used on p. 27).

Seneca *Apocolocyntosis* ed. P. T. Eden. Cambridge: Cambridge UP 1984 (extract used on p. 49).

Sherk, R.K., 1988. *The Roman Empire: Augustus to Hadrian. Translated Documents of Greece and Rome 6.* Cambridge: Cambridge UP (extracts used on pp. 68, 98).

Tacitus *On Britain and Germany* trans. H. Mattingly. Harmondsworth: Penguin, 1948 (extract used on p. 76).

Wellesley, K., 1989. *The Long Year* AD 69. Bristol: Bristol Classical Press (extract used on p. 60).

Zosimus *New History* trans. R. T. Ridley. Sydney: Australian Association for Byzantine Studies 1982 (extracts on pp.168, 170, 217).

Extract from Nero, p. 55, trans. D. Miller. Extracts on pp. 75, 86, 87, 105, 106 (A. Victor), 111 (Fronto), 153 (A. Victor), 160, 167, trans. C. Scarre.

INDEX